# When the Rackets Reigned

# When the Rackets Reigned

*Ed Taggert*

iUniverse, Inc.
New York Bloomington Shanghai

**When the Rackets Reigned**



iUniverse books may be ordered through booksellers or by contacting:

iUniverse
1663 Liberty Drive
Bloomington, IN 47403
www.iuniverse.com
1-800-Authors (1-800-288-4677)



ISBN: 978-0-595-49689-1 (pbk)
ISBN: 978-0-595-50027-7 (cloth)
ISBN: 978-0-595-61210-9 (ebk)

Printed in the United States of America

# Contents

# *Foreword*

To borrow from Charles Dickens, "It was the best of times, it was the worst of times ..."

This is not the tale of two cities, just one. But the paradox of good and bad marching in lock step 50 or so years ago has left lasting memories for those who experienced that era. Reading, Pennsylvania, in 1956 was an exciting, prosperous place in which to work and play. Unemployment was low as big industry and small machine shops and the hosiery and clothing makers and the Reading railroad were thriving, and the Democrats were back in office in a town where unions flourished. Entertainment was plentiful, Penn Street was a shopper's paradise with department stores and shops of all types, and its theaters and restaurants ands bars gave it the aura of Main Street U.S.A. We all spoke with pride about our workforce, skilled and diligent, and crime was of the non-violent variety, for the most part. Why we even had Friday night cruising for the young people. This was typical America, so it seemed on the surface. But having recovered from sacrifices and trials of World War II, Reading was about to enter a period of inordinate disregard for the rule of law by politicians and racketeers. It was an era that caused the Pretzel City to become known as Sin City.

I arrived at the *Reading Times* early in 1956. With little knowledge of Reading's style of rough and tumble politics, I was assigned to the police beat. During the next eight years of the insidious partnership between government and vice merchants, it was an exciting time and place to be a newspaper reporter. Although I was somewhat removed from the frontline battles that developed between the press and suspect elected officials, I saw firsthand that it was indeed a war.

Our editorial staff and that of the *Reading Eagle* played a variety of roles in keeping the public informed during that era of unbridled politics when Abe Minker controlled most of the vice activities.

Drexel Bradley and Gene Friedman were the *Times's* infantrymen who day after day had to face corrupted city officials. Bradley was the City Hall reporter all through the administration of Mayor Daniel McDevitt. Drex and others shared that assignment when John Kubacki was mayor. Friedman was assigned to the Berks County courts and federal court in Philadelphia during the entire period when political and criminal figures were constantly testifying before local and federal juries. He had that beat throughout the eight years District Attorney Fred Brubaker was in office. Gene and Drex took plenty of verbal abuse, but shrugged off the snide remarks. Sparring with those who bobbed and weaved when asked for straight answers, the pair came to work every day wondering how draining or embarrassing the next confrontation would be. Those years of asking hard questions of politicians experienced in warding off such queries wore on the newsmen but they didn't flinch.

I earned my stripes early in the war while covering the appearance of a former policeman at a veterans organization meeting. He accused McDevitt of failing to remove gambling machines, or reduce prostitution as he had promised before being elected. New on the job, I didn't think to call the mayor for his reaction before the story appeared in the next morning's *Times.* When I followed up the next day by going to the mayor's office, I took one of the early volleys he would fire at the press in the years ahead. First he talked so softly I couldn't understand him. As I moved closer and bent to hear him, he bellowed a bruising denial of the cop's charges, filling me in with the cop's poor record before quitting the force. Although I towered over the diminutive Dan, I had no height advantage by the time I left. That was the only time I felt his wrath, but for Bradley it was daily combat as he questioned the mayor about the complaints being made from many quarters.

Directing the extended drama for the *Times* during those exciting years was Richard "Old Pete" Peters. Pete, our courageous city editor, was ever alert to making a good story better by keeping reporters on their toes, always looking for new angles to pursue. He put them to the test and they usually passed with fine marks. Pete inspired loyalty, accuracy, and creativity among the ranks.

So, it is to those I've singled out, and to others I might have forgotten on that winning journalistic team years ago, that I dedicate this book. In addition to Friedman and Bradley, other *Times* reporters who contributed most of the articles in this retelling of those good old days, were: Nick Yost, Marty Salditch, Ben Livengood, Ray Koehler, Andy Billy, and Bill East. Photographers Cliff Yeich, Jackie Evans, and Chick Harrity provided photographs almost daily of men and women not happy to have their pictures taken.

Over the years I had conversations with several of the principals in this book. Many have died but I vividly remember the tales they told because of my interest in crime. Others have lived into the 21$^{st}$ century and I interviewed them and took notes when I realized I wanted to write a book about those years when a cascade of crime stories drenched the city of Reading.

I would also like to give special thanks to Robert Gerhart for the tales he recalled from his days in City Hall during that era. Bob was a protégé of U.S. Rep. George Rhoads and publisher of *The New Era,* a labor publication, before serving as a state assemblyman and senator, successful businessman, and philanthropist. He also assisted financially in the publication of this book.

Without the technical help offered by my son, Brian Young, and my nephew, Josh Taggert, I would still be wandering around in the digital jungle that so frustrates me. My wife, Mary, spent endless hours editing the constantly changing copy I handed her, correcting my spelling, grammar and typos. To her, my profound thanks for that brief moment of encouragement near the end: "I really thought you'd never finish it."

**Ed Taggert**

# 1

# *An early history of notoriety*

Vice is nice is a notion that prevailed in Reading, Pennsylvania, for a long, long time. In a community noted for its proud work ethic and productivity, gambling and prostitution provided a certain mystique that cast a long shadow over the city during much of the 20$^{th}$ century. Reading's good image as a booming industrial town suffered the blemish of a political heritage in which the rackets too often had the deciding vote.

When it was still considered naughty to gamble, the betting fraternity could feed its habit at the illegal slot machines in the many clubs and social quarters of volunteer fire companies. Horse parlors served the racing patrons, and numbers writers abounded all over the city and in most blue-collar plants. Politicians, police, and many citizens winked at easy-to-find houses of prostitution. Conventioneers loved the locally brewed beer and its variety of hometown pretzels. And the voters were reconciled to the possibility that no matter whom they elected, the vice-is-nice system was in good hands.

In 1935, a Berks County grand jury handed a written recommendation to Judge H. Robert Mays that he should not give jail sentences to numbers writers. The jurors felt fines were penalty enough. Judge Mays responded: "I indulge in games of chance myself, but I do not approve of any commercialization of any violator of the law. The whole business is part of a racket."

Indeed, the judge was telling the truth. For years, starting back in the 1920s, Mays played the numbers at Ike Marks's cigar store on Court Street. And by 1935, Reading was deluged with numbers banks operated not only by local racketeers, but by Philadelphia mobsters who frequented the city during the Depression.

Some would trace Reading's cultural appetite for illegal pastimes to Prohibition. But a variety of gambling choices was available by 1920, and prostitution in Reading's tenderloin dated back to the Gay Nineties or earlier. It wasn't only the racketeers who were setting bad examples. During the early decades of the 20th century it was common practice to buy an appointment to the police department. Men in their forties were hired, then loafed through the years, often on sick leave. But it was Prohibition's illicit trade in beer and booze that gave Reading its sin city image. With the arrival of slot machines and the numbers lottery, smart purveyors consolidated, and soon Reading racketeers were fringe players in national organized crime.

Although beer baron Max Hassel rose higher in mob ranks than any other in Reading, he made his name by acquiring interest in numerous breweries on the East Coast. While master brewers helped make him rich, Max protected himself as a master briber. His well-paid lawyers always found ways to keep him out of jail. Although known as a nonviolent philanthropist, Hassel took political corruption to new levels during his years as one of the top bootleggers in the country. The local reaction to his murder at the hands of New York mobsters was indicative of the city's attitude toward vice, and the men who profited by it. An estimated ten thousand mourners packed a two-block area of North 5th Street as they waited in line to move past his coffin in Henninger's funeral home in 1933.

For the next dozen years, the poster boy of the city vice crowd was Tony Moran. Born Anthony Mirenna, Tony's climb to the top was gradual and not well documented because his arrest resume was slim. But every gambler in town knew Tony ran a couple of large numbers banks, prostitution was pretty much under his umbrella, and he dabbled in the slot machine business. Ralph Kreitz and John Matz were considered the one-armed bandit kings of the 1930s and '40s. At the time of his death in 1945, Moran owned 15 properties in the city and county, including 608 Cherry Street, one of the whorehouses managed by Dutch Mary Gruber. Soldiers from Indiantown Gap created gridlock at 6th and Cherry on weekends during World War II.

The numbers game was the most profitable racket ever devised. It originated in England during the 18th century, arriving in the U.S. with the steady stream of immigrants who brought along their good and bad cultural habits. In England, the outlet for numbers gamblers was at the so-called policy shop. Thus, this form of gambling was originally called the policy game. Back in the post-Civil War era of Boss Tweed's reign in New York, Al Adams, with his 1,000 policy shops, was the big numbers racketeer. During the Prohibition-Depression years the numbers game gained added popularity in Reading. Many corner grocery store owners added to their small incomes by writing numbers for the Philadelphia mob, headed by Herman Stromberg, an import from New York City. Better known as Nig Rosen, Stromberg was on trial in 1935 as head of Philadelphia's policy racket. One witness testified that he overheard Nig tell a friend that Reading wasn't any help when a $44,000 hit left Nig short of cash. Nig was the layoff man for Simon Applebaum who was running a numbers operation from his Wyomissing home. Simon could not come up with the cash Nig needed because the state police had clamped down on his operation. When Applebaum came to trial in Reading, a couple of his writers testified that when he had hired them he promised to pay for lawyers and bail if needed. When he reneged, they said he was paying them $30 a week and taking in $400 a day. Applebaum received a bigger fine and jail sentence than his employees, but Nig Rosen was acquitted after a three-day trial in Philadelphia. Nobody called it organized crime in 1935, but the Rosen-Applebaum relationship could be seen as a continuation of the bootlegging partnership Max Hassel had with Philly's BooBoo Hoff during Prohibition. And for decades to come, Reading racketeers always had shadowy connections to the New York or Philadelphia Mafia.

Productive Reading numbers writers in Rosen's employ occasionally would be treated to all-expense paid trips to the Quaker City. While Moran controlled a large share of the local rackets, there was seldom any conflict with outsiders.

Abe Minker was a small-time bootlegger during Prohibition. When his North 8th Street Gang waged war with the South 7th Street Gang in 1922, Minker won the battle but lost the war. Several of the Southerns went to jail, but Minker joined them when he was found guilty of perjury for lying about Philly gangsters who tried to abduct him. During the Depression the small profits from his attempts at legal business ventures did not satisfy his big ambitions, so he drifted back into the rackets. With the help of New York mobsters, Abe made his pitch to take over the local mob in the mid 1940s.

Johnny Wittig became a legend in local crime circles by shooting Moran in Tony's gambling joint behind Cole Watson's basement poolroom at 529 Penn Street. Just weeks before Germany was defeated in World War II, Johnny's execution of Moran changed the course of vice in Reading, although it didn't become real noticeable for several years.

Wittig received a 10-to-20-year sentence for third-degree murder, but was back on the street within six years. It was never documented, but insiders claimed Abe Minker paid Wittig to eliminate the competition. This theory gained credence when Johnny returned to Reading and tried to veil himself in respectability by taking legitimate jobs for four years. Then in 1956 he surfaced as Minker's No. 1 guy.

With Moran out of the way, Minker began his consolidation move. By the spring of 1951, he was on the verge of completely controlling vice in Reading.

Ralph Kreitz was still an independent, as were several others, but Abe was considered the heir apparent. However, his rise to eminence occurred just at a time when the U.S. Senate began looking into organized crime.

Senator Estes Kefauver was the original head of a Senate committee that held hearings all over the country. Certain national crime figures became household names as Kefauver's group revealed that a national crime syndicate did exist, despite J. Edgar Hoover's denials to the contrary. Reading's reputation as a wide-open town landed it on the committee's suspect list. The reason Reading was brought into the investigation was to show that interstate mobsters were stretching their tentacles to draw small cities into organized crime. Reading's population in 1950 was close to 110,000.

Federal investigators swarmed into Reading the spring of 1951. They talked with ministers, bankers, businessmen, and second and third level racketeers to compile a thick dossier on Abe Minker and his henchmen. The basement of the old post office at 5th and Court streets was humming as cops, gamblers, and city officials joined the parade of people questioned. Late in May, thirty-two men and women were subpoenaed to appear at a crime committee hearing in Reading. Heading the list were Abe Minker, Ralph Kreitz, attorney Sam Liever, and Chief of Police William Birney. At the last minute the hearing was shifted to Washington.

On June 28, by telephone link, radio station WEEU broadcast the hearing to Berks County listeners. Earlier, Kefauver hearings had been televised, allowing the nation to watch and hear the testimony of notorious crime figures such as Frank Costello, Jake "Greasy Thumb" Guzik, Abner "Longie" Zwillman, Frank Erickson, Joe Adonis, and Ben "Bugsy" Siegel's moll, Virginia Hill. Reading had its own star-quality witness who charmed the senators and the press with his down-to-earth version of politics in Berks County.

Ralph Kreitz did not dress for the occasion. He showed up coatless, tieless, disheveled. Unlike others who hid behind the 5th Amendment, the 50-year-old Ralph was candid and philosophical regarding his long career of providing mechanical devices to those who ignored the odds. As the self-appointed spokesman for his hometown's horde of gamblers, Ralph delivered an unabashed account of the way things worked in Reading. In his heavy Pennsylvania Dutch accent, he enraptured his listening audience with words of wisdom about how to win, or lose, the vote up home.

Reminiscent of Irvin S. Cobb or Will Rogers, a couple of early radio homespun, comedic philosophers, Kreitz was not afraid to lay it on the line. The Senate committee was not accustomed to such honesty and audacity. Ralph's self-incriminating testimony was met with smiles and outright laughter. About gambling in Reading, he told the panel, "It's openly known, but nobody figures it's notorious. You do, but our people don't."

About reports of bribes to city officials, he said he had no personal contact with the police; didn't even know Police Chief Birney. He told the panel he gave Detective Lt. Albert Hoffman $800 eight or nine years earlier when Hoffman was sick but, "It was not a bribe. I gave Hoffy the money as a gift to be used to save his life when he was sick. I never gave any other state or city policeman money. If you needed money to save your life and I had it, I would give it to you."

That was probably the truth, although his denials about political payoffs almost certainly were not. At the home he shared with his mother on Windsor Street it was open house the year round. Just about everybody was welcome, including politicians and policemen.

The senators questioned him about raids on clubs and saloons where his machines had been seized. He explained what everybody already knew: after raids, the clubs would stay closed for a short time then resume business as usual. Asked if the clubs were currently operating, he said, "No."

As long as the committee's counsel asked questions about himself, Ralph was ready to answer, but when asked about Abe Minker, he clammed up. He didn't bother taking the 5th, he just pled ignorance or said he had no opinion about the activities of others. Because of his other straight-from-the-shoulder responses, nobody pressured him. His rumpled shirt, suspenders, baggy gray pants, torn belt, and scruffy shoes gave him the appearance of a man who had just slopped the pigs. Unpretentious and approachable, he was elevated to star of the hearings by the Washington press corps. He advised Sen. Herbert O'Conor, who had replaced Kefauver as chairman of the investigating committee:

"Why senator, if you was to come to Reading and run for political office, and promised to close down these places and clean out the machines, you couldn't get elected no how."

Ralph and O'Conor got into a debate about the federal tax levied on each slot machine. Kreitz saw the tax as a federal license to gamble, but O'Conor said it was a penalty. If he paid the tax, then it was legal to operate the machines, wasn't it? Ralph wanted to know. The senator was unable to answer that one, possibly unaware there were Pennsylvania laws banning money paying gambling machines. Ralph also took a poke at religious leaders who were forever complaining about gambling, but were happy enough to take his money when he answered their requests to support church activities.

One columnist called Ralph "the chummiest, biggest hearted hoodlum I ever met." Other information Ralph disclosed about himself: he netted about $60,000 annually, was sentenced to a 60-day prison term in 1948 for evading $42,953 in income taxes, and usually had about 100 active slot machines. Also, he had a few punchboards scattered about the county, and he knew no bookies because he never played the horses.

The sociable tenor of the hearing took a sharp drop in the afternoon when Abe and Isadore Minker and their nephew, Alex Fudeman, testified, along with a surprise appearance by Police Chief Birney. During the morning session, Birney was rolled into the hearing room on a litter, having recently suffered a stroke. Soon he was wheeled out, and it appeared he would not be asked to testify. But there he was in the p.m. telling the senators all he did was follow Mayor John F. Davis's orders regarding gambling and prostitution. He claimed his job was to respond to complaints, not initiate raids on bookie joints, card games, or gambling machine violators. There were no complaints filed, as far as he knew, for the past 20 or 30 years.

The questions asked of the Minker brothers told more about their vice operations than did the few answers Abe and Izzy provided. Almost always they responded with the phrase made famous by Mafia figures who had preceded them at earlier hearings:

"I refuse to testify … etc, etc, etc."

The 5th Amendment protection against self-incrimination was spouted time and again as the senators and committee counsel asked the Minkers about their relationship with various known criminals. Had Abe Minker been to Hot Springs, Arkansas, with Frank Costello? Did Abe know Nig Rosen in Philadelphia? Was Izzy a stockholder in Western Union, which supplied bookie joints with racing results? There was plenty of name-dropping, leaving the impression the Minkers were well connected to organized crime.

The Minkers' local lawyer, Sam Liever, had been subpoenaed, but was excused because his father, Hyman Liever, had just died. Alex Fudeman, Minker's nephew, was another silent witness, the 5th again at work. A few Minker employees were elusive in describing their duties.

Testifying for Reading's opposition forces was the Rev. James D. Matchette. He did not support Kreitz's theory about the futility of an anti-gambling candidate running for office. As an activist for Reading church groups and community organizations, Matchette claimed to have approached both Mayor Jack Davis and Berks County District Attorney John E. Ruth about gambling in the city. These are the answers he said he received:

Davis—"Gambling is part of the nature of our people."

Ruth—"Gambling is part of the life of the community."

At the end of the one-day hearing, the senators were left with the strong impression that Reading politicians were under the heel of the local racketeers who in turn were connected to organized crime. Everybody was left wondering whether the voters of Reading got that message and what they would do about it.

# 2

# *Small city on a national stage*

Frank Costello and Abe Minker were among the few losers that came out of the Kefauver Committee hearings. Costello never regained his status as senior statesman of the Mafia, and Minker's influence in Reading dwindled during the next four years. Virginia Hill's prestige as a gangland floozy was diminished, but that really had no bearing on organized crime.

Change in the status quo of Reading politics began in 1950 when cracks in the solid Democratic City Council began to appear. Mayor Jack Davis's proposed solution to battling crime was to reduce by eight the number of detectives in the police department and return them to patrolman duty. Only Councilman Charlie Stoner voted "No" and the change went into effect—but for only a week. In 1951, three weeks before the July 25 primary election, the mayor offered a similar resolution, this time with no support at all from his party conferees. They were backing Stoner, now Davis's opponent in the primary. If it had not been for the organized crime hearing, it was likely Jack would have run unopposed for a second term. He certainly was one of Reading's most popular mayors, a humorous after-dinner speaker who was always in demand.

Stoner was a power in the Democratic Party. He believed the fallout from the crime hearing would be serious—Davis had to go. Stoner cast himself as the only savior able to retain the Democrats' supremacy in City Hall. Davis claimed City Council had taken away his power as head of the police department by constantly rejecting his attempts to put more uniformed policemen on the street to protect the citizens. The supposedly smart money was on Stoner because of his close ties with the volunteer firemen and his influence with other party leaders.

But Davis pulled an upset, narrowly winning by 196 votes. The Democratic voters evidently didn't blame the mayor for the black eye dealt them in Washington, or more likely, didn't care. Jack, whose jokes and quick wit had charmed his constituents for four years, won on personality against the party machine. He openly supported gambling and was betting there weren't enough Republican voters in Reading to defeat him. The Republicans nominated James B. Bamford, a drug store operator and former Chamber of Commerce president. Gambling and intimations of political corruption in the current administration were the two issues on which he campaigned.

Rev. Matchette and his Joint Committee on Crime kept up the pressure on Jack Davis and City Council. At an October City Council meeting, Matchette and the Rev. Mervin Heller crossed swords with Davis and Democratic Councilmen J. Clinton Bach and John Gingrich about the legality of bingo and other forms of gambling. The clergymen read some of the many uncomplimentary passages about Reading in the Senate Committee on Organized Crime report. Not much was settled in this war of words and interpretations, but Davis made it clear he supported local gambling because the people wanted it. Matchette rebutted that opinion claiming 52 anti-gambling Protestant ministers were on the local Joint Crime Committee and were urging their congregations to vote Republican.

The GOP hoped the two-term jinx that marked the history of mayoral elections would continue in this one. That cycle was not broken in 1951 as Jim Bamford beat Jack Davis by almost 3,000 votes despite a much smaller registration of Republican voters. With the election of Samuel Russell and Edward Harper to City Council, it was the first time in 29 years the GOP controlled a Reading administration. Without doubt, the crime hearing had finally awakened the Reading electorate.

It was naïve to expect the rackets to disappear just because Jim Bamford had led the resurgent Republicans to major victories in both city and county. Although Bamford continued to promise a thorough cleanup of the rackets, he probably would have needed the state's 28th National Guard Division to accomplish such a monumental feat. Bamford was not naïve and it wasn't long before he was defending himself against a former city solicitor and Rev. Matchette's followers.

John Wanner, who had served as an assistant district attorney under the outgoing D.A., John Ruth, handed the mayor a list of 22 clubs in Reading where Ralph Kreitz either owned or supplied gambling machines. "Nothing is easier to break up than the slot machine racket," he stated at the second City Council meeting of the new administration. Democratic Councilman Jerome Stabb supported Wanner by asking Bamford, "Would you care to make a report on what action you have taken so far on the slot machine question?"

"Not at this time," Bamford replied.

Bamford would eventually explain the philosophy he adopted regarding gambling and how he thought it worked out:

"We picked out our spot as one being described as pearly gray purity. We weren't against people gambling. This meant gambling would be tolerated if not controlled by the rackets." He admitted it didn't work.

"What we did, however, for those four long years—we annoyed those people who wanted a more liberal policy than we were willing to put up with. And the people who wanted absolute purity felt we had disappointed them."

Before 1951 there were no federal laws that specifically said gambling was legal or illegal. Congress felt it was the states' business to govern vice. But the Kefauver Committee exposed organized crime as an interstate problem, so it was time to bear down on the mob—and make a little tax money while doing it. Federal reformers passed legislation in the fall of 1951 requiring all professional gamblers to buy a $50 stamp each year. Added on to that was an occupation tax of 10 percent of the gambler's income. Another twist in this latest attempt to legislate morals was that stamp holders had to file monthly returns of their gambling winnings. This wide-reaching legislation also extended to gambling machines: annual $150 stamps on pinball machines with cash payoffs, and $250 stamps on slot machines.

Pennsylvania already had anti-gambling laws, which were pretty much ignored by Reading's wagering element, so the fast money crowd did not pay much attention to the new federal tariffs either. If local gamblers did adhere to the federal laws it would put them in a Catch 22 situation: buy a stamp and pay the tax and you were announcing your violation of Pennsylvania laws. So Reading's racketeers shrugged and ignored the new federal legislation.

And so it went over the next four years. More than once the mayor would call his administration pearly gray, meaning it was focusing on organized crime rather than targeting homegrown racketeers. This, Bamford explained, meant that no single mastermind Mafia-connected crook like Abe Minker would be able to control vice in Reading with the help of outside mobsters. This did not sit well with the reformists, but the slot machine operators were very pleased to get out from under Minker's sway.

The independent gaming operators formed a cooperative to divvy up the pie without a large slice being allotted to an all-controlling rackets boss. It was called the Berks County Amusement Operations Association. Policemen under the new chief, Robert Elliott, were alerted to report any sightings of Philly or New York mobsters who might be edging in. In prostitution circles, Mable Jones and Freddie Williams were becoming dominant among several whorehouse operators as folk hero Dutch Mary Gruber was being eased out.

Newly elected Republican Councilman Sam Russell tried harder than the rest to restrict Minker. He introduced a letter to council that he wanted sent to U.S. Attorney General James McGranery. The Justice Department had announced it was making up a list of major organized crime figures who, it concluded, should be deported to their native countries. This project resulted from the recent Kefauver Committee findings. Russell's letter informed McGranery that Reading City Council approved of having Abe Minker denaturalized, and suggested his name be added to the Justice Department's deportation list.

As Council debated Russell's motion, the two Democrats refused to support it. John Gingrich voted "No" because he didn't believe "in crucifying a man when he was down," and Jerome Stabb just wouldn't vote. So the letter was sent on the approval of Russell, Mayor Bamford, and the other Republican councilman, Ed Harper. McGranery ordered the Immigration and Naturalization Agency to look into the matter. Abe repeatedly refused to appear for questioning. Twice he ignored I&N subpoenas. His lawyers appealed the issuance of those orders and eventually argued the case before the Third District Court of Appeals, which upheld the I&N action. In November 1955, Minker's attorney argued the case before the U.S. Supreme Court, and won.

On the brink of losing his citizenship, Abe hired Jacob Kossman, a prominent Philadelphia criminal lawyer to take his case before the U.S. Supreme Court. This would begin a client-attorney relationship that would bring them together many, many times in the next 15 years. The well-paid Kossman responded by arguing the case in a sterling defense for the 57-year-old racketeer who dreaded the thought of being sent back to Russia. The case was argued before Justices Felix Frankfurter, William Douglas, and Hugo Black in November 1955. All three had been appointed to the high court by President Roosevelt in the late 1930s.

Two months after the Supreme Court hearing, the three justices released a unanimous opinion, overturning the Third District Court's ruling. "Witness" was the key word in their decision. Although I&N rules gave its agents the authority to subpoena witnesses for questioning, the trio of legendary justices agreed Abe Minker was more than just a witness who would give testimony in an investigation. Since he was the person I&N was trying to build a case against, he had the right to ignore a subpoena. Justice Black went even further in his opinion:

"The respondent Minker is a naturalized citizen of the United States. He was subpoenaed by an immigration officer to appear and give testimony as a "witness." But Minker was not to be a witness in the traditional meaning of the word.

This is one that testifies in a court proceeding or in a public hearing of some kind. The immigration officer who summoned Minker was not a judge or grand jury of any kind, nor was he at the time acting in any quasi-judicial capacity." Black pointed out that policemen, sheriffs, and the FBI did not have subpoena powers, so why should I&N agents conducting investigations have that authority.

Justice Douglas offered other opinions favoring Minker. He pointed out that Congress provided for canceling a certificate of naturalization on the ground that it was procured "by concealment of a material fact or by willful misrepresentation." At that point Abe had not been found guilty of that. The justice claimed there was no pretrial administrative procedure provided in the I&N rules section governing denaturalization." Kossman had used these same arguments in his defense of Abe. It was a groundbreaking case that led to a clearer understanding of what was needed to rescind a naturalized person's U.S. citizenship. No move to denaturalize Abe surfaced again, although I&N later withdrew his passport when it feared he would make an unauthorized flight out of the country.

During the stir that Russell's letter caused in City Council, he revealed that a valuable piece of county property had "fallen into the hands of an open and notorious racketeer." Minker had purchased a tract where Route 582 and Route 422 meet at the eastern tip of Mount Penn. It was indeed a choice location and eventually became the site of Minker's White House Market. In future years Abe would often step outside the market to conduct racket-related conversations in a car on the parking lot. He feared his legitimate business would be compromised if he were caught arranging illegal deals inside the building.

In later years, gamblers would sing the praises of the rackets during the pearly gray administration when all the boys received a fair share of the take. The Republican administration in Washington didn't pay much attention to Reading during those years, not making any headline grabbing raids or investigations. So it was a peaceful, profitable four years for the fellows who hung at 6$^{th}$ and Penn flashing their rolls and dropping into the Crystal for a bite.

Johnny Wittig was back in town, having received a pardon from Gov. John S. Fine just before Christmas 1951. Abe Minker's influence and money were believed to have helped Wittig win a governor's commutation, which was a fairly common practice at the time. Having served six years of his 10-to-20 sentence for killing Tony Moran, Wittig might have gone right back into the rackets had Davis been reelected, thereby giving Minker a free hand to expand his operation. But the Minker drive to the top was temporarily delayed, and Wittig had to take real jobs for the next few years. First he was hired as a laborer by Garman Construction, a local contractor that often won bids for city projects. Then his job as a timekeeper at Alcoa near Myerstown allowed the calluses on his hands to soften up a bit.

Johnny was a ladies man, the strong silent type. He wasn't much for small talk, which made him more effective as an enforcer when he did give an order. Other than being convicted in a crooked lottery in 1939, Johnny did not have much of a police record. Moran and Wittig received 9-month sentences and $1,000 fines for running a phony charitable weekly drawing for the Elks Crippled Children Benefit. Moran served his minimum time, paid his fine and was released. Johnny, however, couldn't raise the $1,000 fine, and when Tony refused to help him, Wittig had to stay behind in BCP to serve his full term.

Supposedly, that's when the feud started between Moran and Wittig. Although they were not on good terms, they managed to stay out of each other's way, with Johnny drifting into Minker's circle. Although Wittig was tried and convicted of Moran's murder, there was a small and secretive faction among the racketeers that hinted Johnny was not the hit man. The theory floated was that Johnny was paid to take the rap, but somebody else pulled the trigger. Although a good size group was in the gambling den that night, none testified he actually saw Johnny shoot Tony. Of the 20 or so witnesses, none ever came forward to accuse anybody else. And no smoking gun was found, although it was .38 caliber bullets that killed Tony, and Johnny was known to have purchased a .38 Colt some years before. The tale persists to this day that the murder was planned, with Wittig agreeing to pose as the gunman, serve a short sentence if convicted, earn a generous bonus, and be assured of a well paying job with Abe when he got out of prison. Harold "Tiny" Hoffner, a close associate of Moran's for many years, was the shooter, according to this long whispered conspiracy theory. Tiny, supposedly, was standing behind a railing watching the card game when the fatal shots were fired.

Wittig had acquired a tough-guy reputation before the shooting, and when he came back from prison he was treated with fear and reverence in the local underworld. Solidly built and slightly taller than average, he had the rugged, menacing good looks of a Hollywood gangster. As the 1955 political picture came into focus, Wittig was prepared to play a major role in the reemergence of Abe Minker as Reading's indisputable rackets boss.

# 3

# *Fruits of Prohibition attract huckster*

When Prohibition opened the floodgates of illegal beer and liquor, Abe Minker swam with the flow. Like many young adventurers of his generation, he joined the army of bootleggers keeping thirsty Americans from going dry. Abe got his start in crime when 18th Amendment supporters staged a successful campaign for legislation they hoped would remove taverns from the social face of America. Instead, Prohibition offered easy riches to those willing to ignore the ban on alcoholic beverages, and gave the speakeasy added notoriety in the nation's lexicon. Minker and his friends and enemies careened around the countryside hauling bootleg spirits, unaware that they were planting the roots of organized crime. Abe, the poor émigré, would one day wheel and deal with the former slum kids from New York City who would eventually top the public enemy list. In a culture that favored aliases and nicknames, Abe Minker became known as the Baron, the Brain, or the General.

America's Prohibition was a stage for first and second generation aliens to act out their fantasies of becoming rich and famous. Most were poor, not too well educated, and with little social or work skills. Most of the bootleggers who rose to the top were born around the turn of the 20th century and arrived in this country as youngsters. Abe Minker fit that mold.

Not a lot is known about his early family life. Abe was born into a poor Russian family that migrated from Brest Litovsk on the Bug River sometime around 1903. Brest Litovsk is now Brest in Belarus. Abe's father, Samuel, was believed to have moved north from the Odessa region of the Ukraine on the Black Sea. Samuel and Ida were young teenagers whose Jewish parents probably arranged their marriage. Max, the first of eight children, was born in 1883. Ida was 14, Samuel, a year older. Ida continued to have children over the next 26 years. A few died in infancy, and Sadie, the first daughter, died as a young child. Two more daughters, Emma, 1894, and Gertrude, 1896, were born in Russia. The last two native Russians were Abraham, 1898, and Alexander, 1901. The father served a tour in the Russian army before leaving his homeland with his family. Isadore and William were American-born in 1907 and 1909 respectively.

Samuel, a devout Jew, spent much of his life studying the Torah, although he never became a rabbi. His wife, in addition to bearing many children, was the family breadwinner—literally. Baking bread was her vocation. Because of Samuel's daily devotions at the synagogue, the children were expected to share the financial burden by going to work at an early age.

As the principal provider, Ida operated a bakery in their house. Max, the eldest, was a young adult by the time the family settled in Reading. He worked as a laborer and later became a huckster with his own horse and cart, peddling fruit, vegetables and bread in northeast Reading. He also was young Abe's role model. Abe left grade school at an early age to become a familiar little merchant with his pushcart full of produce, selling to his neighbors and contributing to the family's small income. When Alex was only five, his regular job was to groom the family horse after Max and Abe returned each evening at the end of a long day peddling food staples. Like Abe, neither Izzy nor Alex finished elementary school. Although Abe had little training in math, his innate ability with numbers was evident at an early age and led to some success as a businessman, legal and otherwise. Alex, the most scholastically minded in the family, earned his high school diploma as an adult by attending night school at Reading High. William, the youngest, was the only sibling to reach high school, graduating from RHS in 1927. Max was the first to gain his American citizenship in 1911.

The earliest recorded Reading address for the family was 533 Moss Street. By 1914 Max had saved enough to buy a two-story brick row house at 818 Elm Street for $1,600. Within a few years Max took a bride, Hattie, and moved to 143 Moss Street. The rest of the family remained in the Elm Street dwelling until Max sold it in 1925 for $2,500 to Morris Hassel, who was spreading his wings as a Realtor. Gertrude, starting in her teens, helped to support the family as a seamstress. Abe was always more interested in making money than advancing scholastically.

When the United States entered World War I in 1917, Abe was 19. The military registration card he signed on September 12, 1918, shows a discrepancy regarding his birth. Later documents listed his birth date as October 15, 1898. The military draft registration indicated he was born almost a year earlier on September 3, 1897. In later years, he claimed during a court proceeding he had served with the Army in two wars. No documentation has been found that he was in the Army in World War I, having registered for the draft only two months before the conflict ended.

During the World War I years the older brothers had built a thriving huckster business, with help from their younger siblings. After the war, Max moved to Schuylkill County with his family and started a scrap iron company. As the wave of WASP morality swept across the country and Prohibition appeared imminent, Abe saw an opportunity to increase his income. He was 21 when alcoholic beverages became illegal in January 1920. Despite the strict religious values his parents fostered, Abe was brimming with ambition and could not resist the lure of easy money. From the early profits of his liquor trade he bought the property at 333 North Eighth Street and opened a commission house, a wholesale produce business. The row house was just around the corner from the dwelling he grew up in at 818 Elm.

He named his enterprise A. Minker and Bro. Alex was the brother more interested in selling apples and tomatoes than engaging in Abe's other darker activities. As a young boy, Alex had come under the influence of a small department store owner. This substitute father figure taught Alex the three r's, a good work ethic, how to use the telephone, manners, and why personal appearance would later serve him well. It was with some apprehension that Alex joined Abe in the produce business, well aware that selling fruit and vegetables was not all his older brother had in mind.

Abe now had trucks and knew farmers with stills who had moonshine for sale. Many residents of the city's South of Penn tenement houses had stills in the hallways. Abe bought and sold their wines.

In some ways, Abe Minker's career as a bootlegger paralleled Max Hassel's, who was the older brother of Morris. Abe and Max bought and sold liquor in the early stages of Prohibition but there is no evidence they were ever partners. By 1923, Hassel was concentrating on beer and continued in the brewery business the rest of his short life.

Early in his career, Abe displayed the characteristic that carried him to the top in racketeering circles, but almost cost him his life as a young man. Greed and deceit were weapons bootleggers employed to attain power. Abe exhibited leadership qualities early, and he believed trust among thieves was for losers. When he got involved with the sale of government alcohol, he was moving into the big leagues and taking more and more risks. Hassel, however, would soon far outshine Minker, becoming a millionaire by the time he was 25. He avoided the violence that so many bootleggers reveled in, while Abe took chances that invited trouble. Hassel would go on to become Reading's beer baron, then was a major partner in a North Jersey beer syndicate. Although Max disdained the use of guns to run his business, he eventually was killed by the New York mob that refused to let him become a legitimate brewer as Prohibition ended in 1933. His early death and Abe's long life refuted an old saw about violence: live by the sword, die by the sword. Abe died in bed at 87.

By early 1922, Abe Minker had developed alcohol sources in Philadelphia. Much of the contraband was hauled in high-powered sedans or autotrucks that could outrun the cars of federal agents and state police. Young, reckless fellows with a taste for speed were hired to make the 55-mile run up the Benjamin Franklin Highway, (later Route 422) the most direct route to Reading from Philly. Compared to today's superhighways, the main road was little more than a two-lane invitation to destruction. Crowned and in constant need of repair, the highway was bordered with runoff ditches rather than paved berm. Spotters would warn truckers if police patrols were in the neighborhood. Police radio communications were primitive.

To do his dirty work, Abe recruited a loose-knit gang of local toughs to run high-risk hijacking jobs for a modest fee. On his payroll were the Eyrich brothers, the Wentzel brothers, Ben Myers, Joe Czarnecki, Adolph DiCarlo, and several others. Charlie Eyrich and Otto Wentzel had theft records dating back to 1911 when they stole 30 hams from a Philadelphia and Reading freight car near Blandon. Abe paid his hired help $50 apiece to waylay designated trucks he knew were delivering alcohol to Reading. Now in their early 30s, Charlie and Otto were senior members of the hijackers, most of whom were about 10 years younger.

Twice before, consignments for Abe Minker had been intercepted by hijackers shortly before reaching the city. It was a Saturday afternoon when another Philly trucking crew was transferring its load of contraband to a Minker vehicle at a prearranged site just east of Reading on a back road. Before money exchanged hands, several gunmen sprung from the bushes to take possession of the Minker truck newly loaded with four barrels of alcohol. The Minker driver and his escort acted out their part in this farce, but the Philly teamsters were not fooled.

The Quaker City mob figured Minker had to be in on the heist. A four-man squad was sent to Berks County the following Monday to get an accounting from Abe. The big-city fellows confronted the suspect in front of his house on Elm Street. They were there to take him for a ride. Abe invited his would-be abductors inside to talk, but as they reached to drag him into their Jordan touring car, he broke free and fled down Elm Street. As two shots flew by, he ducked into a corner hotel at 8th Street. The gunmen followed in their car, turning north on

8th. Alex Minker was working in the commission house as their car slowed in front of 333. Several shots were fired into the grocery store, the bullets narrowly missing Alex, and the neighborhood was in an uproar. Police arrived and a description of the car with four occupants was sent out by police radio.

Pottstown received the message. Its patrolman on High Street, Obadiah Rhoads, spotted the car coming east on the main highway through town and jumped onto its running board, gun in hand. As the driver slowed to a halt, Rhoads relieved the occupants of their loaded pistols. The suspects were driven back to Reading.

Police Chief Harry Stroble charged the quartet with assault and battery without even ordering anybody to City Hall to identify them. The suspects were released on $300 bail each and ordered to appear before Alderman Focht the following Friday.

Abe, angry and frightened, offered his hijackers the opportunity to earn even more money by rubbing out his would-be assassins. At the time he didn't realize how much trouble for himself he was inviting. The Eyrichs and Wentzels told Abe they deserved a bigger cut for stealing four barrels of alcohol. Seven participants had divided $350. When Abe turned them down, they refused to become his hit men. Abe, still furious about his close call went to Alderman William J. Cooney to have warrants sworn out against his assailants. Assault and gun charges were filed with Abe and Alex as the prosecutors.

The Philly four showed up for the Friday hearing before Alderman Harry I. Focht, expecting to pay a small fine for disturbing the peace. Then the turmoil began. Constables John Smith and John Sparely suddenly arrived to serve the suspects with the Minker warrants. When the constables handcuffed the quartet and started to haul them away, the out-of-towners became annoyed and threatening. So did Alderman Focht, who angrily lectured Minker and his attorney:

"This intrusion is entirely without justification, is a direct slap at the police department which arrested these men, and it is the worst deal that has ever been pulled off in this court. There is a case to be disposed of and until then common courtesy and practice demands that all other interests keep their hands off."

He then postponed the hearing he had expected to conduct on the lesser charges. It was a costly tactical move by Abe, on whose oath the new warrants had been issued. The gunmen were taken to Alderman Cooney's office, where they were charged on multiple counts. Then bail was set at $1,200 apiece. Although one of the four had $1,000 with him, that was just about the extent of their collective pocket money. They telegraphed friends in Philadelphia and the bail money was quickly forthcoming. But now District Attorney H. Robert Mays decided it was time to intervene. When the next hearing was held on May 4, he was there, the defendants were there, but Abe and Alex Minker were not.

During the interval, Fred Marks, a former Prohibition agent who was closely associated with Max Hassel, stepped into the picture. He suggested that for everybody concerned it would be best if Abe and Alex just dropped the charges. The D.A. thought otherwise. Capiases had been issued and they were brought to Alderman Cooney's office the next day. Abe and Alex now claimed they could not identify any of the shooters who fired at them. Abe said he thought the car was a Buick, and since the Philly Four were in a Jordan, they probably weren't the ones who threatened him.

"Then why had you sworn in the warrants that they were?" Dist. Atty. Mays asked. At the time he thought he knew, Abe said, but since then he decided he wasn't sure, so it wouldn't be fair to definitely identify them as the gunmen. Mays said there was no choice but to drop the charges and return the bail money to the defendants. However, Minker was ordered to pay the court costs for frivolously wasting everybody's time. Mays guaranteed that this was not the end of the case. Perjury, he warned, was on his mind.

The Minkers continued to run booze in and out of Reading despite threats of retaliation from their Philadelphia contacts. Eventually the parties reached a compromise: the metropolitan gangsters would let Abe go on living, if he quit shortstopping their deliveries.

Closer to home, Abe was having trouble with several of his own henchmen. The Eyrich-Wentzel bunch had become disenchanted with Abe's pay scale. They began turning down other Minker hijack jobs or offers to make deliveries that spring. By summer there was a complete break. As the falling out erupted into open warfare, the police began calling the two factions the North 8th Street gang and the South 7th Street gang. The climax of this feud was a high-speed chase equal to anything Hollywood could dream up, resulting in the arrests of 14 wild characters with Abe Minker the focal point of the uproar.

The 7th Streeters learned that another shipment of alcohol would be arriving from Philadelphia the evening of July 19. They were waiting at the east end of Norristown on the Ben Franklin Highway when a Minker & Bro. autotruck approached. The autotruck was a high-powered sedan with the back seat and trunk reconstructed to provide more cargo space. Bill Weidman, a regular Minker grocery driver, may or may not have known what he was hauling. He said he didn't know but it turned out to be alcohol in three 50-gallon drums and three smaller casks. Ed Knarr rode with Weidman, and a Buick followed with several Minker guards.

Two cars of 7th Streeters tried to block the truck when it reached Norristown, but Weidman swerved past them and sent his vehicle racing west on Main Street. The 8th Streeters guard car also flew by as the hijackers scrambled into their automobiles to give chase.

As the vehicles reached the outskirts, Stanley Kozak, driver of the Minker Buick tried to block a fast-closing Stevens driven by Adolph DiCarlo, who tried to pass on the narrow, bumpy highway. As a front-seat passenger with DiCarlo, Charlie Eyrich was cheering him on, hanging out the window shouting profanities at Kozak. After much jockeying, DiCarlo managed to maneuver his car past the Buick. Soon he was closing the gap on the loaded autotruck. Bringing up the rear in the chase was a Haynes with Rocco Curro at the wheel getting lots of encouragement from passengers Clayton Wentzel and a few others. It was like a scene in a Mack Sennett comedy, only much louder than a silent reel—and this WAS for real.

By the time DiCarlo drew even with the autotruck, Charlie Eyrich was on the Stevens' running board, trying to get a grip on the truck to leap aboard. Weidner swerved right, almost squashing Charlie who was waving a knife, but drawing no blood. The other two cars were also jockeying for position as the quartet of vehicles zoomed into Collegeville.

Finally, DiCarlo nosed ahead forcing the truck to stop. Fearing the fiery Wentzel, Weidner and Knarr jumped out and ran. They escaped into the town's Masonic Hall. Wentzel hopped into the truck, clutched the steering wheel and continued west on the Ben Franklin Highway. At Limerick, he veered right onto Swamp Pike, heading for Boyertown.

According to a later report by Abe Minker, he had no role in the hijacking but just happened to be traveling to Philadelphia when the wild riders went flying west as he was traveling east through Norristown. He turned around and followed the speeding procession back to Collegeville where he picked up Weidman and Knarr and returned to Reading.

As Wentzel hightailed it up Swamp Pike, the other three cars continued the chase. Finally a flat tire halted the flight in Gilbertsville, just short of the Berks County line. The autotruck was bumping along till Wentzel pulled off the road in front of Henry Fry's general store. The potential for a real riot grew as 14 members of the two gangs piled out of the four vehicles, some of them armed with handguns. But these former compatriots were not killers, just exuberant young men mostly in their early twenties enjoying the lawless thrills that Prohibition offered.

A truce of sorts was reached as some of the Minker crowd loaded half the barrels of alcohol into their Buick and took off for Reading. After the tire was replaced, a few of the 7th Streeters left in the confiscated Minker autotruck, heading toward Philadelphia. But they soon turned onto back roads looking for a place to hide their loot. They found a suitable spot along a stream, unloaded their share of the alcohol and covered it with brush. They abandoned the truck after driving halfway to Pottstown, completing the trip on foot.

The Buick didn't get far before the wear and tear of the chase caused a tire to go soft. At a garage west of Boyertown the stranded Minker crowd responded as a car loaded with 7th Streeters drove by. Everybody was in high spirits, laughing and hooting and jeering, both sides evidently satisfied they were the victors. When the 8th Streeters got rolling again and returned to Reading, Abe was not happy that half of the delivery from Philadelphia was now missing.

At the age of 23, Abe had developed into a leader who could quickly rally his troops. Within a few hours he was able to round up a large search party of about 35 young men. The recovery team formed about midnight before setting out from Reading in a posse of about a dozen cars. They roamed the back roads of eastern Berks and western Montgomery counties. Earl "Piggy" Snyder, a 21-year-old bartender at Stanley Kozak's bar at 10th and Buttonwood, had Alex and Izzy Minker in his car when DiCarlo's Stevens was spotted—and stopped. Otto Wentzel and Charlie Eyrich, who DiCarlo had picked up after they hid the loot, fled from the car when they saw the size of the gang that was growing with each arriving vehicle. DiCarlo, however, failed to escape.

He was still in the Stevens when Snyder delivered a punch through the driver's open window. That was the beginning of a battering that DiCarlo took until he told his captors the location of the hidden alcohol. It was recovered and taken to another hiding place before Abe Minker sold it. Snyder drove the Stevens, with DiCarlo still getting mauled, back to Reading. After his release, DiCarlo claimed he was robbed of $500 or $600 dollars, quite a bit of pocket money in those days.

The feud heated up again the next afternoon when Otto "Buck" Wentzel and Charlie Eyrich, accompanied by younger brothers, Clayton Wentzel and Dewey Eyrich, showed up at Kozak's bar armed with lead pipes and blackjacks. The target was Piggy Snyder. Before they left, Piggy was as badly beaten as was Adolph DiCarlo the previous night. That was the first round.

Having trashed Kozak's place, the quartet moved on to 333 North 8th a few minutes away and surprised Abe Minker and his father in their commission house. Abe took a few licks from the attackers but, again, quick on his feet, he fled the store. Abe showed a lack of mettle by leaving his aging father to fend for himself, but was unable to do much fending. The Wentzels and Eyrichs worked over the 54-year-old Samuel to the extent that he was hospitalized for a few days with body and head injuries. An unlucky insurance agent and a few housewives happened to be in the store. They became frightened ingredients in the tossed salad the place resembled by the time the invaders left.

That day, any time members of the two gangs crossed paths there was a fight. A near riot developed that night at 6th and Penn, the gathering place for racketeers even in the early 1920s. For almost six months this long-running feud dragged on in the courts. Early on, the two gangs would have been happy to drop the matter, but the authorities wouldn't let go of it.

The Montgomery County district attorney's office charged eight of the Wentzel-Eyrich gang with highway robbery. The 7th Streeters countered by having DiMarco swear out warrants against eight Minker sluggers for assault and battery. Then the original April hijacking incident resurfaced to add to the Minkers' troubles. Dist. Atty. Mays charged Abe and Alex with perjury for having filed numerous gun charges against the four Philadelphia men, then refusing to identify them.

Dewey "Stumpy" Eyrich, a World War I veteran and father of three, insisted from the beginning that he had no part of the July hijacking. But Minker associates had fingered him and he spent several months in jail before charges were dismissed. Dewey's wife and other wives and mothers of 17 children by the 7th Street defendants claimed their spouses were not afforded swift justice because of postponements caused by Minker lawyers. The inelegant eight complained about shabby treatment by Montgomery County Prison guards, who in turn said they were merely reacting to outrageous conduct by the Reading rowdies.

The perjury trial of the Minker brothers began on September 11. The prosecution relied on the testimony of Clayton and Otto Wentzel and Charlie Eyrich to win convictions against Abe and Alex. The 7th Streeters admitted they were paid by Abe Minker to hijack booze from Philadelphia bootleggers and insisted that the brothers could easily identify the men who shot at Abe and brother Alex. The jury believed them and the judge handed down 2- to 3-year sentences to the pair.

Izzy Minker, only 16, added to the family woes by being picked up during a raid by Prohibition agents in Philadelphia the same day his brothers were convicted.

Abe and Alex appealed for new trials but only the younger brother was granted that opportunity to stay out of prison. While Alex continued his battle in the courts, Abe was shipped off to the Eastern Penitentiary in Philadelphia on May 1,

1923. After more appeals and three continuations of Alex's case, the perjury charges were dismissed for lack of evidence.

Two days after the Minkers were convicted in 1922, the 7th Streeters had their day in court—Montgomery County Court. They did not fare well, partly because a few of them were all too candid in describing the madcap hijacking that started in Norristown with spinoff action in several other places for the next several days. The defense witnesses all claimed they planned to turn the hijacked alcohol over to the police, but the Minkers prevented them from doing that. The jury couldn't swallow that alibi. Six of the eight originally charged were tried in court and five were convicted. Otto Wentzel received the longest term, 5 to 6 years; DiCarlo got two and a half years; Curro and Clayton Wentzel, each 2 years. The gang's stuntman, Charlie Eyrich, a 31-year-old father of four, sobbed when his 3- to 4-year sentence was handed down.

Was Adolph DiCarlo assaulted in Berks County or Montgomery County? That was the big question when the trial for Minker's gang started on December 12 in Reading. The question was never really answered as witnesses who roamed the countryside that summer night offered different versions of what happened. When Snyder was asked whether he actually punched DiCarlo, "Only hard enough to knock him over," Piggy said with a straight face.

The jury chose to believe that Adolph took his shellacking on the back roads of Montgomery County, and that's where the case should have been tried. Berks juries, quite frequently sympathetic to liquor law violators during Prohibition, ran true to form by acquitting all eight defendants.

So ended a misadventure of youth misspent and the miscarriage of justice. The Draconian penalties handed out to the Eyrich-Wentzel gang were in stark contrast to the court decision reached in Berks County where judges and juries were often more sympathetic to racketeers.

The month Alex won his perjury case, another run of notoriety began for the Minker family. On May 4, 1924, Alex, now living and working in Allentown, was in a fatal traffic accident. He was driving toward Reading a few miles east of Kutztown when his car broadsided another auto crossing Kutztown Road. Although six people were in the high-powered sedan Alex was driving, only 23-year-old Samuel Israel was fatally injured, pinned under the overturned car. A coroner's jury ruled Minker responsible for Israel's death. In December 1923 Alex was found guilty of involuntary manslaughter. His sentence: 6 months in prison and a $50 fine.

The day after the inquest, Abe Minker learned his first appeal for early release from jail was denied. He served another year before being discharged from the Eastern Pen.

# 4

# *An organized crime pioneer*

Away from his family for two and a half years, Abe Minker was released from prison in the spring of 1925. At 26, the experience of incarceration might have temporarily restrained Abe's freewheeling attitude about making a living, but it did not prove to be a permanent restraint. Although he returned to Reading for a short time, he soon was back in Philadelphia looking for work. Not much is known about his attempts to become a legitimate businessman, but there are lingering reports that his first few ventures were not very successful. It is believed he entered the clothing manufacturing field, but in what capacity we can only guess.

An indication that Abe wanted to go straight was that one of his goals was to become an American citizen. He realized an alien with a police record was not likely to be approved for naturalization. After three failed attempts to have a hearing before the state Board of Pardons, he began working the political system to clear the way. This was the beginning of a rather successful history of paying the right people to advance a personal cause.

In January 1929 he retained Francis Shunk Brown, a former state attorney general and former member of the Pennsylvania Pardons Board. Brown succeeded in convincing the board to listen to Abe's case. The prominent attorney gave an eloquent portrayal of Abe as a reliable businessman who had learned his lesson after a misguided youth. Duly impressed, the board gave Abe a good recommendation. Gov. John Fisher quickly granted Abe a full pardon, wiping clear Abe's criminal record. Although he now was eligible to apply for citizenship, that was put off for the time being while he pursued a more active role in Allentown with his brother and uncle.

Alex Minker, having completed his short term on the manslaughter charge, returned to his previous job in his uncle's construction business in 1925. Rubin Mainker was the brother of Samuel Minker, the father of Abe and Alex. Rubin owned Tri-County Construction Company in Longswamp Township, Lehigh County. As sometimes happened, the family name was evidently misspelled during the immigration process for one of the brothers. Rubin, unlike Samuel, was a successful businessman. He moved to Allentown around 1919 from Bayonne, N.J. In 1921 he started Tri-County Construction and went on to become a successful contractor in the Allentown-Easton area. Alex joined him in 1923 and eventually became secretary-treasurer of the company. He also worked as foreman on some of his uncle's building projects, which included the construction of several movie houses.

Tri-County built the Capitol Theatre on Allentown's Hamilton Street, and the 19th Street Theatre, in 1928. The 19th Street Theatre was described as a first-run silent movie palace just before talkies became the vogue. Four months after the theatre opened it went into receivership. Those two theatres were Mainker's last construction jobs before he sold the business to nephew Abe Minker in January 1929. This was at the same time Abe was probably paying a good sum for his pardon. If he was unsuccessful in the clothing business, it's possible he was involved in some illegal ventures to make ends meet.

When the stock market crashed that year, Alex Minker at 28, and his Uncle Rubin both suffered severe financial losses. An Allentown newspaper article at the time described Alex as "slim of stature with a debonair manner which impresses all who meet him."

In addition to the failed construction company, Rubin Mainker lost Penn Theatres Corp., which owned a chain of movie houses including the Strand and Franklin theatres in Allentown. Alex Mainker, a cousin of Alex Minker's, installed a sound system in the 19th Street Theatre and it was back in business by 1930.

Although Abe bought Tri-County from his uncle, the construction industry was at low ebb as the Depression era began. There were unsubstantiated reports that Abe built houses and apartments in Philadelphia. A more reliable report, however, came from Reading businessman Norman Kaplan, a Minker family friend, that Alex was the builder of Ridge Homes in Laureldale. Kaplan died at 95 in 2002.

When Alex returned to live in Reading in the early 1930s, in addition to his contracting business he worked as a salesman for several years. What he didn't do was get into the rackets with his brothers. Abe by now had plunged full-time into bootlegging and gambling, sometimes dragging his younger brothers along.

Although any financial gains Abe achieved in Allentown were minimal, he did acquire a wife there. He married the former Marguerite Vernon and on January 21, 1931, she gave birth to their daughter, Dona. The marriage ended in divorce the following year.

Despite the repeal of Prohibition in 1933, there was still a big market for bootleg alcohol and beer, and Abe Minker was right in the middle of meeting that demand. He became associated with at least three major bootlegging gangs. Although Abe had avoided arrest since his release from prison in 1925, his police record starting in 1935, and for the next four years, was crowded with court cases and convictions. During this period he was indicted five times, convicted three times, and served more than a year in the federal prison at Lewisburg.

The Alcohol Tax Unit of the Internal Revenue Service was tracking bootleg groups in the Scranton, Baltimore and Philadelphia areas, and Abe was called to testify before federal grand juries in those cities.

It is likely he moved into the numbers racket in the early Depression years. But in August 1935 two of his younger brothers were arrested in a house on Greenwich Street near 11th where a numbers bank had been under surveillance. Izzy and Bill Minker were believed to be running the bank, but local police said there were higher-ups controlling the operation. Bill, the youngest sibling at 24, was found innocent by a trial jury, but Izzy, two years older, pleaded guilty and received a 3-month sentence in Berks County Prison. It seems probable that Abe, by now 37, was connected to the lottery business because his involvement in major bootleg groups provided him with the financial means to bankroll a numbers bank.

In May 1934 Abe was indicted by a federal grand jury in Scranton, but wasn't arrested until June 26, 1935. U.S. marshals and ATU agents seized Abe in his house at 1601 Palm Street at 2 a.m. By that summer he was constantly on the move producing and distributing illegal alcohol over a wide mid-Atlantic area.

In the Scranton case the federal prosecutor called Abe "a big shot" in the Jenelli gang that operated illegal stills and sold untaxed alcohol. Among his peers Abe was known as the Baron because of his leadership qualities and a good mind for figures despite his limited education. The government claimed Abe had failed to pay taxes on $200,000 worth of alcohol he distributed while with the Jenelli gang. Often willing to trust the prowess of his attorneys, Minker was the only suspect of the 62 indicted who chanced to stand trial. Seven defendants became fugitives and all the others, except Abe, pleaded guilty. The purported syndicate chief, Peter Jenelli, received a 3-year prison term. A jury found Abe guilty, but he appealed the 22-month prison term and a $7,500 fine handed down by federal Judge George Welsh. Abe's decision to prolong the case proved to be a wise gamble as he was granted a new trial. Rather than begin another trial after the many convictions in the first one, on April 15, 1938, the federal prosecutor dismissed charges, wiping out the prison sentence ordered by Judge Welsh. By that time, Abe was involved in several other cases.

Minker was indicted with 16 others in Baltimore by a federal grand jury on October 29, 1936, charged with conspiring to evade liquor taxes. He wasn't arrested until December 13 in Allentown. The following May 4 he was found guilty and purported to have played a major role in the four-state operation. His sentence: a 15-month term in the federal prison at Lewisburg, where he was confined on June 4, 1937. He also was ordered to pay a $5,000 fine.

Hardly settled in his new cell, Abe learned five days later he was indicted by a Philadelphia federal grand jury with 98 others, all charged with conspiring to defraud the government of taxes due in the sale of liquor valued at $20.5 million, produced in an unregistered still and sold in four states. Abe got another break when the court entered a directed verdict of acquittal for him on April 1, 1938.

While the illegal alcohol trade took up most of his time, he also was managing a couple of Coal Region breweries. This became public knowledge when he was summoned to court to explain why he had failed to keep his beer licenses current. On July 28, 1937, he was tried and found guilty, drawing a 3-month prison term and a $250 fine. The good news was that he could serve the new sentence concurrently with the 15-month term.

Minker had a busy June 1938. Despite ranging far and wide in the illegal booze trade, Abe spent enough time in Reading for local authorities to add to his troubles. On June 4 he was indicted by a Berks County grand jury for distributing illegal alcohol. A few weeks later the grand jury in Philadelphia again indicted him on tax charges for his role in the three-state bootlegging combine. Before the month was out, so was Abe—he had completed his term at Lewisburg. Before he was released he had to sign a pauper's oath swearing he was penniless and could not pay the $5,000 fine. That September, the Berks grand jury indictment was dismissed by the local court for insufficient evidence.

The Philadelphia case did not go away quite so easily. One of Abe's acquaintances in prison had been Ruby "The Fireman" Gulkis. This Philadelphia racketeer headed the tri-state illegal alcohol outfit. After the feds closed most of the mob's stills, Gulkis's bootleg ring began collecting denatured alcohol, much of it stolen automobile anti-freeze. The contraband was recooked in New Jersey and Maryland stills to remove the dangerous denaturants, then distributed to retailers. Eventually 26 Gulkis associates, including Minker, were arrested. Worn down by the constant court appearances, Abe pleaded no defense, probably after making a deal for no jail time. He was given an 18-month suspended sentence, three months probation and fined $750.

In five bootlegging cases over the past five years, Abe was sentenced to a total of 58 months. There were three convictions, but with acquittals and suspended sentences and concurrent terms, he served less than 13 months in prison.

In his last conviction it was Judge Welsh who levied the suspended sentence. Welsh had seen the 22-month term he gave Abe in the Scranton case go down the drain when a U.S. prosecutor decided not to retry the case. In October 1939, Abe was summoned to appear before Judge Welsh to set some things straight. Abe had petitioned the court to have his 15-month suspended sentence wiped out and his probation period shortened. Hoping to foster sympathy, Abe had purchased the property at 335 North 8th Street and, with Izzy, started up his wholesale house again. He claimed his older brother, Max, and a brother-in-law, Abe Weiner, had advanced him $5,000 to get the produce business off the ground. His appeal was partially denied as Judge Welsh knocked off $500 from the $750 fine, but would not reduce any of the stipulations in Abe's sentence.

"Come back next year," the judge told him. If Abe remained clean, maybe they could talk about leniency. "You have innate abilities in a legitimate business, and if your reputation in the produce business was as high as it is in the bootlegging business, you'd be standing pat today."

His market did prosper, but Abe continued to look for other nefarious ways to line his pockets. In June 1940, he was arrested by the FBI in New York City for attempting to cash in a stolen $5,000 Treasury bond. Through Abe's underworld connections two large bonds that were stolen from a Minneapolis bank courier the previous month came into his possession. Together with a relative who operated a soda fountain in Philadelphia, Abe traveled to New York. While Abe waited outside the Federal Reserve Bank, the relative tried to exchange the $5,000 bond for five $1,000 bonds. The alert teller checked a list of stolen bonds, and Abe and the relative were arrested. Searched, Abe was relieved of a hotel safe deposit box key, which led FBI agents to another stolen $5,000 bond.

Abe's run of good fortune continued as Federal Judge William Bonudy ruled that the agents should have obtained a search warrant before, not after, taking possession of the safe deposit box key. The evidence was declared inadmissible—case closed, Abe had squeezed through another loophole.

In its determined pursuit of justice, the FBI asked the court to imprison Abe as a parole violator. Judge Welsh was assigned this phase of the case and again indulged the career criminal. The jurist accused the FBI of using his court of trying to cover up its own violations of the law. Abe's very capable lawyers were always ready with reasons why he should walk. Since evidence in the stolen bonds case had been suppressed, they said it could not be used to show their client had violated his probation.

Judge Welsh agreed:

"This is the first time this has happened in this court and I don't want it to happen again. I want it understood by every government agency that I will not permit them to do by subterfuge and indirection what they cannot do openly and aboveboard. It seems to me that indirection, subterfuge and circumlocution were used in this case and it was a clear attempt to use our probation department as a whipping boy."

So Abe, who had engaged in a criminal activity by trying to trade in stolen bonds, thereby violating his probation, could again enjoy that autumn day in New York.

His next bit of possible criminality, but again no jail time, occurred a few years later following the robbery of more than 50 craps shooters at the Recreation Billiard Parlors in Reading. Six New York armed robbers were arrested and tried for the February 17, 1941, holdup in the basement gambling den. Although Cole Watson was listed as the lessee of the 533 Penn Street property, it is believed to have been part of the subterranean complex of rooms that was Tony Moran's gambling operation at 529 Penn Street. The gunmen ordered the players to take off their trousers. Pockets were rifled and a safe was emptied. Police reported the crooks made off with an estimated $3,000. After they were arrested in Manhattan, the suspects claimed they took only $1,000.

Abe Minker's name was brought up during the trial later in the year when Berks County Judge Paul Schaeffer, as a witness, related a conversation he had with a Berks County Prison inmate. Judge Schaeffer said the prisoner told him that Abe Minker had arranged the holdup because Moran's craps game was competing with his own gambling operation in the Berkshire Hotel. When the prisoner testified at the robbers' trial he implicated Abe. No charges were placed against Minker because the prisoner was not considered a reliable witness. Other than that, Minker stayed out of the news for most of the decade, but he was empire-building on the quiet.

Possibly his wife had something to do with that. That would be his second wife, the lovely Verna Saltry. His first marriage, which resulted in the birth of his only daughter in 1931, lasted little more than a year. On April 13, 1942, he married Verna. His 35-year-old bride had been a hostess at a Scranton restaurant at the time they met when Abe was dealing in untaxed alcohol with the Peter Jenelli gang. Beautiful and blonde, Verna later was the secretary of State Supreme Court Chief Justice George W. Maxie of Lackawanna County.

How did Abe win such a lovely mate, his hometown buddies wondered. Physically, he could not come close to matching his charming bride, but he romanced her in a fashion that guaranteed their partnership for life. At 44, Abe carried 190 pounds on his 5-foot-7 frame. Although he never completely lost his Yiddish accent, he displayed a quiet confidence that associates respected. Possibly Verna felt Abe's past was all behind him when they married, but his past was also his future, and she would bravely suffer the notoriety and humiliation resulting from Abe's criminal career.

After four years of battling for his freedom in federal courtrooms, Abe had received quite an education from his quality attorneys. He learned how to use the law to his own advantage even when it appeared the government had an airtight case against him.

It is tempting to question Abe's motives when he joined the Army a year after World War II started. Surely he saw the possibility of wiping clean his police record if he distinguished himself in the military. There was talk among friends that when he enlisted on December 4, 1942, he had the connections to be assigned to an Army Quartermaster unit and would be commissioned as a major. He certainly had experience in buying and distributing provisions while engaging in legitimate and illegitimate business ventures, but, whatever his plan was, he remained a private only five months before being honorably discharged. Now he returned to Reading where he would gradually help organized crime gain a strong foothold in the city.

His short military tour of duty paid off just after the war in Europe ended. Congress had passed legislation granting immigrants who had served in the war a much easier path to citizenship. At his naturalization hearing some very influential witnesses, including Adrian Bonnelly, a future president judge of Philadelphia courts, praised Abe's character and generous charity work. He became a U.S. citizen on May 17, 1945, but that never took him down the straight and narrow path citizens are expected to follow.

The murder of Tony Moran in April that year caused a major vacuum in the leadership of Reading's rackets community. Was this a second attempt by Minker to remove Moran as the city's gambling kingpin? Ralph Kreitz continued as the top distributor of gambling machines, although Abe began edging into the pinball and slot machine business with his Fairmore Amusement Company. When the war ended that year, the number of Indiantown Gap soldiers making Reading their weekend playground gradually dropped off. Dutch Mary, having lost her not-so-secret partner, Tony Moran, saw a substantial decrease in her bordello business, but still maintained a house or two. And Mable Jones was establishing herself as the up-and-coming madam, eventually making Lemon Street as well-traveled as Plum.

The lottery game did not disappear with Moran's death, but more and smaller numbers banks distributed the wealth. It was more or less every man for himself before Abe Minker gradually built his organization. He partially filled the vacuum in the second half of the 1940s as he consolidated his forces.

During WWII and at the beginning of the Cold War era, federal law enforcement was at a minimum in small cities. All through the 1940s, three Reading administrations pretty much ignored wide-open horse parlors, numbers banks and gambling machines. As Ralph Kreitz told the U.S. congressional committeemen, you couldn't get elected by promising to stamp out gambling. By 1951 Abe Minker had positioned himself as the leader of a strong underworld gang that could give him control of all rackets activity, if he could also control City Hall. But the Kefauver Committee hearings spiked that possibility, and the policies of Republican Mayor Jim Bamford's pearly gray administration further stymied Abe's ambitious plans for another four years.

When Abe's Fairmore Amusement headquarters was destroyed by fire, he moved to 428 North 6$^{th}$ Street. This storefront was next to the Reading House, a neighborhood bar owned by Daniel F. McDevitt, the future mayor of Reading. Whether Minker and McDevitt first became acquainted at that time is not known, but the proximity of their places of business suggests a budding relationship once they became neighbors. It is possible that Abe financially supported Dan when he won a seat on City Council in 1953. And it was obvious he heavily contributed to Dan's campaign for mayor in 1955. Events would prove that a grand alliance was already in place to help Minker's domination of the rackets as soon as Dan took his seat in the mayor's chair.

Although Minker was quietly setting the stage for his future operations in Reading, he also was testing the offshore waters. In 1955 Abe tried to expand his legitimate holdings, although his past history as a racketeer came back to bite him. Through his daughter, Dona, he met Henry H. Held, a lawyer and businessman from Brooklyn. It was Held who formed a fashion design business for Dona and a partner in 1953. Later, she introduced her father to Held at a restaurant in Philadelphia. Eventually, Held and Abe were talking business: the development of a shopping center to be called Fiesta Market in Puerto Rico. Abe upheld his end of the bargain by having his brother Max's sons in Schuylkill County raise money to buy the land for the market. The nephews, Albert, Elwood, and Arnold Minker plunked down about $90,000 of the $135,000 deal for the land, with Abe supplying the balance. The proposition dragged on for a couple of years as Abe continued to promote the venture with Held. The attorney was on the verge of investing when he received a call from the U.S. Economic Development Corp. An agency representative advised Held about Abe's criminal record over the past thirty years. Held said he was shocked that he almost had become a business associate of a longtime racketeer. The deal collapsed. Abe sold the land for $175,000. His nephews might have made a small profit, but Uncle Abe was stymied from going international.

Minker was patient, waiting for the voters of the city's Democratic Party to bring back a friendly mayor he could control. When that happened, it wasn't long before Reading began being called Sin City in the national media.

# 5

# *Curtain rises on era of deception*

By the spring of 1955, the national exposure of Reading as a rackets town was diminishing as the primary election race was heating up. The Democratic voters who had helped Jim Bamford beat Jack Davis, now realized that no matter who was mayor, the rackets would survive. That segment of the Democratic electorate that had strayed was now ready to return to the herd.

Danny McDevitt had not sat quietly at City Council meetings during the past two years. He teamed with another Democrat on council, Paul Wolf, to battle the Republican majority in an unsuccessful effort to break the city's contract with Gilbert Associates Inc., to make improvements to the city water system. Also, having failed to create a water sewer authority to finance improvements to the sewage disposal plant and the construction of sewers in the $18^{th}$ and $19^{th}$ Wards, the pair worked to have the question of starting an authority placed on the 1954 election ballot. It was defeated, but McDevitt earned the reputation of fighting for a cause. During his two years on council he was director of accounts and finance.

Danny was an aggressive 38-year-old when he ran against the old warhorse, Jack Davis, for the Democratic nomination in 1955. The former mayor's earlier luster had worn thin and he won less than half as many votes as the 9,179 McDevitt received. Mayor Bamford chose not to seek reelection, opening the field for City Clerk Ralph Levan to become the Republican candidate.

Vice was a lukewarm issue in the election, although the GOP used a campaign slogan of "Keeping the Rackets Out." This was a bit hypocritical since the rackets had remained firmly in place during the pearly gray administration even if the Mafia influence had been defused. Republicans planted warnings in their campaign publicity about the blossoming relationship, although it's doubtful they anticipated just how cozy McDevitt and Minker would become.

As expected, McDevitt trounced Levan by almost 5,000 votes. It was a banner day for the Democrats who gained majorities in both the city and county. Among the Democratic winners was John Kubacki, who easily won a seat on City Council, along with Democrat Harold Guldin. To fill his unexpired term on council, McDevitt appointed Charles A. Hofses. Guldin was a labor leader and former Reading School Board member. Democrat Frederick O. Brubaker collected almost twice as many votes as the Republican incumbent, Henry Koch, in winning the district attorney race.

"If you don't like the way we're doing it, why don't you run for office yourself?"

That was the challenge Dan McDevitt accepted some years earlier when he filed a phone complaint about the condition of city streets. This was after his father had been chief of the streets bureau. To his gripe, an annoyed City Hall bureaucrat responded with the political cliché that Dan took to heart. First he helped others get elected, then entered the political ring himself in 1952.

His mother, the former Catherine Heffelfinger, and father, Thomas H. McDevitt, raised 13 children in their home at 1453 Cotton Street. Thirty-one years before his son became mayor, Tom was voted Reading's most popular volunteer fireman in a contest promoted by the *Reading Times*. His prize was an all-expense paid trip to that year's World Series. Tom was president of the Firemen's Union and of the Washington Fire Company, and a longtime employee in City Hall. He died shortly after Dan was elected to council.

As the fourth oldest child, Dan attended St. Peter's parochial school, then on to Reading Catholic High. "We all had to work to get along," he said. His contribution was as a newspaper carrier and selling peanuts at weekend sports and entertainment events. Before being drafted into the Army in 1942, he worked in Cassels and A&P stores.

World War II provided him with a greater sense of achievement as he served with a reconnaissance unit in the 5th Infantry Division in Europe. He rose to the rank of first sergeant of his company, was wounded during the Battle of the Bulge in Belgium, and was hospitalized for seven weeks in Luxembourg. Among his military honors were the Purple Heart and the Croix de Guerre, a French medal for bravery in battle.

After the war Dan and a partner, Bernard Pietrzykowski, purchased the tavern that became the Reading House on North 6th Street. In 1949 he bought Pietrzykowski's share of the business and ran the bar until being elected to City Council. Like most Democratic politicians he was a member of numerous veterans and Democratic clubs, fraternal organizations, and of course, the Washies, his dad's old volunteer fire company.

Dan's wife, the former Isabel Shaner, worked at the St. Lawrence Restaurant in the 500 block of Penn Street for 20 years. She served as manager of that popular eating place from 1943 to 1954. Interviewed by the *Reading Eagle* after her husband was elected mayor, Mrs. McDevitt said she hoped to avoid the political limelight that would shine on her mate. She did remain in the background during his years in office as his battle with the federal government and the local Republican Party intensified through 1964.

Minker had already done the groundwork to build a gambling empire before McDevitt's election. C. Wilson Austin, an attorney closely linked with Democratic Party politics for years, received a call from one of the Bonanno brothers, a prominent family in the mob. The caller was interested in buying the 30-year-old former Northeast Republican Club building on North 10th Street just below Walnut. Austin represented the Samuel Blatt estate, which had obtained the property in 1954 after a mortgage foreclosure. On December 28, 1955, Austin formed a corporation called X-Bex. Samuel, John, and Paul Bonanno were listed as the original officers of X-Bex. Austin, who had no interest in X-Bex, said he arranged a $125,000 mortgage with Reading Trust Company.

In a deposition given in 1961, Austin told about another mortgage loan he once discussed with the Reading Trust president. "This is for a Minker corporation," Austin told the bank official, "because if the bank does not want to do business with a Minker corporation, tell me right now. I want to save your time and mine." The bank official replied: "If the security is good enough, I will loan money to anybody." Austin told the banker the 10th Street property was worth $750,000. Dating back to Prohibition, most Reading banks had no qualms about dealing with known rackets figures, especially Abe Minker and Max Hassel.

Using the Bonannos as dummy buyers, the racketeers had obtained the building just a few weeks before the new administration would take office. The real operators out of Philadelphia immediately begin converting the place into a gambling casino that would operate with rare interference from law enforcement for the next four years.

After the election, but before McDevitt took over as mayor, he sat down with Bob Elliott. The respected police chief had done a commendable job of keeping Minker from bringing organized crime interests into Reading. Elliott was hoping this policy would be continued under McDevitt, but quickly learned otherwise.

"You can stay on as an officer but you'll have to go along with my policies regarding gambling," the mayor said. Elliott had no trouble interpreting that edict.

"Mr. Mayor, I'm going to keep on arresting gamblers no matter where you put me," Bob responded. On day one of the new administration, Elliott was demoted to patrolman and to a place where he could do the least harm—the basement where he became the permanent turnkey of the City Hall cellblock.

McDevitt appointed Bernard Richards as the new leader of Reading's 155-man police force. Bernie was an affable, soft-spoken veteran who faithfully followed his leader down the primrose path. Just the opposite of his feisty boss, Bernie just went along for the four-year ride, seldom speaking out, rarely showing authoritative anger or getting caught up in controversy, but always doing as he was told. With Bernie at the helm, many city policemen were frustrated as they had to ignore the rampant vice that soon became evident to everybody.

In Reading's commission form of government, the mayor was director of safety and head of the police department. So all law enforcement was directly his responsibility. He could hire and fire at will. On his first day in office, McDevitt addressed the second shift of his men in blue as they lined up in the squad room at 4 p.m.

"Assist me and bear with me," he stated. "Make Reading's police department the finest in the entire country. It can be done."

There were the usual promotions and demotions as there were every time a new administration took office. Being a policeman in Reading led to a precarious career. The cops endured McDevitt knowing favoritism rather than performance was politics as usual. Within seven months, McDevitt's vindictive actions would reduce his police force to a laughing stock.

If ever a new administration could be accused of starting out under false pretense it was that of Dan McDevitt's in 1956. In the first week of January, the day after the newly elected city and county officials were sworn in, a team of city police and county detectives raided a few city houses of prostitution. Two madams, Mable Jones and Girlie Williams, were arrested. The two cases were settled at the alderman level as both paid $100 fines. No attempt was made to have the case held for a court trial. This became a pattern that would continue for several years.

The same day as the prostitution arrests, another team of city police raided a small stakes poker game in the Calabria Club, 412 Penn Street. Each of the eight poker players paid $15 forfeits, failed to show up for hearings, and that was the end of that. No moves were made against the numerous bingo games throughout Reading. These initial police actions were little more than obligatory raids to mollify the moral constituency who wanted to believe the new administration really was bent on reform, one of its campaign promises.

Patrolman Bernard Dobinsky, a future president of the local Fraternal Order of Police, and years later a long-term chief of police, was promoted to sergeant when the new team took over. On day two, Dobinsky and detective Robert Bitting were summoned to the mayor's office. Among those present when they entered, in addition to McDevitt and Chief Richards, were Dist. Atty. Fred Brubaker, other police officials—and Abe Minker.

"The red flag immediately went up," Dobinsky recalled. "Then the mayor told Bitting and me, 'You fellows are going to close down the pinball machines. You are our new vice squad.'" That same day the mayor put all Reading operators of multinickel pinball machines on notice: take them out of service. He gave them 24 hours to remove such devices from stores, bars, clubs, restaurants—all places having them in the city.

WOW!!! was the citywide reaction. Was this the beginning of a general cleanup of the rackets? Insiders knew what was happening but the general public did not.

McDevitt's first assignment to Dobinsky and Bitting: on Wednesday take a squad of men to warn clubs, bars, and stores about the new pinball ban. The new sergeant carried out his orders, and on Thursday a few machines were confiscated. The ambiguity of McDevitt's directive was that the city required $20 permits for places profiting from the pinball machines, some of which cost up to $785. The stores and tavern owners and distributors that unplugged, but did not remove, their machines were in danger of having them confiscated by the police. Numerous license holders converged on City Hall the next day to have the fee reimbursed. City Treasurer John L. Hoch told them to replace the multicoin pinball machines with single-coin models, which were considered amusement devices, not money-gobbling games of chance. The sale of licenses ceased for the time being. The mayor released a statement concerning 341 active licensees:

"We issued the licenses for amusement purposes and, lo and behold, we find the machines actually are gambling devices. I feel the licenses were taken out under false pretenses and the city is not obligated to return the fees."

During the pearly gray administration, the Berks County Amusement Operators Association was formed to promote harmony and prosperity among the independent distributors of pinball and slot machines. After a few years of dwindling interest, the association was now revitalized by the mayor's unprecedented action. An assistant district attorney, Russell R. Yoder, quickly handed his resignation to Fred Brubaker because Yoder belonged to the law firm Ruth, Weidner, Woerle and Yoder. John Ruth and Henry Koch, two former district attorneys, were hired by the BCAOA to take action against the city of Reading. Yoder felt there was a conflict of interest, so he quit.

The biggest catch when the vice squad went into action was Charles "Chuck" Schwambach, who with his wife operated Queen of the Valley Diner at Lancaster Avenue and Morgantown Road. He also had a profitable pinball machine business at 611 Tulpehocken Street, distributing up to 85 gambling devices, shuffleboards, and jukeboxes. His arrest had been ordered by McDevitt to show the other operators he meant business. Schwambach would later report:

"The mayor made a statement to the newspapers that all pinball machines were illegal. So my telephone began ringing from my various customers: 'Please take them out, we don't want any trouble.' I sent my employees to start pulling out machines. Sometimes as our trucks pulled away, trucks belonging to the mob backed up and installed their machines."

The day after Schwambach's arrest, Charles Boyer and his son Warren were charged with setting up and maintaining multicoin pinball machines. That was about it. A few others were charged but most of the operators just sat back and waited.

When Schwambach and the Boyers faced questioning at a preliminary hearing before Alderman Paul Brogley, they refused to cooperate, taking advantage of their 5th Amendment rights. Brogley held them for the Berks Grand Jury. A worker at a store where a Schwambach multicoin pinball was located told the grand jury she paid a playing customer a quarter to leave so she could close down for the night. The grand jury, seeing no point in taking this case, and others like it, to trial, dismissed the charges against Schwambach and a few others who were seized in this charade the mayor soon backed away from.

It became obvious that the crackdown was merely a ploy to drive the independent operators into hiding and open the door for Minker. Bernie Dobinsky asked to be relieved from the vice squad, even if it meant losing his stripes. McDevitt granted his request but did not demote him. McDevitt then assigned another patrolman, his brother Raymond McDevitt, to team with Bitting on the vice squad. Later, Raymond was promoted to captain. Dobinsky eventually became a desk sergeant, and then on to chief of the department from 1968 throughout the 1970s.

Dist. Atty. Brubaker issued a statement on Thursday of that first week in office that he supported McDevitt's ban on city multicoin pinball machines but he was still studying the situation to determine whether the taboo should extend into the county.

Behind the scenes, a scenario that had been plotted before the election continued to be acted out. As usual, Abe Minker had his minions do the dirty work so he could not be directly implicated in illegal activities. Alex Fudeman, Minker's 42-year-old nephew, was his middleman during negotiations with the BCAOA. Alex and his brother Louis had been in the rackets for more than 20 years. Both were convicted in 1934 of running an illegal still in Gibraltar. In the early 1950s, the brothers also went to prison for income tax evasion.

It was Alex who called Mike Carpin, president of the BCAOA, to set up a meeting with the operators. This gathering during the second week of January took place in Carpin's office at 117 Penn Street. Alex palmed himself off as a goodwill ambassador. He invited the operators to employ him as their public relations representative. It was a hire-me-or-else offer. He guaranteed that City Hall and the Courthouse would cause the operators no further problems if they paid weekly fees to him. Alex's day job was running a grocery store—but he spoke for Uncle Abe and his audience listened. Most of the operators caved in to the extortion threat. Some, whose machines had been seized, figured this kickback was the only way to get their devices back in action.

The mayor took exception to a statement by the former district attorney, Henry Koch, that the purge of multinickel pinball machines was part of a shakedown racket. Dan fought back:

"I challenge Citizen Koch to disclose the names of the men he claims are pressuring so-called pinball operators for 'tribute,' so that formal charges can be prepared." Koch and McDevitt, although running for different offices in the last election, had exchanged some bitter words on the campaign trail.

Another poke at McDevitt was taken during a hearing for Clyde F. Snyder, whose restaurant was one of the first places raided the previous week. Dobinsky said he had been ordered on December 21 to investigate places where multinickel machines were available, well before the McDevitt administration took office. Dobinsky, still a patrolman on that date, had been given his instructions by Det. Capt. John Feltman, the only officer above the rank of sergeant who was not demoted when the Democrats took office.

Ex-Mayor Bamford, commenting on his successor's rush to put his plan into action, claimed, "Anything of that kind was done without my direction or knowledge." Former Police Chief Elliott also denied knowing about the premature investigation. Bamford said he never moved against the pinball industry because he did not consider it a threat to law and order in the city. Capt. Feltman took the blame by stating that complaints of children playing the machines were being investigated. As for Mayor McDevitt, he had no comment for the press. This was McDevitt's first small skirmish with the newspapers.

Having secured deals with the independent operators to make regular payments to Alex Fudeman, Minker gave McDevitt the OK to end the 19-day ban. The mayor was ready with a good excuse. He dragged out a 1943 ruling by the Superior Court of Pennsylvania that pinball machines were not gambling devices. Danny said his police force was still on notice to arrest any owners who paid off on pinball machines that were licensed for amusement only. It was an idle threat that soon became all too obvious.

When Josephine "Jessie" Maione's whorehouse at 117 North Seventh Street was raided on March 17, nobody was too excited. For Readingites, raids of this type were commonplace for years. Usually they were settled in the office of a city alderman who levied a small fine, took the money and let the girls and johns run. But this time Jessie and three hirelings were held for criminal court and had to pay total fines of $950. Josephine got the message. Despite numerous arrests over the next six years, Jessie and her girls of the night never again had to appear in criminal court. Well into the next administration, all prostitution cases were settled at the alderman level or in police court.

A clash in April between a newspaperman and McDevitt turned into a full scale war in the weeks and months ahead. The opening shot was fired by *Reading Times* reporter Charlie Kessler, who wrote about a City Hall meeting from which he was barred. After the meeting of Department of Public Affairs employees, a few annoyed employees told Charlie they were asked by the mayor to voluntarily contribute 2 percent of their annual pay to the Democratic Party. Macing was just traditional politics in Reading but was always conducted in private. After Kessler's news story exposed this practice, McDevitt was livid because earlier administrations had gotten away with it. At fifty cents a week, politicians felt they were not placing any hardship on their workers. The mayor promised there would be no retaliation to those who didn't ante up. Kessler went to the trouble of computing 2 percent of the city's $2 million dollar annual payroll—$40,000. That would be a nice start for the next election.

In May, *Times* reporters found multicoin pinball machines in stores within a short distance of Reading High School. They were in violation of the mayor's ban of such gambling devices near city schools. As he always did whenever the newspapers revealed vice operations, McDevitt insisted there had been no complaints made to his police department. Therefore, since his cops didn't waste time chasing rumors until such official complaints were filed, there was no evidence gambling devices were available to teenagers. He said it was his policy to brush off criticism of his administration because such negativity was merely media speculation.

But it obviously was more than speculation. In March, Julian Hanssens had issued a warning through the media that the Internal Revenue Service was going to clamp down on all proprietors of places where unlicensed gambling devices, including pinball machines, were available to the public. Hanssens was supervisor of the IRS office in Reading. His announcement came shortly after IRS raids in Schuylkill County resulted in 11 arrests. Get ready, Hanssens promised, his agents were out there checking, and there better be a $10 or $50 or $250 federal stamp displayed for every machine. If not, the machine would be seized and the proprietor would be in further trouble with the IRS if he or she wasn't paying the 10 percent gambling occupation tax. A couple of state police raids during the spring resulted in arrests and the seizure of unlicensed machines, indicating the operators were flouting state as well as federal laws. But gamblers, proprietors, and machine distributors continued to run the stop signals that were flashing in Berks County.

In another small community of associates, unanimity was ephemeral. By summertime, several of the pinball machine operators were not living up to their commitments to Minker. Alex Fudeman told his uncle not all of the BCAOA members were meeting their quotas when they came to his Penn Street office. By now the operators were calling Alex's place the shakedown office. Occasionally, Abe would make personal appearances to remind those in arrears to pay up if they didn't want a visit from the police. He also was angered by their refusal to disband the BCAOA. Then he found out that Ralph Blankenbiller Sr. was trying to rally his fellow members to revolt. At an operators meeting in June, Blankenbiller told the membership he no longer would pay the PR fee, and urged others to do likewise.

That summer Johnny Wittig was earning his pay as the mob enforcer. Warnings of personal injury or property damage seemed to be idle threats at first. Then, shortly after Blankenbiller's defiant stand, reality stormed in. It was a late June afternoon as Meredith Hagan, an employee of Chuck Schwambach's, was leaving Mike Carpin's office next to the Penn Street Bridge. Hagan saw Alex Fudeman drive by, then stop his car to let two very large men out. Hagan went back inside to tell the half a dozen loungers that he thought they were getting visitors.

When the strangers entered Carpin's place, one stood blocking the front entrance as the other announced, "Break this up. If you don't break it up I'll come and take you out of the house." He grabbed Carpin by the shirt, ripping it, and shoved him toward his rear office. On the way he slapped Mike on the head, still threatening further damage. In the office he continued to manhandle his victim, ordering an end to the BCAOA and its lawyer, Henry Koch, or else.

Out front, the bulky thug guarding the front door advised, "Don't anybody get any funny ideas. Just keep out of it and you won't get hurt." His hand hovered threateningly near his jacket pocket.

Hagan managed to slip out a side door and call City Hall. He said he hustled up Penn Street to a phone booth "with visions of a bullet in the back." By the time the police responded hours later, the sluggers were probably halfway back to their Hoboken or Brooklyn pads.

While the police dallied, Judge Warren Hess heard about the ruckus and called Carpin's wife. He then contacted Fred Brubaker who proved less than excited about Mike's health. According to the judge, in so many words the district attorney said he would look into the matter if Carpin filed a complaint. Mike didn't and the only investigation conducted was by a patrolman who showed up at the scene of the crime much later that afternoon. Some cursory questions put to those idling in the storefront indicated they really didn't want to talk about it. With no complaint—another case closed. The battering of Mike Carpin was a hot midtown topic for a few days but soon became old news and went into hibernation.

On July 7, county detectives Warren Heinly and Lester Sell visited Blankenbiller's Diner in Shillington and removed a multicoin pinball machine. More pressure was applied two weeks later when the same detectives seized two more of Blankie's machines in the Temple Diner on the 5th Street Highway. Ralph was never charged by the district attorney's office, but Brubaker obtained a court order to destroy the three devices at considerable cost to the owner. There were no other confiscations of other operators' machines during this period.

The strong arm tactic and the machine seizures served as a good argument when the operators weighed their options. Yearning for the old pearly gray days, most operators continued to pay their protection fees and many places where the devices were located bought $50 or $250 federal gambling stamps. The revolt continued to simmer for the next year as Johnny Wittig was kept busy issuing warnings. It was a rocky marriage of convenience.

# 6

# *Shootout adds violence to big picture*

During the spring of 1956 a fatal police shootout drew attention to Reading's burgeoning vice with the help of outside outlaws. It was the city's wide-open reputation that attracted a couple of dangerous holdup men from Lehigh County. They were suspected of staging a brothel robbery in Pottsville several weeks before they tried a similar job in Reading.

Erbor Worseck had served more than eight years in prison for having taken Allentown Police Chief James Elliott hostage during a stolen goods investigation. His 16-to-32 year sentence was later commuted by Pennsylvania Gov. George Leader. This proved a fatal mistake as Allentown police soon suspected the 31-year-old Worseck and his 29-year-old partner, James Redline, of staging a series of holdups in Schuylkill and Lehigh counties.

On the night of April 11, 1956, the pair came to Reading in a late-model car loaded with handguns, numerous packets of heroin, and bent on terror. Their first stop was at the Hand In Hand Café at Cherry and Lemon streets. They were looking for women, and the bar manager, Raymond Hershman, offered to drive them to the Midway Restaurant for some action. Redline said he was willing to pay $20, somewhat over the going rate. Hershman drove them to the Reading Company train station parking lot on South 7th Street. The Midway was directly across the railroad tracks.

For more than a hundred years, the Reading Company's train rails had replaced what was originally 7th Street. If you stepped off the curb in front of the restaurant, it was wise to make sure a westbound train from Philadelphia wasn't pulling into the station.

Thinking he was just helping a couple of out-of-town guys making the rounds, Hershman pointed them to their destination. On entering the dingy eatery, they ordered coffee while taking mental notes of the layout. Redline followed another male through a door to the living room where several women were lounging. The Midway's waitress, Burnell Quick, was on her way to the kitchen when she encountered Redline holding all the frightened occupants at gunpoint. Redline angrily questioned the women about where the money was kept. Everybody in the room, five women and four men, was relieved of wallets, purses and loose change. Worseck took $24 from the cash register in the restaurant, then searched all the rooms. Finding only a few dollars and change, not enough money to satisfy them, he decided to go look for the madam. Since Ardella Smith mentioned she had been with Mable Jones at the Grand Hotel a short time before, she was chosen to accompany Worseck while Redline kept an eye on the hostages.

On the short trip up the 7th Street sidewalk to Franklin Street, Worseck warned, "Don't act suspicious. Walk like a movie star, like Lana Turner … and you won't get hurt." He also mentioned that he had already murdered one person and wouldn't hesitate to kill again.

Turning at the tracks at the Franklin Street grade crossing they entered the barroom of the Grand Hotel just after midnight. They stood at the bar before Worseck sent Ardella over to a table where Mable was seated with Nathan "Nate" Liever, proprietor of the Grand and reportedly the local agent for rotating prostitutes around the southeastern Pennsylvania circuit. Phil West, owner of the Hand In Hand Bar, was seated with them.

Ardella told Mable the stranger wanted to talk with her in private. As Mable conversed with the new face in town at the bar, Liever and West, both experienced at reading body language of shady characters, did not like what they saw. Mable returned to the table. Without saying as much, her tone and expression signaled trouble was afoot, "I have to leave, be right back."

Surprisingly, Worseck left the bar with Ardella, allowing Mable to tell Liever and West that there was a holdup in progress at the Midway. Worseck and Ardella were waiting when Mable came out. Liever immediately followed them outside and notified two patrolmen on the corner, Michael Perate and John Kowalski, what was happening.

The policemen approached the trio from the rear, ordering the women to walk away. But Worseck spun around, .38 caliber revolver in hand, and disarmed the cops. The women fled as Worseck ordered Perate and Kowalski to walk ahead of him to the Midway.

The restaurant was empty, but in the rear, Redline had been terrorizing his prisoners. He pistol-whipped three of the working girls, Ruth Tyler, Mary Taylor, and Burnell Quick, trying to pry from them suggestions about where money might be stashed. He also had poured himself a tall glass of whisky which he proceeded to drink—evidently too fast as he suddenly vomited while still holding a gun on the detainees. Perate and Kowalski were directed to a bedroom, forced to the floor with a death warning if they moved. Still unable to find any large stash of cash in the house, the robbers prepared to leave, taking along handguns confiscated from the cops. After seeing the patrolmen taken captive, Liever phoned City Hall from the barroom and several police cars immediately converged on the scene. A shootout was shaping up.

First to arrive were Patrolman Harold Bean, a World War II veteran, and Patrolman Clarence Derr, who one day would become Reading's chief of police. They hid momentarily in an alley next to the Midway as Sergeants Donald Ray and Douglass Palm arrived across the tracks in another squad car.

Bean stepped out of the alley just as Worseck and Redline exited the restaurant. Redline aimed the first shots at Bean, but the patrolman returned fire before going down. A bullet glanced off Bean's trouser zipper and missed his spine as it spun through his lower body. Worseck was almost face to face with Bean as he too began firing. The 36-year-old Derr came out of the alley shooting. He was hit in the arm but scored a bullseye to Worseck's body. Redline, firing as he ran, raced across the railroad tracks as Ray and Palm opened up on him. Redline took a shot in the stomach, lurched across the station parking lot before diving under a car. Thirty or more shots were fired during the gun battle. The car shielding Redline was heavily damaged as he continued to fire. The sergeants, Ray, 49, and Palm, 36, were not injured as bullets whizzed past them. When his weapon was empty, Redline was dragged from beneath the auto by Jerome Bosold, a 27-year-old patrolman.

On the sidewalk in front of the Midway, despite a bullet wound in his left forearm, Derr overpowered the fatally injured Worseck. An unidentified man, possibly a john held hostage moments before, assisted Derr in subduing the bandit. Harold Bean sat bent over on the curb, blood flowing from his stomach wound.

Ambulances rushed the four casualties to hospitals. Worseck died at 6:30 that morning after surgery in Community General Hospital. Bean survived surgery in the same hospital but his condition was critical for more than a week. Redline's plight was similar to Bean's although his recovery was faster. After recovering from surgery in St. Joseph's Hospital, he was committed to Berks County Prison on a first-degree murder charge. Derr's arm wound was treated in Community General and he was released the following day.

At his trial in October, Redline was represented by M. Bernard Hoffman, who insisted the first-degree murder charge was inappropriate since the accused had not killed anybody. But Judge Warren Hess rejected Hoffman's petition to have the charge reduced. The jury found Redline guilty as Dist. Atty Fred Brubaker argued a murder was committed during the commission of a crime in which Redline took part. Judge Hess imposed a life sentence on the defendant. Barney Hoffman vowed to appeal the case all the way to the U.S. Supreme Court if necessary.

Mayor McDevitt praised his police for their bravery, but avoided any mention of the setting for the widely reported shootout. The Alcohol Tax Unit, however, was definitely interested in finding out more about the 57 packets of heroin found in the gunmen's car. Redline claimed they had stolen the heroin in the Pottsville robbery. Although he admitted being high on heroin the night of the Midway robbery, he denied ever being involved in illegal drug trafficking.

In 1958, a Pennsylvania appellate court reversed Redline's conviction. Instead of first-degree murder he was charged with armed robbery to which he pleaded guilty. After serving eight of a 10-year term in Berks County Prison and another six months in Schuylkill County Prison on a robbery charge, the 41-year-old Redline was released. He was lauded by officials at both institutions as being a model prisoner, a remorseful, hard-working trusty who never gave them any trouble.

Harold Bean slowly recovered from his gunshot wound, returning to duty eight months later. He retired as a policeman in 1962 and lived to the age of 86.

Despite Reading's sin city image, its persona did not include an overabundance of violence. Not until the infestation of drug gangs in the last decades of the last century could Reading be accused of being a dangerous town. Violence at the height of the racketeers' power was not excessive. The gun battle was an anomaly that occurred in a neighborhood that already had a bad name, if not to a frightening degree compared to its reputation shortly before and after the turn of the 21st century.

A spinoff from the 7th and Chestnut shootout was a major drug bust on Pottsville's Minersville Street in May 1957. Following up on Redline's admission about stealing heroin from the Pottsville whorehouse, the state police began an investigation. It proved an honest confession by Redline that culminated in the arrest of 30 prostitutes and johns. Drugs with a street value of more than $5,000, a considerable amount in 1957, were confiscated. Although not caught in the raid, Melvin "Bo" Washington was arrested at his Reading residence and linked to the drug ring operating in several houses on Minersville Street. Because of recently passed federal drug laws, Washington received a 5-year sentence.

Mable Jones now felt vindicated. Despite Redline's confession about the source of the drugs found in his car, rumors persisted that the bags of heroin had been taken from her house.

One of the few positive reports about crime in Reading came a week after Bo Washington's conviction. Harry J. Anslinger, the legendary U.S. commissioner of narcotics, came to town to address the 23rd annual convention of Pennsylvania District Attorneys Assocation. He announced that dope sales in Berks County were surprisingly light, considering Pennsylvania ranked sixth in the country in the traffic of illegal narcotics. Although Philadelphia was rife with heroin and marijuana at the time, the dealers and pushers were being thwarted in Reading.

This made Capt. Feltman happy because his orders were to avoid initiating investigations of prostitution or gambling without the mayor's okay, but he had a free hand to clamp down on drug dealers at any time, which he did.

# 7

# *IRS takes aim at tax cheaters*

Reading was no stranger to federal law enforcers by the 1950s. The first big contingent of government crime fighters to target Reading was in 1918 when the U.S. Department of Defense sent close to 100 agents into the city to wipe out rampant prostitution. During Prohibition it might have paid the feds to rent a house in the Berks County seat, rather than pay travel and board expenses for its agents headquartered in Philadelphia and other cities. In its extended campaign to close down Max Hassel's breweries and the city's numerous speakeasies, agents from one federal agency after another spent as much time in the Pretzel City as they did in their home office. The Senate Committee on Organized Crime in 1951 used Reading as its poster town to demonstrate how the national syndicate was connected to small city racketeers. Five years after that extravaganza, the Internal Revenue Service was laying the groundwork to prove once again it was more powerful than any defiant municipality.

Jules Hanssens, chief of the Reading IRS office, was keeping his superiors posted on how little regard local stores, bars and clubs had for federal gaming laws. In April of '56, Hanssens announced that enforcement of federal regulations was about to begin. Although Reading and Berks County officials might have been winning points with the betting community by ignoring state laws prohibiting gambling, the IRS had its own agenda regarding tax dodgers. On visits to places with gambling machines agents were refining their pinball skills in and around Reading and gathering evidence by cashing in games they racked up. More important were the notes they were taking about payoffs to slot machine winners.

Fireworks of a different nature came a day after the July 4 celebration in 1956. The usual Fourth of July firecracker and cherry bomb casualties were published in the next morning's *Times* but a much greater explosion of news occurred that afternoon.

Daniel L. Tucker was intelligence division chief of the IRS's Philadelphia District. For the next six years he would become a regular visitor to Reading, usually bringing along a large contingent of raiders. On July 5, Tucker led 30 agents in a roundup of multicoin pinball machines in Reading and its suburbs. All afternoon and early evening, working in pairs, agents seized 44 gambling devices from 23 places. The owners had signs on them "For Amusement Only" or "No Gambling Allowed," but the skilled players could earn cash instead of being awarded free games. Hotshots of that era will recall the flashy names the machines displayed: Bolero, Beauty, Starlet, Pixies, Broadway, Variety, Jack in the Box, Big Time, Singapore, Beach Club, Gay Time, and Dude Ranch. They were the current rage, sucking up nickels as fast as the suckers could feed them. The confiscated machines, some empty, some loaded with coins, were taken to the Berks County Courthouse basement.

The raid was the first in the Eastern Pennsylvania (23-county) District. The IRS said Berks County was selected as the kickoff point because "observations by special agents showed that violations of Internal Revenue laws regarding gambling were flagrant in the area."

The agents experienced no problems as they served search and seizure warrants on proprietors or bartenders. At first one large truck was sent around to collect the devices. But because of the large number removed, a second truck was needed. A few seizures were made as proprietors were loading their machines into get-away vehicles.

If the T-men met no opposition, it wasn't quite that easy for newsmen at the American Legion's Gregg Post at 10th and Penn streets. Tipped about the raid before the 1 p.m. starting time, *Reading Eagle* reporter Irv Rollman and photographer Ed Schneider were in the Gregg barroom when the agents arrived. Schneider started taking pictures, but several patrons and post officials shouted their objections. Leon McCall, post home association manager, waved his arms yelling, "You can't take pictures here." Another growling suggestion from a burly customer: "Throw the bums out."

Several pictures of agents and gambling machines inside and outside of clubs and at the Courthouse graced the news pages that day and next. But the feature story was about the mayor's former bar, the Reading House at 424 North 6th Street, being knocked off. T. Nathaniel McDevitt, one of the mayor's brothers, said he was the proprietor, all the while berating the T-men. Politics was behind the raid, he insisted. And Danny echoed that sentiment when he was asked to comment:

"I find it quite amusing and also quite interesting that this should happen at this time, in this year, 1956, which is just a coincidence that it is a congressional and presidential election year. I pose a question: I want to know where they have been in the last four years when the machines first made their appearance while the Republicans were in office?" (The slots in Reading actually dated back to the early 1920s.)

This became McDevitt's chant for the rest of his three and a half years as mayor. He claimed politics was behind every legal action taken by federal or state law enforcement units in his hometown. Unfailingly, he cried politics whenever the IRS, the ATU, the Pennsylvania Liquor Control Board, and the state police visited city establishments in relentless pursuit of racketeering. It became a standing joke that politics meant not only the Republicans in Washington but also the Democratic Party in Harrisburg.

McDevitt's first run-in with the Liquor Control Board was in 1953 after he was elected to City Council. The LCB regulations stated an elected official was ineligible to hold a liquor license. That's why the board refused to renew his license when he was elected. McDevitt lost his appeal in the Berks court, and the title to the bar was turned over to his brother, Nate, who was now, in 1956, in jeopardy of losing it.

Harold "Hoagie" Guard, owner of the Guard House, North 6th and Spring streets, took legal action after three of his machines were hauled out during the July 5 raid. Hoagie wasted no time hiring Jake Kossman, Minker's Philadelphia attorney. The court papers Kossman filed declared the IRS had illegally seized Guard's amusement machines and should return them immediately. Dan Tucker, back in Philadelphia when he learned of the petition, had a hearty laugh as he explained:

"The seizure warrants were issued by U.S. Commissioner Henry Carr on affidavits by our men that they played the machines and when they hit, they were paid off in cash." In addition to the three Guard machines seized, agents grabbed a note pad containing "records of payoffs."

Fred Brubaker arrived at the same conclusion as did Mayor McDevitt. He, too, characterized the raids "more of a political maneuver than a law enforcement exercise." Fred told about offering the feds evidence about multicoin pinball machines four days after he assumed office. He had prosecuted two proprietors, gained one conviction and a second indictment. The D.A. claimed the T-men shunned him, just as they did on July 6 when he again tried to offer assistance.

"In January," Brubaker stated, "the Washington agents were not interested, but in July the Washington agents have picked Reading and Berks County from among the 67 counties in Pennsylvania. And in so doing, they failed to ask for coordination from local law enforcement officials." He then said, "However, if it is a sincere effort of law enforcement in spite of its circus-like birth, I offer 100 percent cooperation from the district attorney's office of Berks County." The T-men never did seek his cooperation in the years ahead.

Like other attorneys before and after him, Kossman argued that the machines were clearly marked "For Amusement Only." Since pinball machines had been declared legal by a Pennsylvania court, he pointed out, the feds had no right to seize the expensive devices. The insignificant amounts of money being paid out seemed like small potatoes to rate such a show of force by the IRS, but the tax people were looking at the big picture. They were after the man at the top who was pulling in hundreds of thousands of dollars from various sources in the gambling chain.

One segment of watchers that was "happy with the support of the federal government" was the Christian Community Life Committee. Its president, the Rev. Paul Z. Ebersole, said his group was formulating a system to monitor multicoin pinball machines being used for gambling. This committee of the Greater Reading Council of Churches invited FBI agents to lecture in Reading and show movies on how pinball machines and other amusement devices could be set to lower the odds of winning, and bilk the players out of money.

Again there was a stream of proprietors seeking refunds on their $20 city pinball permits. No dice, city treasurer John Hoch reiterated. He tossed the ball back to the mayor when questioned about whether the city was checking proprietors concerning payoffs. By Thursday, two days after the raid, McDevitt was no longer talking to the press. In a subsequent *Times* story, Charlie Kessler belittled the "usually loquacious chap" for clamming up, further alienating their once friendly relationship. Danny decided how he could get even with the monopoly press, as he frequently referred to the Reading Eagle Company dailies.

When *Eagle* reporters tried to enter the City Hall pressroom the following Monday it was locked, the word Press removed from the door. When McDevitt had taken office, he made available to reporters a room next to his office. The new quarters were certainly better than the closet-like enclosure where reporters had to work during the previous administration. It was left to William Morgan, head of the public buildings bureau, to tell the press it had been dispossessed. "The mayor said he needs the space," Morgan stated, and that was that. The first *Eagle* reporter on the scene was told to remove the typewriter and any other personal belongings of the press corps. Over the weekend none of the councilmen had been informed of the eviction, and no new accommodations were made available. When the mayor left his office that Monday morning the reporter asked for an explanation but none was forthcoming. "Too busy," was all Danny would offer as he hustled out of the building.

Unaware of the lockout, Charlie Kessler arrived in City Hall at 1 p.m., only to find his workplace no longer available. Unable to get an explanation from the busy mayor, Charlie called his city editor, Richard Peters. Familiar to readers as author of his Page 1 column headed "Old Pete," Peters sent his chief photographer, Cliff Yeich, to City Hall. Peters suggested that Kessler borrow a typewriter and start writing his story on City Hall's front steps. Charlie did a bit of creative begging to borrow an Underwood from one of the departments. As Yeich snapped a shot of Charlie at his new workstation, the mayor was watching from the window of his second floor office.

He reacted like a good soldier spoiling to counterattack. He felt persecuted and unfairly wounded by the steady barrage of criticism the *Times* had been throwing at him. His Irish was up—the consequences be damned. There would be no Purple Heart after this battle, only black and blue smudges on his political career that he would wear with defiance.

After the photo op, Charlie reentered City Hall, started up the broad staircase leading to the second floor, carrying the typewriter. There at the top glaring down at him were the mayor and the chief of police.

"Lock him up," was McDevitt's biting command. He turned and strode back to his office. Charlie grinned, believing the mayor was just going along with the farce. He soon realized the chief saw no humor in the order he had to carry out.

To describe Bernie Richards, low-key comes to mind. Rarely showing much emotion, he looked more like a big, gentle grandfather, than a ranking law enforcement official. Bernie had a long and undistinguished career on the police force until he hooked up with McDevitt. When he was chosen to replace the respected Bob Elliott, the rank and file wondered what was in store. Nobody could accuse Bernie of being anything but a faithful follower of his scrappy commander.

"When I saw that Richards looked grim and determined, I asked him," Charlie wrote, 'Was the mayor serious?'"

"Yes, he was." the chief replied, "Come with me."

"On what charge?"

"Disorderly conduct."

Specifically, the warrant for his arrest stated Charlie was obstructing a public passage. Actually, City Hall's broad flight of front steps was partially divided by two broad stone pillars. Charlie positioned himself to the left of the left pillar leaving the central steps clear for people entering through the main entrance.

Mayor McDevitt was bent on revenge. His reaction to the Kessler stunt was definitely spontaneous, but what followed a short time later possibly was a sinister weekend plot in response to the raid on his tavern.

Kessler had a slight speech impediment that became more noticeable when he was excited. Flabbergasted, he sputtered but smiled, while taking the short trip down to the basement cellblock. First, however, he returned the typewriter to the office from which he had borrowed it. To quote Charlie:

"It's a frightening, bitter feeling when Gestapo methods are used to jail an innocent person."

That was the lead to Charlie's front-page story the next morning. As he explained, "It was supposed to be a humorous picture poking fun at some of the strange antics that go on in Reading's city government these days." It was just the first act of a three-ring circus lasting more than a week.

About the cell he occupied for half an hour, Charlie noticed "one word scrawled in pencil on the wall: 'Repent.' I looked at it and wondered if the message could not be directed more profitably to some of the men who run the city's government."

During his brief stay, several cops dropped by his cell to offer condolences. One said. "And we have to work for a guy like this. You know how we feel."

Charlie's employer posted a $15 forfeit for him to appear in police court the next morning at 8 o'clock. The reporter continued to be amazed when Alderman John J. DeMott added to the absurdity by finding him guilty as charged. Chief Richards was the only witness. Reading Eagle Company appealed DeMott's quickie decision and entered $200 bail for Kessler's release. Charlie would have to wait more than a week before the wheels of justice rounded back into shape.

# 8

# *Tickets plentiful for mayor's dramatic farce*

The arrest of Charlie Kessler was a spur of the moment decision by Mayor McDevitt, but that did not satisfy his penchant for revenge.

While Charlie was idling in a lockup downstairs, McDevitt plotted an even more bizarre way of getting even with the newspaper company for allowing one of its editors to continually heap abuse upon him.

The principal target of McDevitt's wrath was *Times* city editor Dick Peters. In his Old Pete column there had been a steady drumbeat of questions and suggestions about how to eliminate vice in the city. And sometimes his opinions and advice were salted with large doses of sarcasm and ridicule. It was the tone more than the substance of Old Pete that drove Danny Boy to reprisal. Reading Eagle Company publisher Hawley Quier was behind his city editor 100 percent. On Quier's orders, Old Pete's column had been moved from the cover page of the second section to the front page.

Just about the time Charlie Kessler was posting his forfeit to appear in police court the day of his arrest, Reading Eagle Company delivery vans were loading up to make their afternoon deliveries. Before the drivers finished their rounds, the depths of Dan McDevitt's vengeance became evident not only to the folks of Reading, but eventually to newspaper readers and television audiences across the country.

Certain squad car police that afternoon were assigned by Chief Bernie Richards to tail the newspaper trucks as they delivered bundles of the *Reading Eagle* around the city. The police officers had specific orders to ticket the truck drivers every time they stopped in a bus zone, a no-parking zone, double parked, or parked too close to a fire hydrant. Since they stopped in those areas every day to drop off bundles of the afternoon papers, the drivers were taken completely by surprise by this sudden enforcement of parking regulations. Sgt. Bernie Dobinsky and Sgt. Bob Ochs tagged the truck they were tailing six times in 17 minutes.

Two other sets of police in squad cars followed two other *Eagle* vans. The total for those ticket writers: 20 tickets in 30 minutes. Each stop by the vans was a matter of seconds as the drivers followed their daily routine of hustling along their routes. This was just Day 1 of McDevitt's vendetta.

The next morning when the *Reading Times* bundles were about to be delivered, company photographers were assigned to cover this bizarre news event. Cameraman Jackie Evans followed the first van with the early editions. But he quickly noticed another patrol car behind him. Using his Graphflex to capture pictures of this unbelievable exhibition of law enforcement, Jackie made sure to park legally each time he got out to focus on the ticket-writing policemen.

Working under pressure to keep up with the fast moving vans, the officers made mistakes. At one location two tickets marked 2:38 p.m. had the same van stopping too close to a fire hydrant at 9th and Penn streets, while the second showed the same violation in the 1100 block of Perkiomen Avenue. There were other minor slips on the slips that the *Times* and *Eagle* published, further alienating the embarrassed cops.

An emergency phone complaint to City Hall during the daytime ticketing travesty was about a malfunctioning traffic signal at 5th and Spruce streets that had vehicles backed up for a block. The caller was told no officers were available to help untangle the gridlock.

Day 2, the mayor's counterattack was stepped up. Third shift cops were waiting in squad cars at 4 a.m. when the four *Times* vans left the loading docks on their city rounds. One truck was stalked by Sgt. Paul Breton and Patrolman Harold Eveland. A flashlight can be both a help and a hindrance when writing parking tickets in the dark on the run. Bronislaw Soltysik, the *Times* driver, did not dally—like the mail, the papers must be delivered despite all obstacles. Riding with him was *Eagle* photographer Stan Gring, his flash bulbs lighting the scene as his pursuers blinked and penned their violations as fast as they could. Having completed his first run, Solty returned to the newspaper plant at 4th and Court to reload. The policemen tried to catch up on their reporting, but soon had to resume the chase.

At his first stop, Solty was handed nine tickets—a record number in this new game of cops and drivers. And then the patrol car stalled as Solty pulled away at 5th and Penn. The flooding over, the cops ran a red light in their haste to catch up and almost collided with a double-parked milk truck. No time for a ticket there—must concentrate on the business at hand. And so it went, the van driver parking for a few moments, dropping a bundle or two, proceeding to the next drop. But for that morning, no more tickets were issued.

In the police department's continuing crusade against the infidel press, according to the gospel of Danny, 35 more tickets were handed to *Eagle* drivers Tuesday afternoon. In the process of tracking the newspaper vans, the pursuers were guilty of almost as many parking violations as were their targets. Double parking, blocking an alley, stopping too close to a fire hydrant, angle parking—the cops ran the gamut of ways not to park. Of course the newspaper reporters and photogs were present to record these misdeeds. Citizens gathered at paper drops just to watch the fun. Kids cheered the drivers, and jeered the cops. The messengers who were delivering the mayor's unusual approach to law enforcement became the victims in this extended charade. The boys in blue mumbled apologies, grinning and bearing it.

McDevitt added a bit more fuel to the fire by denying police reporters access to patrol car reports. The press was allowed to review accident reports but not the daily summaries of men on patrol car duty. Although the mayor would not discuss the overall situation with reporters, he did issue a written statement that the dailies printed verbatim:

"Because a City Administration should maintain an orderly flow of news to the general public, I sincerely deplore the status of my present relations with the local press.

"However, I think it is high time that a public official summoned the courage to remind the local press lords that, in spite of their tight monopoly here, they cannot ride roughshod and unchallenged over elected officeholders.

"Before setting themselves up as self-appointed custodians of public morals, editors of the morning newspaper might well engage in some personal soul-searching. The mantle of righteousness hangs ill upon them.

"When I read my oath of office, I saw nothing that said the Mayor was to become a docile doormat upon which smart-aleck reporters could regularly wipe their feet so that their editors' dictatorial whims could be gratified.

"Reporters work for a living even as you and I. Generally, I respect their profession. However, I have nothing but contempt for the willful, self-centered man who worms his way into a position of high editorial trust and uses his newfound powers to satisfy his own ego.

"A newspaper should report the news honestly and impersonally.

"Judging by the recent news gathering and writing tactics of the morning paper, its editorial policy has deteriorated into yellow journalism.

"This editorial deterioration, I submit, represents a dark day for Reading, which so desperately needs another newspaper or other type of communication medium so that the general public may get a true and balanced picture of local happenings.

"I am reminded of Abraham Lincoln's celebrated reply to his many critics:

'If I were to try to read, much less answer all the attacks made on me, this shop might as well be closed for other business.'

"I'll do the very best I know how—the very best I can, and I mean to keep doing so until the end. If the end brings me out all right, what is said against me won't amount to anything. If the end brings me out wrong, 10 angels swearing I was right would make no difference".

That same day Mayor McDevitt's message was published, the *Times* ran another story that did nothing to reduce the mayor's rancor.

With front page pictures, the story informed the public that the city's chief building inspector was guilty of blocking the sidewalk with piles of cinderblocks and bricks just up the street from City Hall. Robert McCormack, in addition to his city job, was the contractor converting a former store into apartments. The building at 828 Washington Street was about 75 feet diagonally across Washington Street from City Hall. R. I. McCormack was clearly printed on barriers blocking the sidewalk.

Of course the story compared Charlie Kessler's alleged obstruction of a public building to the piles of blocks and bricks forcing pedestrians to walk in heavily traveled Washington Street. McCormack had issued his company a building permit for the $7,000 renovation job, and a permit to block the sidewalk. But the big question for the appointed department head: was he violating Section 107.7 of the city building code? That section stated: No official or employee connected with the Department of Building Inspection, except one whose only connection is that of a member of the board of survey or of the board of appeal … shall be engaged in or directly or indirectly connected with the furnishing of labor, materials, or appliances for the construction, alteration or maintenance of a building.

Daily news meetings at the *Times* were beginning to resemble high level tactical planning for troops going into battle. The news was not neglected but the search for new and clever tactics to fight the ticket war dominated the meetings.

By the third day of McDevitt's Folly, as the newspapers had dubbed it, the national media was taking notice. Freedom of the press was at issue, but most newspapers and television stations evinced more humor than concern in their coverage. However, one Florida citizen worried in a letter to McDevitt it was wrong to hinder free access to a newspaper. Dan made time on his busy schedule to compose a two-page reply explaining that the monopoly press in Reading was a bigger danger to freedom of speech than was one small town mayor. His repeated reference to rodents might have given V. M. Newton, Jr. in Tampa the impression he (Dan McDevitt) was the Pied Piper of Hamelin trying to rid Reading of ratty reporters and editors.

The policemen assigned to the ticket detail were no longer smiling about this sham as a pursuit of justice. As a crowd of a hundred gathered at the *Times* loading dock on Wednesday afternoon, the squad car drivers were openly complaining about the nuisance campaign they were fronting. In addition to the personal abuse they were taking, they worried about the lack of respect directed at the whole police department in general.

But they carried out their assignments, doling out another 18 tickets, running the total up to 73. In addition to Bronislaw Soltysik, truckers Walter Hoffa, Milton Resch, Donald Columbo and Florence Williams had endured considerable ribbing and annoyance for three days. Flossie Williams, colorful and profane, let more than one police officer know what she thought of the harassment. She knew them personally from long years of touring the city, but her searing expletives added just a bit more emotion to McDevitt's confrontational relationship with the press.

When City Council met that week, the mayor removed the press table that had been situated very close to the council table. He explained that at times he had heard members of the press curse during meetings. The press, he said, could now use another table some distance away where representatives of business sometimes sat to speak with council.

McDevitt's counterpart on radio at that time was Paul Barclay whose "Night Mayor" program was broadcast on WHUM. It was a popular talk show for Reading listeners who liked to discuss local politics and other issues. In the course of the IRS raids and reactions emanating from City Hall, Barclay often took the newspapers' side although he worked for a competing news outlet. When Barclay asked McDevitt whether the press table banishment included him, the mayor said his actions against the Reading Eagle Company monopoly must be broad and bold. Reminded that Reading Eagle Company did not own WHUM, McDevitt replied, "Over the months surely changes will be made again." To Barclay he said, "I'm terribly sorry." Paul discussed his removal on that night's show.

Thursday there was no police escort when the *Eagle* vans moved out to make their drops. The war was over but there was not a formal announcement from the mayor's office. Charlie Kessler tried, unsuccessfully, to see the mayor, but through his secretary he learned, "There is no news today." Reading Eagle Company said it would file a petition to have the parking tickets ruled illegal.

That same morning the *Times* published a story that McDevitt ordered members of the police department to take samples of the type faces of all typewriters in City Hall. He personally visited the *Eagle* newsroom the next morning to state his version of the typewriter incident. The typeface samples were in connection with an unidentified police matter, he stated. According to Kessler's tipsters, the mayor was trying to track down the writer or writers of anonymous, uncomplimentary letters he had received in City Hall the past few days. Just another sideshow in the circus that still had a few more days to run.

By the end of that hectic week, Charlie Kessler's disorderly conduct case began to heat up. Having appealed the $51 fine levied by Alderman DeMott, Eagle Company attorneys argued before Judge H. Robert Mays that their client had not received a fair hearing. DeMott, an alderman for only 10 days, had ruled Kessler guilty after listening only to Chief Richards's brief and mumbled testimony. Judge Mays ordered DeMott to produce all records of the case for a hearing the next week. In the meantime, City Solicitor C. Wilson Austin notified Chief Richards the disorderly conduct charge would not stand up in court. DeMott's handling of the case was a procedural bust.

Austin also issued an opinion on the parking ticket fiasco. He said momentary stopping of a motor vehicle for the purpose of actually unloading or loading, does not constitute a violation of the Motor Vehicle Code even though the vehicle might be stopped in an area where parking is prohibited. With his own legal counsel telling him he acted injudiciously, the mayor's harassment of the press was proving fruitless.

Judge Warren Hess, at a five-minute hearing, dismissed the charge against Kessler. Then he figuratively tore up the 73 parking tickets by agreeing with Wils Austin's opinion. Much ado about nothing was the unsaid verdict.

Two weeks later the press table was moved back to its former location. Reporters from both dailies insisted they were never guilty of cursing anybody, but obscenities at the council table were not unheard of.

Everything returned pretty much to normal in mid-September when the mayor made available another room for the press. By then, Charlie Kessler had left the *Times* for a short stint as a free-lance magazine and television writer. He said he never harbored bad feelings against Mayor McDevitt.

"By throwing me in jail, the mayor gave me the biggest break I ever had. I've gotten national publicity in newspapers, magazines, and television."

Later, Charlie returned to his first love, the news, by working another brief tour at the *Reading Times* before beginning a long career with the *Lancaster New Era*.

# 9

# *Jules—collector of stampless machines*

Many places in Berks County failed to heed the warning in 1956 that the IRS was going to continue enforcing federal laws regarding mechanical games of chance. There was a modest increase in gambling stamps but not nearly enough to suit Jules Hanssens. On February 13, 1957, IRS agents visited 18 places in the county. Seals were placed on 32 gambling devices with the warning that unless appropriate stamps were obtained, the machines would be confiscated. Although a second visit showed that the violators had purchased stamps, some proprietors had to be told they were required to post the stamps where customers could see them.

Shortly after that warning, IRS agents located three tractor-trailers containing 63 one-armed bandits on a farm near Dauberville. This evolved into a long legal hassle with Ralph Kreitz eventually admitting ownership of the slots that had been used years before at his Dreamland Park off the Pricetown Road. Ralph had completed a short prison term for tax evasion and was semi-retired from the rackets. He still owed the government about $287,500, so the U.S. felt compelled to seize these machines and sell them if possible. By the end of February, Hanssens claimed other unlicensed gambling machines worth about $150,000 were also confiscated.

Berks County was not the only target of the IRS. Hanssens led raids in Lancaster and Schuylkill counties resulting in dozens of fines and seizures. In the summer of 1957, Jules released some startling figures: racketeers in Berks and Schuylkill counties alone had not bought hundreds of the required gambling stamps and had avoided paying an estimated $1 million in taxes.

By early 1957, the gambling casino at 10$^{th}$ and Walnut streets had been doing a thriving business for about a year. It had become an open secret around town that this was a well-attended big league dice game. By now it had also changed ownership, further verifying that organized crime had its finger in the pie. The property was sold by the Bonannos' X-Bex Corp. to Albert DeStefano of New York City for $36,500.

Federal prosecutors would eventually report that Abe Minker received $1,000 a week from the casino operators for providing local protection. The annual casino payroll was $350,000, the government estimated. The racketeers employed as many as 50 "luggers" who nightly chauffeured Philadelphia area and out-of-state gamblers to Reading. There were croupiers, guards and doormen, food handlers, and the ever present mob loan sharks who "faded" the gamblers. The dice emporium wasn't a Caesar's Palace, but at that time it was believed to be the best place available to high rollers on the East Coast.

Numbers writers weren't too hard to find either. Old Pete frequently mentioned this accessibility in his column, but, since the mayor had no faith in much of what the daily newspapers printed, his police force was not encouraged to follow up these unconfirmed leads.

The Joint Committee on Christian Community Life of the Ministerial Association of Reading, and the Greater Council of Churches, sent letters to McDevitt and Dist. Atty. Brubaker complaining that "laxity" was apparent in law enforcement in the city and county, and asked them, "Do you share our concern for the good reputation of our community and good government?"

As usual, Danny found a way to shift the blame. He stated that the federal government was helping the rackets by selling gambling stamps. Following this logic, he claimed the feds were licensing gamblers and he had no intention of becoming a tax collector for Uncle Sam. Not in a shy way, he presented a list of achievements to prove Reading presently had its finest government in years. In 14 months his administration had managed the conclusion of a $4.5 million water improvement program, had repaved many miles of city streets, had reactivated the Redevelopment Authority, and demolished a blighted area between Washington and Walnut streets, and erected new street signs. As for his police force, it had solved 88 percent of the crimes investigated. Traffic fatalities were reduced from 12 to 2, and numerous outside toilets were removed from backyards. The outhouse issue was thought to have been settled decades ago. But he made no promises to crack down on gambling or prostitution, which he believed were no worse than in neighboring cities the size of Reading.

When Mayor McDevitt's brother, Nate, was charged with a gambling stamp violation the previous year in the family tavern, it was assumed this was an IRS warning that no club or barroom in Reading was safe from federal investigators. But Nate wasn't convinced. On September 7, 1957, the tax fellows were back, but this time they got him for running a horse book. Two other bookmaking establishments were knocked off that day with a total of six men taken into custody.

One of the three bookie joints knocked off was the Roundup Cigar Store at 9 North 8th Street. The IRS district office was directly across the street at No. 10. Gas mileage and surveillance costs were minimal on that investigation as government agents could look out the window and observe John Kranis and Tony Lucchese at their daily job of taking horse bets across the way. Jimmie Albert was at work in Vets Cigar Store, 14 North 10th Street, when arrested for bookmaking. Nate McDevitt was identified as manager of the Reading House. Also charged were George Stafford and Nathan Schlechter, Reading House employees. Another bookie, James Kranis, was arrested a month later. A total of $1,100 was seized from the three bookie locations. All seven were charged with failing to buy $50 gambling stamps.

The Reading House raid came at a very inopportune time for the mayor. He left Reading that day to attend a weekend U.S. Conference of Mayors in New York City. After the raids, the Reading and national press tried to reach him by phone but, as he explained in his Monday press release:

"I refused to answer calls placed every hour throughout the night, fully assured that the City of Reading was not threatened by any such catastrophe. The thunder and rumble had the identical tone of prior pre-election campaign thunder that would liken the city of Reading unto the City of Nineveh. The keynote of this thunder being—'Get McDevitt.'"

If nothing else, the constant pressure applied by the federal government inspired the mayor to exercise his literary prowess. He zeroed in on the federal gambling stamp that the Reading House had failed to obtain:

"By a concentrated and well-timed effort, the Internal Revenue Department found certain instances where federal tax stamps were allegedly not procured. This is a situation that can be duplicated in any city in the country.

"From the cities of Pennsylvania (including Reading), thousands of citizens attend the races held in other states—where betting on horses or dogs is legal. Thus when you attend, and perchance, bet on the races in ANOTHER state, you are a law-abiding citizen. If you place a bet on the same race in Pennsylvania, you are a lawbreaker in Pennsylvania.

"Then the Federal Government says in effect—pay the federal tax on horse betting and wherever you are, you are a law-abiding citizen.

"I am not flaunting the laws of our Federal Government, nor the laws of our state. I do say, however, that the legal situation is tangled and unclear. There is no city in the country that is not plagued with these conflicting laws, and as a result, a basic issue is being kicked along from pillar to post."

Several years later the federal law requiring gambling stamps on all mechanical games of chance was found to be unconstitutional after a flood of similar complaints from around the country. It was quite evident that the IRS singled out Berks, Dauphin and Schuylkill counties to enforce the gambling stamp law far more than in other areas of the state. The government was relentless in building a strong case against the man who defied every attempt to close down his operations in vice—Abe Minker.

The arrest of Dan's brother Nate and his fellow bookies had a ripple effect as the U.S. attorney's office in Philadelphia began using federal grand juries to look deeper into Reading's racketeering. Called to testify in November 1957 were Reading City Controller Bruce R. Coleman and two employees of bookmaker Tony Lucchese. Although they were not caught up in the September raid, Anthony Psardelis and Joseph DiBlasi, known numbers writers, were summoned to testify. No explanation was offered about any connection Coleman, a former acting postmaster of Reading, had with the two racketeers, but he was dubbed "an important witness." Bruce would become the first of several City Hall employees called before federal grand juries over the next several years.

As the bookie case worked its way through the court system, Isabel McDevitt, the mayor's wife, sought the return of $443 in cash and checks that IRS agents seized at the Reading House. She was listed as secretary-treasurer of Reading House, Inc. The money was eventually returned and all seven defendants received $1,000 fines and a year of probation.

At a hearing before the Pennsylvania Liquor Control Board 10 months after the raid, it was confirmed that Nate McDevitt and George Stafford were no longer employed at the Reading House. The tavern's license was suspended for 15 days.

Jules Hanssens was something of a cowboy. He enjoyed his reputation as a gangbuster during his stint as the IRS's hatchet man in the Reading district. It was further dramatized when he brought along on raids his good looking secretary, Kay Stover. Often, he invited reporters and photographers from the *Times* or *Eagle* to give them an up close view of his flamboyant crusade to collect the government's taxes. And if there were political implications when his boys made arrests, all the better. But the publicity didn't sit well with the mob. According to the IRS office in Philadelphia, a threat that Hanssens "will be found in a field," was reported. Whether the mob ever considered retribution was never verified, but it added to the hype. The local cops ridiculed Jules' grandstanding, claiming he courted attention after hours in local watering spots. He became something of a minor legend among those who dwelt on the rackets.

# 10

## *Notorious but generous to those he liked*

When Abe Minker bought a few acres at the merging intersection of Route 562 and Route 422, he moved his grocery operation from North 8th Street to the small store on the property. He called it the White House Market. This was in the early 1950s. A fire destroyed that building in 1957, but Abe quickly rebuilt a supermarket on the same site and kept the original name. This became the headquarters for his legitimate business interests as well as for other enterprises he was not so public about. In 1956 when he conspired with certain city officials to protect his rackets venture, he still operated Fairmore Entertainment, his gambling machine company at 428 N. 6th Street.

It was in the White House Market that he spent much of his time. Although titles were loosely distributed among the family, Alex Minker was generally regarded as manager of the supermarket. Izzy divided his time between Reading and Florida, but showed up at the market fairly frequently. Bill, the youngest, had moved to Las Vegas to work in a casino.

Mrs. Anne Brenner was the market's bookkeeper. She had the unpleasant task of explaining some of Abe's business matters to the Kefauver Committee in 1951. She began working for Abe in the early 1940s. The White House Market staff ranged from 20 to 25 employees before closing in 1964.

Abe was noted for his generosity to friends and employees he liked. He would not put up with phoniness or insubordination. If he detected such traits in a worker, quick dismissal was likely to follow.

Now approaching 60, Abe was nagged by chronic back trouble that required frequent visits to the chiropractor. During the late 1950s and early 1960s when he was occupied with legal matters, he suffered through long hours of discomfort in the courtroom because of his aching back. Aging, operations, and mounting stress would take their toll as he lost weight and was eventually reduced to using a cane. Although thinner, he was still solidly built and wore a 38-40 jacket. Izzy was tallest of the brothers, and Abe the shortest.

Abe developed an interesting friendship with George Christman, a young veteran of the Korean War who went to work at the market as a meat cutter, and later became manager of the meat department. George said Abe took a liking to him and often invited him to lunch at Fegley's Family Restaurant on the Philadelphia Pike.

"When we walked in you could see people knew who Abe was. We sat at a corner table out of the way," George recalled. When Abe wanted to just talk he would invite George to the Blue Room in the White House basement. It was a separate room large enough for a conference table where Abe met daily with his No. 1 aide in the rackets, Johnny Wittig. Every morning between 9 and 10 o'clock Johnny would join Abe in the Blue Room to discuss gambling matters.

Christman could not verify that Abe had a safe installed directly under his chair at the conference table. A local carpenter, Frank Novella, however, claimed to have constructed a strongbox under the floor shortly after the supermarket was built.

After Charlie Wade became police chief, he visited The General on Saturday mornings to discuss the continuing disputes they had with Mayor Kubacki. Abe also kept in touch with Joe Bonanno on a regular basis by phone. When Abe called Bonanno's home, if one of Joe's family answered, this was the message: "This is the general, is the colonel there?" Gus Yatron, at that time on the Reading School Board, and later elected to the state House of Representatives and the U.S. House of Representatives, occasionally shopped in the White House Market and was usually invited to the Blue Room to chat.

After Abe was committed to prison in 1963, the market was not the same, George Christman said. When the store closed the next year, George left for a butcher's job at ShopRite in Temple. He later opened his own place in Oley that is currently run by his son, David. At an early age, David was handed a $10 bill for Christmas by his father's boss. And to this day, George still wears one of the two cashmere jackets Abe gave him. Abe had a sweet tooth and a weakness for pies—just the filling, according to George.

"If he liked you, he treated you real good," George recalls. The hundred dollar bills Abe handed him on holidays was very big money for a young family man just getting started. The good side of Abe was always blurred by the clouds of illegal activities. He was generous to his synagogue, Kesher Zion, which he regularly attended. His only child, Dona, knew him as a good father who visited her often after she moved to New York City and married.

The White House Market was a successful business that helped Abe hide some of his tax indiscretions. But his blatant gambling empire would be his downfall once the federal government wanted their share of the take that he defiantly refused to pay.

# 11

# *Big league bingo has short run*

Before it was known as bingo, it was called beano. Historians claim the game originated in Italy in the 14th century, but didn't become established in America till the 20th century. By the Depression years, bingo spread through Reading as a financially rewarding game of chance for entrepreneurs. Bingo sprouted as a much needed source of revenue for charitable organizations and volunteer fire companies. Movie theatres had bingo nights. For some churches, bingo provided funds to run social and educational programs. A Catholic church in Wilkes-Barre credited bingo with helping the parish survive in the early '30s. Many good causes benefited from the loose interpretation of state gambling laws that allowed bingo to exist. As long as the prizes were merchandise, not cash, the authorities rationalized that bingo wasn't really gambling. The religious right insisted bingo WAS gambling, a game of chance, no matter what you won. It was an endless argument local and state officials have never resolved. The debate continues today.

Reading, with its large population of blue-collar families, had a natural affinity for gambling, and a particular passion for bingo. Over the years, bingo flourished, waning only on a few occasions when politicians were pressured by religious groups into anti-gambling stances because of blatant racketeering. City administrations in Reading, whether Democratic, Republican or Socialist, ordered police to ignore bingo operators as long as they heeded the merchandise-only rule. The elderly loved the game, many shuffling off to their favorite bingo hangouts on a regular schedule. Like the numbers game, bingo had a legion of followers. Because merchandise bingo was almost exclusively the domain of charitable and civic organizations, or very small businessmen, live and let live was the general feeling of the authorities. Racketeers generally regarded bingo as small change with insignificant returns. But the day would come when they tried to turn it into a big moneymaker.

By 1957, when chartered bus trips to various entertainment and recreational centers gained popularity, the professional gamblers revised their penny-ante opinion of bingo. More players and bigger payoffs could be incorporated to ensure a very profitable game of chance. It was an out-of-town syndicate that tested the waters in Berks County. Some believe it was one or more of the New York Mafia families involved; others felt orders were coming out of Pittston, near Wilkes-Barre, where the Buffalino family held sway.

The game opened in the spring of 1957 with little fanfare at Oley Township's Pheasantland Park near Pleasantville, about 15 miles east of Reading. A large cement block building that could accommodate a thousand seated players was the off-the-beaten-track venue the operators sought. Dozens of buses delivered hundreds of players from the coal regions and as far away as North Jersey. To give the game a bit of local color, John Hyneman, a longtime Reading gambler, was hired to manage the enterprise. But it was an organized crime unit that leased the building, supplied the gambling paraphernalia, and organized the bus trips. Showcasing merchandise prizes so ubiquitous at local games, Hyneman's display included toys, lamps, and other nonperishables, not the usual fare of hams, meat platters, and fruit baskets seen at Reading bingo sites. But the stuffed animals were there just for show. Cash prizes were the big come-on—lots of cash. Quite probably, Abe Minker was getting a cut by allowing outsiders to operate on his turf. Hyneman was certainly under his wing.

Although the new game not far from Reading was not overly hyped, it didn't take long for the aficionados to learn that a bingo bonanza was about to arrive. The evening of Wednesday May 1, several chartered buses were parked near the Reading Railroad station at 7$^{th}$ and Franklin streets to take players to Pheasantland Park. In the crowd was *Times* reporter Charlie Kessler who observed, then drove in his car behind the buses to the Oley Valley.

An estimated 1,500 showed up on opening night, packing the building well beyond its seating capacity. Traffic was heavy, and Hyneman called Oley Township Police Chief Russell Wren for more traffic cops.

Admission was free with each player receiving a card for two free games. Extra cards for regular games were $1. After the winner of a $500 game was wildly cheered, the professional caller from New York, John Weisman, kept the crowd roiling by promising there would be a $1,000 winner the following Friday night.

*Eagle* reporter Irv Rollman approached Hyneman, with whom he was acquainted. They chatted, nothing special, just small talk. Irv watched as John sold cards, handed out coupons to winners, and left no doubt in the minds of the players and reporters who was in charge. Winners were paid in coupons, the holders going to an office off the main hall where Chief Wren was posted at the door. Two men at a table in the office took the coupons and counted out cash prize money to the winners. Everything was well organized. The announced schedule: Wednesday and Friday nights and Sunday afternoon. But by the second week, a Saturday game was added. The biggest individual payoff was $850 on the second night—not the $1,000 as promised—of the game's 11-day run. Attendance ranged from 450 to 1,000 after the opening night overflow.

Besides Kessler and Rollman, two other reporters were regulars at the game. Gene Friedman and Bob Schoenert scribbled notes while covering playing. They attended seven sessions of the game before the dailies broke the story on May 13. For years the company had carried merchandise bingo advertisements, but that quickly ended when the Pheasantland Park game was reported.

Dist. Atty. Fred Brubaker and state police Capt. Reese L. Davis put their heads together a day after the *Times* made public that illegal cash bingo had arrived in Berks County in a big way. Brubaker released a written statement:

"This is an immediate cease and desist order. This order applies to all bingo, effective immediately."

As he did on several occasions during his two terms in office, Brubaker called on the Reading Eagle Company reporters to turn over to him their findings about the new game. The newspaper company took the stand that its reporters were not being paid to do the district attorney's job. If he read the newspapers he would know as much as they did. The D.A. in turn usually argued that he was understaffed with only a few detectives and in no position to initiate investigations. His job, he insisted, was to prosecute offenders, not to investigate their criminal activities. His philosophy of law enforcement was the source of constant antagonism between him and the press. But when it came time to prepare charges against the operator of the bingo game, he called on newsmen to help make his case.

Brubaker told reporters that Reading Eagle Company was violating the law by publishing bingo advertisements. Publisher Hawley Quier realized the hypocrisy of running news stories about the illegality of bingo, at the same time his firm was making $25,000 a year selling bingo ads. He ordered an end to the advertisements but continued his support for exposing unlawful activities in the community.

The day after Brubaker's all-inclusive bingo ban was announced, a group of 15 bingo operators met at Goody's Bingo on Court Street across from the Courthouse. They could not understand why they were being lumped in with the cash bingo gang that was violating the local understanding about merchandise bingo only. They then crossed the street, took the elevator up to Brubaker's office and had a long confab with him. After the meeting, the group held further private discussions about whether they should file a suit against the group John Hyneman was fronting.

The state Public Utilities Commission also got into the act by starting an investigation of the bus companies that were carrying players to Pheasantland Park. None of them had gained clearance from the PUC to transport gamblers. There were no chartered buses or bingo at the park Wednesday night following Monday morning's expose.

Pro-bingo forces were in a lather as Clarence Ehrgood, operator of Goody's Bingo, announced a protest would be held at the Reading Fair racetrack Monday evening, May 20. Predictions ran rampant as the bingo forces expected 5,000 to attend. Invited to speak were Fred Brubaker and the newsmen who exposed the game. A day before the proposed rally, Brubaker announced he would take part in the debate only if managing editors of the two dailies also participated. When the news executives failed to answer this challenge, Ehrgood called off the protest because without the district attorney it would be a waste of time.

That same day, Hyneman was arrested and charged with running the cash bingo operation. Capt. Davis, had received a complaint about the game the day after it opened. His investigators were present the second night, but left after witnessing winners receiving coupons, not cash, out in the open. Chief County Detective Warren Heinly also went to Pheasantland Park but had somebody else enter the bingo hall and check it out.

Although it certainly was no one-man operation, John Hyneman was the only one linked to the game who was arrested. Although they were not subpoenaed to be witnesses at Hyneman's preliminary hearing, five Reading Eagle Company editorial people agreed to testify when told to by Brubaker. "It is your duty to come forth with evidence necessary to obtain a conviction," Brubaker stated during a radio interview the night before appearing at a hearing before Alderman Paul "Mose" Brogley the next day.

More interesting than most of the testimony were the heated exchanges between the four lawyers in attendance. M. Bernard "Barney" Hoffman, representing Hyneman, was quick with the repartee. Reading Eagle Company had attorneys W. Richard Eshelman and William Lessig Jr. there to protect the rights of the reporters. And Donald Spang represented Clarence Ehrgood, the Goody's operator. The hearing became a noisy, colorful circus with Mose Brogley as the frenetic ringmaster.

County detective Heinly was the first witness. Although Hoffman maintained Heinly's hearsay evidence was not admissible, this was Brogley's courtroom and he let Warren do all the hearsaying he wanted to. The person Heinly had sent into the bingo hall to look things over was never identified, but that mystery man had reported that Hyneman was acting like the game's manager, so Mose let the detective tell his story.

Ehrgood had informed Brubaker he attended the Pheasantland Park game and witnessed people cashing in winning coupons. Now, testifying under oath, Ehrgood took the 5th Amendment on the advice of his lawyer because somebody playing bingo was violating state law just as much as somebody running the game.

Mrs. Edna M. Grauf, despite reminders by Hoffman about incriminating herself, had no compunctions about admitting she was a player and had seen Hyneman selling bingo cards on the floor of the hall. The Bingaman Street resident said she won $20 by having the first four numbers called. She said Hyneman handed her two coupons, which she cashed in for $20 in the office guarded by a policeman. The witness did not see Hyneman hand cash to anybody else, she said. Despite the earlier warnings about testifying, neither Mrs. Grauf nor anybody else was arrested for playing bingo at the park.

Next came the parade of *Eagle/Times* reporters. Irv Rollman recounted his conversation with Hyneman. Charlie Kessler testified that he found out about the game by reading an advertisement of the mob operation in his morning newspaper. Brubaker's examination of the press witnesses was tinged with sarcasm. He asked Friedman whether he had played bingo while covering the story.

"Only on May 4," Friedman said, adding that he spent $7.

"Say, you're a big spender—or else you play a lot of cards," Brubaker remarked.

Of the newsies, Bob Schoenert was the only winner. He told about playing bingo at the park on five occasions. He said he won twice on May 4, cashing in coupons worth $30 and $20.

Dick Peters was the last witness. He and Brubaker sparred about the newsman's Old Pete column in which Peters often satirized mob activities and city officials who seemed to ignore what was becoming an almost daily flow of stories about the rackets. As expected, there were fireworks when Fred and Old Pete went toe to toe. In one loud exchange, Fred asked:

"Do you have personal knowledge of the operation at Pheasantland Park?"

"I was not there." Peters stated.

Up to that point questions and answers were civil in nature. Then Brubaker opened up:

"You mean to say you weren't there and did not witness cash payoffs, but you called me a big, fat liar in your column?"

"If you read it correctly," Pete replied, "you'll find I did not call anyone a big fat liar."

"You said you knew who the big fat liar was."

"I did not say who the liar was, in print."

"I'm glad to get the record straight on that."

That concluded the first round of the legal portion of this case.

When it reached the trial stage on June 11, Barney Hoffman tried to convince the jury that bingo was a game of skill, not just a game of chance. Hoffman had used that defense almost 20 years earlier when he represented five bingo players at an October 1938 trial. He won acquittals for his clients from a jury that decided the issue in 15 minutes. Brubaker argued that the skill aspect of bingo did not matter, it was still gambling and gambling was illegal in Pennsylvania. This time the jury was out for a little more than two hours before finding Hyneman guilty of unlawfully managing a lottery and selling lottery tickets. However, he was acquitted on another count of setting up a lottery. In effect, the jury was saying Hyneman was not the boss. There was never any public announcement of an investigation being initiated to find out who was the real backer of the game.

The only new witness at the trial who did not appear at the preliminary hearing was Drexel R. Bradley, another *Times* reporter. He testified that he too covered the bingo games and on one occasion saw Hyneman in the payoff room handing a winner cash. That added a little to the smattering of evidence the prosecution presented.

This was the first time in the memory of gamblers that a bingo operator was found guilty in Berks County. Hyneman's conviction might have convinced some operators to lay low for the time being but it didn't deter John from giving it another try. A little more than five weeks after losing his battle in court, Hyneman was back in business at the same location, with a new payoff twist.

Instead of cashable coupons for the winners, cashable U.S. savings stamps were offered as prizes. With John Weisman at the microphone, the Pheasantland Park bingo game resumed on Thursday, July 17, with a crowd of less than 300 seeming even smaller in the large hall. It was explained to the players that the stamps could be redeemed at any bank or post office. Merchandise, such as toys, lamps, portable TV sets, percolators, irons, food items, or merchandise coupons from local department stores also were available to the winners. Unanimously, they chose the $10 books of stamps.

The first night the game ran smoothly with much of the same personnel as in May. Missing, however, was any sign of law enforcement. Only 10 chartered buses were lined up on the parking lot with about three dozen cars. Top prize for the night was a War Bond Special worth $1,000 at maturity.

Fred Brubaker had no comment when asked about the game by reporters that night, and Capt. Davis said he would act only if asked to by the D.A. The following day the IRS got into the act. Treasury agent Charles Saul handed Hyneman an IRS Form 1099. Such forms, John was told, had to be filed with the IRS showing the names of all winners of prizes valued at $100 or more. This meant those able to yell bingo had to give the government its cut of their winnings. That was enough to worry the operators and make players lose interest. Attendance dropped to 200 the second night, and the place was closed by the weekend.

That ended the tale of Pheasantland Park bingo other than Hyneman losing an appeal to have his conviction overturned. With no attorney representing him, Hyneman was sentenced to 3 to 12 months in Berks County Prison by Judges Mays and Forrest Shanaman.

The roots of bingo in Berks County were too deep to shrivel and die just because of this setback. Merchandise bingo soon returned and thrived under future district attorneys. Indifference by the state allowed cash bingo to flourish in the later part of the century on the condition that operators were charitable organizations. Finally in 2001, Dist. Atty. Mark Baldwin stirred up a fuss by closing down games whose operators were obviously not charitably minded. Rackets figures had gained control and were taking the lion's share of the profits, much more than they had agreed to in deals with various charities.

At another time, the IRS probably would not have taken an interest in bingo in 1957, but aware of the mob's tentacles reaching into so many other types of gambling, Pheasantland was added to the hit list.

That summer, Jules Hanssens issued a statement explaining why his investigators had been so busy in Berks and Schuylkill counties for the past year and a half. The racketeers in that area had built up a tax debt of almost $1 million dollars—$973,023 to be exact. And that figure did not include the major cases still in litigation that were getting special attention by the IRS rackets squad. Other tax delinquents—individuals and businesses owing withholding and Social Security taxes—in the Berks-Schuylkill area had good records, ranking lowest in the Philadelphia District.

# 12

# *Strong extortion case turns sour*

Warren Hess, president judge of Berks County's common pleas court, watched for more than a year as the mayor yelled politics every time outside law enforcement was needed to fight the blatant activities of the Minker mob. In 1956 when Judge Hess first heard about the Mike Carpin beating, his complaint to Fred Brubaker was ignored. This brush-off by the district attorney rankled the judge.

It was September 7, 1957, raids by IRS agents when the mayor's brother and six other bookies were arrested that piqued the judge's disgust with local law enforcement. Four days after the raid, Judge Hess sent a letter to Thomas D. McBride, the state attorney general. Berks Judges Forrest Shanaman and H. Robert Mays supported it with their signatures. The judges were seeking outside help to bring the racketeers in line. Mayor McDevitt immediately blamed the Republicans for stirring up the pot again. Shanaman was a Republican, but Hess and Mays were Democrats. Pennsylvania's governor, George Leader, was a Democrat. Mays, in particular, was well acquainted with Minker's activities over the years. He was the county's district attorney in 1922 when he prosecuted Abe on perjury charges and sent him to prison for almost three years.

In his letter to McBride, Hess laid out the racketeers' record of the past 15 months and how city and county law enforcement had dodged their responsibilities. It was a damning indictment of the present political leadership, and Hess requested intervention by the state. The attorney general wasted no time in acting.

On September 20, McBride came to Reading to learn in detail about the recent dominance of Minker over just about every form of vice in the city. After a long meeting with the three judges, McBride declared a state police probe would begin immediately. A day later Lt. Russell K. Knies arrived in Reading from the state police headquarters in Harrisburg with Sgt. Willard J. Stanton to conduct an investigation. It was no undercover job, no sneaking around to place horse bets or trailing gamblers in big cars. Much of it was interviewing gambling machine operators who were being fleeced by Minker. The investigators did not ask for local assistance, although Fred Brubaker was quick to offer support by his small detective staff. McDevitt also said he would cooperate but declared the charges of vice in Reading were merely spectacularism (sic) and politically orchestrated by the Republican Party. He also referred to *Times* and *Eagle* reporters as headhunters. At a press conference on the same day McBride was in town, Danny offered his opinion:

"We are in the midst of a political campaign that has hit a new low level, if that is possible, and I would caution citizens of Reading and other readers of the local press to think for themselves and not be influenced by bylines in the local press, knowing full well the local press is in cahoots with our unethical opponents. I again put emphasis on the readers of the local press to continue to think for themselves. Period."

By the end of October, the press was asking McBride whether the case would end up in a grand jury investigation. He said wait a little longer, things were shaping up. Houses of prostitution closed down, the numbers writers took a vacation, and the luggers from Philadelphia were no longer dropping off craps shooters at 10th and Walnut.

After seven weeks, Lt. Knies and Sgt.Stanton compiled enough evidence to do what McDevitt's police force had been directed not to do: they built a solid case against Abe Minker and his immediate subordinates.

On November 13, 1957, Abe Minker, Johnny Wittig, and Alex and Louie Fudeman were arrested by state policemen. Minker was charged with conspiracy, the other three with extortion and conspiracy. Several of the threatened and harassed pinball operators were spoiling for revenge and had given Knies and Stanton an earful. A hearing was scheduled for two days later. Judge Hess was assigned by McBride to serve in the role of magistrate. Brubaker suggested that the case go before a special investigative grand jury "to clear the air," but McBride nixed that idea:

"We are aware of the great cost and time needed for such action because of our recent proceedings in Dauphin County. We felt that we would not petition the court for convening such a grand jury at this time, as we felt we could get the same results through these proceedings." He didn't mention not trusting a local panel to reach an honest decision.

McBride appointed his deputy, Victor Wright, to prosecute the case on information received from the two state police investigators who had submitted a nine-page report. On the eve of the preliminary hearing, Wright released the findings of the seven-week investigation to the press. Regardless of the outcome of the criminal case that the commonwealth was now pursuing, publication of the report allowed the public to pass judgment on the racketeers. The report covered mob activities from the beginning of 1956 up to September 1957. According to the document, city police had not seized a single multicoin pinball machine after the mayor had lifted his ban on them at the start of his administration.

The most explosive area of the report was Wright's summary of the evidence which indicated to him: "One is inescapably led to the conclusion that, at best, the local law enforcement officials were less than diligent in the discharge of their duties in respect to the conditions described above." The report did not single out the mayor, the chief of police, or the district attorney, but law enforcement was their mandated responsibility.

In rebuttal, Brubaker answered questions from out-of-town newsmen:

"I most certainly do deny that there was any collusion or understanding or payoff between my office, myself, and any racketeers or other underworld elements. I want a grand jury investigation and I will continue to fight for it. As a last resort, I'll petition the court for it myself."

For the November hearing, Wright subpoenaed 13 witnesses for the state. But the first one he called, Ralph C. Blankenbiller Sr., arrived late. So George A. Reifsnyder, another pinball machine distributor, opened the floodgates as accusations poured out against the defendants. Like others who would follow, George stated that shortly after Mayor McDevitt decreed all multicoin pinball machines illegal, Alex Fudeman met with the Berks County Amusement Operators Association. Reifsnyder said Abe Minker's nephew offered to serve as a public relations representative for the group and would guarantee that Reading and Berks law enforcement authorities would not bother BCAOA members. He also described the scene at Mike Carpin's place that June afternoon in 1956 when two thugs entered the place, manhandled Mike, and threatened others to observe the rules Abe Minker had dictated. Reifsnyder testified he paid Alex Fudeman $125 a week in public relation fees for almost 18 months. He estimated his total payoff at $6,250.

The latecomer, Ralph Blankenbiller, was next on the stand but he proved to be a reluctant witness. He claimed Alex Fudeman never mentioned that he had connections in City Hall or the Courthouse. That's when Wright read Blankenbiller's statement to the state police investigators:

"We were told we could not operate, which represented a considerable loss in income. It would be better to go along. I agreed to go along against my better judgment."

Blankenbiller admitted paying Fudeman $100 a week for 16 weeks, "then I quit." He remembered Abe Minker was present when he paid his weekly fee at "his shakedown office." And Blankie told about the pep talk he made to BCAOA members to rebel against the mob, and the fact that his speech resulted in three of his machines being seized at two diners by county detectives.

When the hearing was recessed for several days because of a death in Judge Hess's family, the state police staged a couple of side shows to the court drama. First they arrested two Reading sisters, Rosemarie Pastore and Mrs. Phyliss Rohrbach, near Baumstown on the Philadelphia Pike. Sgt. Edward Strickland and Trooper Arthur McNally had been tailing them as they drove around eastern Berks County picking up numbers slips.

The next day, December 10, Knies led a five-man squad from Harrisburg in a raid against a Reading bookie and numbers operation in a grocery store at North 2nd and Washington streets. Although Victor Wright's report had mentioned that vice operations were closed down during the state police probe, it was now obvious the mob was already back in business.

Abe Minker was not included among the suspects in this latest raid, but Knies and his team had no doubts about who was behind the operation. Joseph Fiorini and Morris Salvi were identified as the pair in charge of the numbers bank, with help from Gerald Thompson, Sebastian Zampelli, and Louis Carrozza.

When the extortion hearing resumed, six more BCAOA members testified about making payoffs to Alex Fudeman. Chuck Schwambach, who had been the initial target of city police when the mayor banned multicoin pinball machines, admitted paying Fudeman $5,350 in 1956, and $3,900 in 1957. He testified that on one occasion when he went to Fudeman's office, Uncle Abe said, "What's this, you're cutting down on payments? You have an obligation to meet and you're not meeting it." Minker glowered as he rose from the defense table and accused Schwambach, "You're not telling the truth." Chuck, exchanging glare for glare, firmly stated, "I certainly am."

The witness also told about going to Minker's Fairmore Amusement Company, which had moved to the 700 block of Penn Street. This was in the spring of 1957 after Chuck had been visited by Johnny Wittig. Schwambach said "the enforcer" told him if he continued to miss payments he would send somebody else around to see him who would be more difficult to get along with than Fudeman was. When Chuck went to Minker's office, he said Abe proposed they form a partnership with their gambling machine businesses, but he turned Abe down.

Leonard Esser, a partner in Barry Amusement Company, termed the $2,000 he paid to Fudeman as shakedown or protection payments. George Siekierka said his partner, Esser, told him the payments came out of their profits. Charles Kerns, owner of Kerns Amusement Company, said he paid $150 a week to Fudeman, but halted payoffs only after handing over $2,225. Raymond Williams, another operator, said he paid $100 every Monday morning for 44 weeks in 1956, and for 22 weeks in 1957, a total of $6,600.

Mike Carpin was called to the stand to describe the scenario at his office that June afternoon in 1956. In detail he told about being threatened and slapped on the head by one of the two strangers who dragged him into his office. Mike also added to the shakedown total by claiming his fee was almost $100 a week and his total loss was about $4,000, all paid in 1956.

All told, 12 machine operators testified. In the end, Wright estimated that at least $50,000 had been paid to Fudeman by BCAOA members.

Asked by Wright whether any attempt had been made to influence his testimony at the hearing, Carpin said he received a call from Alex Fudeman on November 15, two days after the four defendants were arrested. He said they met that night under the Penn Street Bridge in Fudeman's car. "No one needs trouble," again quoting Fudeman, Carpin said, "you could be charged with perjury if you testified."

When Blankenbiller was recalled to the stand, to Wright's question about whether he was approached, Ralph appeared to be mystified and said, "I haven't been approached."

But Reifsnyder gave Wright the answer he wanted when asked the same question. The witness said he had received a call Wednesday evening, November 13, from Alex Fudeman, who was already out on $3,000 bail after his arrest that afternoon. Reifsnyder said Fudeman drove to his house and they sat in Alex's car and talked. He said Wittig was also in the car but was not threatening.

"Fudeman knew we had a meeting of the Berks County Amusement Operators Association scheduled for Thursday," Reifsnyder said, "and asked me to convey a message that we all would be better off to take the 5th or we would be arrested." Wright then told Jake Kossman, the defense attorney, "I won't tolerate your clients calling our witnesses before a hearing."

"He didn't tell them to lie or run away, he only asked him to convey a message," Kossman countered.

After Wright rested his case against Minker, Wittig, and the Fudemans, he immediately asked Judge Hess to allow him to present witnesses who were contacted by the defendants in an attempt to dissuade them from testifying. Judge Hess immediately granted the motion, noting it was very serious for anyone to attempt to hinder, dissuade or prevent a witness from attending and testifying in court. And that was just what Fudeman was charged with when Wright ordered him arrested before he left the courtroom that day. Alex retaliated 10 days later by swearing out a warrant against Schwambach, charging him with perjury. In the warrant Fudeman claimed Schwambach lied when he testified that he paid only $5,350 to Fudeman in 1956. Alex claimed Chuck paid a lot more than that. Another lie Chuck told, according to Alex, was that Abe Minker was present when Schwambach paid his weekly dues.

When Sam Liever arrived to represent Fudeman at a hearing for Schwambach, he expected the Berks district attorney to handle the prosecution. But Victor Wright stepped in to inform Liever that he (Wright) would represent the state in this case. He said he saw Fudeman's warrant as an attempt to silence Schwambach, and Wright had no intention of letting him get away with it. Wright said he and Fred Brubaker had an agreement that any case growing out of the state police investigation would be handled by the state attorney general's office. So he trumped the mob by keeping the case under his control.

For the next year the case against the Minker crowd was bogged down by numerous motions by the defense. A Berks grand jury indicted the four defendants and those indictments were contested in January 1958. One of the jurors, Thomas Williams, was arrested and charged with embracery, attempting to influence another juror. Then there was a turf war about who should try the case growing out of the December bookie/numbers raid. The state finally agreed to let Fred Edenharter, an assistant Berks district attorney, handle the case. Edenharter eventually gained convictions against Morris Salvi, Joe Fiorini and two others in June 1958. Fiorini, who was moving up in Minker's mob, served a month in jail on that conviction, the first of three he would receive in the next few years.

The state won a couple of victories when Alderman Charles Lease tossed out Fudeman's perjury charge against Chuck Schwambach, then held Thomas Williams for grand jury action on the jury tampering charge. Williams was eventually convicted but died a short time later. Fudeman's case of trying to influence witnesses moved through the grand jury but never reached the trial stage. Minker, Alex Fudeman, and Wittig filed petitions to quash their indictments, to no avail. Appeals were filed with and rejected by Pennsylvania's high courts. And finally, in early December 1959, the U.S. Supreme Court declined to review a final appeal to quash the Minker gang's indictments. That was the end of the appellate line.

Although the legal circus attracted a large, if confused, newspaper audience, the public was not aware of the shadowy drama being played out in gambling circles. The mob had waved a club at the BCAOA in 1957, but failed to stop its members from testifying at the November hearing. But during the next two years as the case dragged on, constant persuasion and generous offers eventually proved to be a winning strategy for Minker and his minions.

The trial finally got underway on Wednesday, December 12, 1959, in Berks County court before Judge Burton R. Laub of Erie County. He had been brought in to avert any possible partisanship, one way or the other, by a Berks judge. While Victor Wright was engaged in jury selection, his assistants rounded up prosecution witnesses who were showing signs of wavering. After the jury was selected, Wright held a pep rally, trying to bring the doubters back in line. He went to bed that night with ominous feelings. The next morning his fears were realized.

When court opened Thursday morning, Wright immediately called for a recess because of "a new development." Judge Laub granted the delay and asked Wright and the defense attorneys, Jake Kossman and Sam Liever, to talk things over in his chambers. Now the dealing began. Wright told the judge his witnesses were backsliding and without their testimony he had little chance of gaining convictions. The evidence against Abe Minker and Louis Fudeman was practically nonexistent if certain witnesses would not testify. Ralph Blankenbiller, Ralph Kuzer, and Chuck Schwambach had testified Minker was present when they made payments to Alex Fudeman. Now they were refusing to repeat those claims before a trial jury.

On returning to the courtroom, Wright repeated his fears to the judge and jury: "There was not only a general air of reluctance among the witnesses to testify, but also an instance of outright refusal." He said he could call the witnesses and direct them to testify. If they didn't, contempt of court charges could be entered, but "You don't win cases that way," he concluded.

In Judge Laub's chambers, a deal was agreed to: all charges against Minker and Louie Fudeman would be dropped on Wright's recommendation. As for Wittig and Alex Fudeman, they would plead guilty to extortion charges and pay $500 fines apiece and $678 court costs. The two charges of hindering witnesses against Alex would also be dropped.

Kossman tried to sugarcoat the shakedown by claiming the machine distributors had paid public relation fees voluntarily and the Fudemans had paid federal taxes on the $50,000 turned over to them. The violations Wittig and Alex admitted to did not deserve prison time, Kossman stated.

Before imposing sentence, Judge Laub let it be known he was not pleased with the plea bargain he was about to carry out:

"My instinct is against it. This is the type of thing that is to be deplored when it is minor, but this was a major matter. These defendants have done this community a disservice and it will take many generations to erase it. The commonwealth's evidence in the case is falling apart, and I suppose I would not be justified in ignoring the recommendations of the attorney general."

Victor Wright held his composure in the courtroom as he watched two long years of warding off legal maneuvers by Minker's lawyers go down the drain. He vented his true feelings the next day to an *Eagle* reporter. He berated the citizens of Reading for electing public officials who allowed the mob to thrive. His voice reeking with disgust, the deputy attorney general stated:

"You can't try a case without witnesses. I'll tell you exactly what I told them (the reluctant witnesses) yesterday, I am not a resident of Reading. I was never here before I was assigned here. While I like your city and think highly of your people, I don't expect to be back or become a resident of Reading. It's up to you people if you like this kind of situation, you can wallow in your own filth."

He said he was fully prepared to try the case when he walked into the courtroom Thursday morning. Then some of the witnesses revealed they would not testify. Some were on the fence, Wright said, but he felt they would take the witness stand even though, for reasons of their own, they were either fearful or just hesitant about testifying. "Without their testimony, the cases would have folded. It would have been a waste of the jury's time and my time," he stated. "We could have attained only the same results with those witnesses as we did. There was no point in going on and on when the end result would only be the same."

No official report was issued about why the operators changed their minds about testifying. But there was no shortage of theories inside and outside of the mob, however. One operator told a friend and client that Minker had relinquished to him his interest in a local beverage company. The same operator intimated to another acquaintance that he had come out of the extortion case "all right." Other reports had Minker repaying the protection fees he had extorted. Another rumor was that even though the fees were discontinued, there would be no pressure from local law enforcement. Minker supporters would claim the operators feared they would incriminate themselves if they testified. That idea could be discounted because they already were on the record of having distributed gambling machines. After two years no charges had been filed against them by the state police, and they further protected themselves by obtaining federal gambling stamps. The state prosecutors felt it was a waste of time to charge the witnesses with giving false testimony at the hearings in 1957. They no longer trusted anybody in Berks County.

Before Minker left the courtroom a free man, he walked over to the prosecution table. Abe extended his hand to Victor Wright and said: "I wish you a Merry Christmas and a Happy New Year." Many believe Abe played Santa Claus several weeks or months before Christmas that year.

A month before the trial fizzled, the voters of Reading elected John Kubacki mayor. Despite having opposed Dan McDevitt on many issues, and campaigning as a reformer who would fight racketeering, Kubacki's record of corruption exceeded his predecessor.

Despite years of criticism from the daily press for failing to take an aggressive stand against the mob, Dist. Atty. Fred Brubaker was reelected, and for four more years continued the pattern of leaving all investigations of vice up to the state and federal authorities.

# 13

# *The giant still nobody noticed*

The production of alcoholic beverages was a profitable cottage industry in Berks County long before Prohibition. Many farmers and immigrants made their own wine or moonshine at home. The practice became even more pronounced when the 18th Amendment took effect in 1920. Although the U.S. government placed a ban on the making, sale, and delivery of all beverages containing alcohol, the Great Experiment would eventually fail in its attempt to drive saloons out of business and reduce the consumption of alcoholic drinks.

Stills, large and small, dotted the landscape, often blowing up, occasionally causing loss of life and considerable damage. The sizable list of illegal still disasters in Berks County tells us that many citizens and racketeers felt the profits of bootlegging were worth the risks involved.

One of the early incidents of Prohibition in Reading occurred at 37 North 7th Street. Complaints by neighbors of odors emitting from the house were ignored by the police. Then on August 3, 1924, a fiery eruption of four stills in that one residence caused a major fire. Twelve barrels of mash and 125 gallons of moonshine were hauled away. A major row in City Council followed the demotion of several in the police department. Two months later two men, their clothes afire, escaped as another still exploded close to the Central Abattoir Company on Grape Street near Front. A truck containing 1,800 gallons of alcohol was seized. Nobody showed up to claim it.

When a Greenwich Township still exploded that same year, tenants Mary and John Hoffman were sued $3,200 by the owner of the property, Joel Gruber. The Hoffmans claimed they sublet the building that was destroyed to Clarence Stump, who was operating the still without their knowledge. Such were the vagaries when trying to find out who the true bootleggers were. The following year in the hills near Mertztown, federal agents arrested eight men and seized a distillery plant with the capacity to produce 150 gallons of moonshine a day as crews worked around the clock.

One of the worst tragedies in Berks County history happened on July 9, 1927, as a Bern Township farmhouse was demolished by a still explosion, killing a mother and six children. A farmer, Mark Fehr, had rented the cellar of his home to racketeers who set up a large still. He was outside the house and survived when the 100-gallon operation erupted in flames that consumed the rest of his family. Reading and Philadelphia bootleggers were held responsible. The road where the catastrophe occurred was later named Bootleg Road several miles east of Bernville. The explosion and fire were so fierce only unidentifiable bones were found.

Fehr was severely burned. He and four others were charged with involuntary manslaughter and liquor violations: Nicholas Ernesto, Ben Myers, Thomas DeMaio, and Angelo Consulio. Ernesto had survived a 1926 bombing by members of the Black Hand, an extortion gang believed to be seeking revenge. Nick's home on Carsonia Avenue was damaged but his family was uninjured. Fehr was eventually sentenced to two years of parole. The other four received two-year prison terms.

After dozens of small stills had been knocked off during Prohibition, the feds scored big when they closed down a Philadelphia-run operation in the old Gray Iron Foundry building in the 1400 block of Mulberry Street. The October 2, 1928, raid netted 10 suspects, with only one, Stanley Kozak, from Reading. The cost of installing modern distillery equipment in that plant was estimated at $250,000. Alcohol seized was worth $18,000.

The Prohibition agency had concentrated on closing down Max Hassel's breweries during the early years of Prohibition. But the raid at the Gray Iron Foundry demonstrated the Treasury Department's determined efforts to go after the still operators, too. And to discourage the homegrown bootleggers, the feds closed down Tip Top Products Co., 205 North 9th Street, a year after the Gray Iron raid. The company specialized in all types of kits and equipment for producing beer, booze and wine. When the agents checked Tip Top's customer list, they found the names of many of the city's prominent professional men.

Despite helping to nurture the roots of organized crime, Reading's history of racketeering during that era was not one of violence. The racketeers did not often resort to guns to have their way, but their dangerous practice of making alcohol eventually caught up with them. It was February 16, 1930, when the lid blew off. Two years earlier a gang fronted by Harold Nathan had purchased a building at Front and Court Streets that had been a distillery during the Civil War. Later it housed a paper mill but as 1929 ended, it had come full circle and was producing illegal denatured alcohol. Old pros from Philadelphia and Brooklyn were brought in to set up a big still.

On February 6, 1930, a Sunday afternoon, the western section of downtown Reading was rocked by a gigantic blast. Two pedestrians, Thomas Maggerio, 42, and Jacob H. Labe, 59, walking near the building were killed. Eight others were injured, including four of the crew working inside. A long-running investigation revealed that Harold Nathan was an alias used by Alex Kligerman, a well-known racketeer from the Philadelphia area. Later it was learned Hyman Goldstein, a New York real estate mogul, financed the Reading operation. Kligerman and three others served prison terms ranging from three to six years. Alex was on parole from Berks County Prison when he was arrested in Reading in a 1935 numbers raid.

Before liquor regained its legal status, three more wildcat stills were discovered in Berks County. In October 1931, a 1,000-gallon still was seized by the Pennsylvania state police on an abandoned farm near Leesport. A large still was uncovered on a Friedensburg farm by federal agents in October 1932. When four men drove up to service their open-air, 1,000-gallon contraption near Shartlesville, state troopers nabbed them in the summer of '33.

When drinkers could buy whisky, rum, and wine across the counter after December 1933, most of the remaining illegal stills were for private use. But racketeers knew there always would be barmen and speakeasy operators buying untaxed hooch. There were a number of still raids in Berks County during the ensuing years, but by the mid-'50s, the racketeers were so heavily engaged in gambling that bootlegging seemed passé. But the metropolitan mobs were still reconnoitering the countryside to expand their activities. On February 22, 1955, a veteran of the Prohibition wars led a combined county-state enforcement unit to an isolated property in Richmond Township, about three miles west of Kutztown. Two men were arrested as another escaped into the nearby hills.

Mike Reilly, now the Berks County chief detective after years as a state cop, had with him two other county detectives and two state agents. The 1600-gallon-a-day still they found in a barn was virtually new, having been in operation only a few weeks. The still had been built by members of the Greaser mob from Philadelphia and South Jersey. The raid was a harbinger of growing organized crime in Berks County.

In 1956, with the 10$^{th}$ and Walnut gambling casino prospering, Philadelphia racketeers were assured by Abe Minker that Reading was a safe place to invest in a large distillery. With city officials on his payroll, Abe convinced the mob the Reading police would not be snooping around when equipment was trucked in to erect a giant still. The same would be promised later when tons of sugar and other ingredients arrived on a regular basis. An ideal site was located in the southeastern section of the city. Much of the once thriving Penn Hardware complex had recently been sold. The area was in decline with many of its buildings unoccupied. Also in that neighborhood were a tannery, a slaughterhouse, a cannery, and a chemical plant, all giving off their peculiar emissions to mingle with the odor of cooking mash. The residential population had become used to the scents of industry.

In 1954, the 77-year-old Penn Hardware Company was sold to Fred Gerson, a prominent New Yorker in the hardware business. The company complex was made up of about 20 buildings, by 1956 only a few of them occupied. In 1955 David Realty Corp. purchased a few of the buildings along Spruce Street. Abe Markowitz, the company president, was looking for occupants for his properties.

Nobody was paying much attention when the Greaser mob, led by Charlie Veneziale, quietly moved into the neighborhood. Veneziale selected Angelo Sgro as front man to acquire property and set up possibly the biggest illegal still on the East Coast since Prohibition. Using the alias Joe Brown, Sgro became acquainted with numerous people in Reading, but he also remained a mystery man for almost a year after the government tried to pin down his true identity.

Abe Markowitz would one day tell federal agents how he happened to hook up with the bootleggers. It was early in December 1956 when he received a phone call from a fellow who called himself Joe Brown. Joe said he was interested in a couple of properties in the Penn Hardware complex. Abe invited him to his Spruce Street real estate office. A few days later an average looking guy in his early 60s entered David Realty Corp. Joe Brown asked Abe if the three-story brick building just across the courtyard from David Realty was for sale. Abe took the buyer prospect on a tour of Building 8, as it was designated on a diagram of the Penn Hardware complex. Brown indicated he was also interested in two adjacent one-story buildings, one fronting on Spruce Street housing Penn Electric Service Co. Markowitz suggested $50,000 as a price for the three properties.

When he returned a few days later, Joe bargained Abe down to $45,000 and they shook hands. Joe agreed to pay $3,000 down with monthly payments of $500 on a mortgage that Markowitz reassigned to him. Harold Blumberg, the first assistant district attorney for Berks County, and a partner in the law firm of Yaffe and Blumberg, represented David Realty in the sale. Blumberg talked twice on the phone with Brown but said he never met Joe face to face. The attorney sent by registered mail a recorder of deeds receipt for the property titles and the terms of the agreement of sale. These documents were dated January 10, 1957, and sent by mail to Angelo Sgro at the address, Spruce and Canal Streets, Reading, Pa. Sgro had no recorded address at that location so the registered letter ended up back at the Reading Post Office. It was January 30 when Sgro showed up at the window of postal clerk Robert Turner to claim the letter. When Turner asked for identification, Sgro produced a receipt that registered mail for him was being held at the post office. Sgro used the name Joe Brown when he signed for the letter.

The David Realty secretary, Maria Architas, got to know Joe rather well when Markowitz turned over mortgage payments to her whenever Brown dropped off his monthly check. Then she would see the two of them wander over toward Building 8 and gab for awhile before Abe returned to his office. Maria, who worked for Markowitz from January 1956 to July 1957, saw Joe and Abe together on numerous occasions. However, she never saw her boss enter Building 8 with Brown.

Markowitz was leasing Building 16 to Joseph Nawa, owner of Penn Electric Service. He notified Nawa his company would have to move by the end of January because unauthorized Penn Electric equipment was stored in an area of the powerhouse, the third building Brown purchased. As the company prepared to vacate the site, some of its employees noticed quite a bit of activity at Building 8. Windows were being removed and boarded up or walled in with cinderblocks.

After Penn Electric moved, city government was openly drawn into the bootleggers' web when Councilman Paul O. Wolf left a phone message for James L. Mengel, chief pump operator of the Water Department. Wolf's directive was to install a waterline that would service Building 8 at the Penn Hardware complex. "At your earliest convenience," the order read. Mengel was foreman of the crew that completed installation of the line and meter in February.

For the next few months a steady stream of equipment arrived, usually at night, and was installed by out-of-towners who kept to themselves. The government never quite got a handle on exactly when the still was operable or when the first cans of alcohol were shipped out. But it was probably early spring of 1957 because the cesspools handling sewage for Building 8 were blocked by disposed mash in April. At first still workers tried to flush the overflowing cesspools, but eventually a cesspool cleaning company was called in. The problem continued through the summer until City Hall answered a second call for help from the mob.

A letter signed by A. Markowitz was received by Mayor McDevitt and submitted to City Council on September 11, 1957. Abe claimed the substandard drainage system was discouraging industrial and commercial clients from buying or leasing his properties. David Realty was prepared to foot the bill for a 10-inch sewer line that would be connected to the main Spruce Street sewer. A month later another letter from Markowitz to Councilman Harold Guldin included plans for installation of the line.

On October 18, a resolution was approved by council, and the Registry Department issued a permit to install a 387-foot connector line. Assistant city engineer John Wayne Seifarth was handed the job order to oversee the work. J. Wayne noticed one significant omission on the blueprints: there was no mention of meters for the line or where to connect it inside Building 8. He pointed this out to his supervisor and mentioned several other shortcuts in the plans that violated city building codes. According to Seifarth, city engineer Francis A. Heine told him to just do it and not ask any questions.

When McDevitt found out Seifarth was a registered Republican, he called him onto the carpet. Mayor Dan held out a change of voter registration form and told the assistant engineer to shift his party affiliation to Democratic. "It will only hurt for a little while," McDevitt predicted with a mirthless grin. Seifarth refused. He quit and took a job in Florida. But he willingly came north almost a year later to explain to a federal grand jury flaws in the work order.

N.H. Garman Bros., one of the administration's favorite contractors, was awarded the job and began digging immediately, completing the project in just over three months. Now, with a plentiful water supply and adequate disposal facilities, the tax dodgers were able to dramatically increase their production.

Donald Noecker, chief of the revenue control office in City Hall, disclosed that water consumption in the still building jumped from 15,200 cubic feet in January 1957 to 78,700 cubic feet by June 1958.

Bootleggers plan for the short term and hope for the long term. The seasoned purveyor of bootleg alcohol understands that you must operate at full capacity as fast and as long as you can because the revenuers will eventually come a'knockin'. After a very successful run of well over a year, the honeymoon ended. On a tip, an investigator for the Alcohol Tax Unit was dispatched to Reading on June 4, 1958. Agent Joseph James parked on Spruce Street about 5 p.m. to observe the courtyard next to David Realty Corp. He saw men milling about at the far end of the courtyard outside Building 8. The distance was too far away for him to recognize faces. He lingered till midnight but saw no suspicious vehicles coming or going.

James and another agent, Stephen Milewski, returned at 8:30 the next morning. About 2 p.m. they detected the odor of mash. Eight hours later the scent was even stronger and seemed to be emitting from the one-story building with a drop door next to Building 8. Later that night the agents saw Dominico Perferi and Henry Kush, two North Jersey men they recognized as bootleggers, leaving a restaurant at 3rd and Chestnut streets. This was not far from the Penn Hardware complex.

The government decided to strike fast and build a case later against the mob. The report about mash fumes plus the presence of two well-known Jersey racketeers convinced the Treasury brass to move immediately before the mob realized its plant had been discovered.

Under the direction of Francis Wills, assistant supervisor in charge of the U.S. Treasury office in Philadelphia, a team of 30 agents led by Victor Fezio was organized. It was after 11 o'clock on Saturday morning June 7 when the Alcohol Tax Unit and several state Liquor Control Board agents broke into Building 8. Within the hour, federal agents went to City Hall seeking additional support. Six patrolmen and three detectives were dispatched to the Penn Hardware complex by Detective Capt. John Feltman. He didn't wait for permission from Mayor McDevitt.

Despite this sizable force surrounding the suspect buildings, mobsters on the job that morning fled through a maze of corridors and dilapidated structures taking a prepared escape route. There were no initial arrests, but the hardware in the building was a sight to behold for the raiders. The 30-inch, two-story high copper cooker was capable of producing more than 4,000 gallons of 180-proof alcohol daily. There was a large hole in the floor of the second story as preparations were in progress to install a second cooker. Five large fermenting vats each containing 5,200 gallons of mash, and two small vats holding 2,950 gallons of mash now belonged to the government. A pre-cooker and a cooler, coils, pipes and wiring strung along, under, and through walls and ceilings made the place look like a Rube Goldberg contraption. Utility, not aesthetics, was the mob's architectural priority.

In the courtyard, a tractor-trailer waiting to be unloaded had arrived that morning. It contained a large cargo of 100-pound bags of sugar. More than 300 five-gallon cans, 30,000 pounds of sugar, 16 cartons of yeast, and fermenting chemicals were in the building.

Wills, the Treasury Department's top man in Philadelphia, said the small work force had made its escape but he promised numerous arrests in a short time. Five agents were injured as they stumbled into what they believed were traps. In several spots, very weak flooring collapsed under their weight. One agent broke a finger, another needed 28 stitches to close a leg laceration.

Wills's office had a good line on members of the Greaser mob from a raid in Vineland, New Jersey, six weeks earlier. Wills claimed the bootleggers were cheating the government out of $40,000 a day in taxes, at the rate of $10.60 tax on a gallon of 90-proof alcohol. Wills noted the raid on the Greaser still near Kutztown three years ago was a losing operation, having been knocked off only a few weeks after production started. At Penn Hardware, the feds were not sure exactly how long that still had prospered but the government believed its loss in unpaid taxes was well over $1 million.

Abe Markowitz was interviewed shortly after the big bust. In his office he was questioned by ATU Agent John Smith. Abe told Smith that he had sold Building 8 to Joe Brown in January 1957. The Realtor said he talked with Brown only 10 or 15 minutes when Joe came to his office the previous month. All transactions after that were handled by mail or on the phone, he claimed. Markowitz told about Joe Brown paying his $500 mortgage payments by leaving them outside the office or shoving them in an envelope under the door. Except for their initial meeting, he said he didn't see Brown again face-to-face, but he thought he might be able to identify him.

Although he never entered the distillery building after he sold it, Abe told agents, he did have suspicions about what was being produced inside. Smith jotted down in the notes he was taking, "On several occasions Markowitz had smelled an odd odor and he inferred from that, that everything was not according to Hoyle."

Now began the Alcohol Tax Unit's difficult task of trying to recoup the government's losses. The confiscated sugar and yeast would be sent to government hospitals and institutions, a miniscule benefit. The distillery equipment would be sold as scrap metal, recovering only a fraction of its original worth, and much of the other ingredients and machinery were worthless.

Nine days after the raid, ATU agents arrived in City Hall to question city officials and workers. According to Harold K. Wood, who would later prosecute the case, the mayor "resented the interviewing of municipal employees, particularly the performance of their duties in regard to water and sewer services." Wood claimed the mayor had advised certain employees not to discuss the matter with agents except in the presence of the city solicitor.

Wils Austin, the city solicitor, said he received a call from the mayor concerning city employee complaints about the rudeness of agents conducting interviews. Austin said he was never requested by the mayor to sit in at the interviews.

Because the still was raided so soon after its discovery, the ATU now had to assign a large team of investigators to build a case against a known enemy, but an enemy that was elusive and very good at covering its tracks. But each scrap of paper, the serial number on every piece of equipment, brand names and other identifying marks helped the government detectives track down the perpetrators. And within a short time the first suspects were rounded up.

With Victor Fezio in charge of the investigation, Dominico Perferi and Henry Kush, the two Greasers seen in Reading by Agent Joe James, were taken into custody in Jersey 11 days after the raid. Perferi was nabbed in Trenton, Kush in North Plainfield. But Joe Brown remained among the missing for quite some time, even after Angelo Sgro was caught.

# 14

## *Major trial, small penalties*

During the summer of 1958, ATU agents interviewed dozens of people in Reading and Berks County who had even the remotest connection to known bootleggers from Jersey or Philadelphia. Suppliers of materials and still equipment were questioned and shown photos of suspects. Eventually, the case against the Penn Hardware bootleggers was built on information received during federal grand jury hearings. The witness list included a who's who of veteran racketeers in the Philly-New Jersey area.

The prosecutor, U.S. Attorney Harold Wood, said he would not release the names of those subpoenaed to testify unless they were potential defendants. He took a few shots at Mayor McDevitt and City Council by reporting it was doubtful that a huge still could be operated "five blocks from the main street of Reading without it being known to some of the city officials and without protection at some level." He then announced that McDevitt, councilmen and others in the city engineering and water departments would be among the 200 witnesses scheduled to appear. The mayor did not hesitate to retaliate. On opening day of the grand jury hearing he fired off a telegram to Wood. It was a backhanded attempt at scorn for Reading Eagle Company as well as Wood:

"A week has elapsed since local newspapers quoted you as saying that the Mayor and City Council of Reading were being subpoenaed to appear before a Grand Jury in Philadelphia.

"As you know, we have not been subpoenaed. This leads us to believe that your statement was distorted or garbled by the press in order to place a cloud of suspicion over this City Administration.

"We can appreciate your chagrin upon learning that your statement was twisted into a disregard for the facts. You, too, must be disturbed at the manner in which the press distorted your statement. At no time did you say City Officials would be subpoenaed, yet the press flatly said we would be called before the Grand Jury."

The mayor went on to say a single phone call from the prosecutor would clarify the misleading news report. Then he added that he and council members would be only too happy to appear in court to clear their names by fully cooperating as they have done in the past.

Among those who were served warrants were Alex Fudeman, named by Wood as the contact man between the Reading mob and the Greasers, and Charlie Veneziale, a Philadelphian believed to be the Greaser chief. James DiNatalie was another suspect ordered to testify. His specialty was obtaining raw materials for use in bootlegging and distribution of the final product.

Even before the first witness took the stand, Wood announced that investigators were looking into a report that one of the potential witnesses was threatened. He said proving such an allegation was difficult but an investigation was underway.

The hearings got off to an explosive start. Abe Markowitz and Alex Fudeman refused to testify, taking the 5th Amendment along with four other mob witnesses. One of those was Anthony Caponigro, bodyguard for the boss, Charlie V.

When Big Tony left the hearing room he spotted Jackie Evans, *Reading Times* photographer, focusing on him. As Evans snapped his picture, the irate Caponigro came at him. Shorter by a foot and outweighed by a hundred pounds, the diminutive cameraman took off down the long courthouse hallway. The chase went around one corner, then another with Evans lengthening his lead, all the while trying to insert a stronger bulb on his flash attachment. Then he made a bad turn into a dead-end hall. Coming at him with balled fist, his cursing assailant was blinded by the flash as Jackie clicked off one last close-up shot—so close, Tony blinked. The mobster managed a wild kick that caught Evans on the thigh. By then, Treasury Agent Francis Grimes arrived, only to receive a kick in the face from the flailing Tony as Evans executed a strategic retreat. Deputy marshals quickly subdued the outraged hood.

When Charlie V marched from the hearing room after taking the 5th the following day, he smiled broadly for Evans who again waited with loaded camera.

"You're doin' pretty good, huh?" said the portly mob leader.

"Just doing my job," responded Evans.

"Yeah." Charlie V was still smiling as he waddled into the elevator. Jackie said he feared Caponigro would retaliate in some way. But when they met again several months later at Tony's assault hearing, the defendant was complacent. He pleaded guilty and got off with a $300 fine.

Three members of the Reading Water Bureau were among the first to testify before the grand jury. Offering the most damaging testimony to the mob was J.

Wayne Seifarth, the former city assistant engineer, who took the stand right after his ex-boss. The chief engineer, Francis A. Heine, was called first to give his version of how the installation of the connector sewer line came about. His testimony was not revealed. Next to testify was Seifarth who told the jurors about being handed plans to install a sewer connector line without a meter. J. Wayne also stated that Heine ordered him not to question the faulty diagram—just do his job.

During the second week of the hearings federal prosecutor Harold Wood kept the pot boiling by again pointing the finger at Reading law enforcement.

"Organized criminals such as we are involved with in this enterprise," he said, "do not go into a locality, set up an illegal operation of this magnitude, unless they have assurances in advance that they will not be molested by local authorities. We think the people of Reading are entitled to know who provided this protection insurance and if it is possible to do so we will expose them."

Mayor McDevitt again exercised his literary talents in a telegram to remind the U.S. attorney that if the ATU had included city police in the June 7 raid from the beginning, all the men operating the still that day would have been captured. Again, the mayor insisted he and other city officials and employees had fully cooperated with the federal government in this case. Two days later McDevitt reiterated the politics theme by insisting Wood was using the still case "to further his own selfish ambitions to become a federal judge." He even accused the feds of bungling the case on purpose by letting workers escape from Building 8, the site of the distillery.

Finally on October 25 the mayor received the subpoena he so fervently challenged Wood to send him. Five days later he had his say under oath. He was in the hearing room for a little over an hour. Smiling, brash, wisecracking, McDevitt was not shy in showing his disdain for Wood and the federal government. He told the press he had answered all questions put to him, and denied to Wood and the grand jury that he had any knowledge of the existence of the Penn Hardware still.

City Councilman Harold Guldin and city solicitor Wils Austin offered a few comments after their short appearances in the grand jury room. Austin observed, "It was hardly worth the trip. What he asked me he could have asked on the phone." Guldin stated, "The only thing he seemed to be interested in was the original letter that came before council from Abe Markowitz requesting permission to run a sanitary sewer line down Spruce Street to the vicinity of the hardware building."

That same day the grand jury indicted 16 suspects, including Abe Markowitz, the only Reading defendant. All the others were from Philadelphia or New Jersey. If Alex Fudeman was the contact between the Reading and Philly mobs, the jury decided the evidence did not justify an indictment.

The parade of almost 200 witnesses ended on November 15 when Wood released the grand jury. He said the investigation was likely to continue with a new panel because of considerable evidence that still had to be studied. Additional indictments were added in the next few weeks until 27 defendants faced trial. Wood took still another poke at the city fathers of Reading for allowing such a huge still operation to continue for well over a year without detection. But he could not provide the evidence to indict a single elected official or city employee. Despite the U.S. attorney's steady barrage of accusations, Danny McDevitt appeared to have won the war of words.

Before dismissing the grand jury, Wood explained why the government felt it was important to try members of the Greaser gang. He stated that during the 18 months the mob owned the property where the still was located, it had the potential to produce 375,000 gallons of 180-proof alcohol. The tax on that quantity of alcohol would have been $3,935,000. It was a bloated figure, but without true accounting and inventory reports no exact amount was ever established.

Where did all these thousands of gallons of alcohol wind up? Not in legitimate bars, Louis DeCarlo explained. He was assistant regional commissioner for the ATU Division headquartered in Philadelphia. Speakeasies, unlicensed joints operating in the shadows where strong drinks at low prices were served, were the outlets for alcohol distilled in Reading. DeCarlo's region covered southeast Pennsylvania, New Jersey, Delaware, Maryland and Washington, D.C., where 163 illegal stills were raided in 1958. Prohibition ended in 1933 but speakeasies did not. The Greasers were selling a five-gallon can of pure alcohol for about $45, the federal man said. He estimated the cost of erecting a large column still between $40,000 and $50,000, including fuel, heat, and motors. Rather than risk insulting some forgotten bootleggers, DeCarlo said the Reading still was ONE of the largest illegal stills raided since Prohibition.

A spin-off from the grand jury hearings was that the government learned that people who did business with the City of Reading didn't always pay their taxes. The jurors heard details about certain contracts that appeared to be under-the-table deals. For 51 years Dominick Maurer and his son, Dominick Jr., had been the contractor of choice when Reading received bids on much of the heavy-duty work to improve and repair the city's superstructure. Now for the first time, somebody other than city officials studied the details of those contracts and the amounts of money the Maurers' company received for the work. The accountants at the IRS office at $8^{th}$ and Penn Streets were kept busy sifting through financial records the government had subpoenaed. Corporate taxes due on some recent jobs appeared well in arrears. Dominick Jr. was indicted, but a kindly federal judge took pity on his father, letting Dominick Sr. off with a $10,000 fine, which was paid by check before he left the courthouse.

The still trial was assigned to federal Judge Edwin D. Steel Jr. of Wilmington, Delaware, and Assistant U.S. Attorney Joseph J. Zapitz would be the lead prosecutor. When witness subpoenas were drawn up, 50 of the 93 were delivered to people in Reading and Berks County. Most prominent in that group were City Councilmen Bruce Coleman and Harold Guldin; Samuel Rothermel, city clerk; and Wilford Heckman, plumbing inspector. Wood announced that he had no intention of calling Mayor McDevitt.

The mayor smiled knowingly when Wood was nominated to fill a federal judgeship vacancy in Philadelphia.

The horde of defense attorneys filed a steady stream of petitions. They wanted detailed information about the grand jury witnesses, dismissal of charges against their clients, more time to prepare for trial, etc. Putting these bootleggers in jail would not be easy. The diminutive Louis Lipschitz, prominent Philly lawyer representing Markowitz, was fighting every inch of the way for his client. His motion requesting a separate trial for Abe was rejected by Judge Steel, although the jurist did make such a concession for three other defendants.

On March 16, 1959, opening day of the trial, six defendants pleaded guilty to charges of conspiring to manufacture illegal liquor. Charges against four others were dismissed, reducing the total of those who would stand trial to 17. Several of the remaining suspects were seen as little more than blue collar workers at the still, hardly qualifying them as conspirators in this major operation. This led to courtroom gossip that more charges would soon be dropped.

With eight lead attorneys, several with assistants, the defense tables were squeezed for seating space. And with that many legal minds and egos fighting for attention, there was a steady stream of interruptions, objections, squabbles, and grandstanding. Not until the second week of the trial did Steel, presiding in his first criminal case as a federal judge, lay down rules to prevent further delays. The 47-year-old Zapitz, a self-described coal cracker from Schuylkill County trying to perform above the fray, was calm and gentlemanly, never wilting under the barrage pouring out from the high-powered defense forces.

ATU agents John L. Smith and Bryan M. Smith testified about questioning Abe Markowitz the day of the raid. Both said Abe claimed he only talked face-to-face with Joe Brown for no more than 15 minutes that day in December 1956 when the prospective buyer came to the David Realty office to inquire about Penn Hardware buildings. After that, all transactions regarding the sale of real estate were conducted by mail or phone, not person to person, Abe had told them.

Abe's secretary at the time, Maria Architas, testified that Joe Brown hand-delivered mortgage payments to Markowitz every month and Abe would turn the checks over to her for bank deposit. She testified seeing Abe and Joe frequently walk from the office toward the still building, chatting all the while. She said she never saw Markowitz enter Building 8. However, when the prosecutor asked her to look at the defendants to see if she recognized anybody who had visited the David Realty office, she said none of the faces resembled Joe Brown's. Angelo Sgro was in that group.

In direct testimony, Markowitz claimed he was unable to give them a description of Joe Brown because he was in the stranger's presence for such a short time. Later in the trial, ATU agent John Kern said Markowitz did recognize Joe Brown as the man "who paid him rent once or twice" when he was shown a photo of Angelo Sgro two months after the raid. This information had not been released to the press before the trial, thereby elevating Joe Brown to the role of mystery man in numerous news accounts leading up to the trial.

Zapitz's main thrust was to call witnesses who could identify defendants seen in the close vicinity of Building 8. But the prosecutor had no witnesses willing to testify to what was going on inside the brick structure. Suppliers of fuel and materials used to produce the alcohol willingly pointed to defendants they had dealt with. Joseph Nawa, brother of Penn Electric Service owner, testified that in January 1957 defendant Anthony Farese borrowed a wheelbarrow from him before Penn Electric moved from Building 16. Farese was the first of the remaining 17 witnesses to be identified.

The next day Joe Brown was again identified as Angelo Sgro. It was Robert Turner, Reading Post Office clerk, who handled the registered letter from the Yaffe and Blumberg law firm to Joe Brown after the Building 8 sale. Because of an address mistake, Brown had to pick up the letter at the post office. During the investigation, Turner had viewed ATU photos and easily identified Angelo Sgro, who was using the Joe Brown alias. Now the courtroom was tense as he pointed to Sgro, ending the Joe Brown mystery. Then it was revealed another defendant had used the Joe Brown alias, too.

That same day, Arthur Auchenbach, another Penn Electric employee, fingered Sgro and Charlie Veneziale as members of a group replacing windows with cinder blocks on Building 8. Now two of the top Greasers were linked to the still operation. Things were looking up for the prosecution.

Unlike the burly Auchenbach, another witness had trepidations about incriminating a member of the mob. Oliver Bleacher, also a Penn Electric employee who observed mobsters in the courtyard, rose from the witness stand and was walking toward Anthony Farese to identify him. Not loudly he said, according to a consensus of several within hearing distance, "This is where I get shot." Other versions of his remark: "I'll get shot," or "I'd rather get shot," or "I feel like a big shot."

What was heard very clearly was Judge Steel's parting shot as he declared a mistrial after two hours of debate between squabbling attorneys and the prosecution. Members of the jury had heard Bleacher's damaging comment. His expressed fear was enough to prejudice the jury, the judge ruled, so another delay in this costly case was deemed necessary to give the defendants a fair trial.

Federal Judge Thomas J. Clary was assigned as Judge Steel's replacement when the case was brought to court for the retrial on June 8, 1959. The 56-year-old Clary had presided at the arraignments of the original 27 defendants six months earlier. Thirty people from Berks County were subpoenaed to return to testify at the second trial. Abe Markowitz's continuing pursuit of a separate trial also was rejected by Judge Clary. One year and a day after the raid at the old hardware complex, jury selection began. Within four days, testimony that took eight and a half days the first time around was completed.

Charles Nawa, owner of Penn Electric Service, denied Lipschitz's claim that he owed Markowitz money, which is why his company was evicted. Nawa said the true story was that Markowitz owed him money for work his company performed in Abe's office.

Two more defendants, Ignatius Esposito and Albert DiMechle, both of Philadelphia, were acquitted by Judge Clary for lack of evidence a few days before the trial ended.

Several witnesses testified seeing Markowitz talking with some of the defendants over the 18-month life of the still. Betty Suender worked for Rueben H. Donnelly Co., an advertising firm renting a second-floor office just above the David Realty office. The attractive secretary said she witnessed the downstairs Realtor conversing with Alfred Salerno, James Chieppa, James Randazzo, and Henry Kush, all Jersey mobsters whom she identified. Suender said she had a good view of the courtyard from her desk, and also saw those four entering or leaving the realty company building.

A witness who said Markowitz directed him to do work for the bootleggers was Abe's maintenance man, James H. Althouse. He said he changed a fuse for Charlie Veneziale and "he gave me several dollars and said 'thank you.'" Althouse also testified he told Markowitz he was suspicious of what the new tenants were up to:

"I told him I'd bet him money there was a still over there. He said 'never mind, what they do is their business, I shouldn't worry about it.'" Althouse said he also helped Farese clean up the blocked cesspool with a fire hose, and loaned him a chain hoist, sledgehammer, and a wheelbarrow to haul cement.

Agents identified out-of-state companies where the bootleggers obtained materials and ingredients to make the alcohol. They also provided Berks witnesses who sold the defendants fuel. Harley Mohn Jr. and Gerald Mohn, operators of the White Front Service Station a few miles east of Reading on Route 422, and an employee, William J. Stichter, all identified several of the defendants who bought kerosene at the station. Veneziale, Kush, Joseph LaMacchio, and Anthony Capoferri were present on different occasions when an 850-gallon tank truck was filled and driven away, the White Front men testified.

The defendant list was whittled to 13 when Joseph Melillio could not be identified in the courtroom, although two witnesses had picked him out previously from ATU photos. Then Joseph Pagano, believed to have purchased the tractor-trailer confiscated at the time of the raid, was discharged. It turns out the large vehicle was registered in the name of somebody else.

Salvatore and Joseph DiPaola, father and son from Baltimore who supplied yeast and sugar in large quantities to the bootleggers, were no longer regarded by the judge as conspirators and crossed off the defendant list. Several witnesses told of seeing Philly mobster Alfred Salerno at or near the still site. It was revealed, he also used the Joe Brown alias. Salerno's motion for acquittal was accepted by Judge Clary. When the three-week trial ended on June 29, only nine of the 17 original defendants remained when the jury retired to ponder their fate.

Five of the defendants had taken the stand to deny they were part of the conspiracy: LaMacchia, Farese, Sgro, Capoferri, and James Randazzo. Markowitz did not testify but was supported by several character witnesses.

The jury's verdict: eight guilty, including Markowitz, and one acquitted, Capoferri, who was seen driving the kerosene tank truck. Lipschitz petitioned for a new trial for Markowitz, as did attorneys for the other seven defendants.

Dan McDevitt thought it was time for a bit more gloating. On July 15 he revealed to City Council he had sent a letter on May 26 to U.S. Attorney Wood.

Confident that he would not be called to testify at the second trial, the mayor had told Wood:

"There was a widespread impression by others to the effect that my being called to testify before the grand jury was tantamount to an indictment and would surely be followed by a conviction as a principal to the operation of that still."

And now, he reported to council he would like to read part of Wood's reply which he received only a few days after sending his note, but did not make public because the second trial was about to begin.

"It is most unfortunate that anyone could arrive at such a ridiculous conclusion," Wood had written.

There was never any shortage of sarcastic repartee when those two swapped missives. Wood pointed out that several dozen other witnesses from Reading appeared before the grand jury, too, and only one was indicted.

A variety of motions was argued in July, Markowitz continuing to insist he was not aware that a still was producing illegal alcohol across the courtyard from his office. Comments made by Judge Clary gave Abe hope that his cause was not lost just yet. "Markowitz had some apparently valuable real estate which was a secondary kind of industrial real estate development," the judge stated. "If a person wanted to buy some of that real estate, I doubt if I or if you would require character references." On another occasion the jurist said unless the government could prove that Markowitz knew what the connector sewer line was to be used for, he could not be charged with conspiring with the racketeers in their illegal still enterprise.

Finally on September 16, Judge Clary overturned the conviction of Abe Markowitz. He ruled the jury had wrongly found Abe guilty of conspiring with the alcohol ring. The evidence did not support their finding, he said.

Judge Clary also acquitted James Randazzo, and granted Angelo Sgro a new trial. Convictions of the remaining five were upheld: Charlie Veneziale, Tony Farese, James Chieppa, Joe LaMacchia, and Henry Kush.

Two Brooklyn men, Pasqual Aurrecchio and his nephew, Joseph Brancalli, who supplied the Greasers with five-gallon cans, were tried in October and acquitted by Federal Judge Thomas C. Egan. Before Sgro stood trial a second time he was acquitted by Federal Judge Allan K. Grim.

When Judge Clary handed out sentences for those found guilty and those who pleaded guilty, seven of the 11 received jail time. Kush, Joseph Mazzio, and Farese got 30 months; Perferi and Chieppa, two years; LaMacchia, one year, and Benito Tedesco, 10 months.

Charlie V, known as leader of the pack, was the last to be sentenced because "Í didn't know what to do with you," Judge Clary told him when he sent the others to jail. He pondered more than a week then gave Veneziale four years probation. After the government spent untold thousands of dollars investigating and prosecuting an illegal operation that brought an estimated million or more dollars in profits to the mob, Clary asked Charlie whether he went to church.

"Off and on," the aging gangster hedged.

The judge advised him to make it, "more on than off and get there Sunday. You hold the key to your cell door."

While the still trial was running its course, Angelo Bruno, a formidable extortion racketeer, was angling to take control of the South Philadelphia underworld. Dominic Pollina was head of the Quaker City Mafia, but various branches of racketeering, including the Greaser mob, operated independently. Bruno approached the Mafia's national commission in New York City with a plan to organize the various factions under his leadership. With the blessing of his old friend, Carlo Gambino, the boss of all Mafia bosses, Bruno pulled off the consolidation without eliminating Pollina, not the usual path of ascension to a rackets throne. "The Docile Don" became Angelo's sobriquet in the press, if not among his henchmen. Pollina lived to a ripe old age, but never held any power again.

Anointed by Gambino, Bruno soon had a few Berks County lawyers and racketeers making weekend visits to his modest row home on Snyder Avenue in South Philly.

Twenty years after Tony Caponigro chased *Reading Times* photographer Jackie Evans around the halls of the federal courthouse in Philadelphia, he was rubbed out by the New York mob. The ambitious Tony had over-stepped his authority by engineering the murder of Angelo Bruno, whom he hoped to replace. Caponigro's retaliation slaying then led to an extended intra-family war that lasted for years.

# 15

# *By the numbers, agents trail pick-up men*

Although the IRS was socking it to the multicoin pinball and slot machine operators, and stores and clubs offering gamblers the mechanical money grabbers, the numbers game had yet to feel the federal pinch in Berks County. Abe Minker took advantage of this. Although the state police had knocked off his numbers/bookie place in December 1957, Minker started up another almost immediately. In the '57 raid, one of Minker's rising stars was nabbed. Joe Fiorini was one of five suspects arrested when betting paraphernalia was found in a grocery store on North 2nd Street. Fiorini and Morris Salvi were regarded as the operators of the bank. Those two and Louis Carrozza, Gerald Thompson, and Sebastian Zampelli were convicted in June 1958. The IRS figured if Fiorini and Salvi were fronting the bank, Abe Minker was the man in charge.

After a couple of years studying the rackets situation in Reading, the feds worked up a numbers game organizational chart. It went like this: 11 sub-banks reported to Minker's accounting office. Each sub-bank employed between five and 30 writers. Thirty-five percent of the gross receipts went to the writers. After deducting for winnings and expenses (mostly protection payoffs), Minker divided the profits equally with the operators of the sub-banks. That share fluctuated according to how much Abe had to lay off to a Mafia banker when a popular number broke the bank. And, of course, he paid his top lieutenants decent salaries and still had a nice chunk left for himself. Since he had no board of directors or shareholders or union to answer to, Abe could make financial adjustments as he pleased.

The government knew Abe Minker and his top numbers operators were not bothering to pay their gambling occupation tax. At this time, Minker's legal team was locked in battle with Victor Wright, the commonwealth's deputy attorney general, trying to keep the extortion case from reaching the trial stage. Abe was also bribing BCAOA members not to testify if a trial was held.

The government, too, was busy that summer organizing a major investigation to topple Minker from his throne. The IRS had a pretty good idea about the worth of Minker's numbers operation: in the neighborhood of $1 million a year. So the tax service decided to go after him from that direction. Five of the top IRS agents in the Northeast were summoned to Philadelphia where they met in the lobby of the Ben Franklin Hotel for the first time on July 27, 1958. In a hotel conference room, the plan of attack was laid out by Frank Rucker, chief of intelligence for the Philadelphia IRS office. He briefed his group about the rampant rackets situation in Reading. The agents were provided backgrounds and photographs of the numbers bank principals and warned not to expect any cooperation from Reading's politicians or police.

Two agents of Irish descent, Fran Larkin and Jack Dalsey, were assigned to zero in on Abe Minker. Both were 39 years old and 14-year veterans of the revenue service. Irv Dubow, Joe Toscano, and Ed Quarry rounded out the squad. When they left Philadelphia that afternoon they headed straight for Reading and found lodging outside the city. The next day they reconnoitered traffic patterns in town, familiarized themselves with certain addresses, and found a few stores where they knew numbers were sold.

Dalsey and Larkin were especially interested in checking out Abe Minker's place of residence in the Hampden House at 1955 Hampden Boulevard, a two-story apartment house. They also began scouting the neighborhood for suitable places to park for surveillance. On their many future visits to this well-to-do northeastern corner of the city they would often see Abe's bronze colored Cadillac parked in front of the Hampden House.

Joe Toscano began playing the numbers at three locations the next two days. He made his first 25-cent bet on July 29 in Nate Hindin's Smoke Shop, 522 North 9th Street. A female sales clerk was behind the counter. A little small talk and Joe was on his way. Next was Steve Arthur's News Stand, 946 Penn Street, where Georgine Arthur, the owner's wife, took Joe's quarter for another bet. Then it was off to J&J Confectionery operated by Joe Venezia on the first floor of his home at 247 Washington Street. For the third time, Toscano played No. 723, exchanging his quarter with a clerk for his lottery ticket. Twenty-five cents was a modest wager—not too high, but certainly no lower than lots of local bets. With odds of 600 to 1, Joe could have made $150 with a winning ticket.

The next day Toscano repeated his tour of these small wagering sites again playing the same amount on the same number each time. There were dozens of other stores where he could have placed his bet, but three locations were enough to help prove a small numbers business could become big business for those at the top.

On August 4 and 6, Toscano continued his routine at Steve Arthur's News Stand. On one of those occasions, a lad about 12 or 13 took his quarter and gave Joe a receipt. It was the owner's son doing his bit to support the family. On other days, Agent Irv Dubow was collecting backup evidence. He wagered a quarter in Nate Hinden's Smoke Shop on July 30. Two months later as the investigation was winding down, Joe Toscano retraced his steps on the last three days of September, buying numbers at the same three locations as he did in August. His regular number, 723, was never hit of the day.

Gathering evidence of actual gambling was the easy part of this investigation. The serious surveillance that summer demanded patience, dedication, and some quick thinking. Within a few days of taking this assignment, the agents knew all they needed to know about Johnny Wittig, Dominic Quatieri, Tony Bonanno, Mike Augustine, and Louie Fudeman. They knew where these racketeers lived, what kind of cars they drove, their license plate numbers, where they ate, and most important, where they were going to be almost every hour of the day. In their unmarked government cars, the agents were trailing the Minker pickup men as they made their rounds collecting slips, tabulating their ticket sales, and moving adding machine tally tapes up the ladder to Abe Minker in his Hampden Heights apartment.

Toscano was sitting in his car near Nate Hindin's shop on August 3 about 12:35 p.m. when Tony Bonanno arrived to make his daily pickup of betting slips. Tony stayed only a few minutes before moving on to his next stop. This routine was documented by Toscano and other agents who took turns as watchers. Each pickup man followed a tight schedule, seldom varying his arrival and departure times by more than a few minutes. When an agent parked near Reading Home Bakery at 609 Bingaman Street about 2:45 p.m., he knew Dominic Quatieri's light green Mercury was parked nearby or would be arriving within minutes. The same could be said for Mike Augustine's two-tone green Mercury and Tony Bonanno's two-tone gray Dodge. Like clockwork, the boys were always punctual. Reading Home Bakery was soon identified as the present headquarters of the mob's floating numbers bank.

After getting the lay of the land, Jack Dalsey and Fran Larkin chose Quatieri as their first target. Mickey Shush was Quatieri's mob sobriquet. Mickey moved about in gambling circles for years. His most recent arrest was in 1955 when he ran a crap game in a Chester County barn. Seventy-five dice players at a farm attracted the state police and Mickey spent a few months in jail on that one.

It was the second day of surveillance, early afternoon when Mickey entered Steve Arthur's place on Penn Street as he began his daily gathering of the slips. When he returned to his Mercury with several small brown envelopes he was not aware that Larkin and Dalsey were watching him from a distance. The rest of the afternoon they put a tail on him that led them out of town. Soon they noticed signs denoting they were approaching Oley. That's where they were renting their room in a motel. Now on Route 73, they saw Mickey's sedan turn into a driveway. A small sign announced Oley Upholstery Company. The agents didn't get any closer that day, satisfied they had found a future target.

Two days later they were hiding in the woods when Mickey Shush arrived in his car with Louie Fudeman and Katherine "Kate" Farrara. All three entered a dwelling that previously housed the upholstery company. A few minutes later Mike Augustine and Tony Bonanno drove up in Bonanno's Dodge. This house was serving as numbers bank of the day and would again in the weeks ahead before another location was found.

Dalsey was in the Hinky Dink Pool Room at 311 Schuylkill Avenue the afternoon of August 4 to observe a clerk take and record several numbers bets. Jack saw Mike Augustine come in, talk to the clerk, then leave in his Mercury. Later, about 4 p.m., Dalsey parked near the Reading Home Bakery where he got out of his car, wandered around and saw the parked sedans of Augustine, Quatieri, and Bonanno. Inside the bakery on the second floor rear the day's numbers wagers were being tabulated on adding machines.

Louie Fudeman, who lived in Lincoln Park, always seemed to be riding with one of the other three. No car of his was mentioned in the investigators' daily reports. Conveniently, Louie's day job was bread salesman for Reading Home Bakery. Bonanno also had a decent income from the luncheonette he owned and operated in the city. Augustine's night job was door attendant at the gambling casino on North 10th Street. So these fellows were all putting in long hours.

The next few days either Dalsey or Larkin arrived at the bakery location about 2:35 p.m. Sometimes the watcher would walk around the block, sometimes he would sit on a bench on Bingaman Street. On August 5, Augustine walked right by the seated Dalsey before turning down the alley next to the bakery and entering through a side door. On the 6th of September, Dalsey was strolling along Bingaman Street when Bonanno passed him going the opposite direction. Jack worried he was becoming a familiar face, so Larkin began patroling the area. No doubt about it, the bakery was the numbers bank that week.

Early evening of August 12, Larkin and Dalsey were parked at 4th and Walnut streets when Mickey Shush arrived and entered 203 North 4th. Johnny Wittig lived in the corner apartment house on the second floor directly over the Golden Band Café. Rumors at the time had it that Johnny owned the neighborhood drinking spot because he was often seen there, but the building was owned by John Muthard Jr. and the Golden Band was operated by Bill Koehler.

As the agents watched from their car, Mickey entered the building carrying what appeared to be a cloth bank bag. When he came out a few minutes later he was empty-handed.

After two weeks in Reading, the agents knew where and when and by whom the numbers slips were being picked up, but no contact with Abe Minker had yet been observed. That would change the following week.

On August 17 they discover another location of the numbers bank. About 2.45 p.m. Larkin and Dalsey are staked out at 13$^{th}$ and Exeter Streets, watching Fudeman and Augustine standing on the corner watching all the Albright College coeds go by. Along comes Mickey Shush in his green Mercury and picks them up. The agents' late model Ford falls in behind them as the trio heads out Pricetown Road. Near Epler's Park, Shush turns where a sign says L. Kiehl in front of a house. They park and enter the house as the T-men pull off the road and duck behind high brush where they can observe. Sure enough, there's Tony Bonanno's gray Dodge parked outside the house. All four are inside going over that day's take and summing up for Abe, or The Brain, as they liked to refer to him. Now the IRS boys know they have discovered a third numbers bank site in the revolving operation.

The next day their routine continues: at 13$^{th}$ and Exeter at 2:45 p.m., Shush picks up Augustine and Fudeman, and off they go to their adding machines in the Kiehl residence. Bonanno shows up 10 minutes later and joins the counters. The computing job usually takes about two and a half hours. Not waiting till the pickup men leave, Dalsey and Larkin head back to the city to put the binoculars on Johnny Wittig's place. At 6:10 p.m. here comes Shush with his cloth bag, drops it off with The Enforcer, whose other duties include dealing with writers or runners who try to shortchange the boss. Having lost Wittig in traffic when they tailed him from his home the previous evening, the agents play a hunch and find a suitable lookout site hoping Johnny will eventually show up at Minker's apartment house. They parked on Rockland Street where they had an open view of the Hampden House. Rockland was tree-lined and offered good shadow cover. They were posted about 300 feet from Abe's second-floor apartment. Using high-powered binoculars, Jack Dalsey could see the living room curtains were open and observed Abe moving past the front window. He also viewed Verna Minker, a very attractive woman who appeared younger than her age.

Traffic was light as they waited. Finally at 9:30 p.m. they saw Wittig's Oldsmobile park in front of the apartment house. Jack, with binoculars, saw Wittig get out, straighten the felt hat he always wore, wrap a copy of the local newspaper around a package about the size of a cigar box, and enter the building. In less than a minute, Wittig came into view through the living room window as he handed the package to Minker. The investigators felt certain the package contained tapes showing that day's total of number plays. The long hours of surveillance had been worthwhile.

During the five-week investigation, the agents witnessed this scenario 11 times. Sometimes they saw Wittig passing his boss the package, other times it was a large envelope he delivered. Wittig never stayed more than 15 minutes. Although Johnny and Abe communicated by phone every day at Minker's unlisted number, these nightly visits were the only face-to-face meetings between them observed during the investigation.

Not much excitement in this job, Jack and Fran think, until one night their cover is almost blown. They are posted in their usual spot, the Rockland Street trees offering good cover as Wittig arrives. Larkin is logging the time as Dalsey squints into his binoculars. Suddenly a Reading patrol car approaches from the rear, lights out, and stops next to them. The smiling face of a young patrolman peers across as he asks, "Looking for something?"

Fortunately he doesn't beam his flashlight at them or he would have seen two very red faces and momentarily rattled veterans. Larkin recovers first and offers the excuse they had prepared in the event such an intrusion would occur.

"Ah yes, officer," his voice steady, "we're studying stars."

"Stars?" the cop questions, "On a cloudy night like this."

"With powerful binoculars like ours we can occasionally catch a glimpse of the pattern we're interested in. We're doing some experimental work for the gang down at the college."

"I understand some of the kids at Albright are really wacky about this astrology bit," the cop notes. He is still smiling, and the agents would like to smile at his lack of knowledge about celestial science identification—but they don't.

Dalsey joins in, "They sure are. That's why the bigwigs at the college asked us to take a leave of absence from our jobs at Temple in Philly to help out on this project. We're like consultants, you know—$50 a day from Albright and still get our pay at Temple."

Obviously very new on his beat, the affable officer says, "OK men, if you see any interesting females up there give me a call."

As he drives away the relieved agents wonder whether Minker and Wittig have witnessed the encounter from the apartment window. Or, will the inexperienced policeman report the incident to his superior who in turn might inform his chief, who is very close to the mayor, a crony of Abe Minker? That apparently never happened because Wittig did not alter his routine in the weeks ahead.

Dalsey would later testify in court that he had witnessed Wittig going into Minker's apartment house with a package or envelope five times in August and six times in September. Nobody asked, so Jack didn't mention the star-gazing near fiasco.

There were quite a few 14-hour working days, irregular meal times, and always the fear of being discovered as government agents. Working together or separately, Dalsey and Larkin never ate together in city restaurants. The same could not be said for their prey. Quatieri, Augustine, and Bonanno met almost every morning for breakfast in The Crystal at 6th and Penn. Jimmy Mantis, manager of the family-owned restaurant, had posted a wooden wall plaque reading

> "This House shall not permit, suffer or have any
> playing of dice, cards, worts or loggets."

But professional gamblers were not banned. Actually, they were welcomed as an attraction for diners enamored by the racketeers. It was definitely not bad for business when Johnny Wittig and his three pickup men frequently had dinner in the popular restaurant. During the investigation, either Dalsey or Larkin occasionally joined them—within lip-reading, or even listening distance, if possible.

During the first month of the investigation, a few agents were granted weekend leaves to visit their families. Later the entire team was ordered back to Philadelphia to organize their notes and work with the U.S. attorney's office to build a case against the racketeers.

When the agents returned to Reading on September 14, Dalsey and Larkin again began spotting Wittig on his nightly trips to 1955 Hampden Boulevard. They stayed on the alert for nosy cops, too. One change in the routine, however, was a new pickup site for Wittig. Instead of Mickey Shush going to Johnny's apartment early each evening, Wittig was driving to the Roundup Smoke Shop at 9 North 9th Street where Mickey was waiting out front with that day's tally sheets. The Roundup was a long-time gamblers hangout. It had been raided one early morning in 1954 when seven players were busy around a poker table in the rear. Leroy Fricker owned the place. The cigar store was Johnny Wittig's last stop before driving straight to Minker's apartment about 9:35 p.m.

Also, after the 24-day hiatus, the agents made daily checks at the Reading Home Bakery, observing the cars of Augustine, Bonanno, and Quatieri in the neighborhood. They would hang around to watch the trio leave before or shortly after 6 p.m. Now and then Alex Fudeman would also put in an appearance.

Then near the end of September the pickup men did not show up at any of the locations of the previous numbers banks. After a few days of frustration the T-men picked up the scent again. On September 28, Dalsey and Larkin were driving in the 800 block of Lancaster Avenue just west of New Holland Road when they spotted Louie Fudeman. He was standing outside the Pensupreme ice cream store. They parked, waited, and watched. Shortly, Dominic Quatieri parked his Mercury on the Pensupreme lot. Fudeman and Mickey Shush began walking west, crossed Angelica Street and entered the end house at 728 Lancaster Avenue. Fifteen minutes later when Mike Augustine parked his car on Angelica Street, the agents suspected they had located the new numbers bank. Verification arrived in 10 minutes when Tony Bonanno parked his Dodge behind Augustine's sedan. All three drivers were carrying bags when they entered 728.

The next afternoon, within a 10-minute span, the same three entered the same dwelling while Dalsey and Larkin watched through their spyglasses from a parking lot across Lancaster Avenue.

Minker was never seen at any of the dropoff points or at the numbers bank. The agents believed all Abe was receiving from his messengers were tapes listing the number of bets and the amounts wagered each day. But when, where, and how the money was transferred to Abe was never revealed. It was surmised that Fudeman's role was to pass the money on to his uncle.

Thus ended the legwork as the IRS team returned to Philadelphia to draw up final reports. The climax of their long-running probe would occur five days later.

# 16

## *Big fish slips the hook*

Despite his underworld history, Abe Minker was a faithful member of Kesher Zion Synagogue. October 3, 1959, a Saturday, started with the celebration of Yom Kippur but ended badly for the Reading rackets boss. He and Verna dressed for the occasion that morning unaware they were under the scrutiny of the Alcohol Tax Unit. The agency did not realize its day of reckoning coincided with an important Jewish holiday.

Jack Dalsey and Fran Larkin arrived in Reading early. Their first bit of business before the main show was to ride past Minker's apartment to make sure he was home. Still a block away they could identify his bronze colored Cadillac, but to their dismay Abe had just closed the passenger door and was walking toward the driver's side. This was not good. The plan was to arrest Abe at his apartment at 2:30 p.m., the exact time the Lancaster Avenue numbers bank would be hit.

"Wouldn't you know he'd pick this day to go somewhere," Dalsey complained.

Dalsey pulled to the curb, watching as Abe made a U-turn on Hampden Boulevard and headed south past the enemy. In their unmarked government car the agents reversed their direction, staying three cars behind the Caddy. Notifying headquarters became a problem, especially if the Minkers were heading out of town. Then these two Irish Catholics remembered it was Saturday, the Jewish Sabbath. They breathed easier as Abe parked, then entered Kesher Zion Synagogue on Perkiomen Avenue.

Although they had been looking at Abe through binoculars for two months, Jack and Fran had never seen him up close. As worshippers returned to their cars after the service, they mistakenly thought one gentleman with a blonde wife was their prey. But the couple did not enter the Cadillac. When they did identify Abe, he was shorter than they expected. After following Minker to his apartment, they went to 8th and Penn Streets where the local IRS office was located.

During the planning stage that week, Special Agent Ed Quarry had pored over IRS records and worked the phone to determine whether any of the 13 suspects on the arrest list had ever paid the 10 percent gambling excise tax. None had.

Having identified 728 Lancaster Avenue as the busiest numbers bank in recent weeks, Dalsey and Larkin recommended that it should be the principal target. Dan Tucker, intelligence chief at the Philadelphia office, was running the show. All that week he was fine-tuning a growing team of special agents and U.S. marshals on their specific assignments. The raiding team would include 30 agents and 12 U.S. marshals. Two state policemen, familiar with the Reading rackets scene, were invited along. A dozen places would be hit, including the three other suspected numbers bank sites, several pickup locations, and the residences of Minker and Johnny Wittig. It was anticipated that Louis Fudeman, Mike Augustine, Dominic Quatieri, and Tony Bonanno would be in the Lancaster Avenue house when the feds struck.

One possibility the raiders had not considered: a big firemen's parade on Penn Street that Saturday afternoon. A few of the agents, including Dalsey and Larkin almost missed the jump-off time. But that pair worked its way through traffic to arrive at the numbers bank area on schedule, and quickly identified the cars of the pickup men parked near the target. Within minutes they were in position to kick in doors. Two other young agents supported the veterans. One of the rookies cut his wrist on broken glass as he entered through the front door. Jack and Fran barged through the back door, shouting, "Federal agents! Nobody move! This is a raid!"

Upstairs, the big four knew the jig was up. Only Dominic Quatieri ran from the counting room. Dalsey and Larkin raced to the second floor with drawn guns, pushing open the first door they came to. There sat Bonanno, Augustine, and Fudeman looking sheepish and frozen in their seats. They were caught in the act of totaling up number plays. Piled on a table were stacks of money separated into different denominations. Dalsey could see somebody was missing and went looking. He yelled through the door of another room, "I'm coming in!" He swung it open … and broke up laughing.

"Hey look at this," he yelled to the two young agents. There was the paunchy Mickey Shush unsuccessfully trying to squeeze under a bed.

Back in the counting room it was determined that money stacked on the table totaled $4,068. From future evidence the government would accumulate, this appeared to be a fairly normal take for one day. U.S. marshals took custody of the money.

The raid was only one reason for the gamblers to fret. They also took a beating from their customers that Black Saturday: winning ticket holders hit for $11,856, resulting in a $7,788 loss for the mob. Payoffs were a little late that week, but the racketeers had to make good or risk losing customers. Besides the money, several new adding machines that Quatieri had recently purchased in Philadelphia, a handgun, other gambling paraphernalia, and hundreds of betting slips were confiscated.

Meanwhile, at the other end of town when an ATU team led by Agent Leo Zynel arrived at Minker's apartment house, Abe's car was not parked outside. And nobody answered when he knocked on the apartment door at precisely 2:30 o'clock. It wasn't a long wait, however, as Abe and Verna returned home about 20 minutes later. There wasn't much holiday spirit as Zynel ushered Abe into his own apartment and began opening drawers and closets. Abe let the agents know he was highly offended to have his Yom Kippur ruined by this intrusion, which did not stop the feds from searching him. They found two numbers slips in his coat pocket—small but suggestive evidence indicating what Abe's line of business was. They also found several phone numbers that proved helpful in the prosecution of the case.

The other eight suspects taken into custody that day were less put out, accepting their detention in varying degrees of concern or annoyance. Johnny Wittig heard a knock on his apartment door, then did not take kindly to his arrest. He swore at his captors but did not resist when he was cuffed.

Agent Bill Glase led a team that bucked the parade crowd as they picked up Steve and Georgine Arthur at their apartment above the Penn Street News Stand. Mrs. Arthur admitted she was selling numbers for Minker but thought Abe was paying his gambling taxes. At Nate Hindin's place, he and three of his clerks who took numbers bets, Irene Moyer, Helen Schaeffer, and Rose Toor were apprehended. They certainly felt discriminated against knowing that dozens and dozens of other numbers writers all over the city were still running free. The same group of agents that grabbed Wittig, then picked up Joe Venezia at his J&J Confectionery on Washington Street.

All 13 suspects were taken to the local IRS office where they were booked and fingerprinted. Except for Minker's short absence from his apartment, the raid had been engineered with no surprises or delays. U.S. Attorney Joseph McGlynn and U.S. Commissioner Edward Furia were part of the raiding detail. They processed everybody in custody to prepare for bail hearings that evening. The specific charges for all 13: engaging in the business of accepting wagers without having previously paid the special occupational tax.

That evening, Minker put on quite a show when he entered the hearing room as the first suspect to appear before Commissioner Furia. When an agent asked his name, Abe responded, "I don't want to talk to you." The questioner said, "I'm a U.S. Treasury agent." Abe was not impressed. "I don't care who you are, I don't want to talk to you," and he began to walk away, then shouted, "You ought to be ashamed of yourselves … all of you … making a big show on a Jewish holiday." He didn't seem to mind that his flunkies had been illegally raking in thousands of dollars every Jewish Sabbath for the past few years.

Furia, with authority, asked, "Who are you?"

"I'm Abe Minker."

"You better watch yourself or I'll hold you for contempt of court," Furia warned. "I'll put you in jail so fast you won't know what happened to you."

The tension eased as Furia wanted to know where Minker's attorney was. Abe said Sam Liever would arrive shortly, then started popping off again:

"I'll tell you what I'd like to do …"

"You better be quiet," Furia warned a second time.

Sam Liever arrived just as Furia issued his warning. The attorney listened as Jack Dalsey and Leo Zynel testified about the two-month investigation and the ensuing raid. Then Liever requested that the bail hearing be delayed until a more definitive hearing regarding evidence could be held. The commissioner denied that request, saying bail would be fixed right away, and evidence could be discussed at a hearing the following Thursday.

Then, another interruption as Fred Brubaker showed up. He wanted Furia to hold off setting bail for everybody until he could view the evidence for the issuance of local arrest warrants for all the suspects. The commissioner said "no" to that, too. Bail for Minker, Wittig, Fudeman, Bonanno, Augustine, and Quatieri was $1,000 apiece. That was twice the amount set for the other detainees. All posted bonds and were released that night.

Five hours after the raid as reporters were tracking the story, Brubaker phoned the *Reading Sunday Eagle* to have the newspaper publish his reaction to the raid:

"I congratulate them (the ATU agents) on using the information that was furnished them and I'll assign an assistant district attorney to cooperate with them in determining what local laws have been violated."

The cleverly worded statement was rebutted by U.S. Asst. Atty. Joe McGlynn a few days later:

"The raid was conducted on the basis of the Internal Revenue Service's own agents' investigation and they did not receive any information from the district attorney of Berks County."

On the assumption that Saturday was an average day for the numbers racket, the U.S. attorney's office felt justified in announcing that the annual worth of Minker's operation was at least $1 million. It was a nice round figure, easy to remember, and was generally used by the government to emphasize that Reading was the gambling mecca of the East Coast. Although it had taken no action against the 10th Street casino, the Treasury Department was certainly well aware the Philadelphia mob was running it. Minker's involvement was never revealed, but it was generally understood he received his cut for affording the mob protection. At the time of the raid, Abe was preparing to stand trial for having forced the independent gambling machine operators to pay protection, another source of his gambling income.

If the IRS felt it had an airtight case against Minker, U.S. Commissioner Furia burst that bubble in a hurry. He had five days to review the reports filed by Larkin, Dalsey, and other agents before holding a preliminary hearing in Philadelphia on October 8. It was well attended. In addition to the 13 defendants, contingents from both the state police and Brubaker's office were on hand. Furia did not claim he was misinformed when he issued the arrest and search warrants, but was left with a false impression about evidence against the principal defendant. He lectured the IRS:

"No jury in the land would convict on the evidence in this case," Furia said in dismissing the charges against Minker. "Last Friday when I spent three and a half hours with agents from the IRS reviewing the evidence in affidavit form, upon which I was asked to issue search warrants in this case, I was reasonably sure that the premises to be searched would produce evidence of the crime alleged.

"I was reasonably certain that Mr. Minker's apartment, based on the evidence submitted to me, would produce cash, master sheets, ledgers, and other evidence usually found in the headquarters of a numbers bank."

He said the easy way out would be to hold Minker for the grand jury, but he felt duty bound to dismiss the charges rather than let Abe's case advance to the next stage. "This would be consistent with a vast public opinion that he is allegedly the kingpin of the numbers racket in Berks County.

"I may have my own personal impression that this is correct and in this particular case Mr. Minker was involved in the unlawful business that was uncovered at the Lancaster Avenue address, where the defendants were caught adding up the daily take which approximated $4,600 in their possession."

The commissioner said there was nothing to show what was in the packages delivered nightly to Minker or whether there was someone else in the apartment that received them. To a reporter he admitted, "In my heart I believe Minker is guilty, but that is not legal evidence."

Minker had retained Jacob Kossman, the noted Philadelphia criminal attorney, who argued before the U.S. Supreme Court in 1955 when Abe was targeted for deportation by the Internal Revenue Service. Kossman also defended Wittig, Fudeman, Bonanno, Augustine, and Quatieri, with Sam Liever representing the other seven.

Fred Brubaker, the frequent target of anti-gambling forces and the local press for not initiating action against the racketeers, used the hearing to heap a bit of scorn on the T-men. As the proceeding wound down, he asked Furia if the hearing was over. When informed it was, Brubaker loudly announced:

"Attention, all agents who testified. The Young Men's Republican Club invites you to put on your show at their club in Reading before the election." Fred was intimating that the raid was a GOP plot to embarrass Democratic candidates, including himself, in the general election the following month.

Joe McGlynn, the federal prosecutor, and U.S. marshals at the hearing, tried to throw their weight around with contempt warnings for disrupting a federal hearing, but the wily Fred was ready for them.

Too bad, he grinned, "He (Furia) said the hearing was over. I cannot be held for contempt."

"You are a guest in a federal court," McGlynn responded.

"I am a taxpayer as well," the district attorney reminded.

Furia ignored the confrontation, continuing to fiddle with documents in front of him. Nothing more came from the exchange although it might have added to the Treasury Department's determination to turn the screws a bit tighter on Abe Minker. And that's exactly what happened.

Brubaker carried out his plan to enter local charges against the numbers defendants but shortly before their preliminary hearing, U.S. Attorney Walter Alessandroni met with Fred in Philadelphia to discuss the case. Alessandroni, the former Pennsylvania attorney general, had recently been appointed to his federal post.

A few days after the Brubaker-Alessandroni meeting, Alderman Ralph Breneiser started a preliminary hearing in Reading by calling his first witness, Jack Dalsey. A long silence followed. Then Alessandroni stood up to announce, "I have instructed all Treasury agents under subpoena not to be here to testify."

He said the disclosure of evidence at local hearings or trial could jeopardize the federal case. Brubaker had successfully fought this same battle three years earlier when he piggy-backed prosecution of other gambling operators who were already charged by the IRS. In that case an IRS agent testified and Brubaker won convictions.

Although the IRS refused to bend this time, the state agreed to allow two state policemen who had accompanied the feds on the Lancaster Avenue raid to testify. But without the testimony of Dalsey and other agents, Fred knew he would not have much of a case. The stakes were much higher in this instance than in the earlier case when the IRS assisted Brubaker. Alessandroni said the agents might be allowed to testify after the federal case was settled, but that might be a year or more. Local charges were then dismissed.

The Justice Department now introduced a familiar name, but an unfamiliar face, into the battle. Thomas F. McBride was appointed special prosecutor for organized crime and would become Abe Minker's nemesis for the next few years. This 34-year-old attorney was not to be confused with Thomas D. McBride, the Pennsylvania attorney general who launched the state police investigation in 1958 that led to the aborted extortion trial against Minker, his two nephews, and Johnny Wittig. McBride with an F, would become the lead prosecutor in two drawn out cases against Abe and others.

Although Minker slipped the hook after the October 3 raid, the IRS soon began baiting another line, and an entirely different method would be employed to land its prize.

# 17

# *Will election bring better government?*

With the long shadow cast by the federal government across Reading Towne, Abe Minker doubted Dan McDevitt could be reelected in 1959. When John Kubacki announced he would oppose McDevitt, The General was not overjoyed. Minker felt Kubacki could be bought, but at what price? So he sent out his scouts to reconnoiter the city for an unknown, a fresh new face with a clean record who would play by Abe's rules.

Frank Heim operated a soft pretzel shop just off the lobby of the Embassy Theater on Penn Street. Frank was a former Central Catholic High School quarterback, a congenial fellow who made friends easily, a family man with a beautiful wife and three kids living in Cornwall Terrace, Spring Township—and, no ties to the mob. Frank knew some of the underworld fellows who stopped by for pretzels, but he wasn't selling numbers or dodging taxes or even skimping on the salt. Frank was just a nice good looking guy who enjoyed gabbing with characters like Harry the Hat, a numbers writer who hid slips under his derby, or Sandwich Joe, who ran errands for hungry racketeers lolling at 6$^{th}$ and Penn. John Gatto was another racketeer with a taste for Frank's handmade twists.

As the 1959 primary elections approached, Gatto began feeling out Frank about whether he ever considered running for office. Plant an idea in Frank's mind and more often than not he would run with it. A pessimist he was not.

"How would you like to be mayor?" Gatto asked one day.

From pretzels to citywide politics was quite a leap, but Frank wanted to hear more. So the mid-level racketeer explained. His people, Gatto said, could engineer the election so that Frank would become the next mayor of Reading.

"But I don't even live in Reading."

"We'll get you a house in the city." And there would be other perks including a car—and probably a lawyer.

"But I don't know anything about politics."

"Ya gratchuated from high school, dincha?"

"Sure."

"So you're educated enough to run this town. My people will help you."

The next step in the process was to earn the approval of Joe Liever, the bail bondsman who knew his way around all the dark corners of Democratic politics. For that meeting, Gibraltar Joe Biancone was Frank's escort. Joe, an ex-boxer of local repute who became a middleman of disrepute in the stolen goods racket, led Frank over to Liever's Washington Street office. Frank passed this initial test as the boys figured this newcomer had enough of the devil in him to meet their requirements. As a visionary, Frank had no clue how he would run the city, but he certainly liked the idea of being the top guy in town. And he had the perfect wife to be a first lady. The boys wanted to meet her—and they wished they hadn't.

Annette, tall, blonde, and intelligent, was the family rock. She steadied the ship when Frank's impetuous nature led them into rough waters. When she found out who was trying to convince her husband to make such an outlandish career change, she issued an emphatic "NO!" Frank's hopes of fame and fortune (more likely notoriety and potential disaster) were dashed. The cooler head prevailed and the mob lost its dark horse candidate.

Before the 1959 primary, Jack Davis tossed his hat into the ring again, but having lost in 1951 and 1955, the former Democratic mayor had little chance of regaining his earlier popularity. Having opposed McDevitt at every turn, Kubacki gave hope to the voters that he would curb racketeering. Minker watched and waited, hoping Davis was capable of pulling an upset if McDevitt didn't win. The mayor campaigned on how much Reading had improved on his watch:

- Construction of a new $4.5 million sewage disposal plant without a sewer tax
- Development of off-street parking lots for hundreds of cars
- Establishment of a long-range planning program for the city's growth
- Paving of more city streets than any other administration
- Construction of the West Shore Bypass
- Planning for senior citizen housing projects
- Modernization of Reading Municipal Airport

- Urban renewal programs

It was an impressive list, but the almost daily news reports about illegal gambling, prostitution, corruption, and City Hall's inability or refusal to combat vice, revived memories of the Kefauver Committee findings all over again. Organized crime was tainting the city.

Behind the scenes in City Hall, the various elements of the Democratic Party were sparring for position. The McDevitt loyalists feared the two-term jinx would strike again because of the cloud that hung over their champion. Although many Democratic pols were offended by Kubacki's brazen style, they sensed he was electable. A third faction, the old guard, wanted Jack Davis back in the mayor's chair. They still liked Jovial Jack, and hoped the voters did, too. So he had considerable support when he announced his fourth straight run for the top job.

It wasn't even close when the primary votes were counted: Kubacki, 7,355; McDevitt, 5,607; Davis, 2,845; Pellicciotti, 1,381. Kubacki's Republican opponent would be J. Edgar Hilgendorf, an easy winner over Thomas E. Schaeffer.

City detective Charlie Wade had ambitions of becoming chief of police. Bernie Richards preferred retirement rather than being demoted back into the ranks as would have happened when the next mayor took over. McDevitt had been kind to Wade, allowing him to work nights in the detective bureau. Charlie operated four home improvement companies during the day. On the graveyard shift, midnight to 8 a.m., there was usually some naptime available. Despite his debt of gratitude to McDevitt, Charlie switched allegiances when Kubacki asked for his support in the primary. Kubacki knew Charlie was gunning for the chief's job. When Jack Davis was mayor he had threatened to remove Charlie from the police force if he didn't give up his businesses. That didn't happen, but Charlie knew Davis, if elected again, would never promote him, and neither would McDevitt who now felt double-crossed.

Wade learned the real facts of political life in August when Kubacki and city detective Bill Focht visited him at his rural home in Cumru Township.

"You're going to have to pay for the job," Charlie quoted Kubacki. "The chief's job is worth $10,000. That's what Abe told me."

Wade claimed he replied, "You told me you had no connection."

He quickly learned John was intimately linked to the mob, but that did not dissuade him from pursuing his dream. Kubacki and his wife had been seen in a New York restaurant dining with Abe Minker the summer of 1955 by a Reading resident who notified the *Reading Times* newsroom.

As a down payment, Charlie gave the mayor-to-be $5,000. Wade could afford it and his goal was soon to be realized. Abe Minker came out on the short end of the deal because he was supposed to get the other $5,000 when Charlie sold his country home. As it turned out, Charlie never did pay Abe the additional money because of the many twists and turns of events that erupted during the next few years.

Nine days before the general election, Wade was involved in a standoff with an armed parolee. Fred Miller, a 20-year-old convicted burglar, fired four shotgun blasts at police when they came to his sister's Buttonwood Street home to arrest him for parole violation. Nobody was injured but the scene was tense by the time Wade arrived shortly before dawn. He stood under a streetlight coaxing the self-professed cop-hater to let him come inside to talk. Miller watched as Charlie handed his revolver to another detective, then was admitted into the house and upstairs where the parolee was holed up. With the shotgun pointed at him, Wade promised the young man he wanted to help him, explaining that he had given jobs to numerous ex-convicts. Miller recalled seeing the businessman/cop on a TV show, "Man Behind the Badge," depicting Wade's efforts to rehabilitate ex-cons. Detective Capt. John Feltman soon joined Charlie, and together they convinced the distraught young man to surrender his gun after three harrowing hours.

The standoff gained Charlie considerable media attention. No doubt about it, Charlie loved the spotlight because he truly enjoyed the adventure of being a cop. It was a counterbalance to the more mundane business of dressing up houses with siding. After his heroics, some saw Charlie as a publicity hound who paid his marginal help marginal wages. Others praised him for giving criminals a second chance to rebuild their lives.

In the final year of the McDevitt administration, two 750-gallon pumpers costing $38,214, and an aerial ladder truck for $42,671 were purchased for the fire department. City Council voted 4-1 to buy the trucks with Kubacki providing the only "nay," as expected. Four years later a month before the 1963 general election, the fire trucks became a campaign issue, one the Republicans were only too happy to exploit. Talk of kickbacks by the vendor, was just talk at that time, but would eventually lead to serious trouble for McDevitt.

Kubacki showed his true colors during the campaign when anything placed him in a negative light. The Liberty Three, a folk group appearing at Beef and Beer, a $5^{th}$ Street nightclub, added special lyrics to a popular song that chided Kubacki's campaign promises to clean up the city. It didn't take long before the candidate learned about the satire. A few nights later a very large fellow with a low brow visited Beef and Beer to talk to the entertainers. The threats he mentioned were frightening enough that the Liberty Three dropped the political lampoon from their repertoire.

When Big John made a speech at Albright College that fall, some of the student activists began throwing hardball questions at him, so he walked off the stage. Stan Michalak, Al Seifarth, the son of J. Wayne Seifarth, and a few other students showed up at a City Council meeting the next week to again take on the candidate. There was a heated debate but not too many straight answers to the students' tough questions. The session ended in an angry draw. Not too long after the election the police started a campaign of ticketing all illegally parked cars around the Albright campus. (Shades of Dan McDevitt's ticketing fiasco.)The activists were sure it was retaliation by the new mayor.

At 4:30 p.m. on election eve, Kubacki stood on the corner of Washington and Poplar streets, a block from City Hall, talking with a *Times* police reporter, author of this book. In an expansive mood, he pulled from his pocket the largest roll of currency the newsman had ever seen.

"Gotta go down and spread this around," he said with a sly smile as he turned to walk away. Down was south of Penn where small cash often bought important votes. After a few steps he stopped, turned and winked:

"That's off the record, you know. It would be your word against that of the next mayor of this great city."

The next day, the 47-year-old prognosticator proved right by being swept into office by a generous margin over the Republican candidate, J. Edgar Hilgendorf. The vote: almost 19,000 for Kubacki, 12,690 for Hilgendorf. Democrats Bruce Coleman, Harold Guldin, and Joseph Kuzminski won equally easy victories for seats on City Council over Republicans Thomas Dwight, Neil Morrison, and Charles Zellnar.

Fred Brubaker was reelected, giving the Democrats complete control of local law enforcement in Reading and Berks County once again. So it was no surprise when the federal government continued to clamp down on the rackets, with the help of the state police and a rogue assistant district attorney over the next four years.

# 18

# *They liked to call it honest graft*

John Kubacki was an enigma—how else can he be explained?

His intelligence was never questioned. Charisma—he was loaded with it. He was mentally quicker on his feet in the political ring than he was as a championship college boxer. His star qualities were exemplified on the gridiron at Reading High School and Bucknell College. He married well, he was a leader, he had a crude sense of humor, and he certainly knew right from wrong. Simply put, he had an awful lot going for him. He could have been ranked high among Reading's long list of mayors, but never will.

Abe Minker, John Kubacki, Charlie Wade—three bright men with different understandings about success. Abe was succeeding as a wholesale grocer when the lures of Prohibition tempted him. From then on he mingled legitimate business with the rackets and paid the price more than once. With Charlie, he seemed to have found the pot of gold at the end of his rainbow, but more than money, he craved prestige, and that was his downfall. John made a good start in politics, but was too deeply infected with Reading's style of governance to rise above it. Their legacy was an era of corruption rarely seen in any small American city.

Kubacki's Polish immigrant father, Bernard, was a foreman at Reading Car Wheel Company. From his mother, Leona, he inherited her broad facial features. Raised at 642 Bingaman Street, John and his family moved to 1558 Mineral Spring Road where he lived the rest of his life.

After attending grade school at 6th and Chestnut, Kubacki showed signs of becoming an all-around athlete at Northeast Junior High School. At Reading High, he lettered in football, basketball, and track. As a triple-threat fullback of the 1929 team he was the passer, top runner, punter, and extra point kicker. On passing plays his brother Stanley was often the target. Stanley was also a bulwark at defense end, with John right behind at linebacker. As a senior John captained the track team, teaming with Stanley to regularly earn 30 points in dual meets. John won District 3 gold medals in the 220-low hurdles and broad jump, and competed in three other events, high jump, javelin, and shot put. Stanley was RHS's top sprinter.

As a freshman at Bucknell College John won a letter in boxing and competed in football and track. Fighting as a middleweight and light heavyweight, he was undefeated in the regular season, then won the Eastern Intercollegiate middleweight title as a senior.

In football he won more honors. As a sophomore quarterback he led his team to an 8-0 season, the only college in the East not to lose a game, thereby winning the mythical eastern championship. He earned All-American honorable mention as a fullback on the 1932 undefeated team. Bucknell played a major schedule at that time as John kicked both conversions in a 14-13 victory over a very good Fordham squad. His only extra point miss was against Georgetown University in his last game.

The Depression was in full bloom when he returned to Reading following graduation in 1934. He became a supervisor in the Federal Adult Education program, coaching Civilian Conservation Corps youths in boxing and football. Then he moved to Wyomissing Polytechnic Institute as athletic director and English teacher. When he became the school's basketball coach, the Engineers compiled a 65-11 (.855 percent) record over five years.

In 1939 he married Mary Eleanor Stocker, the daughter of Dr. and Mrs. Joseph Stocker of Wyomissing. This was a big step up the social ladder for the young man who never lost his rough edges. Mary was a graduate of Sharon Hill Academy and Trinity College, and attended the University of Pennsylvania's College of Women.

The Stockers treated the newlyweds to a European honeymoon despite the gathering war clouds. They were on the S.S. Normandie returning home when World War II broke out in September 1939. The last three days were sailed under blackout.

During the war, Kubacki served in the Navy as a physical training officer and boatswain's mate. He was 33 when discharged from the military. Instead of continuing his career as an educator, he took a job in public relations with a local distillery. Next he became a salesman for Reading Display Service. But the idea of running for public office intrigued him. He liked the challenge it presented and had the confidence to believe he could win and be a good public servant. He first ran for a seat on the Reading School Board in 1948, but lost in the Democratic primary. The next year among 10 candidates he placed third in the voting, to become a school director. But this was a non-paying, part-time position that did not fulfill his ambition to wheel and deal.

Kubacki did not take a back seat on the school board. Everybody quickly became familiar with the bulky activist who had an answer for every question put to him, and a question for anybody who made a proposal. He was a politician of the Jesse Ventura mold, not a party line wimp—big, imposing and ready for a scrap. In 1950 the voters sent him to the state House of Representatives. Now he was on his way. In '52 and '54 he made it back to Harrisburg, each time by a bigger margin. He also served on the Reading Recreation Commission during that period. Then he made a bizarre decision, at least it was judged that way by many.

Why would he want to return to Reading and run for City Council in 1955? That was not the usual progression of local politicians who had followed the same path he did to the state Capitol. Why did John not run for mayor? His chances appeared as good as Danny McDevitt's or former mayor Jack Davis's. It was one of the few times he showed any caution. Always his own man he was wary of a three-man race, preferring to seek a council seat where the odds favored him. He and Harold Guldin easily won as the Democrats dominated by a large margin. With McDevitt riding to an easy victory, it appeared to be smooth sailing for the Democrats for the next four years. That optimistic view did not last long, thanks to John Kubacki.

During McDevitt's administration, Kubacki was the disloyal opposition. He seldom agreed with the mayor, almost always going out of his way to distance himself from the other councilmen while leaving the impression he was an anti-rackets crusader. In 1959, after Kubacki was elected mayor, but before he was sworn in, he continued to promote this image. He promised a crackdown on racketeers in the 7th and Franklin neighborhood, the city's tenderloin for decades. That area was a haven for prostitutes and bars that had little regard for the Pennsylvania liquor laws. Kubacki, standing in front of future Police Chief Wade and Detective Capt. John Feltman, announced:

"I am definitely going to put one or two of our best and toughest patrolmen there, with orders that they carry nightsticks, and under no condition will loitering and assembling, as they do now, be tolerated." In hindsight, this was a rather innocuous promise compared to his campaign talk about routing the racketeers. Nudging a few loiterers off the street was hardly going to make a dent in prostitution. There was no mention of gambling or political corruption in his edict.

Less than three weeks into his administration, Mayor Kubacki tagged along as his police force raided three places in the neighborhood he promised to sanitize. The police action was a show of force that was really a smokescreen. Two whorehouses and a gambling joint were knocked off. Although 43 men and women were arrested, the fines were light and the charges watered down. Mable Jones ran her girlie parlor at 129 Lemon Street, but conveniently wasn't at home when the cops arrived that Sunday morning at 4:30 a.m. Four girls and a few fellows were sitting around but no real action was interrupted. Over at Freddie William's place at 124 Plum Street, it was the same story—more smoke than fire with Freddie not on the premises. The big catch was a backroom card game in a building on 7th Street in the 100 block. Twenty-seven gamblers were arrested.

None of the unoccupied women was charged with prostitution, just disorderly conduct. The out-of-town dawdlers paid $15 fines and were warned by Capt. Feltman to get out of town and stay out. The public was led to believe that was just the beginning of a major cleanup. Not until minutes before the raid were patrolmen and low-level officers ordered to the Nut, a taxi stand at the 7th Street Station. But when it happened, most of them suspected it was a sequel to the drill Mayor McDevitt staged when he launched his phony anti-pinball crusade four years earlier.

The farce continued five nights later when Wade's cops hit 18 more spots suspected of after-hours vice, but to no one's surprise, no hanky-panky was discovered at any of them. Adding to this show of force the mayor was armed with a water pistol. Patrolman John Halstead was not laughing when he was sprayed by his boss. At one of the bawdyhouses a couple of girls were painting by the numbers while cops searched their empty bedrooms. Pinochle, not poker or dice, was the game of choice at the gambling sites. "At least we're keeping them on edge," Chief Wade stated.

Kubacki solicited the aid of tavern owners to keep out the bad element that was giving the city a bad name. He and Wade continued their PR campaign at numerous public gatherings. In the middle of February, Wade, Capt. Bill Focht, and Lt. Ed Cwiklinski broke into the gambling casino at 10th and Walnut streets, only to find Johnny Wittig and John Hyneman playing rummy. The charade was getting ridiculous. Wade's next stop was at the S&S Cigar store at 7th and Cherry streets. Several men were playing pool and a few others were engaged in a game of barbut. The hangers-on watched with amusement as Wade swung a double-bladed ax, ripping apart the gaming table, the dice scattering on the floor.

"That was known as barbut, but now its kaput," Wade growled.

John Kubacki trailed along as Wade and his assistants then went to the 10th Street Cigar Store at No. 14. In a back room a dozen players were engaged in a poker game, but claimed they were playing rummy. The players were hauled into City Hall and charged. All told, the trio of police brass plus one, raided seven places that night and made 55 arrests. Every gambler posted a $15 forfeit; none showed up for a hearing the next day. Fines for all this police activity totaled $1,155.

The raids continued throughout the year as gamblers and prostitutes and johns paid their small forfeit bonds and fines, then went on their way. There were dozens of arrests, but to any close observer it was evident the city was wide open and no sincere effort was being made to bring top racketeers to trial.

Behind the scenes another campaign was being waged, one that was a well-kept secret and of a darker image. Only weeks after the new administration was sworn in, a salesman from a company that sold parking meters visited Charlie Wade. Rodger Weidlich from Bangor, Pa., was a former policeman who had met Wade at police conventions. Now a salesman for Koontz Equipment Corp., Weidlich called on Wade to find out if Reading was in the market for parking meters. Wade offered to set up a meeting with the mayor. They met, discussed the number of meters the city might purchase, and Weidlich agreed to work out a proposal. At a February luncheon/meeting in the Berkshire Hotel with Wade also attending, Kubacki told the salesman he wanted to buy 500 of the company's $59.50 Duncan-Miller meters. According to Weidlich, the mayor then added:

"You know we fellows run for office. I would like to get at least about $12 to $15 per meter for a political donation." Weidlich said he would have to discuss that with his supervisor.

Abe Minker was furious when Wade told him Kubacki had been negotiating with Weidlich. Quoting Abe, Wade said, "When meters are going to be purchased, Joe Liever and I will handle the purchase. We'll handle it. I'll tell Johnny what he is going to buy. He'll mess the whole thing up."

When Wade relayed Minker's orders to the mayor, Kubacki questioned Charlie's loyalty to him. According to Charlie, the mayor complained:

"Abe and Joe want to run everything. The other departments don't split with me, but I have to split with them."

Wade's answer to his boss was more of Minker's thinking: "Abe says we have to feed an army, we've got to take care of a lot of people."

Kubacki replied, according to Wade, "He never says that when it concerns Bruce Coleman, Harold Guldin or Ruoff's departments."

Weidlich was back in Reading a week later ready to do business, but Wade said he first wanted the salesman to meet "Joe" who had the final say on city purchases. They drove to Abe Minker's apartment house on Hampden Boulevard, where Weidlich went inside and talked with Joe/Abe.

Having just returned from the hospital after an operation on his ailing back, Abe was in a robe and slippers as he explained the real deal to the ex-cop in his kitchen. The price of the meter was fine, Abe told Weidlich, but he said there had to be a reimbursement of $10 per meter. Arguing that he doubted his company would pay that much, Weidlich suggested a figure that Minker rejected. But they agreed to talk again.

After a discussion with Koontz president, Alfred Roach, Weidlich returned to Minker's apartment a few days later with an offer: $6 extra for each meter, a total of $3,000. Minker stalled a few more weeks but finally gave the OK to close the deal "cash and tax free."

In the second week of April, Weidlich brought a check to Reading for $3,000 made out to him by Roach. He asked Wade to go with him to a city bank to cash the check. Wade provided ID and vouched for Weidlich as he received the cash in a large envelope. Now outside the bank at 6th and Washington streets, Charlie gave an order: "See the fellow in a white shirt standing halfway down the block. That's Joe. Hand the money to him."

That Joe turned out to be Bobbie Frank Johnson, an employee of Wade's Air Spray Corp., who returned the envelope to his boss who then went to City Hall and handed it to Kubacki. Wade admitted receiving $300 for his role as middleman. He would later claim under oath that he didn't really want the money, but as a member of the Kubacki-Minker team he had to play along and take what was offered.

The 500 meter heads were purchased in June, the kickback known only to the few involved. As Wade would testify a few years later, Abe Minker, not John Kubacki, made the deals for parking meters.

There was no public bidding for the meters. Other negotiations were progressing at the same time Weidlich was trying to peddle his product. Walter Hughes, general manager of Karpark Corp., received a call in his Starkville, Miss., office from Joe Liever. Hughes, who was no stranger to Reading, was asked to come to the city to discuss the purchase of meter heads. In 1948, the first year of Jack Davis's administration, Hughes had met Liever when Joe was a sales representative for Karpark, but Joe's contract expired in 1959. When Hughes arrived in Reading, Liever drove him to the White House Market. Abe Minker came out to Liever's car on the parking lot to talk. Abe never conducted illegal business inside the market.

They didn't dicker about the meter price, $51, but as for the kickback, Hughes's offer of $12 per meter was $3 short of Minker's asking fee. Abe suggested Hughes go to City Hall to talk with the mayor. Remembering the hall clock he received when Karpark sold meters to the city in 1948, Abe suggested a similar gift to Kubacki might swing the deal. At City Hall, the mayor also declared a $12 kickback was too low. (Hughes always referred to kickbacks as commissions. With a straight face in court he would claim his company never paid kickbacks.) Hughes showed the mayor a brochure from Herschede Hall Clock Co., the parent company of Karpark. Hughes claimed Kubacki suggested an $880 grandfather clock he pointed to in the catalog might sweeten the deal. Hughes claimed Herschede, of which he was plant superintendent, did not give clocks away but he felt the company could work something out.

There were other meetings till finally on June 15, Hughes went to City Hall where he and Kubacki negotiated a contract for the purchase of 500 meter heads. Although Karpark again claimed his company did not give grandfather clocks away, Hughes said he felt he could accommodate the mayor so he wouldn't have to pay for one. But the $25,500 contract sat idle for a year as the mayor stalled and waited for a better deal.

By July 1961, a new proposition was offered by Karpark. To get the deal moving again, Hughes told Minker that $1,600 in meter spare parts was included in the $25,500 contract. But, if the city decided it didn't want the spare parts, that $1,600 could be added to the commission. Understandably, Abe chose the cash.

Still needing a middleman because Joe Liever had refused to sign a new contract, Hughes contacted an old friend in Covington, Ky. In gambling circles, Covington was every bit as notorious as Reading. The friend Hughes chose to be Karpark's sales rep in Reading was George Gradel, an established bookie. In the often complex and shady kickback business, Gradel was offered 20 percent of the $7,500 kickback for doing practically nothing except inserting his name as the middleman in the transaction. City Council approved the contract.

It was August when Hughes arrived in Covington to hand a check for $7,500 to Gradel. They cashed it, then at the request of Hughes, Gradel handed back $375 because "it would be nice" to do something for the widow of a former Reading meter maintenance man named Peters, "who did us a lot of favors." Hughes wanted to show his appreciation by sending her the money as a Christmas gift.

Now the pair drove to Reading, Gradel's first visit to the city. In Joe Liever's office there was a heated debate about whether Gradel or Liever was Karpark's legal agent. Abe Minker argued for his longtime buddy, while Hughes supported the bookie he had known for 15 years. Since Gradel kept about $1,125 of the money, it appears he won the debate.

According to later testimony by Hughes, he handed an envelope containing $6,000 to Liever in a dark hallway outside Joe's office. Joe then gave the envelope to Johnny Wittig to take to City Hall and turn it over to Mayor Kubacki.

Fearing things were getting out of hand, Abe called a meeting in Liever's office with Kubacki and Wade to formulate a cover story. Abe warned everybody to deny there was an extortion conspiracy. Kubacki ordered Wade to refuse to talk to IRS investigators if they came back to question him again. According to Wade, Abe told him he should take the 5th Amendment if he was questioned under oath. Charlie said he refused to do that because it would ruin his credibility as a policeman. The meeting at Liever's place did not resolve the matter, Kubacki remarking as he left, "Whatever you work out is okay with me."

The mahogany hall clock was shipped to Kubacki's Mineral Spring Road home shortly before Christmas. Hughes and Gradel came north to help set it up.

All the principals in this bit of graft ate their Christmas dinners that year quite satisfied to get it over with. But what they thought was a done deal would later come back to become a drawn out scandal over the next three years. Weidlich and Hughes had caved in to IRS investigators and the Reading crooked clique's road to prosperity was getting bumpy.

In 1962, another deal was in the making between the Reading Parking Authority and Karpark, but by July, IRS investigators were asking a lot of questions of the people involved in the previous extortions. But the wheeling and dealing continued as Minker began negotiating with Duncan-Miller Company for another large purchase of meter heads for the new Franklin Plaza parking garage, with Liever as the agent. But that deal was never culminated. Instead, in May 1963, the city parking authority purchased 580 meter heads from Magee-Hale Park-O-Meter Co., of Oklahoma City. IRS investigators proclaimed the deal perfectly legal: $43.50 per meter; total cost, $23,968. Instead of a kickback, the company offered a cash discount of $2.20 per meter.

Mayor Kubacki never attempted to win any popularity polls. He continually stepped on toes in his four years as mayor, never seemingly too worried about winning friends. What was best for him, not for his constituents or party, was his apparent political philosophy. When his authority was challenged, it was not his nature to step back and negotiate or compromise. Counterattack, not diplomacy, was the tactic he employed when the opposition faced up to him. And as the feds continued to press their case against him, he continued to deny any complicity in the charges he would soon face.

# 19

# *The mob trashed by a hero*

Anthony Damore is a rare patriot. He didn't just wave the flag or trumpet allegiance to his adopted country. Forty-six years later, he did not want or seek credit for going above and beyond what is expected of a model citizen. In 1959 he was a hard-working taxpayer who felt those who cheat the government deserve to pay the price. When he read about the Lancaster Avenue numbers raid, then saw that charges against Abe Minker had been dismissed for lack of evidence, Anthony realized he was in a position to help the government. Anthony was Abe's trash man. Rather than avoid involvement, as so many in his position would have done, Anthony did not shirk his civic duty.

Thinking like a detective, the 39-year-old Damore began rummaging through the trash he collected at the Hampden House. He wasn't sure what he was looking for, but soon realized adding machine tapes he found in Minker's rubbish might be of interest to some federal law enforcement agency.

Four and a half decades after the Lancaster Avenue bust, the 83-year-old Damore was reluctant to talk about his role in the prosecution of Abe Minker. In a brief telephone interview he was asked, "Who was it at the IRS that first contacted you?"

Testimony at a 1961 trial had not answered that question. It appeared the IRS agents had approached Anthony with a request to turn Minker's trash over to them. But his answer during the recent phone conversation indicated otherwise.

"Nobody contacted me," be insisted. "Who said I was contacted? I called them because I should as a good citizen."

He did not need the IRS to ask for his assistance. He initiated that phase of the investigation. Law enforcement agencies often complain that volunteers of Damore's stripe are indeed hard to find. His inquisitive action gave the Alcohol Tax Unit another chance to capitalize on its earlier findings.

But at a much later date, Anthony was still reluctant to talk about his role in bringing down a major racketeer. He didn't want to talk to the press in 1961 and he's of the same disposition today. Other than his brief admission, "Nobody contacted me," he refused to further elaborate.

After the October 3 raid, the racketeers took a very short vacation, but within a few weeks of tightened security, Abe's runners, writers, and pickup men were as busy as ever, but more alert to possible ATU observers. Abe was not so openly defiant as before, but the bucks continued to roll in. It took the T-men a while to find the new numbers bank, but something like that can always be uncovered with patient surveillance.

The Trash Man Cometh would be an apt title for this drama starring Anthony Damore. He collected the rubbish at the Hampden House three times a week. Beginning a few weeks following the raid, after each pickup he carefully separated trash in Abe's container from the other collections. As a prosecutor would one day note, if they didn't get Minker on the tax charges they could get him for mixing garbage with trash, a city ordinance violation.

Abe's trash was easy to identify because he always placed it in a bag or box. Envelopes and newspapers addressed to him, initialed napkins, messages from New York Mafioso, tapes showing daily numbers and slot machine takes, summary sheets, and notes revealing information about his other vice operations were found.

It was in November when Damore contacted the IRS. The Alcohol Tax Unit immediately sent agents to Reading to wade through Anthony's valuable cache. Some of the paper trash was ripped or shredded but ATU technicians put the puzzles together. After each collection a T-man would visit Damore at either his home or at his storage area at 7th and Laurel streets. The agent then carted the rubbish to Philadelphia where it was sorted and evaluated.

The probers were able to estimate amounts of money that Minker's bank was taking in daily and monthly. There were other figures that told them Abe was paying at least one elected official $850 a week. Lesser city officials, according to the investigators, were raking in $250 a week. Other jottings indicated a monthly retainer fee of $1,740 was going to a New York outfit that covered big hits suffered by the Reading bank. Other information about the 10th and Walnut casino was obtained, but this was before Congress passed interstate gambling laws a few years later.

Rebuffed on its first attempt to indict Minker, the ATU stepped up surveillance in Berks County in December when it was evident the numbers game was back in business. Special Agent Harry Gegenheimer tested the numbers waters in Chink's Shoe Rebuilding Shop in the 400 block of North 13th Street. No questions were asked as he placed a quarter bet on a number in early December.

Things heated up for the T-men when Gegenheimer saw four familiar faces climb into a car on Fairview Street in Reading. So he tailed them. The quartet was Tony Bonanno, Mike Augustine, Louie Fudeman, and Dominic Quatieri, all nabbed in the Lancaster Avenue raid. The agent was led down through Mount Penn on Route 422. The mobsters' car turned right at Neversink Road heading south for more than a mile. The agent watched as the racketeers entered an isolated frame farmhouse. For more than two months the house was under observation before the feds mounted their attack.

A week before the ATU was ready to make its move, it was upstaged by Cumru Township Police Chief George Baltasser and state cops from the Reading barracks. The chief had been hearing rumors for a couple of years that Charlie Lucchese was running numbers and bookmaking operations out of his home off the Cedar Top-Knauers Road. A copse shielded three sides of the split-level, and there was a quarter-mile-long macadam driveway leading back to it. Neighbors were suspicious of all the traffic turning in to the drive. The first complaint was filed in 1957, so Baltasser began checking on Lucchese's past history.

It turned out that Charlie and his brothers had compiled quite a police record over the past two decades. In rackets circles they were known as Jimmy Peters, Charlie Peters, and Louie the Lug. The eldest, Anthony Lucchese, used the alias Jimmy Peters when he wanted to hide his true identity. Charlie Lucchese, the middle sibling, sometimes went by Charlie Peters. And Louie the Lug, the youngest, grew up as Louis Lucchese. All were short, dark and attracted to women.

Anthony, a barber by trade, and Charlie got their start in the rackets shortly before World War II. Their idea of helping the war effort was to supply our boys in uniform with girls. In 1943 they were arrested for running "a full-scale white slavery syndicate" in southeast Pennsylvania. According to the state police, it was Charlie who recruited a 15-year-old girl among other teenagers to perform in hotels in Reading, Lancaster, Harrisburg, and Lebanon. Originally sentenced to 6-to-12 years in prison, his term was reduced to 3-to-6, and he served less for good behavior. Anthony's term was 5-to-10 years, but he also got a reduction and was released after two years. Even though Tony violated his parole and was returned to BCP, in 1950 Gov. James Duff commuted his sentence. For selling numbers in1953, he got off with probation and a $1,000 fine. Louie was granted a promoter's license by the Pennsylvania Boxing Commission several weeks before the Cumru numbers bank was uncovered in 1960. A "very thorough" investigation by the Boxing Commission before Louie's appointment obviously wasn't thorough enough.

After his prison sojourn, Charlie tried his hand as a salesman. Then in 1956 he formed G&G Novelty Company, retailing toys, games and novelties in a store at 758 Penn Street. It appeared to be a legitimate business that did $50,000 to $100,000 annually according to Dunn and Bradstreet reports. The numbers bank and bookmaking were bringing in more than that during its four-year run before the law moved in.

When a second group complained to Chief Baltasser in September 1959, he looked closer at the matter and eventually got the state police involved in February 1960.

Capt. George Sauer, Troop C commander at the Reading Barracks, began preparing for a raid. After three weeks of surveillance it was noted Charlie drove the short distance each afternoon to a nearby school bus stop to pick up his daughter and another pupil. On March 17, state police Lt. Rocco Urella and Chief Baltasser arrested Charlie as he waited for the bus. When the kids arrived, they were escorted to a township building by a Cumru policeman for safekeeping. At that same time, Cpl. Leroy Lilly and Troopers Arthur McAnally and Donald Holloway were serving a search warrant on Charlie's wife, Edith, when she answered the door of their home.

Charlie wondered aloud whether his arrest was the fair thing to do. "Why bother us. There are a lot of bigger people than us in this county." Urella couldn't deny that, knowing exactly who Charlie was referring to. Something was said about the luck of the Irish on St. Patrick's Day, but Lucchese failed to see the humor.

Evidence popped up even before Urella and Baltasser got Charlie back to his house. Settle-up sheets were plucked from his shirt pocket. He explained the sheets showed what he owed to numbers writers and what they owed him.

The team at the house was impressed with the furnishings, the swimming pool, the seven telephones. It was all quite luxurious. Charlie claimed he had been in business only two days, but the investigators estimated it was more like four or five years, since he moved onto the 30-acre property in 1954. On another point, Charlie came up short: instead of the $300 a day he said he was pulling in, records of numbers and horse bets that were seized indicated it was a $1,000-a-day business. Whether Charlie was connected to a syndicate was never revealed, although there was talk that he was backed by the Philadelphia mob which was why Abe Minker had not drawn him into his net. It was revealed 40 people were on Charlie's payroll.

Baltasser described the scene after Charlie was brought back to the house:

"We found horse action being taken over the phone, and numbers action, and we were kept busy for half an hour answering calls. We took the results of races that were coming in from various race tracks throughout the country." Some of the callers probably were not happy to learn later on that the win, place, and show finishes being fed to them were not the true results.

Edith Lucchese was charged with the same gambling violations filed against her husband but the arrest warrant was never served. Fred Brubaker pointed out she would not have had to testify against Charlie, so why bother. The state cops agreed to drop the charges since Lucchese indicated he wasn't going to fight the law. He pleaded guilty to one charge and five others were dismissed. He received a four-to 11-month term in Berks County Prison, had a heart attack two days after sentencing, had a second seizure a few weeks later, then recovered and served his minimum time. Because of his heart problems, Charlie was crossed off the list as a potential witness in the impending federal grand jury probe in Philadelphia.

The IRS waited a few years, then came after the Lucchese brothers again. On April 3, 1963, Charlie, Tony, and Louie were charged with owing the government $101,000 in unpaid income taxes. The Cumru Township numbers operation wasn't just Charlie's game. According to the government's investigation, all three shared in the profits: Charlie and Tony, 40 percent each, and Louie the Lug, 20 percent. Charlie had failed to obtain a gambling occupation stamp and his reported income in 1958 should have been $95,308, according to the IRS, not the $6,443 figure he filed.

The feds wished they could dispense of the Minker case as quickly as Lucchese's numbers case had been wrapped up, but it wasn't to be. They still had a dozen unindicted suspects on their hands from the Lancaster Avenue raid as they prepared to hit the Exeter Township numbers bank. Their ace in the hole was the trash barrel evidence.

Several of the Alcohol Tax Unit agents in the Lancaster Avenue raid returned to Reading five and a half months later on March 25, 1960, to wind up another major investigation. Owen M. Morris, group supervisor of the intelligence division in Philadelphia, and Dan Tucker, chief intelligence officer, led the 11-man strike force. Two agents hid in a gully near the house to alert Tucker when the racketeers arrived. With radio communication among four cars staked out near the target area, Minker's men showed up in two cars for their daily counting session shortly after 3:30 p.m. Trees on three sides of the house made it easy for the raiders to close in without warning. Tucker gave the signal to charge at 3:35 p.m.

Without a hitch, the agents swarmed into the house to arrest four suspects just beginning their tabulations.

Tony Bonanno was the only numbers repeater, having been nabbed in the Lancaster Avenue raid, too. John Hyneman, now 66, was winding down a career in the rackets dating back to Prohibition. He was the front man for the money bingo game at Pheasantland Park. William "Sonny" DeCamillo, 25, was in the early stages of his career as a numbers writer. Earl Borrell, at 64, was a veteran numbers writer who was among a dozen pickup men for Tony Moran when he was arrested in a major numbers sweep in 1939.

In the Exeter raid, $4,143 in cash was seized on the counting table, very similar to the daily amount raked in at the Lancaster Avenue bank. So it was obvious to the T-men that it was business as usual for Minker's crowd. The threat of jail time and fines certainly had not slowed down the racketeers. The usual paraphernalia was hauled out of the farmhouse, including more new adding machines that had replaced those seized in the October sweep. A .38 caliber Colt was found in Hyneman's car. Also the autos of Hyneman and DeCamillo were impounded. The suspects were relieved of their pocket money: $1,215 total. Hyneman at his bingo trial had promised a judge he would never again be involved in illegal gambling.

For a month things were relatively quiet on the numbers front in Reading. Individual writers set up their own banks, operating independently and running the risk of taking big hits that could wipe them out. Knowing the situation, many customers looked for other gambling outlets. Although the big bank was out of business for the time being, the IRS knew it had to nab Minker or the game would be resumed in a short time.

# 20

# *Colorful cast for grand jury probe*

A federal grand jury began looking into Abe Minker's earnings in the spring of 1960. The mob, a few politicians, and some businessmen twitched as the U.S. attorney prepared witness subpoenas. John Kubacki and Abe Minker could see to what extent the IRS was willing to go to collect the government's tax money, but that did not prevent the newly formed team from carrying out its extortion plans. Graft was so thoroughly ingrained in the city's political culture, they saw it as no more than plunder for the victors, too small for Washington to pursue. Minker was brokering the parking meter deals primarily to keep peace in the family rather than making a big score.

Walter Alessandroni, newly appointed U.S. attorney, was selected to conduct the grand jury hearing because of his knowledge of the Minker crowd. It was he as Pennsylvania's attorney general who ordered the investigation of rackets activities in Reading in 1958 that led to the failed prosecution of Minker, the Fudeman brothers, and Johnny Wittig the following year. First Assistant U.S. Attorney Joseph McGlynn Jr. would support Alessandroni in the present grand jury hearings. At first the government focused on the numbers cases. Then, witnesses with no connection to that racket were summoned, indicating the government aimed to look into other aspects of vice and corruption.

Eighteen witnesses received subpoenas to appear when the grand jury convened on April 25, exactly one month after the Exeter Township raid. Rackets figures swelled the witness list and from the start they showed their loyalty to The General, as some called Abe. It didn't take long before the 5th Amendment escape hatch was opened.

Joe Fiorini and Kathryn "Katie" Farrara led the parade of witnesses called to testify. Plenty of sex appeal here, but not much cooperation. The attractive brunette and the dapper gambler were showstoppers in the first act, citing the 5th for their refusal to testify.

Katie was a 45-year-old looker, shapely, and stylishly dressed. Her brother, Chester "Chet" Farrara, had been in the numbers game but presently was better known as the owner of the California Shop, an upscale men's store in the first block of South 5th Street. In the early stages of the 1959 IRS investigation, Katie was seen by agents Jack Dalsey and Fran Larkin in a car with Dominic Quatieri and Louie Fudeman. They were tailed to a house off Route 73 near Oley.

From the opening question she wasn't talking. She wouldn't talk about the numbers bankbooks, her brother's business books, or the book of the month—nothing. Alessandroni warned she might face contempt charges if she didn't open up, but Kate just kissed him off. The prosecutor left the jury room to discuss the situation with U.S. Judge Harold Wood. Indeed, agreed Wood, the lady in the cream colored blouse was risking a contempt charge.

For the time being, Alessandroni gave up on her and tried to pry open Joe Fiorini. But he, too, cashed in on his legal right not to incriminate himself. Judge Wood had enough of the stalling and scheduled an open hearing for the next morning. He listened to the questions that had been put to Katie the previous day by McGlynn, then ordered her to answer them.

Sam Liever, representing Farrara, said she couldn't testify because she was being investigated for not paying income taxes the past few years. He said she might incriminate herself. This open hearing provided hints about what was happening in the grand jury room. Agent Patrick O'Brien's testimony was read to the judge. O'Brien offered a glimpse of Reading's recent gambling history:

"This was shortly after McDevitt took office. The numbers and horse business under Bamford was subdued." O'Brien was quoting from an interview he had with John Venezia in early 1956. According to Venezia, who had a candy store on Washington Street, he was informed that Joe Bonanno would be coming to his place to pick up numbers slips now that the new administration was in City Hall. Bonanno was a trusted Minker lieutenant. Venezia took the 5th when asked to testify before the grand jury.

Two weeks into the proceedings, Judge Wood decided Katie Farrara WAS justified in refusing to testify. These are a couple of the questions she refused to answer:

"Were you ever employed as a bookkeeper or tally clerk, or some kind of clerk in a numbers bank ... since 1956 in the city of Reading? Did you ever perform any services of a clerical nature in a numbers bank in which you did not know that the banker, which is the principal, paid the excise tax?"

Wood said his decision was not based on those questions but rather on the fact that Miss Farrara was under IRS investigation for having failed to file tax returns for four years and could incriminate herself in that regard. Although the judge let Katie off the hook, he offered his private opinion that she wasn't so worried about herself as she was about protecting higher-ups. Whatever pressure was being applied, or inducements offered not to testify, was never revealed.

Places like the Zanzibar tavern, Chink's Shoe Rebuilding, the Horseshoe Inn, and other familiar businesses were mentioned as being frequented by numbers players. A Who's Who of Reading numbers writers dotted the witness list during the second week of the hearings: Santo Damiano, William Guiles, Clarence "Chink" Banks, John D. Bonanno, Leon Wertz, Tony "Jimmy Peters" Lucchese, Anne Lucchese, William "Bill" Kozier, Arthur "Mike" Bauers, C. Hunter Biehl, David Pizzo, Henry "Rabbit" Martin, Theodore Slabik, Leo Ertel, Henry Martin, Larry Spinnata, Russ Dusenberry, Louis Cavallucci, Anthony Carabello, and Louis Apsokardu. These were mostly working people trying to add to their income by peddling betting slips—bartenders, operators of cigar stores and luncheonettes and shoe shine stands and other small businesses. From them the feds picked up smatterings of information that added to the file the government was developing on Minker's domain.

The makeup of each day's grand jury witness list suggested how broad the investigation was becoming. More straightforward than many of the previous witnesses was Abe's accountant. William E. Hartman arrived with loads of documents covering Minker's financial history dating back to 1949. He was also questioned about the financial affairs of Abe's wife Verna. Minker's daughter, Dona Nives, told about Isadore Minker's attempt to buy into a Las Vegas gambling casino in 1954. It failed, she said, because the Nevada gambling board learned Izzy was only a front for four other persons with criminal records.

Musa J. Eways, president of Mast Engineering Co., was questioned by the grand jury about four checks totaling $10,700 his company paid to bail bondsman Joe Liever. Mast had received a contract from the city to upgrade the sewage plant and sewer expansion in the 18$^{th}$ Ward. Eways denied the payments had anything to do with the rackets. However, he said, as a matter of principal he would not say why the money was paid to Liever, a close friend of racketeers.

The story behind that deal was revealed many years later by a public relations associate of the now defunct Gilbert Associates. Mayor McDevitt approached him, the PR man recalled, offering the contract to Gilbert's if a $10,000 gift from the company was forthcoming. The associate refused to be the middleman in the deal, although he agreed to carry the message to the company's top officials, who he doubted would accept such an arrangement. He was right, they didn't. The same deal was offered to Mast, which ended up doing the work. Joe Liever declared the money he received from Eways was listed on his income tax return as a finder's fee. The government could not prove where the ten grand found its final resting place, so nobody was ever charged with extortion.

Ray Wagonseller, John Venezia, Earl Groff, and Louie Casale tried the 5th Amendment dodge. Judge Wood conducted another open hearing to determine why they shouldn't hold them in contempt. More bits and pieces about vice in Reading became public. So many sessions on so many different issues were held over the five-week length of the secret inquiry, newspaper readers back home had trouble keeping track of what was happening.

The recently resolved Penn Hardware still case was inserted into the grand jury hearings when Augustine "Gus" Mazzio was called to testify. The Philadelphia mobster was one of five defendants who pleaded guilty to conspiracy and was now serving five years probation for having purchased kerosene used in the still operation.

Although the feds had not paid much attention to the 10th and Walnut casino that escaped the scrutiny of local law enforcement for four years, former officials of a company that bought the property in 1955 were now called in for questioning. In typical mob fashion, the officeholders of X-Bex Corp. were regularly shuffled in order to mask the real owner of the property. Benny, Sam, and Paul Bonanno denied having any official status, although the government had documents listing them as officers. Robert Ganter, a Reading tavern operator, was shown to be the current X-Bex president, but to no one's surprise he knew nothing about a casino being operated in the building. Another reluctant witness with a short memory was George Barrow of Yeadon, a Philly suburb. Better known as Skinny Barrett, he was the manager of the 10th and Walnut game. Justice Department attorneys learned that Barrett worked for Joe Profaci, the godfather of one of New York's five Mafia families. Court documents revealed that the Profacis received 30 percent of the earnings from gambling ventures Barrett ran.

Believing Minker was connected with another New York family, the feds subpoenaed Anthony "Fat Tony" Salerno to testify. The 48-year-old boss of Harlem's biggest numbers bank was a member of the Genovese family. Although he spent much of his time in Miami, he was a principal suspect in a current federal investigation in Manhattan. He was the highest-ranking racketeer subpoenaed by the Philly grand jury.

Phyllis Nonnemacher, employed by Boscov's, was in Manhattan on a business trip in the late 1960s. With other buyers, she often ate in a restaurant operated by Fat Tony. On one occasion it was Phyllis's birthday when the portly racketeer came to her table to offer congratulations. He then picked up the tab for the Reading group. When he learned Phyllis and others were from Reading, he asked:

"Any of you know Abe Minker?"

He received a unanimous "yes." Tony smiled:

"Tell Abe hello from Fat Tony."

The grand jury hearings took on an aura that only the Mafia could excite when Salerno flew in from Miami on the last day of the proceedings. He wasn't too happy when a *Reading Times* photographer snapped his picture, and he wasn't too talkative in the jury room. There was strong evidence over the years that he and Abe Minker had more than a nodding acquaintance. It is believed the government asked him about his involvement in the 10th and Walnut dice game. Judging from his brief appearance in the jury room, he used the 5th to good advantage.

Another latecomer to the hearings was Alex Fudeman, sporting his signature bow tie. Government agents had been hunting him for more than a month, unaware he had moved to New York City. But he received word there was a summons for him, so he stopped by and became the last of 36 witnesses to testify, excluding federal agents.

The repeated raids and prosecutions by the federal government were becoming a growing concern in local gambling circles. The machine operators were doing a thriving business, and the private clubs, volunteer fire companies, and service organizations that offered gambling were raking in sizable profits. By the end of May 1960, the IRS revealed that 109 places in Berks County had obtained U.S. gambling stamps. Seventy-seven Reading establishments had purchased $50 or $250 permits for 134 devices, and 57 county clubs had stamps covering 57 devices.

# 21

## *The tax man closes in but trial stalled*

Charges against Abe Minker in the Lancaster Avenue case had been dismissed five days after the raid, and since he was never charged in the Exeter Township raid and was not called as a witness by the federal grand jury, his status was still in limbo when the grand jury wound down its investigation. But when the panel presented 16 indictments on May 26, 1960, Abe's name topped the list, dashing any hopes he had of escaping still another prosecution.

The main charge against Abe: failing to pay the 10 percent excise tax on $1.3 million, the gross amount his numbers banks were believed to have earned from September 1959 through March 1960. According to the IRS, he owed Uncle Sam $130,000. He was charged with "attempt to evade excise tax due on wagers by failing to file an excise tax return, and by concealing and attempting to conceal the true and correct amount of wagers accepted."

Eight others were indicted on charges of having failed to pay the excise tax and not buying $50 gambling stamps: Johnny Wittig, Tony Bonanno, Dominic Quatieri, Louie Fudeman, Mike Augustine, Sonny DeCamillo, John Hyneman, and Earl Borrell. Seven numbers writers charged with failing to pay their gambling occupation taxes were: Ernest "Steve" Arthur and his wife Georgine, Nate Hindin, Mrs. Helen Schaeffer, Irene Moyer, Mrs. Rose Toor, and Joe Venezia.

U.S. Attorney Walter Alessandroni could hoist a toast to more than just the indictment of Minker and his workers. The prosecutor had won the early battle in the grand jury hearing without introducing some of his best evidence. Anthony Damore was still in the closet as were the tapes and other papers he had fished from Abe's trash can. It was a bit of a gamble on Alessandroni's part, but his ATU witnesses had carried the day. A week after the grand jury retired, Abe appeared at the U.S. commissioner's office in Reading to post $500 bail. He looked thinner and older and was using a cane. The worst was still to come.

If the IRS felt it was playing with a pat hand, the Pennsylvania state police were wrong to believe they could do as well back in Reading. The same day Abe was posting bail, a Berks County grand jury tossed out three gambling cases. That spring, the staties had been dropping in on the social clubs of county volunteer fire companies with games of chance. Three were knocked off. When the cases reached the Berks grand jury, the panel's decision mirrored local sentiment that a little gambling never hurt anybody. It refused to send the cases to trial. Punchboards, a jackpot lottery, and a 180 club were the types of wagering choices that the grand jury felt were not worth prosecuting. You would have had to search long and hard in 1960 to find a county or city volunteer fire company social quarters that did not cater to gamblers. Add slot and pinball machines to the mix and you had the source of much of the revenue it took to keep clubs operating.

Although all the defendants in the federal case pleaded not guilty when arraigned in June, at a later meeting of the minds, economy prevailed. It was decided that the two top guys would stand trial, but all the other defendants would take the fall. Just before their trial got underway on September 28, all but Minker and Wittig pleaded guilty. Abe wanted to proceed with his trial but Stanford Shmukler, now representing him in place of the absent Jake Kossman, asked for another delay. Kossman was behind the request. He was recovering from eye surgery, and he also was representing Jimmy Hoffa in a Florida case. U.S. Attorney Alessandroni said a postponement till November was acceptable, but not to January as Shmukler asked. They bickered about the significance of their case. Alessandroni called it, "The largest and most important case concerning organized racketeering the U. S. attorney's office in Philadelphia had ever handled. This case concerns wagering in excess of a million dollars a year."

"You call it racketeering," stated Shmukler. "This business about a million dollars gambling, those are just figures." Then he compared the case to the tax unit's indifference to Philadelphia violators. "It is interesting to know that this is another Reading case. Although there are three to five thousand persons arrested (annually) in Philadelphia for gambling and no one ever gets a gambling tax stamp or pays excise taxes, yet there is never a prosecution there or in any other large city. This stems from the desire of local efforts to settle private grudges. It's always Reading that does something wrong."

Abe himself mimicked his ex-neighbor on 6$^{th}$ Street, Danny McDevitt, in one of his rare interviews with the press: "Some of my Republican friends admit the prosecution is political and I am certainly inclined to believe it. If the government has something on me, and not manufacturing evidence, I would plead guilty … but if it's political I'll fight it with every ounce of strength I have."

He reminded reporters that former Mayor James Bamford's administration tried to have him deported. And this, he claimed, after he had performed his patriotic duty by serving his country in two wars. He was in the Army for a short time in World War II but no records were found showing he served in World War I, although he did have a draft card.

When the trial for Abe and Wittig began on November 28 with Judge C. William Kraft on the bench, it had a very short run. A jury was quickly drawn that Monday morning. Then six large shopping carts loaded with numbers paraphernalia were wheeled into the courtroom, and testimony from government agents got the proceedings off to a flying start. A *Philadelphia Inquirer* headline over the trial story on Tuesday morning read 2 Gamblers Called Tax Evaders. Kossman, now back at the defense table, showed a copy of the paper to Judge Kraft. A poll of the jury indicated seven of the 12 jurors had read the headline. Kraft then declared a mistrial, much to the dismay of everybody but Kossman. "Why this headline writer has undertaken to prove what the government so laboriously hopes to prove, I don't know why?" the judge questioned. The word "gambler" was a no-no. Minker, despite his disappointment, rationalized: "I was never charged with gambling … maybe bootlegging, but never for being a gambler."

The delay again weakened Minker's legal team. Jake Kossman, reputed to be one of Philadelphia's foremost criminal attorneys, could not devote much time to Abe's case because he was working overtime trying to keep Jimmy Hoffa from being indicted in Florida. For three years Hoffa and Bobby Kennedy had been insulting each other during the McClelland anti-crime hearings. It was the longest and most expensive congressional hearing since the Teapot Dome scandal in the 1920s. Although leadership rules regarding unions were eventually strengthened, Hoffa came out of the hearings with a bad reputation but no penalty for his fast and loose control of union pension funds. The Justice Department, however, had picked up on a shady land deal in Florida involving Hoffa. It was during the 1960 presidential campaign that Jimmy began scrambling to avoid being indicted by a federal grand jury.

All through 1961 whenever Hoffa demanded Kossman's immediate attention, Abe Minker had to rely on Jake's associate, Stanford Shmukler, and Sam Liever to handle his case. They were certainly capable attorneys but a peg or two below the top-rated Kossman.

The retrial was scheduled for January 9, 1961, but both Kossman and Minker were unavailable. Jake was in Miami defending Hoffa, and Abe was in Philadelphia's Temple Hospital recovering from another back operation. Shmukler was granted a trial postponement until March. Alessandroni then had a request of his own: raise Minker's bail because Abe had applied for a passport on the same day the mistrial was declared back in November. On his application he had listed January 1961 as the approximate time he intended to travel outside the United States. Based on that information, the prosecutor recommended the court place travel restrictions on the defendant because a passport had been issued to Abe for a proposed trip to England, France, and Italy. The court then restricted Abe's travel to the southeastern corner of Pennsylvania.

In March, Judge Kraft handed down sentences and fines for the 14 numbers defendants who entered guilty pleas six months earlier.

Tony Bonanno was hit with the harshest term—one year in jail, a $5,000 fine, and five years probation.

Dominic Quatieri and John Hyneman—one year in jail, $5,000 fine.

Sonny DeCamillo—nine months in jail—$5,000 fine.

Louie Fudeman and Mike Augustine—nine months in jail, $2,500 fine.

Earl Borrell, six months in jail—$1,500 fine.

Nate Hindin and Joe Venezia—each fined $5,000.

Ernest and Georgine Arthur—each fined $2,500.

Irene Moyer, Helen Schaeffer, Rose Toor—each fined $1,000.

Seven of the numbers writers were unable to pay their fines by the June 6 deadline: Hindin, Venezia, the Arthur couple, Moyer, Schaeffer, and Toor. They were given a 48-hour extension by the courts to come up with the money, but only three met that deadline. Partial payments followed in the next few weeks and by July 11 all the men had met their full obligation. Judge Kraft decided to cut the fines of Moyer, Schaeffer, and Toor to $100.

Word had been leaked to the Minker camp that the government possessed papers or documents containing Abe's signature. If these papers were to be used as evidence, Kossman demanded copies of them since no such evidence was mentioned previously. These were the papers taken from Abe's trash container. The defense also learned a color movie film of Abe dumping his trash was available.

At a pretrial hearing Shmukler argued that the government had violated Minker's civil rights by poking around in his trash without a search warrant. As a prime witness, Anthony Damore was now out of the closet as he heatedly insisted the trash he collected became his property to do with whatever he wanted. Judge Clary was in complete agreement. He ruled the ATU investigators and trashman had not broken any laws when they sifted through Abe's rubbish looking for evidence.

Now the stage was set for the government to prove in court it could finally bring down the man who it so ardently pursued. Abe Minker's future, it appeared, rested on discarded adding machine tapes, which did not lie, rather than on human witnesses who often did. Finally everything was on go when all the colorful principals gathered at the federal courthouse in Philadelphia on March 6, 1961.

Although Abe Minker was the big newsmaker throughout 1961, behind the scenes, Mayor John Kubacki was having relative success wheeling and dealing with city business. While he managed to dodge any major investigations for the next few years, he did have one City Hall run-in that caused a flurry for a few days.

When his authority was challenged, it was not Kubacki's nature to negotiate or compromise. In true gridiron tradition he usually plunged right at any opponent who had the temerity to question his actions. Such was the case in September when he held a meeting in council chambers with representatives of the firemen's and police unions. According to the mayor it was a by-invitation-only meeting.

The gathering had barely started when the mayor spotted 18-year-old Edward Binasiewicz, a photographer for Councilman Jerry Kobrin's weekly, the *Reading Record*. "Out!" Kubacki firmly stated, pointing to young Eddie. "You were not invited to this meeting." Binasiewicz pointed to a *Times* reporter, who the mayor said WAS invited. The photographer left but was followed by the mayor into the front hallway.

Exactly how forcefully Kubacki handled the matter was never quite resolved, but the teenager claimed his much bigger adversary roughed him up. So he filed assault and battery charges. Six days later at a preliminary hearing, Binasiewicz testified that Kubacki grabbed him by the shoulders, accused him of harassment, and vigorously shook him until he threatened to have the mayor arrested. Firemen who were at the meeting testified they saw the mayor shaking the youth. Other defense witnesses who observed the pair arguing, said they did not see any physical contact. Alderman Ralph Breneiser dismissed the charges because the youth admitted there were no blows struck and he was not injured. Although Kubacki won this minor scrap, it showed intimidation was a weapon in his arsenal he did not hesitate to use.

# 22

# *Anthony talks; Abe big loser as Wittig walks*

The long and bumpy road to trial was finally traversed on March 6, 1961. Abe Minker and Johnny Wittig were anxious to bring an end to the extended process that was prolonged by the absence of Jake Kossman. The famed criminal attorney was still in Florida defending Jimmy Hoffa. That meant his associate, Stanford Shmukler, was at the defense table when Judge Kraft gaveled the court to order. No major surprises were expected because much of the evidence had already been aired at a plethora of court proceedings.

John Dalsey led a squad of Alcohol Tax Unit agents to the witness stand, all repeating testimony they gave before the grand jury, at hearings, and at the mistrial over the past 10 months. The jury heard at length how the agents had conducted their investigation of the numbers operators and was given a complete rundown on those arrested in the two ATU raids. On the third day, the star prosecution witness, Anthony Damore, retold his account of collecting Abe Minker's trash and turning it over to government agents. A strong and believable witness, Tony offered some of the most dramatic testimony of the 10-day trial. He helped define why Johnny Wittig was known as Minker's enforcer.

One aspect of Tony's voluntary work for the government showed his mettle after the mob got wind of what he had done. As usual when the mob tried intimidation when things went wrong, Wittig was assigned to rectify matters. Tony testified about his confrontation with Johnny a year after he first started separating Minker's trash from the other rubbish he collected. He said Wittig first tried to contact him by phone in the fall of 1960. Then he came knocking at the door of Damore's house in Reading's 18th Ward.

Without introducing himself, Johnny asked, "Are you the guy who collects the Hampden House trash?"

Damore: "I said, 'Who are you?' and he said 'Johnny Wittig.' Then he began asking me questions. He asked if I had a helper. I said a colored fellow in the afternoon, and my brother sometimes helped me. So he asked if anyone was going through the trash and I said not that I know of. He wanted to know if any government agents were around."

"When was that?" Judge Kraft asked.

"I won't forget that date, your honor. I was married 19 years that day." That drew the biggest laugh of the trial as Anthony was more specific, "November 10, 1960."

The witness continued, "Wittig reached in his pocket and pulled out a bill. I said 'no, I don't want anything.' He said, 'Buy yourself a hat.' It looked like a 10-dollar bill." Damore said he refused to accept Wittig's money, and he received no compensation from the government.

"I did this 'cause I thought it was my duty as a citizen of this country," declared the stocky, ruddy complexioned trash collector.

Wittig left, fully aware that threats would have no effect on this feisty patriot. Johnny was not aware that agent Steiney Korlovich had Tony's house under surveillance and witnessed the conversation at the front door.

Isaac Noll, superintendent of the apartment house where Minker lived, testified he was asked by Abe for the name of the man who collected the building's rubbish. This was just before Wittig visited Damore. It had taken just about a year before the government's secret was leaked to the mob.

From the trash barrel litter, the ATU had pasted together bits of paper and adding machine tapes to build a theory of just how profits of the lottery operation were divided. Agent William F. Lynn Jr. deciphered lists of coded names and rows of figures, and offered expert opinions to the jury of how the mob's accounting system worked. Reconstructed adding machine tapes and torn notes were flashed on a large screen for the jury as Lynn explained a crooked money trail within the organization. It was his presumption that the better numbers writers paid a fee to the mob's hierarchy just to peddle the game. Although various writers received 25, 40, or 50 percent of their net sales, they in turn had to pay ice (protection fees) of $50, $125, $150 to $600, depending on how many customers they served. Some smaller writers paid nothing. The weekly total deduction from the writers' cut was usually $1,650, although for one Friday the amount listed was $2,400. Paying ice, according to the coded lists the ATU compiled, were Santo, Billy, Mike, Lee, Earl, Kotz, JV, J, and Z. Joe Venezia had admitted he was JV. The agents who testified did not specifically identify anyone on the list, but in the gambling community the nicknames and initials were easily recognizable.

When Shmukler asked Lynn what he thought the names and numbers meant, the agent said he didn't know. But prosecutor Alessandroni jumped up, suggesting Lynn tell what he really thought the list meant.

"I think it was for protection," Lynn stated. It was believed Minker covered the legal expenses of those writers who paid ice. A second list of abbreviated names pasted together from the rubbish created even more interest. Next to each of the 30 names or initials on that list was a dollar figure. The amounts ranged from $25 to $750. There was no actual testimony identifying the names, only images shown on the large screen. Reporters from the dailies jotted down the following names:

John H., Walt, Jerry, chief, Focht, Joe, John, county, state, Dany, Rob, Mark, Kid, Jake, me & D, Joe L., Rabit, Bloom, Henry, Baby, Jerry, Joe, Wilson, Clo, Fet, and a few identified by a single initial.

Lynn reiterated the significance of the names and figures of the second list: "I believe it's money to pay protection." City and county elected officials and police bigwigs were squirming, wondering whether the feds would eventually come looking for them.

Alessandroni supported Lynn: "I think the agents know everyone on those lists. I would say they do know."

The loosely coded names could be identified by anyone on the street really familiar with the daily numbers game. A few of those in the position of controlling law enforcement of vice activities were most likely receiving three-figure payments. If that was the case, $1,650, or even $2,400, would not cover the weekly graft payments. Therefore, another chunk from the daily take was probably added to the grease pot.

In summing up, Alessandroni described the numbers racket in Reading as "a franchise system, operated by independent businessmen who received 35 percent of what they wrote, with incentive awards paid for additional business after deductions for payoffs. The banker collects all the money, centers the protection, doles it out, providing a service to the writers."

The prosecutor said the ATU investigation revealed some writers regularly cheated the bank. Also, there was considerable evidence that Minker was quite friendly with Mafia bigwigs, but not enough to prove outsiders were involved in the local numbers operation.

When asked by the press if the government would track down and charge those on the protection list, Alessandroni said only time would tell. Without additional proof of identity, the feds decided against another extended, and probably fruitless, investigation.

Minker had been in the hospital for back surgery in January 1960 from the $10^{th}$ to the $21^{st}$. No trash was recovered from his barrel from the $12^{th}$ to the $26^{th}$. But then business picked up again and the adding machine tapes told the story of daily profits and losses in the numbers racket.

Shmukler frequently argued that the only real evidence that connected the numbers operation to Minker and Wittig were the suspicious packages Johnny delivered to Abe's apartment on a regular basis during August and September 1959. Judge Kraft seemed to agree with that argument when he compared Wittig to a faithful bank messenger.

"If he did what you said he did he would not be connected," Kraft stated to Alessandroni. "He would be taking things to the great white chief of the enterprise and have nothing to do with his attempt to cheat the great white father in Washington."

The judge also sided with the defense regarding Wittig's visit to the home of Anthony Damore. Since there was no attempt to coerce or frighten, Kraft said, he believed Wittig was within permissible bounds of surveillance and found Damore "as we did, a terse, not too communicative soul." Things were looking up for Johnny. Before the jury began deliberations on Wednesday March 15, Judge Kraft ruled on a defense motion to acquit Wittig. Charges were dropped against the messenger.

It took the jury only two and a half hours to find Minker guilty on all five counts of excise tax evasion. Unlike the first case against Abe which was tossed out a few days after the October 3 raid for lack of evidence, the government this time drew kudos from Judge Kraft for compiling abundant, undeniable evidence.

"I felt it was one of the best prepared cases I had ever been pleased to see in some 30 years of practice as a prosecuting attorney, defense attorney, and judge," Kraft stated.

Having heard about Minker's plans for a European trip, the judge set Abe's bail at $30,000 with the provision he also turn in his recently issued passport. He was forbidden to travel outside southeastern Pennsylvania pending his appeal for a new trial.

If Abe Minker felt Uncle Sam was singling him out of all the thousands of tax-dodging racketeers, his belief was solidified by another jolt from the government that same day. Before he could leave the courthouse in Philadelphia, a lien for almost $2 million was filed against him for other federal taxes Uncle Sam said he owed.

"He was really shook up, practically in a state of shock," said an agent who was present when Abe learned of the lien. "He didn't seem to know what was going on."

The IRS offices in Philadelphia and Manhattan both would have jurisdiction in this civil case. Minker was charged with failure to pay $1,957,178 in income taxes, excise taxes, and special occupational taxes over a four-year period. Following are income taxes he owed:

1956—$100,103
1957—$320,132
1958—$310,448
1959—$307,141

According to the IRS, Minker owed excise taxes on wagering profits: $479,697 for the period March 1, 1956, to March 11, 1960; and another $440,812 for the period March 12, 1958 to March 25, 1960. To top it off, he was $357 in arrears in his occupation tax for the years 1956-60, the government claimed.

Abe's empire was in tatters. Intransigent federal law enforcement agencies were tightening the noose. While more notorious organized crime figures traveled freely from their Miami mansions to their businesses in Manhattan, Abe was almost reduced to house arrest. Fat Tony Salerno, considered the No. 1 guy in East Harlem's $50-million-a-year numbers racket, made a fortune over the next 15 years without constant harassment from the IRS. As an alleged small businessman, Tony paid taxes on $40,000 a year income. The IRS didn't catch up with him till 1978 when he received a 6-month jail sentence.

Excise taxes and gambling stamp requirements were not IRS high priorities in the 1960s once the illegal drug business started to grow. None of the national Mafia figures was being pursued so relentlessly as was Abe Minker. Jimmy Hoffa, long connected to organized crime, certainly was Bobby Kennedy's No.1 target, but others in the Justice Department had their sights set solely on Abe.

Although Abe's conviction was a major news story that spring, Henry Wolfe, a self-proclaimed city watchdog, stirred up a controversy that again demonstrated that shady transactions in City Hall were the norm, this time involving something that could hardly go unnoticed. But Henry, with a tip from his private spy network, found out that an old 13.8-ton mobile crane that had been sitting idle for several years, was missing from its resting place on the sewage plant grounds. The crane, extending several stories high, was a 1941 relic left at Spaatz Field,

Reading's wartime airport, when the military pulled out in 1948. It was late in 1959 when Wolfe discovered the huge crawler crane was no longer at the sewage disposal plant on Fritz Island.

Continuing to snoop, Henry learned that the crane had been sold for $500 to Alfred Consoli, a Reading contractor whose company was installing sewers in the 16th Ward under a $190,632 contract. Consoli admitted buying the crane, but said he then sold it as scrap iron. Things started to get dicey when the sewage plant manager, Leon Karnat, said he turned the $500 over to city clerk Samuel Rothermel, who in turn gave it to Mayor McDevitt. But Sam and Dan later denied they had any part in such a transaction. And there was no bill of sale, no receipt, no city record of any kind to support or reject these contradictory claims.

Things cooled down when Wils Austin, then the city solicitor, worked out an agreement with Consoli who did the math on scrap iron and came up with a figure, $437, which he paid to the city. He did not reveal who the scrap dealer was that he sold the crane to or how much he received. Austin accepted Al's story and his check—case closed as of December 2, 1959. McDevitt completed his few remaining days as mayor, avoiding a showdown with Karnat about who was not telling the truth.

Henry Wolfe, as usual, was not satisfied. He would not accept Consoli's story that the crane was sold as scrap iron. Sixteen months later, Henry called the *Times* to have a reporter and photographer accompany him to Lancaster County where he believed the crane had wound up. In the town of Marietta, there it was on the property of the U.S. Aluminum Corp. President of U.S. Aluminum, Joseph Sansone, provided records showing the crane had been sold to his company by Consoli for $825 on October 2, 1959.

Now the fun began as Mayor John Kubacki was only too happy to sling some mud at Dan McDevitt, by now in the state Legislature. Kubacki ordered his police to investigate this new turn of events. Consoli, whose claim of selling the crane as scrap iron, was becoming the scapegoat of this reignited issue. As the investigation warmed up, lie detector tests were proposed for the four principals: Consoli, Karnat, Rothermel, and McDevitt.

Karnat welcomed the chance to clear himself and passed a polygraph with flying colors. The city bought the polygraph equipment at that time, although Kubacki claimed it was not because of the crane scandal. Leon stated that he cleared the deal with the mayor before taking the cash from Consoli when they met at 6th and Court streets. In the test he admitted never seeing the five $100 bills Consoli said he placed in the envelope addressed to Sam Rothermel. Karnat said McDevitt had given him direct orders to give the money to the city clerk. By

1961 when the issue flared anew, Dan and Sam were working in Harrisburg. Kubacki wanted Consoli to issue a statement explaining his version of the deal. Within a week Al's written account was made public. He admitted that the deal to sell the crane to U.S. Aluminum was all set before he paid Karnat the $500 in cash, but he didn't know in whose hands it ended up.

When Henry Wolfe showed up at the next City Council meeting, Kubacki and the councilmen willingly let him spout off about the crane deal. Normally, they tried to harness Henry whenever he presented his negative spiels about their mismanagement of the city. This time they welcomed the dirt he was throwing in somebody else's direction.

Wils Austin, still city solicitor, worked up a proposal that Consoli rejected. Austin had computed his own figures regarding the price of scrap iron and decided Al still owed the city another $388, plus $35 interest. Since he already was in the red on the deal, Al felt he did not owe anybody anything. Kubacki, however, was more interested in bringing McDevitt to the bar of public opinion to explain where the $500 went, since the city had no record of receiving it.

As April began McDevitt was starting to fight back against "the smear campaign" and "the comic opera," as he tagged Kubacki's probe. But he would not accommodate the detectives trying to get him to take a polygraph test.

With another check for $458, Consoli eventually settled with the city. In his statement he also claimed to have spent $279 to have the crane's bucket repaired before selling the equipment to the aluminum company. The final payment seemed to put the case to rest since no criminal charges were forthcoming.

Then Rep. McDevitt surprised everybody by showing up at a City Council meeting accompanied by Sam Rothermel on May 24. After a brief introduction by the ex-mayor he handed a two-and-a-half page statement to Sam to read. It was another denial by the pair that they had any roles in the sale of the crane. There was no new information to offer, just extended verbage about the lack of proof needed to verify Leon Karnat's version of where Consoli's $500 ended up.

"The alleged payment for the crane, either by check or by cash in a sealed envelope, was completely without proof," Sam read. "Later the superintendent of the sewage plant, in a sworn statement stated that he did not see any money put in the envelope, and that he could not swear that he saw Rothermel, or anyone else open the envelope.

"Insinuations were again revived when the head of the present city administration purchased a lie detector, and set up a pseudo tribunal of his own, and decreed, without any further proof, pro or con, that the superintendent of the sewage plant was completely cleared, and that the matter now rested with Samuel H. Rothermel and Daniel F. McDevitt."

Without proof that would stand up in a court, McDevitt insisted, he was not going to walk away from this scandal allowing his reputation to be blackened without having his say. When Kubacki made his final challenge to McDevitt that day, "You have the opportunity of going downstairs and taking the same test with an impartial group," McDevitt said lie detector evidence was not admissible in court, so why bother?

Democrats celebrate their 1955 victory:
Coucilman Harold Guldin, Mayor Dan McDevitt,
District Attorney Fred Brubaker, and
Councilman John Kubacki

Charlie Wade

Mable Jones

Angie Martin Wilkerson

Abe Minker
Johnny Wittig
Santo Damiano
Benny Bonanno
Joe Fiorini

Judge C. Wilson Austin

Judge Warren Hess

Richard "Old Pete" Peters

Don Holloway

# 23

## *Where did all the money go?*

In addition to the huge lien of almost $2 million it placed against Abe Minker, the IRS obtained restraining orders for his wife, Verna, and his 41-year-old daughter, Dona. They were forbidden to withdraw anything from bank accounts and safety deposit boxes in their names or fictitious names. The agency ordered Minker deposit boxes in New York City, Reading, and Scranton banks sealed.

Now began a frustrating game of hide and seek as the IRS sought court permission to open the bank boxes. Although it was never proved, it appeared Verna and Dona beat the government to Abe's stash. For a couple of weeks after Minker's conviction, Verna's whereabouts were unknown to the government. She and Dona were included as defendants in the government's civil case as the IRS hoped to recover at least $100,000 when it opened the bank boxes. The revenue service was aware the women used fictitious names when renting some of the boxes, while opening bank accounts under their real names. The government accused both of being fronts for Abe. Jack Heidelberger, IRS investigator assigned to track down Abe's scattered holdings, said:

"Minker leased safe deposit boxes to conceal large amounts of cash and securities ... as part of a fraudulent scheme to place them beyond the reach of the United States government in the collection of its taxes. Shares of common stock were held in the name of Minker's wife, Verna, and his daughter, Dona Minker Nives of New York City, to conceal the true ownership."

Heidelberger compiled a long list of cash transactions over the past four years the Minkers engaged in at several New York and Pennsylvania banks. But in the days ahead when the IRS gained the court's permission to open the deposit boxes the Minkers leased, only two revealed any cash. Records showed Dona and Verna had visited three financial institutions in New York on January 13, four days before the boxes were sealed.

On March 22 a search party that included IRS officials, attorney Jake Kossman, U.S. Attorney Walter Alessandroni, and reporters, first visited an Irving

Trust Company branch in Manhattan. In a box leased to Barbara C. Moyer and Marguerite Moyer, they found $500 in $10 and $50 bills. Dona and Verna later admitted they used the Moyer name when renting the box.

As Alessandroni quipped, "There wasn't enough in that box to pay Kossman's fee for the day."

In a taxicab caravan, the group next moved to National City Safe Deposit Company where $400 was found in another box, again leased under the Moyer name. The president of National City, Roswell Reagan, declared that keeping cash in a company box was prohibited. Reagan remembered Marguerite Moyer (Dona) visiting the company's vault two or three days before it received an order to seal the box.

Two more boxes were empty when searched at Underwriter Trust Company. One was listed under Dona Minker Nives, the other under a dummy corporation, H.&S. Associates, Inc., which Abe Minker had access to. Except for rubber bands, an empty jewelry box stuffed with cotton, and some empty envelopes, that cupboard was bare.

The IRS arrived at a Scranton bank looking for loot the next day, but Verna had been there eight days earlier. Too late, the federal investigators opened an empty deposit box in the Pennsylvania National Bank and Trust Company.

A few days later the IRS searchers had no better luck when they found only Abe's Army discharge papers and a greeting card in his safe box in Reading Trust Company, a city bank where Abe had done business for years.

When a total of only $900 was recovered from six safety deposit boxes, the IRS seized Abe's weekly $231 paycheck from his White House Market. Employees at the market were grilled concerning large and small financial matters they might know something about. IRS accountants were looking deep into every aspect of Abe's financial life, but he had covered his tracks well.

Although the Justice Department was granted restraining orders forbidding father, wife and daughter from withdrawing any money from any type of bank deposits after March 18, most of the money had already been removed by that date. The investigating agents were accused by Abe's legal team "of sinking to a new low," when they questioned his cleaning lady.

"They asked her if she found any money lying around, if there were large amounts of money kept in the apartment, and if Mrs. Minker had bought a lot of new clothes," Shmukler complained at one of several hearings on this issue. The attorney claimed his client's right to privacy was being violated. But no matter how many mattresses they looked under, Abe had found hiding places beyond the government's reach.

After several years of studying Abe Minker's gambling domain, the IRS knew almost as much about the Reading racketeer as did any of his closest associates. Because Abe refused to completely close down his numbers banks, evidence against him continued to mount. During the spring and summer of 1961, U.S. attorneys used still another legal tool to pry loose more information about Abe's overall financial situation. Minker family members, a few of his associates, and some businessmen with whom he dealt were subpoenaed to give depositions. Answering under oath, those questioned collectively wove a blurry tapestry of money, securities, and banking techniques that revealed Abe as a man bent on protecting his ill-gotten fortune.

Still recovering from another back surgery, Minker begged off going to Philadelphia to give a deposition, so the feds came to him. They knocked at Abe's apartment door in Hampden Heights shortly after 10 a.m., July 6, 1961. They didn't leave till almost noon, not knowing much more than when they started. The four-man government team was U.S. Attorney Alessandroni; Homer R. Miller, a tax division attorney; William Hagen, counsel for the IRS; and Carl Melone, an assistant U.S. attorney who would do most of the questioning. Philadelphia attorney Leon Kline represented Abe, who began using his 5th Amendment rights from the start. "I refuse to answer because it might tend to incriminate me, etc, etc, etc. To save time, Kline suggested, why not allow Abe to use a shorter version of the "I refuse …" verbiage. Melone would not bend:

"If he is going to claim the privilege, I think he is going to have to claim the privilege properly. We feel that this action warrants application to the court to compel him to testify. I think the record would be better if it showed what his answer was."

More than half of the 41-page transcript portrayed Abe repeating his reason for taking the 5th 103 times. And that's why the federal four returned to Philadelphia with a tape recording filled with unanswered questions.

Other witnesses had preceded the fruitless questioning of Abe by his inquisitors, as he regarded them, in the deposition ordeal. White House Market was of particular interest to Melone, who did most of the deposing. Those who handled the books for Abe were the first to be questioned. From William Hartman, Abe's accountant, it was learned that Verna Minker was president, Israel Minker was vice president, and Abe was secretary of White House Market Inc. Brother Alex was actually running the business at this time, while Izzy made only perfunctory visits to the supermarket every few months after moving to Florida with his wife. But it was Izzy the feds questioned about store operations.

Anne Brenner had worked for Abe for more than 20 years. As his bookkeeper in 1951 she was called before the Kefauver Committee. Now, Brenner had to endure questioning about the many loans and repayments between White House Inc. and Abe's Brighton Realty Corp. Brenner, also assistant secretary of Brighton, told Melone that stock in the food market held by family members was in constant transition among themselves. Some of the stock transactions she could not explain. As for White House Market business, she said the average weekly sales totaled about $35,000, or close to $2 million a year.

When fire destroyed the original market in 1956, the corporation made two $30,000 loans to Brighton Realty, according to Hartman, but he claimed the loans were repaid. Melone wanted to know where the money had come from since the fire had wiped out Minker's legitimate business. Hartman said the corporation had a substantial bank balance at the time of the fire.

When Dona Minker and Abe's nephew were interviewed they revealed Abe was building a house in Phoenix, Arizona, where he hoped to retire with his wife. In typical rackets fashion, a confusing financial arrangement indicated the nephew, Albert "Sonny" Minker, and his wife, were co-owners of the $41,000 rancher under construction. Sonny was the son of Abe's older brother, Max. Sonny, following in his father's footsteps, ran a scrap iron business in Shamokin. Verna was said to have paid $3,200, using Dona's money, for the lot in the Meadow Palms development. At the time of purchase, the developer's prospectus noted: "Every buyer is a carefully selected member of this neighborhood of prestige." Would Abe have passed muster without Dona and Sonny serving as ghost buyers?

It would be another five years before Abe and Verna eventually lived in the L-shaped, two-bedroom rancher with 2,400 square feet of living space and a 30-foot long swimming pool. The exclusive Meadow Palms development was six miles from the center of Phoenix.

Sonny admitted that he had been involved in another major project with his uncle in the Caribbean. Abe came up with the idea of building what today would be called a strip mall to be named "Fiesta Market" in 1955. He asked his nephew to become an investor. Sonny said he, and his brothers, Elwood and Arnold, scraped together $93,000 to go along with Abe's $50,000 to purchase land in Puerto Rico, the location of the proposed market. The island deal languished for a few years but seemed revitalized when Henry Held, a Brooklyn lawyer, was drawn into the project.

Held met Dona Minker when she wanted to start a company that dealt in designer fabrics. She introduced her father to Held in a Philadelphia restaurant.

Sometime later Abe approached Held about helping him obtain a bank safe deposit box. Abe told the lawyer there was friction between Dona and Verna and he wanted the box to hide possibly $100,000 to be available to Dona in the event of his death. Held, who had an interest in several companies, said he had a corporation seal for a company, H&S Associates, that was presently dormant. He gave Abe the seal, which was then used by Dona to purchase a safe deposit box under that corporation's name. In her deposition, Dona claimed she rented the box for personal belongings, not for her father's money.

Abe tried to use Held to his advantage again by asking him to invest in the Fiesta Markets project. When the IRS traced the H&S Associates seal on Dona's safe deposit box back to Held, the government informed him about Abe's long criminal record. Held quickly dropped out of the picture and Fiesta Markets never became one of the Caribbean's first supermarkets.

The land purchased for $134,000 in 1955 was sold four years later for $175,000 to the International Basic Economy Corp., according to Sonny Minker. In his deposition, Sonny offered some rather confusing figures about who got what out of the deal, but it appears IBEC sent Uncle Abe a check for $25,000. A second check received by Sonny for $150,000 was deposited in a bank before being divided among family and friends who had invested in the planned market. Abe got the biggest share, $43,500.

Izzy was adamant that Abe had no financial interest in the White House Market. He claimed his brother William and he were the principal stockholders when the place was being rebuilt the summer of 1956. Abe had no role in any of the family financial transactions that involved the market or Brighton Realty, Izzy repeatedly stated. He said he was worth $400,000 in 1956 and admitted making several small loans at that time. Whenever he was stumped for an answer, Izzy used memory lapses to explain away his incoherent answers.

The IRS investigators had done their homework before taking the depositions. They asked the dozen individuals who were deposed about the reasons behind many transactions, who wrote checks and who received them, and what they paid for. Numerous stock transactions were asked to be explained, and although there were some "I don't remember" answers, all of the questions were answered, many of them falsely.

Benny and Sammy Bonanno were the only racketeers summoned by the government to explain their connection to Abe Minker. Benny admitted being a friend rather than an employee of The General. He said he took newspapers to Abe's Hampden Heights apartment, he chatted with Abe about horse racing, and he admitted discarding pieces of paper or adding machine tapes in the trash container behind the Hampden House. But he couldn't offer any details about what the numbers meant, those on the slips of paper he threw away. Benny said he thought he and Nate Liever bought Fairmore Music Company from Izzy or Abe Minker and renamed it Berks Amusement Services, a company that dealt in pinball machines and jukeboxes—and slot machines which Benny chose not to mention. The devices were not leased to clubs and bars, he explained, but his company shared the profits, 50-50 with the operators of 30 or 35 places where they were located. His job description: marketing the devices and trying to steal customers from several other competing companies.

Melone showed Benny a Fairmore Amusement bank statement he had sent to Meyer Weiner, the company's accountant. Although he was supposed to be the company's treasurer, Bonanno was unable to explain most of the deposits and payments listed. Several company expenditures Benny tried to ignore by mumbling, "Living expenses." Melone asked, "For what?"

"Going to the race tracks, betting horses," Benny shrugged. "It could be a lot of things." By his own standards it was an honest answer. Like most racketeers, Benny relied on gambling to provide the style of living he was used to as one of Abe's top henchmen.

Sam Bonanno's principal duty at Berks Amusement was to make the rounds on collection day. A third brother, Paul, was merely a mechanic who set up and repaired the machines.

While being deposed, Abe's closest relatives and associates could not hide behind the 5th Amendment because they were not facing any charges, nor was the IRS tax unit investigating them. But their answers to probing questions helped create a picture of a conspiracy to camouflage Abe's wealth.

Did Abe have money in Switzerland, as was rumored around Reading? Dona said she didn't know. When the government pulled Abe's passport and ordered him not to leave southeastern Pennsylvania, Dona and her husband, Fred Nives, took a two-week trip to Switzerland in January 1961. Nives denied he ever took funds of any type, including travelers checks, or securities belonging to his wife or his in-laws to Switzerland for deposit. Dona, who also made trips to Florida, Ohio, and Puerto Rico in recent months, claimed she did not carry money, securities, or jewelry to those places for anybody else.

Melone noticed that Brighton Realty Corp. was often revealed as a source or beneficiary of intra-family loans. Dona was sometimes the intermediary when money changed hands. According to a convoluted tale Dona related, the summer after the White House Market burned down, Izzy Minker decided he would like to invest in the market as it was being rebuilt. At that time he gave Dona $66,000 as a gift because he wanted to see his favorite niece have some security. No, he insisted, the $66,000 was not given to him by Abe to give to Dona. On the same day, June 11, 1956, Dona bought 145 shares of Brighton Realty stock for $20,000, and Izzy bought 177 shares in White House Market stock. The balance of her gift from Izzy she loaned to Brighton Realty. The problem with all this unlikely movement of money, which Melone was trying to prove belonged to Abe in the first place, was that Dona was unable to produce documents to prove such transactions occurred. The IRS shared Melone's concern that this was no way to do business.

From the questions that were asked and the evidence Melone presented, it was obvious Abe's daughter and wife had helped him launder large amounts of money. Dona admitted she and her stepmother obtained a safety deposit box in the names of Marguerite and Barbara Moyer. This was in June 1960 in New York City at the National Safety Deposit Box Co. While being questioned by an IRS attorney, Dona heatedly defended the use of fictitious names:

"Because, since I can remember, I have been hounded. People have been questioned: my friends, intimate friends, people that I live with, my employees. You have tapped my telephone and you have recorded my telephone calls to my father, and I will be happy to tell you how I know. And when you went into my parents' apartment and ransacked it, I would not want to subject myself to that. Since I have a few dollars and a few pennies of jewelry which are mine indisputably, I have no intention of putting those to your scrutiny."

Abe had long ago ceased worrying about his own reputation. Since his bootlegging days and early conviction for perjury he had become immune to public criticism. But the government's continuous probing into the lives of his closest relatives enraged him. No matter how much he spent on legal fees, he realized he could no longer buy his way out of this trouble. Through manipulative dealings he managed to hide his wealth from the revenuers, but he would be in debt to the government for the rest of his life.

For six months after his conviction, Abe continued to run up legal fees as his lawyers filed numerous appeals: for a new trial, to slow the process of searching his bank deposit boxes, and to delay his sentencing.

There was never any lack of surprises when Abe Minker was scheduled for a court appearance. In the fall of 1961 when his sentencing was due, all the principals were on hand when Stanford Shmukler sprung still another stall. The attorney announced Abe was innocent because he could prove some of the evidence that convicted his client was tainted.

It was his nephew, Alex Fudeman, who had framed him and had finally admitted as much, Abe claimed. He and his daughter had visited Alex in New York City three times in the past two weeks and his nephew had confessed to forging Abe's signature on various scraps of paper and placing them in his trash, according to Abe. So the signatures that had been identified as Abe's by a handwriting expert at the last trial were really Alex Fudeman's attempt at forgery, Minker concluded. Alex was willing to confess in court or to IRS investigators, Shmukler insisted. No motive, however, was mentioned in Abe's petition to the court to delay sentencing until this matter was resolved. In street jargon, this was a no-brainer for Judge Kraft. Since neither Dona nor Alex showed up to offer testimony at an October 17 hearing, the judge announced sentencing would take place the following week.

There were lots of hearts and flowers for Abe in the form of letters of commendation and vocal praise by character witnesses at the sentencing hearing. Even Adrian Bonnelly, the president judge of Philadelphia County Court offered a tribute: "He's as good as anyone I know, except for what I read in the papers."

However, it was what Judge Kraft read in the legal papers that passed in front of him over the past months and the testimony he had listened to that weighed more importantly in his decision. Lawyers and ministers and rabbis and businessmen and medical men all vouched for Abe's philanthropic offerings and his devotion to family and synagogue. But the judge would not be swayed.

As one attorney reflected after listening to all the glowing testimonials for Abe: "I feel like an acrobat having to follow an act like that."

On October 25, 1961, Judge Kraft sentenced Abe to four years in prison with a $35,000 fine. He was convicted on five counts of failure to pay excise taxes on his gambling enterprises. This was in addition to the $1.9-million lien placed against him in March.

Prison was not in Abe's immediate future, however, as another round of appeals commenced. After the U.S. Circuit Court of Appeals rejected Minker's petition for a new trial in January 1963, the U.S. Supreme Court, on March 25, refused to give him a hearing, and on the 16th of May Abe appeared before Judge Kraft for the last time. Jake Kossman pleaded to have his client's sentence reduced, to no avail. Verna was with her 64-year-old husband, watching as he was led from the courtroom by federal marshals and taken to Moyamensing Prison in Philadelphia. A few days later he was transferred to the federal penitentiary at Lewisburg, where he was to remain for the next four years.

This was not the end but just the beginning of two more years of Abe being hauled into court by the federal government, the state, and even the county. It was possibly the low point of his life. Failing health, a disappointingly stiff prison sentence, and the delay of his retirement plans combined to present a bleak outlook for the immediate future.

# 24

# *Bandits without masks rob their willing victims*

By 1961 the slot machine element in Berks County had continued its growth pattern for six straight years. For decades, mechanical one-armed bandits had become standard equipment in Reading clubs and fire companies and other public places. By the '60s, however, new electronic consoles were the rage. They stepped up the pace of winning and losing with lots of bells and whistles. The sparkling devices were the early handiwork of the cybernetic era whose monster growth now sucks up hundreds of billions of dollars yearly in fashionable casinos around the world. These moneymakers had seductive names such as Super Wildcat, Big Tent, Trail Blazer, Red Arrow, Galloping Dominoes, Super Circus, Double Shot, Touchdown, Big Three, Gunsmoke, Wagonwheel, Mermaid, and 7-Star. The console models of 45 years ago did not spew out coins to winners. Bartenders or other attendants handled payoffs. Most pinball machines required $50 federal amusement stamps, but the fee for the more complicated multicoin slots was $250.

The gambling machines added to Reading's reputation of an entertainment mecca with its thriving Penn Street movie theaters, after-hours barrooms, and houses where the shady ladies were prone to please. Today's seniors revel in memories of that halcyon era without taking into account the destructive influence the rackets had on the city's political foundation. Was the carefree acceptance of a culture shrouded in corruption and deception the impetus for the city's present struggle to regain its economic and social balance in the new century? Certainly other factors were influential in Reading's descent, but that attitude of let the good times roll left many more losers than winners in its wake.

In the second year of the Kubacki administration, three series of articles published in daily newspapers gave its readers an even closer look at the rackets. The stories incited some positive reaction from law enforcement, but the underworld continued to flaunt its illegal operations despite serious personal and financial setbacks. For the most part, the afternoon *Eagle* and morning *Times* editorial staffs operated independently and competitively. But, in the summer of 1961 reporters and editors from the two news departments combined to produce a seven-part series about Berks County's burgeoning gambling machine business. Entitled *A Community Cancer* it revealed how more and more county places with gambling devices were complying with federal law by purchasing gaming stamps while flaunting state laws prohibiting gambling. The Internal Revenue Service began its crackdown on establishments lacking stamps in 1956. That year by the end of June, there were 26 places that had stamps covering a total of 41 machines in Berks County. In the past five and a half years, according to the IRS, Berks was the No. 1 county in the number of federal stamps purchased in Pennsylvania. As a tax, the stamps had cost Berks proprietors a total of $183,000 during that period. From 46 licensed machines in 1957, the county number had now grown to 226 in four years. Reading places covered by stamps was 137.

The latest figures showed Dauphin County, which included Pittsburgh, ranked second with a total levy of $135,000 collected over the same period. The tab for Philadelphia and Bucks and Delaware counties was zero. No drinking establishments or other kinds of spots with gambling machines in the state's biggest metropolitan area had bothered to purchase a single stamp. The IRS was certainly exhibiting a double standard in its campaign to clean up Berks County and Coal Region counties. The statistics proved Dan McDevitt's oft-uttered complaint that Reading was Internal Revenue's patsy.

Reporters working on *A Community Cancer* articles found that whoever was assigned to pay the winners was trained to be wary of strangers. The word had gotten out that newsmen were on the loose and checking. One reporter visited 46 places where he was not known, and at only six spots was he allowed to cash in his winning games. Newsmen heard other players being told that there would be no payoffs because the heat was on. But some suckers continued to drop nickels and dimes and quarters into the slots expecting to be paid despite the warnings. When the heat was off, a nickel wager could earn as much as $50 or 1,000 free games.

For owners of gambling devices, capital investment in the 226 machines that were licensed in Berks was estimated to be about $250,000. The distributors usually split the take with proprietors, 50-50, although a few clubs bought their own machines and kept all the profits. That was a risk few clubs were willing to take, because if Treasury agents seized an unlicensed machine they were likely to dispose of it.

*Times* newsmen were invited along when a detail of IRS agents loaded a Cape May Coast Guard patrol boat with Ralph Kreitz's old one-armed bandits that had been seized and were now to be deep-sixed a few miles out. Jules Hanssens, leading the dumping party, observed as five of his seven landlubber mates fed the fish in the angry sea:

"Well, old Ralphie had the last laugh."

Jules suggested sinking the next shipment in the Schuylkill River. While the bandits had been stored in the basement of a Philadelphia federal building, janitors and other service people were known to have dropped coins in the slots hoping the relics had one more jackpot left in them. The government had not paid Ralph a dime for his 63 slot machines before burying them.

A year after the newspaper series ran, Ralph finally settled his tax problems with the federal government. He was at rock bottom after selling his one-third interest in a three-story property at Moss and Exeter streets for $7,500. He turned that over to the IRS. Unlike Abe Minker, who owed far more in back taxes than Ralph ever did, the star of the Kefauver hearings wasn't much for putting money in the bank. He loved buying gifts for kids, and his home on Douglass Street had a well-used welcome mat. His sponsorship of VVV sports teams was appreciated by scores of amateur athletes. Judge Joseph Lord III made the decision to let Ralph off the tax hook when the aging racketeer turned over the $7,500 which was well short of the $72,348 still due. Ralph died a short time later knowing he had paid as best he could.

When Mayor Kubacki was asked to comment on the gambling machine series, he was ready and willing. He used the occasion to give a lengthy dissertation, something of a philosophic viewpoint on the evils and benefits of gambling as seen by himself and demonstrated by the general public's support and participation in games of chance. For almost two hours in a give and take with newsmen, the mayor was at his expansive best, parrying every question with an answer that made sense—if the baser frailties of Everyman take precedence over the rule of law.

"The whole problem," he said, "is made up of many parts which someone at the federal, state, or even local level has defined as gambling. At what point can we, in charge of enforcement, say that we must stop pinball machines or amusement devices or bingo, which is played for food, groceries and clothing, or punchboards ... lotteries that are sold at hotels and clubs to sponsor baseball and bowling teams, or raffles or turkeys and hams during Easter and Christmas, or at festivals and carnivals, or at hospitals and fire companies to raise necessary funds for necessary equipment to save life and property? Who is there among all of us to say how far we should go?

"There are two definite things that affect this subject. One is the people, and if they desire it, it will remain with us no matter what steps we can take to eliminate it. Therefore, I feel the educational approach has a great deal of importance because without the people spending their money, whether it be for pinballs or any other form of gaming, everyone will agree it cannot exist."

The mayor said a solution to wiping out all gambling would be to hire 12 more policemen to form a squad that did nothing but pursue racketeers. But would the voters want to pay an additional $50,000 a year in taxes to form such a team. No, he didn't think they would.

Seated at his office desk in City Hall, Big John lectured reporters as if they were his students signed up for Gambling 101. Did the general public believe widespread gambling existed because there was a connection between the organized gamblers and public officials or ranking police officials? His answer to this:

"It is evidenced among the public that there is from time to time in one administration or another that there may be some connection between the vendor (supplier) and some police officials. One of the reasons this could be so construed is that at many of the public banquets where there are clubmen or liquor retailers or others in the liquor business … these men, officials and vendors, meet and know each other socially. Because of this, some people may think there is a connection between them."

At the time of this charade, Kubacki was seeking favors from a parking meter company that eventually would lead to his downfall. But this was showtime and Big John was tap dancing to his own tune. He convincingly argued that if the good citizens of Reading wanted gambling, so be it. Who was he to go against the wishes of the people?

"They say let's legalize gambling," he stated. "If the people feel so strongly toward gambling, then they have a right to have it placed on the ballot."

Was it poetic justice that within 16 years, the gambling public would be able to participate in the Pennsylvania State Lottery, or take a bus to Atlantic City and spend as much as they wanted in the Resorts casino?

In the wake of the *A Community Cancer* series, Kubacki and Dist. Atty. Brubaker made overtures to state officials to look into the gambling problems they faced. Both urged the state police to conduct a thorough investigation of gambling in their jurisdictions. Col. Frank McCartney, the state police commissioner, came to Reading on June 22, 1961, to confer with the mayor and the

D.A., who promised their complete cooperation. McCartney fulfilled their request.

That summer local gamblers suffered through a drought at the places they went to lose their money. Slot machines were hidden or hauled away from clubs and bars, and the Cherry Street dice game was closed down. Any poker games still in existence were floating to avoid detection. The numbers game didn't disappear, but the writers took care to avoid detection much more so than usual. It was indeed a dry summer for the big operators.

Just before the staties turned in a final report of their probe in early September, they arrested 48-year-old Bill Noll, and 47-year-old Sam Bruno, a pair of veteran independent numbers writers. Col. McCartney led the raid. In his report, the colonel said his troops at the Kenhorst Boulevard barracks would continue to keep an eye on gambling in the city and county. McCartney also stated that during the two-month investigation, there was no indication that Abe Minker and company were still in business.

All 137 Reading places with federal stamps were identified in the newspaper series. Many were not displaying the stamps as was required by law. The press investigators were seldom asked to show identification at clubs where memberships were required by the Pennsylvania Liquor Control Board. Teenagers were seen playing the gaming machines even after a recent news story told about an 18-year-old who burglarized a city restaurant and broke open a gambling machine where earlier the same evening he had lost $15. He was caught and served time in BCP.

The *Times* published another series in November with the catch line, *Uncle Sam vs Abe Minker*. This was a summary of the depositions the Justice Department lawyers had taken the previous summer.

Gene Friedman, the *Times* reporter who covered the courts all through the McDevitt and Kubacki administrations and beyond, teamed with City Hall reporter Drexel Bradley to condense the 782 pages in eight volumes of deposition papers. The first part of the series was published only a week after Minker was sentenced to serve four years in federal prison for evading gambling excise taxes.

The power of the press is questionable. It apparently did influence the outcome of the 1959 general election when Mayor Dan McDevitt was unseated by John Kubacki. The McDevitt-*Times* feud probably tilted soured city voters toward Kubacki, who had become the media's standup guy at City Council meetings. In the same balloting, however, after the *Times* had offered its readers a steady stream of stories that could be considered anti-Brubaker, Fred retained his job as district attorney.

In December the *Times* continued its anti-rackets crusade with a third series, calling it *Operation Vice Den.* The girlie business suddenly was stripped bare of any pretense that it wasn't big business. This seven-parter led to a string of arrests, court actions, law enforcement surprises, and more official denials. The green light the red-light district had enjoyed for so long would soon turn amber as Abe Minker's regime continued to crumble.

# 25

## *Newsman lifts the curtain on bordellos*

Reading Eagle Company had no stated policy "to get" the racketeers and the suspect politicians and police officials, but with all the vice activity and ensuing court cases against the mob, the press was feeding its readers a steady diet of sensational news. But the newspapers often were just the messengers delivering to its readers accusations made by other politicians and civic reformers voicing their opinions. Times city editor Dick Peters regularly questioned why federal investigators could uncover large gambling operations while city and county law enforcement feigned ignorance about these very public pursuits. In his "Old Pete" column, Peters dispensed a steady stream of satire critical of Danny Boy McDevitt and Fearless Freddie Brubaker for picking and choosing their targets. Brubaker sometimes answered by declaring he needed a much larger staff to properly investigate the mob. Since the county commissioners turned down his requests for more detectives and assistant district attorneys, what could he do? McDevitt claimed his 155-man police force always checked out complaints and regularly made arrests. However, a full-scale campaign to shut down gambling and prostitution was never initiated on his watch.

The Times hired Donald Barlett as a rookie reporter in 1956. He was assigned the Boy Scouts beat, soon piling up so many stories about the good deed lads that he was told to slow down. Before enlisting in the Army in 1958, he broke a story about a clergyman trying to raise funds for a nonexistent boys camp. Donald served 26 months, much of it in Army counterintelligence. Returning to the newspaper in 1960, he was given special assignments in which his military investigative experience was put to good use. When he noticed a story in an Allentown newspaper about the increase in venereal disease, he decided to see where Reading stood on that issue. His investigation naturally led to prostitution, which was flourishing in the city.

In October 1961, Peters turned loose the diminutive, unimposing reporter to do a series on prostitution. A few other reporters assisted in the probe, including Earl Ruthardt and John Hilferty. Ruthardt spent quite a bit of after-hours time in Eddie Guard's bar at Franklin and Lemon streets. That's where Mable Jones nightly held court. She was a good-natured lady, now middle-aged, who spent freely on her good-time friends. Earl got friendly enough to join the madam at her special table. In his quiet, inquisitive manner, the slim reporter picked up odds and ends. But when it was learned he was a reporter, from then on a signal light on the jukebox would start blinking whenever he walked in. That cued Mable and her pals not to talk business within hearing range of "Earl the Squirrel."

Reporter John Hilferty was more direct, going right to the source for his information. He visited Freddie Williams's house at 124 Plum Street one night, selected one of the four young ladies and appeared ready for action. But when his choice asked for her money in advance, John could only come up with four dollars, six shy of the going price. "Not tonight, dearie," he was informed. Before he left he learned that on other nights as many as six girls were available. If you had the deep pockets to spend the entire night, a room with hostess was for rent.

Barlett rented a third-floor room at the YMCA located across the railroad tracks from the houses of Claudia Glenn and Josephine Maione. Night after night, binoculars focused on the 7th Street sidewalk traffic, he sat by a window taking notes as men entered the pleasure joints. Donald also roamed the tenderloin, asking questions of taxi drivers, bartenders, shady ladies, even neighborhood kids. During his month-long investigation, Barlett perused courthouse documents and police records to sketch biographies of Josephine from her early days in Scranton, and of Mable Jones when she worked the avenues of Brooklyn and Manhattan till she wound up as Reading's madam queen of the post-war years.

Donald compiled enough facts and figures to write a seven-part Operation Vice Den series that first appeared in the December 12, 1961, edition of the Times. He identified five whorehouses located in Reading that were using women shuttled from city to city on a regular basis. This, plus one-girl bordellos, streetwalkers, and bar girls, combined to make prostitution a business that totaled an estimated half a million dollars a year. The going rate was $10 to $15 per customer.

During his probe, Barlett charted the traffic entering the two houses on North 7th Street. For Jessie's brothel the daily average of customers was 40, providing a conservative estimate of $2,000 a week income, which the madam split down the middle with her girls. Since some of her employees lived in the house, they repaid part of their earnings to their employer. No bar girls were connected to that operation, and cabbies who brought customers received a small gratuity from Jessie.

Josephine Florence Yemen was born on the Fourth of July, 1900, in Freeland, Luzerne County. When she married Nick Delorenzo in 1927 she was calling herself Jessie while living in Wilkes-Barre. Nick left after two years. By then, Jessie was available for a price. Some said it was Nick who set off the dynamite that wrecked her bordello at 8 Jefferson Street in 1931, but he was never charged. The house was repaired and she and her girls went back to work. During the Depression, the cops hauled her in so often she finally moved to Reading where her mother was living in 1940, the same year her divorce from Nick was finalized. Also that year was her first prostitution arrest by Reading police. It was no secret to Ralph Maione what profession his fiancée was in when he married her in 1942. For the next 15 years she prospered in relative obscurity, but shortly after Danny McDevitt came into office she was closed down and spent six days in BCP.

Barlett's stories disclosed a 107 percent rise locally in venereal disease in the past four years as reported by the American Social Health Association (ASHA). The Vice Den series took swipes at the city police department for its halfhearted record of sporadic vice arrests. And the state police, it was pointed out, had not made a major prostitution raid in the city for almost three years. As for the district attorney, Barlett wrote, he had taken no action against any local organized crime figures so far that year. The Pennsylvania Liquor Control Board was accused of failing to raid bawdyhouses where liquor and beer were being sold.

Barlett quoted a boy about 11 or 12 who evidently was paid to direct customers to one of the 7th Street houses:

"Do you wanna know a good house," the boy asked a man ambling along the street.

"Where," the man asked.

"In there, 111. You have to go in the back way." Claudia Glenn had gained another customer.

By the time Part 4 of the series appeared, readers were informed that teenagers could test the adult waters, and most of the houses were open seven days a week. Only Josephine's girls got days off. After a week of Barlett's extended report there wasn't much left to the imagination about the city's red-light sororities.

On Wednesday December 14, the series had to share the news spotlight with the beginning of a criminal trial. The case involved four men who had taken part in an armed robbery at Claudia Glenn's place the previous May at 4 o'clock one morning and made off with $339 from her purse. Two male customers from

Topton witnessed the robbery by the armed intruders wearing silk stockings over their faces. The trial would have caused little notice had it occurred at any other time, but the robbery aspect was easily overshadowed by events that suddenly burst into a torrent of court actions on the bawdyhouse front.

As Judge Hess read Part 3 of Operation Vice Den Thursday morning, he was incensed by an accompanying story that reported Claudia's place was still open for business even as the robbery trial was being held. He quoted Barlett's latest revelation in court that day and ordered a temporary restraining injunction served on Glenn immediately. The madam and June Miller, an inmate, were arrested and charged with prostitution violations.

Glenn, who was a principal witness against the accused robbers, then got on her high horse when the questions being asked of her hit too close to home. Now needing a lawyer, she quickly hired John S. Speicher, who advised her to take the 5th Amendment. Seemingly in as much hot water as the four defendants, Claudia took the constitutional route a dozen times. Although she wouldn't admit to running a bordello, Judge Hess informed the jury that 111 North 7th was just that. Police witnesses also testified about Claudia's impressive police record the past two years: four arrests in 1960 and two, plus the latest, in 1961. None of the cases had reached criminal court, all having been settled in an alderman's office by paying $50 or $100 fines.

On the opening day of the robbery trial, Arthur Nester, one of the two male customers at Claudia's house that early morning of the robbery, reported that he was accompanied by Wayne J. M. Kern. The 50-year-old Kern, father of three, was served a subpoena to appear in court on Thursday. That morning at 7 o'clock he drove to an isolated spot near the Topton reservoir, attached a hose to the exhaust pipe of his car and died of asphyxiation. Asst. Dist. Atty. Peter Cianci said he had not planned to put the World War II veteran on the stand, but wanted him present in the event defense counsel called him to testify. In present day vernacular, Kern would be regarded as a collateral casualty of the rackets. The defendants, Robert E. Barry, Leonard Fisher, Rodney Kline, and Richard Eberhardt, all from Reading, were convicted.

Fred Brubaker tried to capitalize on Barlett's thoroughly researched series by pressuring the newspapers to release Donald's sources to him. Barlett refused, claiming the state shield law protected his sources. On the day the final Vice Den story appeared, Barlett received a subpoena to testify in the civil cases against Mable and Claudia. State and federal shield laws gave reporters the right to protect the names of news sources, but interpretations of the U.S. Constitution have often placed this issue in limbo. More than a few news people have spent time in jail for contempt when they defied court orders to reveal their sources.

Hess ordered an immediate hearing to resolve the debate. Eight members of the city police department testified they took part in arrests at Glenn's whorehouse, but Barlett refused to answer questions about where he obtained his facts and figures. Although Brubaker admitted he probably didn't need Barlett's testimony to prosecute Mable Jones, Claudia Glenn and June Miller, he still felt the 25-year-old reporter was in contempt for refusing to answer some of his questions. In the end, Judge Hess ruled in favor of the district attorney although voicing suspicions that the case might have to go before an appellate court for a final decision.

A related story to the steady stream of prostitution news was another Barlett expose revealing Jessie Maione's hiring of one of Police Chief Charlie Wade's home improvement companies, Air Spray Inc., to do a $780 stucco siding job on a house she owned at 113½ North Poplar Street. The rear of this small house was centered only a short distance from the rear entrances to the bawdyhouses run by Jessie and Claudia. Wade denied any knowledge of the siding contract until Barlett's story came out. Charlie said the management of Air-Spray did not notify him about jobs the company contracted to do.

The Times's star reporter checked tax records and found that Mable Jones was in arrears of her city, county, and school taxes on her two bordello properties. The delinquencies dated back to 1957 and totaled almost $2,000. Mable's accountant, Councilman Bruce Coleman, had some uneasy moments explaining how such a mistake could have happened. The city filed liens against her two places. By March 1962, Mable paid her $76 city water bill and $785 toward her school tax bill. City Hall halted proceedings to sell the houses but reminded her she still owed $949 in school taxes and another $153 on her late county taxes. It took several months before those bills were paid in full because city cops, on orders from the chief, closed down the girlie joints in April and May.

For six years Fred Brubaker had brushed off accusations by the press, federal prosecutors, the local Republican party, and civic and religious groups that he was not fulfilling the responsibilities and obligations of a district attorney. Sometimes he would answer his critics, sometimes he would ignore the bad press and censure. Then on February 5, 1962, he filed a civil suit against Reading Eagle Company, claiming he had been harassed, badgered, embarrassed, and libeled because of politics. The libel petition cited 14 articles published in the Times, including five stories in the seven-part Vice Den series. Fred was asking in excess of $5,000 in damages, plus punitive damages, claiming the stories were published "recklessly, wantonly, and from improper motives." His suit said the articles were intended to show that "he received and accepted payoffs from the operators of such illicit and vicious establishments ..." The civil case would not come to trial for another 15 months.

Maybe Josephine Maione thought the Times would quit peeking, at least until after Don Barlett's contempt case was settled. But that wasn't to be. In late February, Don wrote another story after a real John posed once again as a randy john in Jessie's playground. John Hilferty took his pick of the three girls available, paid $10, then climbed the stairs to her room. But on that wintry night he conveniently got cold feet. His excuse: fear of being caught in a police bust. The mock john really did feel wanted, however, as Jessie and the other hirelings coaxed him to stay. The madam even promised to pay his fine if the cops intruded. But his orders were to reconnoiter, not engage the enemy. Jessie returned his fee—good faith money to prove she really wanted him as a regular customer. In their conversation, Hilferty wheedled as much at he could out of Jessie before departing. The madam told him she did not cater to all-night customers because she was usually too busy to spare a room for that long. Barlett's story about Josephine and Mable continuing to operate was ignored by the local authorities for several weeks.

When arguments in Barlett's contempt case were heard in March, Judge Hess pointed out that both he and Judge Albert Readinger, who were presiding, were members of the Pennsylvania House of Representatives in 1937 when the state passed its shield law. So they were certainly familiar with it. Charles H. Weidner of Stevens and Lee law firm presented the newspaper's side in the matter. A.D.A. Peter Cianci spoke for the commonwealth. The crux of the case was Reading Eagle Company's contention that sources meant not only what other informants told Barlett, but also any information he obtained by personal observation. Cianci's problem was that he could not find any previous cases that defined exactly what a source meant. Some of the questions Barlett had refused to answer at Claudia Glenn's hearing in December were about incidents he had observed during his investigation. Weidner pointed out that Barlett was his own source and not required to testify. Cianci argued that any eyewitness to a crime was obligated to testify. Weidner disagreed. He stated that Barlett was given an assignment to write about prostitution, he carried out that assignment, and was not, by state law, required to reveal where or how he got his information.

Judge Readinger posed the question: what if a reporter was the only eyewitness to a murder, should he have immunity? The judge also asked: if a reporter wrote a series of articles that put law enforcement agencies in a bad light, could that writer refuse to help these agencies in court proceedings? Weidner countered with the current example of the Glenn case where Judge Hess had stated there was no reason to make Barlett testify because other witnesses had given the prosecution all the evidence it needed to win a conviction. The deadlock was broken a few days before the trial for Claudia Glenn and June Miller when Barlett agreed to testify. The contempt charge was dismissed by Judge Hess.

"This is a more desirable result," the judge stated. "I read the articles with a great deal of interest when they appeared in the Times, and I state publicly I think he (Barlett) rendered a great public service in exposing such conditions, which apparently have gotten some action since then."

In January 1962 the Reading Junior Chamber of Commerce had formed a new committee, naming it PAUL (Political Action Under Leadership). PAUL's goal was to stamp out rackets in the city and county and to obtain good government. It launched a long range program in March by inviting the mayor of Canton, Ohio, to speak to a Reading audience that supported the Jaycees' project. A crowd of 600 listened in the Abraham Lincoln ballroom as James Lawhun explained how he, with the help of honest cops, the local newspaper, and others ran the rackets out of Canton.

Lawhun, elected the previous year, said ASHA's 1961 report stated Canton had 30 gambling and prostitution sites. When elected authorities made no effort to close those places, 35 policemen took it on themselves to stage raids without orders from the police director or mayor. That started the ball rolling and with lots of publicity from the press, new city officials were elected and the gambling providers and madams were either arrested or left town.

The young visiting mayor quoted from a recent Reading Times editorial:

"Because it seems it is the good citizens who are the last to be aroused by the political muck encroaching on a community and by their nature, being without organization, they are in many ways almost helpless to cope with it."

"It says it much better than I ever could," Lawhun stated.

Canton was similar in size to Reading. It took eight years at the polls by Reading voters before the mob's grip on their nefarious businesses was loosened. Reading's policemen never staged a rebellion like that of their Canton brethren. In this game of wills, PAUL now became another player on the side of those who would regain control of law enforcement in Reading. Mayor Kubacki and Dist. Atty. Brubaker were in the audience the night of Mayor Lawhun's address.

In the spring of 1962 the IRS was going after unlicensed machines and gamblers all over the country. On the weekend Mayor Lawhun addressed the Jaycees, the IRS conducted raids in 33 cities from Manhattan to Ogden, Nevada, from Miami to Peoria, Illinois. Just so Reading didn't feel neglected, a few days later the T-men quietly scoured Reading bars and clubs, confiscating 14 devices for which no federal stamps had been purchased. Some were late-model, multicoin machines with innocuous names: "Lots of Fun," "Barrel of Fun," and "Fun Ways."

Matt Whitaker was a familiar name in Reading gaming circles, but in the lower coal region he was a gambling icon for decades. It is likely that Matt and Abe Minker had an arrangement: "You stay out of Berks County, Matt, and I'll leave you alone in Schuylkill." The same day IRS agents were nosing around Reading watering holes collecting "Fun" games, a few more agents entered Matt's Cigar Store at 116 Norwegian Street in Pottsville to arrest the 47-year-old Whitaker. The significance of this arrest was that the Justice Department's FBI, and Treasury Department's IRS combined forces to knock over a widespread interstate gambling operation. The two departments were seriously pursuing violators of new federal gambling laws. Whitaker was brought to Reading before a U.S. commissioner. In later years he would be forced to make other trips to the Pretzel City for similar reasons.

Bill Lilley, often operating as a lone ranger in the South of Penn district of Reading, was becoming a well recognized figure in that part of town. Working primarily in the 7th and Franklin Street area, often in the Grand Hotel barroom, he was ever present when women offered their wares to the opposite sex. He tailed streetwalkers to their rendezvous, whether in a rooming house, a car, or a bordello. In a two-year period he would be credited with almost 50 prostitution arrests.

Some of Lilley's arrests were easier than others. Following a tip, he entered an unlocked room in the Crystal Hotel, 733 Penn Street. He arrived too late for the main event, but not the payoff. He was amazed as he watched and listened to the conversation between 44-year-old Bonnie Winters, a former Maione house inhabitant, and her 66-year-old satisfied customer:

"Give me the money."

"How much do I owe you?

"Whatever you think it's worth.

Grandpa, a big spender, took $20 from his wallet and handed it to an indifferent Bonnie, who offered no change. "Times are tough," she observed.

The old gent paid a $15 forfeit at City Hall, which he, like many johns before him, lost by not showing up for a hearing the next day. Bonnie was hauled off to BCP.

# 26

# *High rollers crapped out by feds*

The oldest of old-timers will tell you it was a sure bet you could always find an illegal gambling establishment in Reading without too much trouble. The Greeks had a well attended card game on Cherry Street across from Dutch Mary's during the pre-World War I years. During Prohibition and the Depression a couple of bookie parlors in the Court and Church streets neighborhood were connected to national horse betting wire services. A full house was commonplace at Tony Moran's basement card game at 529 Penn Street before and during World War II. Philadelphians and their suburbanites and coal crackers from Schuylkill County usually knew where the action was in the Pretzel City. The horse book at 6th and Franklin streets run by Moran continued long after Tony was killed, eventually closing down because of the Kefauver Committee heat.

The poker game that ran for several years in a loft at 9$^{th}$ and Penn streets is still remembered by World War II veterans. A couple of local entrepreneurs organized the nightly games, which soon drew an ever increasing number of players, and a growing audience. It was open house—no peephole through which to whisper a password or a "Joe sent me." In a few years larger accommodations were required as craps became more popular than cards. The game was moved to a vacant storeroom near 10$^{th}$ and Penn. As the 1950s dawned, outside interests had muscled in. Racketeers from Harrisburg and Philadelphia were not only banking the game but staffing it, too. The mob, both local and area-wide, was sharing the profits that continued to grow. One high roller, who also shared controlling interest, was his own worst customer, and the game eventually folded because he owed so much to his partners. Local law enforcement generally ignored these obvious violations of state gambling laws, giving credence to long-standing scuttlebutt that local politicians got their cut of the pot.

In many cities and towns, gamblers had to find out where the floating crap game was scheduled each night. In Reading, from 1956 to 1962, the dice were rolled in the same locations night after night. The racketeers occupied permanent quarters without fear of being knocked off by local authorities. This could happen only if gambling became profitable to elected officials as well as to the racketeers, according to various state and federal law enforcement officials who pointed their opinions directly at Reading's City Hall and the county Courthouse.

With the election of Dan McDevitt as mayor in 1955, the mob was ready and waiting for a bigger and better wagering venue than the gambling community had ever experienced in Reading. The building at 149 North 10th Street was built by bigwigs in the Republican Party in 1924. They felt their membership had outgrown their former social headquarters, a row house in the 700 block of Franklin Street, a few doors down from the home of Max Hassel's family. It was called the Coolidge Club. Actually, it was a wealthy man's speakeasy during the early years of Prohibition. After a state police raid, instigated by Pennsylvania's Republican prohibitionist governor, Gifford Pinchot, club officials decided it was time to move. The Northeast Republican Club was built on North Tenth and became the county GOP headquarters. The building is now in its eighth decade, housing the Genesius Theatre for many years.

In the 1950s, the Grand Old Party moved its social quarters to Wyomissing when it opened the Young Republican Club. In 1956, when the 10th and Walnut casino started up, crime families from New York, Jersey, and Philadelphia all had an interest in it. Many gamblers boasted that this was the biggest and best craps game this side of Las Vegas. With fancy tables and trained croupiers, the game ran nightly for more than four years with only a few brief interruptions when the state police launched investigations. Once the heat was off, the large gambling hall was filled to its capacity of about 200 people on many nights.

George Barrow, a career gambling operator known as Skinny Barrett in and around Philadelphia, became casino manager shortly after it opened. Regular limousine service was available from the Quaker City. Chauffeured sedans left 13th and Market streets each night about 10 p.m. to bring the Philly and Jersey high rollers to Reading. Luggers, the drivers who traveled the Pennsylvania Turnpike each night, were low-level Mafia soldiers or wise guys, many with nicknames: Skidley, Credo, Flivvie the Fish, Snorky, Husky and on and on.

While Abe Minker supplied the protection through his local government connections, the out-of-town mobsters refurbished the vacated building. Reading was centrally located for gamblers from Allentown, Harrisburg, the Coal Regions, Lancaster, Jersey, and Philadelphia. They came in droves to the largely residential neighborhood. Less than two blocks from City Hall, the game gained considerable notoriety. Reading Times city editor Dick Peters wrote about its charmed life in his "Old Pete" column week after week, but the pols and cops paid no heed. Charlie Wade, then a detective, said police sent to check out complaints always found nothing but pinochle games. "We should have gotten Oscars for the acting jobs we performed," he later noted. Forewarned, the dice operators would move the tables out of the main gambling quarters, and the place was generally vacated.

The craps game was shut down in late 1958 during a state police investigation, but its customers were properly notified to keep their dollars ready because the closure was only temporary. By 1959 the game became such an attraction that it was decided a new location in a less conspicuous area had to be found.

Government prosecutors later reported the Philadelphia mob paid Minker $1,000 a week, plus a percentage of the take, for the protection he provided by keeping the local police at bay. The feds also figured that the casino's annual payroll was $350,000. An estimated 50 luggers were employed to bring gamblers to Reading.

In early 1960 the large craps tables and other gambling equipment were moved to the first floor of the building at 235-237 Cherry Street. By February the new setup was back in business.

Alfonso "Fonsie" Comito became the listed owner of the two-story structure, and Ralph K. Blankenbiller, a local amusement and gambling machine distributor, held the mortgage. The second floor was occupied by the Calabria Society Club which had moved from its Penn Street location. The popular late nightspot was a good cover for the large number of people coming to and going from the dice den below. The gambling area was not as expansive as was the big room at 10th and Walnut, but the three large craps tables and other smaller card tables were enough to accommodate the 100 to 150 players admitted nightly. The building was off the beaten track and New Jersey license plates were not so noticeable parked in that area. But it was no secret to police patrolling the neighborhood.

Hailing from Yeadon, a Philadelphia suburb, the 57-year-old Skinny Barrett continued as the major domo of the dice game after it moved to Cherry Street. For local flavor, 49-year-old Benny Bonanno served as Barrett's deputy and was Minker's man on the spot. Most of the other principals running the game were members of the Philadelphia and New Jersey mobs. Barrett rented a room at the Berkshire Hotel, usually leaving for work about 10 p.m.

Gamblers from far and wide began showing up at the front door of 237 Cherry about 10:30 o'clock. Players had to pass through three doors to gain entrance. The front door was unlocked. The second was usually controlled by an electric buzzer. The third sturdy door, always locked, had a small window peephole through which the doorman could see the customer. Benny Bonanno occasionally was the doorman. At other times it might be Fred "Whispers" DePatrizio, a Camden resident. They knew all the regulars. If you brought a friend and vouched for him as a responsible gambler either Skinny or Bennie had to give the okay to admit him. It was best to speak up if Whispers was at the portal because he was hard of hearing.

There was an office with a safe off the main room. That's where enough money was brought by Benny to start each night's play. Skinny usually laid out piles of bills at the first table as the early birds waited for the signal to start. Pasquale Pillo or Dominic DiCaprio took turns as the "shuffler," the moneyman. He kept tabs on the fast moving bills as bets were won and lost. He straightened the piles of $1s, $5s, $10s, and $50s after each round of betting. At 11 p.m., he or one of the others would then loudly announce:

"Let's play craps!" or "Craps are open!"

As the crowd grew, more money was provided by Skinny for table two, and eventually for table three. At each table was a stickman to rake in the dice, two dealers to pay off or drag in the money, a shuffler to make sure the money was kept in order, and two men sitting behind the stickman on a ladder to watch for cheaters. The games moved with incredible speed; no place for beginners. By today's A.C. and L.V. standards, the scene was pretty rustic, but in 1960 it was a gambler's paradise.

The game became so popular that Saturday and Sunday matinees were added to the weekly schedule. The night games sometimes ran till 6 a.m., but usually closed two or three hours earlier.

All this covert action did not bring much business to Reading. The Daniel Boone Hotel was the big winner. LeRoy Stieff, the third-rate hotel's manager, set up special $3 weekend rates for gamblers who usually stayed one and a half days. But when many started stretching the hours to two full days he upped the rate to $4. He also gave group rates. Other than stimulating bar and restaurant businesses, and giving the ever-bustling bawdyhouses a boost, the gamblers added little financially to the community.

The luggers who had time to kill often went up to the Calabria Club to drink, flirt, and sometimes antagonize the local yokels. Paul "Tucson" Lavigna doubled as a bartender and bouncer in the club. Tucson, of average size, had been a traveling bar fighter after a short-lived career as a boxer. He gave that up because Marquess of Queensberry rules hampered his brawling, no-holds-barred style. He gained a minor reputation on the bare-knuckles circuit after the war, eventually turning to bartending and numbers writing to earn a steady income.

It was a summer night in 1961 when a couple of Philly luggers came on too strong to a lady at the bar in the Calabria. Tucson was on duty that night. Defending the lady's honor, according to Tucson, he went the limit, sending both of Angelo Bruno's henchmen to Community General Hospital. Several stranded gamblers had to find other rides back to Philly that night.

The next day, Tucson was called onto the carpet by Benny Bonanno. Bruno, the new Mafia godfather in the City of Brotherly Love, was demanding a personal Lavigna apology, or else. Tucson lived to tell the story, but almost choked saying, "I'm sorry."

In the fall of '61 there were rumblings that the state police commissioner Col. Frank McCartney had posted investigators in Reading to begin another rackets cleanup. The casino was closed down for a few weeks, but again the regular customers were informed that when the probers went back to Harrisburg, it would be business as usual. The tables and other gambling paraphernalia were moved out during the hiatus, fearing the staties might break into the place and damage the equipment. The investigation ended without conclusive evidence. The game resumed but only on weekends. By the end of the year, it was full steam ahead, seven days a week.

During Dan McDevitt's years as mayor, he and other Democratic officials sang the same tune whenever the feds came after local racketeers. Politics! Politics! Politics! The Republican administration in Washington merely wanted to show up Reading's Democratic Party. With Democrats now in the White House, that old plaint was hardly valid.

In November 1961, President John F. Kennedy signed a federal law that persons who aided and abetted gambling by crossing state lines conspired to do an unlawful act. The luggers driving gamblers to Reading from New Jersey and other out-of-state locations were in violation of this new rackets-busting legislation, and Bobby Kennedy, the President's brother and attorney general, was eager to test it. Bobby ordered FBI Director J. Edgar Hoover to look into reports of a major dice game in Reading, Pennsylvania. After years of publicly denying there was such an entity as organized crime, the FBI chief was now about to prove that the Mafia did exist. It would come out later that the FBI knew about the game since its inception in 1956.

As part of Bobby Kennedy's promised crackdown, a team of 40 IRS agents, led by Thomas F. McBride, special prosecutor for the Justice Department's organized crime and racketeering section, swept through Reading in December, arresting seven men at six locations on numbers charges. Patsy Spadafora, a future Reading alderman, and Frank Donato, a future victim of the Mafia, were arrested, along with proprietors and bartenders at five cafes or luncheonettes: Robert Schearer, John Paladino, David Pizzo, John Ocksrider, and Santo Damiano. They were charged with failing to buy $50 occupation tax stamps while selling lottery tickets.

Once again Fred Brubaker went to Philadelphia to ask U.S. Attorney Drew J. T. O'Keefe to turn over to him evidence in the numbers arrests so he could prosecute the gamblers. Not right now, O'Keefe said, maybe later that could be arranged.

Of the eight years Dan McDevitt and John Kubacki occupied the mayor's office in Reading, 1962 could be considered the turning point when Reading's racketeers began losing their clout. With federal agencies continuing to arrest tax evaders, and local and state authorities stepping up their law enforcement, 1962 was the year the black cloud over the city began leaking, further drenching Abe Minker with legal problems.

FBI agents saturated the area around the Calabria Club for several weeks. Frank Kauffman, senior resident agent for the FBI's Reading office, and his sidekick, Special Agent William Davis, spent many a cold night recording the arrival and departure of limos, the names of the luggers, and even identifying some of the players.

On December 29, lugger Anthony LaMonica was turning into the Calabria parking lot when the wheels of his large sedan began spinning in the snow. Special Agent A. R. Christinsen came out of hiding long enough to assist a taxi driver and two of Tony's passengers free the vehicle from the slush. It was dark but the agent got an up close look at the driver whom he would one day identify in court.

Two agents managed to gain entrance to the game by duping local players into vouching for them. The pair was never identified nor called on to testify when defendants came to trial, but the information they gathered was invaluable as the agency prepared for a major raid.

Ten days before the feds were ready to strike, the FBI agent who would lead the raid was caught in an embarrassing position. Fred Frohbose, special agent in charge of the Philadelphia office, was reconnoitering the Cherry Street neighborhood, not realizing somebody was tailing his car. It was detective Bill Lilley, the city's lone vice officer who had picked up the scent. Bill had a way of smelling trouble and usually got his man. This time it was Frohbose who Lilley felt was acting suspiciously, so Bill pulled him over. Just what transpired after that is unknown because Fred gave a creditable excuse and was released.

After midnight January 20, Frohbose was again back in the area, this time with a hundred agents to back him up. They had been bussed from Philadelphia and were moving into designated positions to launch the biggest raid on East Coast gambling in recent years.

It was a Friday night, a light dusting of snow covering the ground. By 1 a.m. the game had been underway about two hours when 25 agents fanned out around the 200 block of Cherry Street to cover escape routes. Another 26 stood by to enter the casino. Armed with a sledgehammer, Special Agent Irving Dean led the pack at 1:04 o'clock Saturday morning. He passed a patron coming out as he entered through the unlocked ground floor entrance. Right behind him was his boss, Fred Frohbose. Dean opened the second unlocked door. At a heavier, reinforced third door he pressed a buzzer to be admitted, shouting "This is the FBI, open up!" Receiving no answer, he smashed a small pane of glass in the door with the butt of his sledgehammer. Reaching through the window frame Dean lifted a wooden two by four used to bar the door. He then broke down the locked door with his sledgehammer.

At that moment, another team of agents was streaking up a staircase leading to the Calabria Club. Binky Dee and his band with singer Ellie Daye had arrived a short time earlier after completing a gig at the Embassy Bar on Penn Street. The club was packed. It was just as popular with the in crowd as was the casino downstairs with the sporting crowd.

"Five guys came charging up the steps swinging those billy clubs—they looked five feet long. And that shotgun, I never knew a shotgun was that big. Then I saw that armband on one of them. FBI it said." That was the reaction of a patron in the Calabria that night. The noise of the inside metal door being battered down was clearly audible up above.

"Santo Damiano, the club manager, told us we should go home," Ellie Daye recalled. "He paid us double and we left."

Behind Frohbose, the troops poured into the casino as gamblers drew away from the door hunting another way out. Frohbose jumped onto the elevated platform used by spotters. Through a bullhorn he announced. "FBI, hands over heads!" Well over a hundred gamblers crowded about the craps tables were shocked by the armed intruders, but nobody panicked. Four agents with shotguns were posted in the corners of the room. All the raiders wore side arms. None of the gamblers resisted, but it was several minutes before order was completely restored as some milled about. With hands raised, every gambler in the place was frisked for weapons. After a short time several suspects expressed discomfort and were allowed to place their hands on their heads. Soon all were ordered to just stand with arms folded across their chests.

Skinny Barrett was quickly identified and seized, but Benny Bonanno could not be found. Ten arrest warrants had been brought along. The first was served on Barrett. Other employees, stickmen, dealers, ladder men, and doormen, were also singled out as the Guys and Dolls look-alikes tugged at their caps, sneaked money into their pockets, and assumed poses ranging from forlorn to sheepish to defiantly cool.

Once inside, Dean headed for the casino office, which was locked. One swing from his utility tool took care of that. His job was to find the money. But first he found a loaded snub-nosed handgun and ammunition in the drawer of a roll-top desk. With advance knowledge, he ripped up two floor tiles and found a strong-box containing $25,000.

A bulge was felt in the lower pants leg of one fellow. It was a roll of money he had stuffed into his sock. Agents assigned to sweeping the gambling tables clean of money picked up another $20,000. Patrons were allowed to keep the bills and coins in their pockets. Later, another $10,000 was found under the floorboards as the place was thoroughly searched. The total cache was $55,000.

Agent J. Robert Pearce stayed inside a few minutes before exiting to a parked car where U.S. Commissioner G. Fred Steinrock and prosecutor Tom McBride were waiting. Steinrock now signed a search warrant and Pearce returned to the casino as the hunt for money and other evidence continued. The case in the months ahead would turn on this seemingly minor procedure. The crack team of criminal lawyers hired to represent the eventual defendants sought to exploit a very large hole in the government's case.

Agents/bus drivers had arrived, parking their vehicles on Cherry street in front of the casino. Another large contingent of agents waited at the U.S. Naval-Marine Reserve Training Center on Kenhorst Boulevard where the players and operators of the game would be taken.

About 1:30 o'clock the suspects, hands again held high, were led from the building. Marching music was provided by the Calabria jukebox: Prez Prado's appropriate melody, "Cherry Pink and Apple Blossom White" filled the snowy night air along Cherry Street. Seemingly more annoyed than worried, the dice players strolled into the waiting vehicles for the 10-minute ride to the Reserve Center. Night shift state policemen at Company C headquarters across the boulevard watched as the steady procession of suspects was unloaded from the buses at the Reserve Center.

I happened to be among the first reporters on the scene. Having covered a Friday night high school basketball game near Harrisburg that evening I returned to Reading, wrote the story, then retired to Harold Leifer's Peanut Bar on Penn Street across from the Reading Eagle Company. Still on my first beer and seated near the front door, I was suddenly jolted into action when a fellow burst in yelling, "They're raiding the Calabria." He was close but one floor off the mark.

John Hilferty and I jogged down to 3rd Street a half a block away, turned the corner and could see a crowd gathering at Cherry Street. An FBI agent was at that corner blocking anyone from going down Cherry to the Calabria Club. While I stayed there talking with the agent, Hilferty went looking for another way to get closer to the casino.

It was snowing, and when I noticed the agent shuffling his feet and staring down I asked did he lose something. He said his FBI badge had fallen off his jacket. Just then, word was sent up from the casino that the press could go down Cherry Street to the club. After the gamblers were led out of the casino and into the buses, I was permitted to go inside and view the interior of the place, but not take notes.

It was after 2 o'clock when I got back to the editorial room and began writing my story about what I had seen and from information picked up by other reporters. We went to press that morning shortly after 2:30 o'clock, and I headed for the Reserve Center where all the post-raid action was. On entering, I was met by Dick Peters. Our city editor seemed a bit grim when he told me to follow him to the temporary headquarters the FBI had set up. Fred Frohbose was there waiting for me. His first words will be embedded in my mind forever.

"NO FBI AGENT LOST HIS BADGE!!!"

I could tell he was upset but didn't realize the significance of my little attempt at humor in the story when I wrote, "Efficient, alert and courteous, one of them proved human by losing his badge in the snow."

So my answer to Fred, "Oh, did he find it?" only enraged him more.

"NO FBI AGENT LOST HIS BADGE!!!" He roared a second time. By now I could see this was a one-way debate I couldn't win. I was unceremoniously excused from his presence with the admonition to get my facts right the next time. The buzz around the Reserve Center was "Who lost his badge?" Another agent later told me that losing your FBI badge was comparable to losing one's virginity, only with a negative spin. Although it never happened, I feared I would get a call from J. Edgar himself. As for the treasured badge, I never did find out what happened to it.

Each of the 105 gamblers arrested was booked as a material witness. Although many of the detainees had not violated any federal gambling laws, they did have to post bail to make sure they would appear to testify against the operators of the game. Bail bondsman Joe Liever soon arrived, almost watering at the mouth when he saw the crowd of nondescript characters being processed. Unfortunately for him, the big majority still had the $25 cash bail required. Liever did come to the rescue of a dozen or more gamblers.

Only 13 in the crowd were from Reading. Philadelphia led the pack with 47. The Coal Regions were well represented as were Jersey towns across the Delaware River from Philly.

As the night wore on, U.S. Commissioner Steinrock determined who among the detainees was employed to run the game and set bail for them. First to be arraigned was Skinny Barrett. His bail was $100,000. Benny Bonanno heard through the grapevine the feds had a warrant for his arrest. He arrived at the Reserve Center a few hours later and was handed an arrest warrant. His bail was $10,000.

Over the weekend, an interstate roundup of suspects began. By Sunday night, 10 more were arrested. The raid was announced in blaring headlines in Pennsylvania and regional newspapers, as well as being the top story on major television and radio newscasts. William "Bud" Tamblyn, a cartoonist for the Allentown Morning Call, drew a caricature of the raid that so impressed J. Edgar Hoover, he gave it a prominent place on his office wall. By Monday, the cleared out first floor of 237 Cherry had lost all its former charm as a gambler's paradise.

Mayor Kubacki declared he was surprised by the size of the game and number of FBI men employed in the raid. He said that early in his administration while following up on complaints, his police had visited the building housing the casino but found no dice tables or any other signs of gambling equipment. Fred Brubaker said he had received tips from businessmen and residents in the Cherry Street area some weeks before the raid. He claimed only an agency, such as the FBI, could employ a force large enough to stage such a raid. The FBI had provided neither the city police department nor the district attorney's office any advance notice of the raid.

Taking a page out of Allentown's ordinance ledger, Kubacki talked about proposing a local law requiring all visitors with police records to register at City Hall while staying in Reading. That might have kept quite a squad of registrars busy in his city. The proposal was soon forgotten.

Tom McBride immediately assembled the grand jury in Philadelphia to begin questioning witnesses three days after the raid. The panel met, off and on, for the next two months, a steady parade of Philadelphia's who's who in gambling circles marching in and out of the jury room. The hearings ended on April 25 with John Kubacki and Fred Brubaker as the last two witnesses called. Charlie Wade was also among the more than 140 witnesses questioned.

Since the beginning of 1956, the craps game at two locations had enjoyed almost uninterrupted success. Millions of dollars had changed hands, most of it ending up in the pockets of the Mafia, some of it sticking to the politicians who allowed it to remain in business. Now it was up to the IRS to figure out the amount of unpaid taxes the racketeers owed.

The big dice game was soon moved to Philadelphia by the same group that had controlled the action in Reading. Almost to the day, three months after the FBI raid in Reading, a South Philly game was broken up by that city's police. Of the 42 arrested on gambling charges, 18 had also been apprehended in the Reading raid. Owner of the residence where the Quaker City game was operating was Eugene Curzio, 59, one of the 17 Philadelphia defendants awaiting trial since the January bust.

# 27

# *Trouble at the top, chief surprises mayor*

The Franklin Athletic Club sponsored a football team in the Greater Reading Football Conference. Smash-mouth football was the brand of sandlot fare offered in the fall on Sunday afternoons in the post-World War II era. Located in the 300 block of Cherry Street, the Franklin AC was also a hangout for some of the local racketeers. Abe Minker occasionally dropped in to scout recruits for his various illicit activities. It was after one of those Sunday afternoon battles that the Franklin players were celebrating a victory when Leroy Zweizig, the team's tall, rawboned center, was summoned to a backroom by Minker. Abe made an offer that Leroy found hard to refuse. He was making $30 a week lugging furniture on a truck. Abe said he could double that if the ex-sailor would come work for him as a pickup man in his numbers racket. Zweizig was fearless on a football field, but there was one person whose wrath terrified him: his mother. No, he told Abe, if he got in trouble with the police his mom would kill him. The fear was really love—he respected her too much to cause her that kind of shame.

So Minker continued to look around. Francis "Fat" Pepe, the league's dirtiest player, was another power on the Franklin AC line. He was available, but Abe didn't trust this short, heavy bruiser to handle his money. Then he spotted Joe Fiorini, a young, good-looking gambler who showed potential for what Abe was looking for. He was hired. Joe eventually gained the notoriety Leroy chose to avoid. He began to be noticed in 1957 when he was arrested that December in a state police raid of a city numbers bank. Joe served his time on that conviction but didn't cut his mob ties. By 1962, Fiorini had moved up in the Minker stable and eventually became Abe's patsy when somebody had to take the fall to protect the boss.

The antithesis of Fiorini was Bill Lilley, the city's one-man vice squad who had become the scourge of prostitutes. But he was always on the lookout for other violators as well. As the FBI was preparing to raid the Cherry Street Casino, Lilley was running a solo investigation of a numbers bank at 872 North 8th Street. That's where Joe Fiorini had a poolroom and a card room on the first floor, his apartment on the second floor, a numbers bank in the basement, and a third-floor room where the numbers money was counted.

After the Cherry Street bust, John Kubacki knew he had to at least make a show of cracking down on the rackets. What the mayor did not know was that his police chief was already planning to put on a show of his own. A secret never revealed: did Charlie act on his own or did Minker give him the okay to stage a raid. Events of the week following the FBI extravaganza certainly left the impression that such a plot might have been developed.

On August 24, 1961, Joe Fiorini had become the first Berks County gambler to be issued a $50 federal occupation wagering tax stamp. The Junction Billiard Parlor on the first floor of his 8th Street house was a front for the lottery bank he was operating at that location. He claimed he needed a stamp in case any of the pool players wanted to make small wagers. The stamp meant Joe was responsible for paying a 10 percent tax on any gambling that took place on the premises. He posted the stamp in the first-floor room dominated by a large card table. The real action, however, was not on the first floor. Several pickup men who visited Joe's place every day, dropped off their bundles at the basement numbers bank—that's where Joe's tax obligation was being accumulated.

In December 1961, the IRS had announced it was auditing Fiorini's monthly tax returns, sending a strong hint the agency believed Joe was not declaring all of his gambling income. Fiorini's big enterprise was the numbers game Mike MacDougall, the gambling expert, had mentioned earlier that month when he addressed the Berks County Medical Society shortly before the FBI raid on the Cherry Street dice game.

Following that dice raid, reporters received four days of "no comment" from Mayor Kubacki. Then on January 24 he called in City Hall newsmen to listen as he lectured the officers of his police force. It was a stirring address/pep talk/sermon to 21 sergeants, lieutenants, captains, and Chief Wade. He issued a 30-minute ultimatum to the department leaders that they must do a better job of curtailing all forms of vice in the city of Reading—or else!

"I want each and every one of you to hear what I have to say, and to remember it," Kubacki stated in the most no-nonsense speech of his years as mayor, "because I hope it's the only time I have to say it."

Like a coach delivering a half-time rallying cry, there was none of his usual flippancy or clever analogies to make his point. It was straight from the shoulder as he decreed an all-out campaign to rid the city of every type of gambling, close down every house of prostitution and street pandering, draw the curtain on lewd shows, and wipe out pornography. And don't forget punchboards, he reminded. He also included a ban on bingo, excluding games run by charitable organizations. A fundamentalist minister could not have made a more inclusive case against evil than Big John did that afternoon.

"I need your help," he implored his officers, "but we need the help of the people. If the people aren't in back of us, I don't see how you or I or we can do this job alone." He suggested the Reading Ministerial Association name a committee to sit down with police officials and "say what we can do to help you put this program across."

Inwardly, Charlie Wade was smiling—if only John knew how soon his orders were going to be carried out. This was a Wednesday and there was about as much validity to Kubacki's declaration of war against vice as there was in Danny McDevitt's 1956 heralded attack on multicoin pinball machines.

On Thursday, a dozen witnesses, most of them from New Jersey, were called before the federal grand jury as the government already was preparing its case to break up the interstate gambling syndicate that ran the Cherry Street dice game. That same day, Wade launched Kubacki's anti-vice drive by checking out four suspected poker parlors. Police found two of them had $250 federal gambling stamps but no gamblers. Two others without stamps, ditto.

The next day, Friday, Bill Lilley would make the mayor look very good, and very angry. For the past two weeks the detective had been tailing pickup men as they made numerous stops before heading back to Fiorini's house to drop off the daily numbers take.

Wade selected detectives Anthony O'Reilly, Walter Romanski, Walter Nawoczenski, Leon Zerkowski, and Michael DeMarco to join Lilley and himself in a raiding party. Until now a one-man investigation, Chief Wade, with Lilley's input, hurriedly arranged to close down the bank. Unlike the large squadron of ATU raiders used in the 1959 numbers raid, the much smaller police team managed to come up with equally strong evidence at the crime scene.

Nawoczenski made the first arrests. The detective began tailing Richard Hock and Paul "Tucson" Lavigna as they picked up packs of numbers from various writers in center city. Then he followed them out to Glenside in the northwest for more pickups, then back into town. On Windsor Street between 4th and 5th, Nawoczenski pulled the suspects over at gunpoint. Hock tossed a bagful of slips out of the car, but the pair of 33-year-olds offered no resistance and was hauled off to City Hall.

O'Reilly and Lilley, stationed near the pool hall during early afternoon, observed eight pickup men delivering bags or packages to the house. The detectives were joined by Chief Wade, DeMarco, and Zerkowski about 2:50 p.m. When they entered Fiorini's house, five teenagers were playing in the billiard parlor. As Wade read the search warrant to the surprised youths, Fiorini entered through an outside door and stood beside him. Charlie, acting as if this was the first time he ever saw Joe, asked, "Who are you?" Zerkowski identified the stranger for his boss. The ruse certainly did not fool his fellow cops, but Charlie reread the warrant for Fiorini's pleasure. The fact that Joe was not in the house when the raiders entered became an arguing point in the extended legal process that followed.

Meanwhile, Nawoczenski arrived at 872 and joined the search. With DeMarco, he located a locked door in the basement. Bashing it in, they found a paneled room serving as a numbers bank. All the familiar paraphernalia was there: adding machines, that day's numbers slips, a numberless phone, and many slips from previous days. But no suspects. Leading from the room were other doors, one to a stairway that took them up to Fiorini's apartment. While poking around in a clothes closet, Nawoczenski tugged on a hanger and ala kazaam, a magnetically controlled door that blended with the closet walls was unlocked. Beyond the door were more doors, one leading to another closet, then up a few steps and finally a door opening into the bank's money counting room. Cash from horse bets and records of the illegal operation were found. A thorough search of the place brought forth a few more adding machines and about $2,000 in cash stashed in a drawer under the kitchen sink. The raiders carried off several cartons of adding machine tapes and other records, evidence of how this numbers operation compared with the previous Minker banks knocked off in 1959 and 1960.

Police marveled at the plush furnishings in Joe's apartment. A huge television set dominated the richly appointed living room. Statuettes, deep-pile carpeting, sectional furniture, wall carpeting, and late-model kitchen appliances were all of the best quality. It was obvious Joe was doing pretty good. The investigators estimated his furnishings and appliances cost between $20,000 to $25,000. His style of living was definitely well above what most of his fellow gamblers could afford. A 12-gauge shotgun and a loaded revolver provided a bit of racketeer-modern to the décor. Joe also maintained a residence in the Brookline Manor Apartments, which was also searched.

While the raid was in progress, 29-year-old William "Chicken" Shearer walked in. Lilley recognized him as one of the pickup men he had been tailing.

Chicken was taken to City Hall where he provided the information that his car was parked near the numbers bank. In the unlocked car, police found about $500 in numbers bets under the passenger seat. Other pickup men seen earlier dropping off betting slips were not arrested.

Fiorini's $50 gambling occupation stamp, the only one in the city, was displayed on the wall. At one point as a news photographer took Joe's picture, he angrily grabbed the stamp from the wall. Later he turned it over to Wade.

"Aren't you going to handcuff me, Charlie?" Joe asked.

"No," was the chief's sharp reply as he led his suspect out to a waiting police car.

If a fly on the line was listening when Minker called Charlie Wade a few hours after the raid, it might have heard Abe telling the chief, "No, Charlie, not at the market; we'll come to your house in the morning," because that's where they hashed things out the next day.

With Johnny Wittig chauffeuring, Minker arrived at Charlie's Cumru Township home Saturday morning. The previous night, Fiorini, Lavigna, Hock, and Shearer were bailed out, with Joe immediately getting in touch with Abe to assess the damage. Joe told his boss that adding machine tapes confiscated by the police from the third-floor room could be troublesome if the feds found out how well the bank was doing. With daily totals listed on the tapes, the IRS could figure out how much Fiorini had dodged in unpaid taxes. And now Minker was telling Charlie to stay in touch. Charlie assured Abe he would cooperate.

Later that day, Fiorini joined Minker and Wittig for a meeting in Baer Park near the Schuylkill Avenue Bridge. When Charlie Wade arrived, Abe told him there was considerable evidence the police had grabbed that he wanted returned to its rightful owner, the bank's manager, Fiorini. Charlie said he would do what he could. He went to City Hall to collect certain cartons of papers for his colleagues' inspection. On Charlie's return to the park, Wittig and Fiorini rifled through the boxes to withdraw whatever they deemed damaging. Charlie returned most of the safe stuff to City Hall, but also took numerous worrisome tapes and papers back to his residence and stored them in cookie jars. That weekend caper remained the quartet's little secret for a year and a half.

Although everybody suspected Minker was financing the bank, the quickie arrests prevented Wade and his understaffed team from collecting any evidence linking Fiorini to Abe. However, Charlie was certainly prepared when it was time to deal with the press after the raid. He issued a lengthy written statement which promised the good citizens of Reading his police force was now in attack mode. Entering the third year as chief, this was his department's first major numbers raid. Wade vowed to launch a permanent crusade against all violators of the law "even if it costs me my life." According to his detailed and passionate decree, "I solemnly promise that Reading will be not only white, but shining white, when I get through cleaning up this city and as long as I remain chief of police. I also want to emphasize the phrase, as long as I am chief of police, and can run my police department.

"I promise my immediate superior, Mayor Kubacki, he will not have to take personal reign (sic) of the police department regarding gambling, vice or other corruption because I will carry out every order he requested at Wednesday's meeting of all superior officers, and will personally stand responsible for the men under my command to achieve this goal."

Reading between the lines and in retrospect, this statement of Wade's was an extension to his simmering alienation with the mayor. The chief resented sharing the blame with Kubacki about the city's lax attitude on vice. However, when he agreed to pay for his job, Charlie had crossed the line. He was in the impossible position of wanting to improve the police department, yet knowing he had committed to the racketeers. So he had to go along with Minker, and get along with the mayor if he wanted to retain his job. It appears Charlie decided to strike while the mayor's very public and fiery announcement to his officers was still fresh in the public mind. He evidently felt Kubacki could not fire him for following such well defined orders.

A year earlier Wade had won a dispute with the mayor about an independent prostitute, Angie Martin Wilkerson, whom Charlie advised not to pay Kubacki $75 a week to stay in business. Charlie came out of that flap on top, and possibly from then on he tried to improve his image by periodically standing up to the mayor on issues that rubbed his boss the wrong way. When Charlie defied the mayor by staging the Fiorini raid, he certainly was not helping Abe's business. But in the nefarious rackets culture, it was not easy to understand the twisted motivation behind certain actions that defy common sense.

Wade was on good terms with Minker whom he usually conferred with in the White House Market on Saturday mornings. The mayor's greed was often the focus of their conversations. Kubacki wanted a piece of every rackets enterprise in town, Abe would complain. The chief's statement to the press had been larded with intimations that he, not his boss, made the decision to raid the numbers bank. And this was just the beginning of his personal crusade against the mob. But would Charlie go against Minker's wishes just to assert himself as a gangbuster, at the same time making points for the mayor? Or was Minker calling the shots to take the heat off City Hall for the time being?

The day before the Fiorini raid, Abe Minker's wife and daughter had appeared at a federal grand jury hearing. This was a follow-up on depositions they had given the previous summer and fall. Abe seethed that Verna and Dona had to undergo more questioning to help the government unravel the financial puzzle he had created. He did receive a little good news in Philadelphia that day when a federal judge gave him the OK to travel in six states, but ruled he could not leave the continental United States. Abe was free on bail while appealing his income tax evasion conviction.

The mayor's ban on bingo—except for charity—lasted four days.

The city's bingo bloc let John know it did not want the low-rent gamblers' pet pastime included on his hit list. After a weekend barrage of phone calls, the mayor announced the people had spoken. So he met with the bingo operators. Assuring the public the bingo operators had no ties to organized crime, he rescinded the ban. Insiders suggested the operators opened their wallets a bit to get the taboo lifted.

Fred Brubaker got into the act by announcing there would be a ban on Sunday bingo. A short time later the Times ran a story that a bingo parlor in Laureldale was open Sundays the past three weeks. The next Sabbath it was closed.

All this local wrangling did not escape politicians and law enforcement officials at the state level. Pennsylvania Republican Party Chairman George Bloom tried to win some points by criticizing the state police hierarchy. He wanted to know why the FBI had not asked Col. Frank McCartney for assistance in the Cherry Street raid. Did J. Edgar Hoover not trust them? Was he worried about a leak to the mob if the state police were included in the planning? Should McCartney resign if he could not be trusted? Gov. David Lawrence fired back, declaring full confidence in his troopers and their leader who were always willing to cooperate with federal agencies. He also leveled a lukewarm condemnation at the Democratic administration in Reading. The federal raid, he said, "is a reflection on the local law enforcement officers." The governor did not question the FBI's failure to notify the state before the raid. Fred Frohbose, the FBI special agent who led the raid, was quick to come to McCartney's defense, too:

"We handle many cases where we have jurisdiction with help from the state police. We had the manpower and the equipment to handle the job. If we needed help from the state police, we certainly would have asked for it."

Although McCartney laughed off Bloom's suggestion that he should be fired or resign, the big FBI raid apparently jarred Harrisburg into once again looking closer at Reading's dismal rackets situation. In 1959 the state police had built a solid case against Abe Minker and his closest aides, only to have it collapse because Reading's top racketeer bribed the slot machine racketeers not to testify against him. Asst. Atty. Gen. Victor Wright, who prosecuted the case, tore into the citizenry of Reading for electing officials who allowed the rackets to operate so openly.

In the summer of 1961, Col. McCartney had sent a couple of his top men to Reading to discuss the gambling situation right after the A Community Cancer series appeared in the local dailies. Mayor Kubacki's response to the articles was that he was helpless in wiping out illegal gambling since the people of Reading and Berks County were such staunch supporters of the various forms of wagering. He refused to ban merchandise bingo and said he would not embarrass such organizations as Reading Hospital, with its annual lawn party, and fire companies or other charitable organizations holding carnivals that traditionally raised money by offering games and wheels of chance. The state police commander's emissaries returned to Harrisburg with promises from Dist. Atty. Brubaker, Mayor Kubacki, and Police Chief Wade that they would certainly cooperate with the state police in removing the cancer.

At the same time the U.S. government was stepping up its interest in organized crime. Col. McCartney claimed to have formulated a plan to root out the big moneymakers in the gambling racket. Although there were several local known gamblers called before the federal grand jury in August 1961, there was no noticeable increase in vice arrests that year. Then the major FBI raid on the Cherry Street craps game, followed a week later by the city police raid on Joe Fiorini's numbers bank, sent another message to Harrisburg that gambling in Reading was still running rampant.

This time Col. McCartney didn't bother conferring with local law enforcement. By the summer of 1962, Capt. Rocco Urella had been transferred from the Philadelphia area to take command of Troop C in Reading. Urella proved to be a hands-on guy who immediately organized a new unit to follow up on every gambling tip it received.

# 28

## *Chief allows vice cop to do his job*

At their trial in June, Joe Fiorini was found guilty of operating a numbers bank, while Dick Hock and Tucson Lavigna were convicted of selling numbers. Chicken Shearer was tried separately and, although two charges against him were dismissed by Judge Albert Readinger, he was found guilty of unlawfully being concerned with a lottery. Judge Hess handed Fiorini a 4-to-12 month jail sentence and a $500 fine. Hock was sentenced to a 20-day-to-1-year prison term and fined $300. Later, Hess dismissed charges against Lavigna for insufficient evidence. Schearer and Fiorini both appealed for new trials. It was a losing battle, and in 1963 both served their time. Shearer's sentence was 20 days to 12 months in BCP and a $500 fine. In its written report to the court, the 1962 Berks grand jury said it hoped the recent raids were just the beginning of a general cleanup.

During Fiorini's trial, Asst. Dist. Atty. John Marx put in a plug for the city's vice detective, Bill Lilley. He praised Lilley's surveillance of the numbers racketeers that led to the raid at Fiorini's house. Marx would soon become a central figure in further local actions against Minker's fading empire. He would provide the district attorney's office with some good publicity for a change.

Judge Hess also praised Lilley when the gamblers' attorney questioned the detective's qualifications because he was testifying in Berks County court for the first time. The judge quickly pointed out, "In the last few years it's been difficult to get court experience. There is not much chance for a city patrolman to come in and get experience." This was the judge's little jab at the district attorney whom he had locked horns with on previous occasions. Practically all of the vice cases for the past few years were settled in police court or at the alderman level: small fines and no jail time. On the witness stand, Lilley handled himself like the professional he had become in making dozens of arrests.

By the time Capt. Rocco Urella arrived as the new Troop C commander, there was a noticeable change in the makeup of the numbers hierarchy. Veteran writers who operated independently during the early to mid 1950s, had been bullied into paying Minker to stay in business during the next six years. They were now moving up to fill the vacuum created by three major busts in the last three years. The pearly gray boys were back. Only this time, the state police were paying a lot more attention to them. Without the burden of chipping in with ice to the boss, their profits were soaring. And there was no shortage of entrepreneurs willing to take the risk.

The transition was gradual and Abe's final numbers bank probably was located very close to a familiar address of recent notoriety. The fact that Sam Matz would start up a numbers bank next door to Joe Fiorini's house probably was more than coincidence. Bill Lilley thought so when he started noticing Matz's car regularly parked in the 800 block of North 8th Street. The detective began tailing the familiar numbers writer and, sure enough, there was Sam making daily pickups all over the city. But instead of returning to Fiorini's house, Sam had a key to the house next door at 870. No hole in the wall was ever found, but it's quite possible the money made its way to Joe's counting room. And at the end of the day it would be a good bet that Abe Minker was counting it again. The police were unable to link the three, but by the size of the operation, it's unlikely Sam Matz was getting all the gravy.

On September 8, 1962, Rocco Urella and his boys were waiting when Matz completed his rounds. With warrants they followed Sam into 870 where they relieved him of $400 in cash, found loads of betting slips, a couple of telephones, and other incriminating evidence. When the phones kept ringing, Sgt. Leroy Lilly took 30 bets from horseplayers. What it all totaled up to was an estimate that Matz, and whomever he was fronting for, was running a $150,000 a year business for the past six months. Bill Lilley, who assisted in the raid with John Beemer, Don Holloway, and Sgt. Lilly, had Matz under surveillance for six weeks, spotting 14 hand bookies who turned bets over to the pickup man.

Other veteran numbers writers were picked off in rapid order in the next few weeks. Beemer and Trooper Arthur McAnally nabbed Earl Groff on Court Street a short distance from the Courthouse. Groff, about half the size of Beemer, had thoughts of escaping as he threw his car in reverse gear, narrowly missing the state cop. A second look at the giant sergeant, and Groff meekly surrendered. Incriminating betting slips put him in the cooler.

A few days later Beemer teamed with Trooper John McCann to nail the owner of Tony Julian's Billiard Parlor on Franklin Street. Julian, 55, and Groff, 53, were seasoned racketeers as were most in the numbers game. It was their livelihood. The prosperous ones evinced a certain degree of honesty, and understood customer service. The penny players lauded the likes of Bill Kozier in the 4th and

Spruce area. Loyalty to his customers was repaid a thousandfold. It was Kozier who became a neighborhood folk hero with his ever-extending Christmas displays in his southeast Reading home. In retirement, when the family moved to Bern Township, his outdoor decorations grew and grew until they evolved into Christmas Village, one of the county's favorite holiday tourist sites. Not all numbers profits were so wisely saved and put to good use.

In October at a Junior Chamber of Commerce meeting, Capt. Urella announced that he had received orders from Harrisburg to continue his campaign against the sudden growth of independent numbers banks that kept popping up. "Right now I have a free hand to investigate vice in three counties, Berks, Schuylkill, and Lebanon," said Urella. With Lilley, Beemer, Holloway, and McAnally doing the legwork, next on the hit list was the 9th Ward Social Club at 927 Buttonwood Street. Spencer Wertz, forced to join the Minker ranks in recent years, was now back in business with his own team of writers and pickup men. On November 17, Urella's crew raided the club. In addition to the boss, also arrested were James Madara, a resident at the club and a pickup man; James Gehris, the club bartender; George Wert, a writer and bookie; George Stoyer, also a writer, and Hannah Friedman, nabbed at the next door grocery where she not only sold stamps for the post office, but also numbers slips for Spencer Wertz. All six were veterans of the numbers game, their ages ranging from Gehris at 47 to Hannah's 61.

Holloway, who by now was usually appointed prosecutor when these cases came to court, said the bank was taking in $800 to $1,000 a day. Gehris admitted horse bets were averaging $400 daily for the past three weeks. On the second floor of the club, several dusty slot machines were seized, and numerous punchboards were found in the bar. The place did have a $250 federal gambling stamp, but that didn't mean anything to the staties who charged the six with violations of state gambling laws.

Judge Wils Austin observed at a later court session that racketeers were less specialized than before: "You know it used to be a man was either a numbers writer or a bookie. Here of late they seem to be doing both."

All six defendants in the 9th Ward bust were convicted on gambling charges in 1963. Wertz served a month in jail and got a year's probation which wasn't a very tough penalty for the amount of money he had been illegally raking in. While he was in BCP he was allowed to pursue his hobby, painting. He was given a cell with a good view of the warden's house, which became his subject.

It is quite likely that his family kept the business going while he served his second prison term. This was a possibility because the state police knocked off

Wertz and company again the following year. This time they found evidence that the numbers bank was far more lucrative than it was 20 months earlier.

Nobody answered the door at 440 Moss Street when a policewoman knocked on July 20, 1964. John Beemer asked his cohort to step aside while he smashed his way in. This was the Wertz family home, and the sergeant's first observation was a woman heading for the back door. The lumbering Beemer took chase after the barefooted Dorothy Wertz, the gambler's 40-year-old wife. It appears she was seeking refuge in the familiar confines of the 9th Ward Social Club only a block away. But she stumbled at the intersection of 9th and Buttonwood, where Beemer caught her just short of her goal. Back at the house, other police found 20-year-old Spencer Jr. huddled in a converted coal bin in the basement. Lots of signs of a numbers operation were scattered about the house. Forty slot machines were found in a nailed-tight basement closet.

Dorothy's husband was not at home when Beemer performed his power entry because Spencer didn't live there anymore. He and Dorothy had split romantically but their business relationship remained fairly amicable. Spence was bedding down in dumpy quarters at the club. The cops soon picked him up and hauled him off to BCP as a parole violator. He was nicked just 14 days before his probation period ended.

When the state police inventory was completed, Cpl. Holloway estimated the Wertz enterprise was pulling in between $600,000 and $800,000 in the year or more it had been in place. If Spencer was associated with a layoff bank, it was not revealed. Holloway said the 9th Ward Social Club was being watched for several months. He noted the bank was active six days a week, frequently changing locations.

The arrest list included Wertz, his wife, his son, and George Wert, who was tending bar the day of the bust. Matters darkened for Wertz when it was learned his daughter and a niece, both 11, had been observed delivering numbers and horse slips and money from the club to the Moss Street house.

Then, adding to this all-in-the-family drama was Spencer's mother-in-law resting in a chair outside 923 Buttonwood where she lived. With a front row seat for all the commotion outside the club on the day of the raid, 66-year-old Florence Czarnecki soon got into it with A.D.A. Leon Miller, who appeared on the scene. Florence had been arrested the previous February for allowing a numbers writer to call in bets from her second-floor apartment. She admitted receiving a discount on her daily $8 wager whenever the unidentified writer came to collect. That perk was for letting him use the phone. The ample Mrs. Czarnecki operated a penny bingo game in a 10$^{th}$ and Walnut storefront. Her gripe with Miller was about her confiscated phone. When was it going to be returned?

A couple of other trends in the numbers racket were noted as the independents continued to defy gambling laws. Numerous women were involved, some young, some quite elderly. When Richard Peterson and his wife, Grace, were arrested for selling lottery tickets, he was sentenced to a year's probation and charges against her were dismissed. Six months later their 17-year-old daughter, Christine, was caught up in the same vice trap. Police regarded her as boss of a small numbers setup that included her 27-year-old half sister. The 60-year-old father told his pregnant teenage daughter, "Now behave yourself," as she was taken away to the Youth Study Center. Judge Hess said it was the first time in the past 25 years somebody that young was connected with the numbers racket.

At the other end of the age spectrum, 80-year-old Laura Bayard was charged with serving 14 players alcoholic beverages during a poker game in her Cherry Street home. Within a few days of Mrs. Czarnecki's arrest in 1964, George Otto, 72, and Robert Clinton, 70, were also charged with peddling numbers. Septuagenarians of the '60s, like those four decades later, had no qualms about gambling. But the whitehairs of the 2000s didn't have to be worried about getting arrested.

Spencer Wertz was relatively pleased when he was returned to his former jail cell where he had a good view of the warden's house. When his brush and oils arrived, he again exercised his artistic talents. That's what he was doing in 1965 when Rod MacLeish arrived for an on-camera interview for the film documentary "The Corrupt City." Spencer told about the prosperous years during the pearly gray administration, and the big financial loss the numbers writers suffered when Abe Minker forced them to pay public relation fees to stay in business. Not only were the gamblers threatened with physical harm if they didn't pay, Wertz claimed, some of their customers were also threatened.

"What I'm in for isn't for stealing or anything. What I'm in for will be legal someday, anyhow … numbers writing." Talking about the big change after Minker took control, Spencer continued, "The new crowd wanted everything. They took what the little guy had and kept it for themselves. They made the little guy work for nothing. You write for us or you ain't gonna write. So that's all there was to it."

The numbers racket never lost is appeal in Reading, even long after the Pennsylvania lottery started in 1978. The local writers gave slightly better odds than the state did, and if a player managed to hit for a large amount, no tax collector was looking over his shoulder asking for a cut of the prize.

When the drug culture gained prominence in the 1970s, law enforcement began directing most of its attention on dealers and pushers. The ensuing violence that soon accompanied the sale of illegal drugs pushed gambling well down on the vice charts. However, illegal sports betting remained quite popular.

# 29

# *Few big losers among Runyonesque mobsters*

The Cherry Street dice case investigation spread over a broad area as the government wanted to show that gamblers from several states were being transported into Pennsylvania. Special organized crime prosecutor Tom McBride had plenty of evidence that out-of-state people had a financial interest in the game, and patrons were being offered long distance transportation to the gambling site.

Ownership of the property at 237 Cherry was something of a tough nut for the investigators to crack. Documented sales agreements provided seven possibilities: Izzy Minker, Santo Damiano, Alphonso "Fonzie" Comito, Ralph Blankenbiller, Joseph A. DiGiacomo, attorney John Ruth, and his secretary Joyce Bergman, all Berks countians. Also considered was James Amato, charged, but not convicted, in a 1938 four-man gangland slaying in Schuylkill County. The government settled on Comito as the owner since 1960, with Blankenbiller holding the mortgage. Having resolved that matter, the 45-year-old Fonzie was among the last of the 15 suspects indicted by the federal grand jury. He was the only defendant charged with conspiracy. Charges against the rest were overt acts in aiding and abetting a gambling operation. The only other local defendant was Benny "Big Ben" Bonanno, who was regarded as Skinny Barrett's first assistant.

The Runyonesque sobriquets of the other 12 headed for trial were right out of central casting:

Pasquale "Husky" Pillo—supervisor, shuffler, ladderman, loan shark, lugger
Dominick "Poppy" DiCaprio—supervisor, ladderman
Querino "Quide" or "Weed" Dentino—lugger
Fred "Whispers" or "Flivvie the Fish" DePatrizio—ladderman, lugger
James "Lefty" Gatto—guard
Rocco "Snorky" Grassi—dealer, lugger
Charles "Chick" Hunt—dealer, lugger

Anthony "Skidley" LaMonica—lugger
Frank LoScalzo—doorman
John Marzilli—dealer, lugger
Joseph "Gassy" Mattia—ladderman, lugger
Michael "Mike" Recchia—dealer, lugger

Among the 41 unindicted coconspirators were 11 from the Reading area who were employees in the casino: Michael L. Augustine, his son Michael R. Augustine, Dominic Consentino, James Corriere, Harry Leonti, Samuel "Schoze" Lombardo, John "Brick" Mainwaring, Dominic Mascheri, Michael Natello, Leon Odagis, and Charles Polasky.

The grand jury investigation lasted more than three months. About 140 witnesses were subpoenaed, including those arrested the night of the raid. Four of the dozens of gamblers held as material witnesses were charged with perjury for lying to the grand jury. But a year later the charges were dropped because the indictments "were fatally defective," according to Federal Judge C. William Kraft.

With 15 defendants and half as many defense lawyers, an agreement was reached with the court and prosecution to have Morton Witkin, a prominent Philadelphia criminal attorney, serve as the defense representative. At one of several pretrial hearings, Witkin's two main points of contention were the arrest warrants served at the time of the raid, and the manner of entry gained by the FBI.

In Witkin's 17-page brief he stated the initial entry was not valid because the FBI violated the law." Agent Dean had shouted, 'This is the FBI' and admitted that his announcement was made to no one in particular and he did not know if anyone could hear him or if anyone was inside the third door." The brief continued, "It was not until the agents were inside that the agent in charge announced through a portable loud speaker 'We are the FBI.' Under the law, before entry can be made, those inside the premises must be made aware of the raiders' intentions."

On a second point, Witkin claimed the FBI violated another section of the law that states a search warrant must be procured before the raid. In this case, the first agents to enter the building had not obtained a search warrant, although they did have numerous arrest warrants. One agent who had entered the building for a short time, returned to a waiting car where a U.S. commissioner issued him a search warrant on information the agent had obtained after he entered the building.

Summing up, Witkin's brief claimed that since the search warrant was not valid, all the evidence taken from the building was removed illegally. He also gave numerous reasons why the search and seizure laws the U.S. Congress had passed the previous year were unconstitutional.

A few months later, the trial judge, Joseph S. Lord 3rd, responded with a decision that was a considerable setback for the prosecution, but not exactly a victory for the defense. He ruled the FBI had acted illegally by entering without a search warrant, thereby making the seizure of all physical evidence invalid. However, he upheld the constitutionality of the new interstate gambling laws, and all 15 of the defendants had to stand trial.

Ruling on Fonzie Comito's petition for a separate trial, Judge Lord granted the request because of all the defendants, only Comito seemed to have no role in the operation of the casino. He was charged with conspiracy because his name was on the most recent sale agreement of the property.

When Judge Lord gaveled the court to order on September 11, 1963, all the principals expected the trial to last a month. Prosecutor McBride's first order of business was to sort out and identify the mostly middle-aged defendants. Since a few of the government witnesses knew many of the casino personnel only by their nicknames, McBride began mentioning "Husky" and "Skidley and "Whispers" until one of the defense attorneys, Louis Lipschitz, objected that such names cast a negative reflection on his client. The judge upheld his complaint, but witnesses would often use the epithets without any coaching from the prosecutors. Later in the trial, another of the material witnesses who had shot craps in the 10th and Walnut game, recalled the nicknames of luggers who had driven him and others from Camden. He knew them as "Big Ernie," "Snake," "Weed," and "Cabbage."

An early witness was Charles Wacks, a lawyer from Trenton who was a regular patron at the game. He was quite open as he described how the game was operated, and that he saw large amounts of money being wagered. But when he was asked to identify some of the hired help he balked. During grand jury sessions he had identified most of the defendants from pictures. Now in court, face to face with the defendants, he didn't recognize, or didn't know, any of the principals being tried. "Reluctant witness" and "hostile witness" was being bandied about by the opposing attorneys, and Judge Lord threatened Wacks with contempt if he didn't stop making speeches instead of answering questions. During his second day on the stand Wacks's memory was restored as he identified Benny Bonanno and others, recalling various duties he had seen them perform.

The hard looking group of defendants sometimes seemed surprised about how closely their movements had been watched by FBI agents who were called to the stand. Agent George E. Lee said over a period of six days of surveillance at the Cherry Street site he and another agent took motion pictures of gamblers arriving and leaving the premises. Near the end of the trial, the prosecution said it intended to present the 75-minute film featuring several of the defendants. Judge Lord, after a sidebar with the defense attorneys, excused the jury and had a private showing of the movie. The black and white 16mm film would not have won any photography Oscars. After the first reel, Judge Lord called a halt to the private showing.

"I've seen enough," he stated. "I say in all candor, they were faceless figures to me. The value is so small, it is far outweighed as admissible evidence. I will exclude them," and the curtain came down without the jury getting even a glimpse of that FBI bomb. Others who viewed it said Johnny Wittig was clearly pictured talking with the game's operators, but the night scenes were mostly indistinguishable.

The only other testimony that hinted Abe Minker was linked to the Cherry Street game came from Sigmund "Sig" Johnson, a Sinking Spring man who managed the lunch counter in the craps den. He said he saw a man transport money from the office to one of the tables before play began one night, but that man was not a defendant. When McBride told Johnson to identify the man, Johnson was reluctant to do so. Only when Judge Lord ordered him to give the name, the counterman said it was Louie Fudeman, Abe's nephew.

The defense rested its case without putting any of the 14 defendants on the witness stand. Instead, each of the seven defense attorneys made acquittal pleas to the judge. Sam Liever, who represented Benny Bonanno, sent a young associate, Robert L. Van Hoove, to plead for their client. By the end of the decade, Van Hoove would be elected Berks County district attorney. Reviewing the 14 days of testimony, Van Hoove claimed witnesses remembered Bonanno as only "walking around, sitting around, and taking no active participation of any kind."

He stated there was no evidence Bonanno handled money, hired or gave instructions to anybody. "It would be asking the jury to guess," Van Hoove claimed. "Mere association of a person cannot make a person a coconspirator." He told the judge Benny was not among those arrested in the casino, but turned himself in when he learned there was a warrant for his arrest.

G. Robert Blakey, another U.S. prosecutor, argued Bonanno was identified by several witnesses, sometimes as the doorman at the game, and that a witness had been asked by Benny to move his car with New Jersey plates from its parking spot under the Penn Street Bridge. "He was aware there was something tainted about New Jersey cars," Blakey stated. He pointed out that all the defendants were aware of the interstate aspect of the game because nightly announcements were made in the casino that cars would soon be leaving for Jersey. Blakey later became prominent as a Notre Dame professor who was an influential advocate of federal wire-tapping laws. In 1968, Blakey was chief counsel for the Special Subcommittee investigating the assassination of President John F. Kennedy.

Attorney Samuel Kenon made a successful acquittal plea by pointing out that no evidence was presented that his client, James "Lefty" Gatto, was employed at the casino. A vague reference in the bill of particulars before the trial that he was a guard, was the only mention of Gatto by the government. Judge Lord ruled that was not enough to find "Lefty" guilty. Charges against the Philadelphia man were dropped.

The case went to the jury on October 7, almost a month after the trial started. After a day and a half of deliberations, the jurors found all but Rocco Grassi guilty. "Snorky," who was a snorkeling enthusiast as a youth, was acquitted of the two charges against him. The other 12 were found guilty on a total of 136 counts, all involving violations of the 1961 interstate gambling laws. Bonanno was convicted on 22 of the 25 counts against him. Within a few days, all of the remaining defendants filed for acquittals or new trials. This list of those awaiting resolution of their cases was reduced to 11 when "Poppy" DiPatricio died a few months after his conviction.

The legal battle continued almost three more years. Charges were eventually dropped against Fonzie Comito because of the murky exchange of ownership of the casino building before the 1962 raid. In August of 1964, Judge Lord handed out three-year sentences to the casino bosses: Skinny Barrett, Benny Bonanno and Husky Pillo. Several weeks later he reduced their terms to two years. The jurist said his decision on sentencing had given him more concern than in any case he had tried. He added:

"If this case had taken place in Nevada it wouldn't even have been a crime."

Frank LoScalzo, a 75-year-old grandfather of seven, received three years of probation because of his age. Similar sentences were awarded John Marzilli, Mike Recchie, and Chick Hunt. Weed Dentino and Skidley LaMonica had their sentences reduced from one year in prison to four years probation. Whispers DiPatrizio and Gassie Mattia had six months knocked off their original one-year sentences.

As lenient as Judge Lord was, four of those originally convicted continued to appeal for dismissal of charges. Benny Bonanno was the first to win in the Third Circuit Court of Appeals when all charges were dismissed against him.

The other three, Barrett, Pillo, and Mattia appealed to the U.S. Supreme Court where their bids for a hearing were rejected.

# 30

## *Mention of "ice" has madam on slippery slope*

When William Scranton became governor in 1963, one of his first hirings was Col. E. Wilson Purdy from the Florida state police to be commissioner of the Pennsylvania state police. An early Purdy announcement was that there was no reason Troop C should suspend its current campaign against the rackets in Berks County. With that authorization, Capt. Rocco Urella felt he could continue to operate with a free hand. It wasn't long before the state police headquarters in Harrisburg was calling on Troop C in Reading to help break up an international lottery syndicate.

A tip was received that a multimillion-dollar lottery enterprise was being operated out of the capital city by Murray Baker, son of the late Lou Cohen, who was considered among the elite in national lottery ranks. Berks County became involved when it was learned lottery tickets were being processed in a trailer home in Cumru Township. Dual raids were scheduled for January 8 of the new year, but the prime target at the Reading end, Lewis Krall, failed to show up at his trailer that afternoon. He had been seen frequenting the home of his Mount Penn girlfriend during the two weeks Troop C personnel were watching him. While Murray Baker of Miami, Fla., and Victor Gates of nearby Camp Hill were being arrested in Harrisburg, Lt. Adrian McCarr, in charge of the Berks team, had to report Krall was not at any of his usual haunts. Lew finally visited his lady friend at her 27th Street home at 8:45 p.m. and was nabbed. A squad from Troop C then searched Krall's trailer just off the Morgantown Road, a few hundred yards south of Reading. It was found to contain a numbering machine, a cutter, folder, and stapling machine. Also seized were 30 steel bands, enough to make staples for an 18-month supply of tickets, coded printing plates, and 13 bundles each with 1,000 large sheets of glossy paper. The tickets, priced at $2 or $3, had the potential value of $5 million when sold.

Next to the Irish Sweepstakes, this was to be the second largest lottery in the country, stated Capt. W. Jess Stanton, overall leader of the investigation. Ten cartons, each containing 10,000 lottery tickets, were found in the Mount Penn residence, and another million were found at the racketeers' central Harrisburg office where the 38-year-old Baker was arrested. The state police were satisfied that Krall's girlfriend had no knowledge of the operation, so she was not charged. The gambling operation included a postal box in Haiti where the proceeds from the lottery were picked up by another member of Baker's syndicate.

The $2 tickets were for a $75,000 prize in each of three different lotteries. At the time of the raids none of the three had paid anything to ticket holders. Code names of the three lotteries were "New Mercury," "POA," and "FASA" (Free American Sweepstakes Assn.). This type of ticket was used as a sales promotion gimmick throughout the country. Other phony lottery tickets seized at the Harrisburg office were for the 1963 Kentucky Derby to be sold in Haiti. It was a big league scam with no winners—except the racketeers.

A week later, Clarence Samuel Lewis and Dorothy M. Helfrich, were arrested at their 110 North 4th Street location of Helfrich Printing Co. Sgt. Lilly said the pair printed tickets for Krall which were then numbered and stapled in his trailer. This type of lottery activity was not uncommon in Berks County. Over the years other sports lottery tickets were made by local printers and distributed far and wide.

A year to the day and hour after the big FBI raid at the Cherry Street casino in 1962, Capt. Urella led what might be regarded as an anniversary bust at a Washington Street house where a long-running poker game was in progress. The familiar name of Bonanno was linked to this action. Tony Bonanno owned the property and his brother Sam was suspected of being a partner in the game.

To gain entrance to the property at 148 Washington Street was partially a second-story job. The usual raiders had cased the joint and through informants knew about the alarm system and the heavy metal door at the foot of stairs to the second floor. Trooper Richard Rafter was the point man. On this foggy, misty night he silently climbed an outside ladder to a second-floor bay window. Inside was a lookout—asleep on a sofa. That was 35-year-old Roger Green who woke up too late to press the buzzer beside him which activated flashing lights in the second-floor gaming rooms as a warning of trouble. Instead, the sound of broken glass brought Green to life as Rafter crashed through the window and raced past the guard to get the drop on the gamblers. At that same time, John Beemer broke through the front door. This was possibly the last of many doors he had punished doing his duty for Troop C. With him, in addition to Urella, were Lt. McCarr,

Sgt. Lilly, and troopers Holloway, McAnally, and McCann. They rushed through the first-floor pool room, opened a peep-hole door to the next room before it could be locked, and raced past the heavy metal door before it could be closed and sealed with a sturdy metal drop bar and slide bolt. Upstairs they joined Rafter who was facing down a dozen and one card players. Among them was 53-year-old Sam Magaro in one of the two poker rooms. He was charged with operating the game. Urella said Magaro admitted renting the property from Tony Bonanno, who was not there at the time of the raid.

A sign on the peephole door left little doubt about who was the boss:

House rules
Gin rummy, ten cents a game
Pay after every game
Sam Magaro, mgr.

Magaro said the Saturday night games usually started at 8 or 9 o'clock and ran till the next morning. He admitted making about $60 a week charging players 10 cents a game.

"We know definitely it ran from $30 to $40 a hand, and on Sunday it would run $100 a hand," Urella stated.

Nine card players were arrested as participants and paid $12 forfeits. In addition to Magaro, others charged as principals in the game were Green, Joe Federici, and Sam Bonanno. As owner of the property, Tony Bonanno was also charged.

One player would later testify at the group's preliminary hearing before Alderman Bill Hall a month later. Melvin Remp said he had been playing cards there for the past five years, indicating this was no new arrival on the poker and gin scene. Although he regarded all the principals as friends, Melvin said he was taught to tell the truth and refused to hide behind the 5th Amendment.

Remp testified poker was played that Saturday afternoon at a $1 limit and with $2 raises allowed. The pot ran as high as $20 to $30. He said Federici, Green, and Magaro cut the pot. Melvin said he saw Sam Bonanno playing, but not dealing.

With Sam Liever representing all four defendants, it was verified that Magaro rented the gaming rooms from Tony Bonanno at $65 a month. Liever tried to absolve Tony of any knowledge that Magaro was running card games, but Alderman Bill Hall believed testimony by Lt. McCarr that he was told by Magaro that Tony often visited the premises.

Hall dismissed the charges against Sam Bonanno because the police witnesses could not identify him as a dealer, as charged, but was just another player. When arrested, Sam had $423 in bills in one pocket and $328 in coins in another. Apparently he was the guy to see if you needed change.

Because the district attorney's office failed to send anybody to the preliminary hearing, Holloway and other state policemen had to play lawyer in representing themselves while presenting the state's case against the defendants.

At their trial in April 1964 all four were convicted. Only Magaro did not file an appeal for another trial. Magaro served the minimum of his 72 days on a 2-to 12 month prison term, and paid a $200 fine. The others stood trial again in February 1965. Nothing changed—guilty as charged. The sentence was a bit harsher this time for Tony Bonanno, 58, and Joe Federici, 29. Their jail time was 4 to 12 months, with $300 fines. "Sleepy" Green, however, got off with 3 to 12 months and a similar fine.

Encased in secrecy, the Philadelphia grand jury hearings were usually a source of rumors. At that same time in 1962, a public trial in Reading left observers and the court trying to interpret the testimony of an important witness. Veiled messages from a bawdyhouse madam seemed to support the persistent notion that she was allowed to remain in business because she paid protection money.

When Claudia Glenn came to trial, expectations were high that Times reporter Donald Barlett might offer some explosive testimony because he had announced he was going to take the witness stand. But it was Claudia who let slip an admission that she was paying "ice", thereby stirring the imagination of the presiding judge.

Claudia was the madam at 111 North 7th Street the night four men robbed her of $339 in May 1961. It was during the trial of the suspects that Judge Hess had ordered Glenn and Mable Jones arrested on charges of operating a house of prostitution. Now at her trial on March 13, 1962, Claudia felt she was being victimized by the politics that had grown out of the robbery case.

The trial itself was pretty much a bust. After nine witnesses had testified, including Barlett, Claudia decided to plead guilty. Judy Miller, the other defendant, was acquitted. Barlett had little to offer except to tell about viewing Claudia's house through binoculars for several nights and reporting in his Operation Vice Den series about the variety of men and women seen entering the place. He testified he had never been inside 111. There was no confrontation between Barlett and Brubaker or any surprise testimony by the reporter.

Before Glenn was sentenced, her lawyer, John Speicher, pleaded for a light jail term for his client. He pointed out that the quartet of young men convicted of robbery had received probation, not jail time. "The real offenders are not here, and others got away," he stated. Some, including the judge, believed he was referring to politicians and mob bosses involved in payoffs.

Fred Brubaker was trying this case, determined to show that he was not soft on vice defendants. To each Speicher plaint that Claudia should be left off easy, Fred proposed to Judge Ralph Body that the madam deserved the maximum penalty possible. It was after Glenn spoke of paying protection to keep her house open that Brubaker challenged her to name names. Enough of the insinuations and innuendo that had been hinted, he stated:

"If Claudia Glenn will give to this court, or to me as district attorney, any information she may have regarding these matters, whatever police officials, officers or anybody did for protection, we will ask to defer sentence. We would take a different position on her sentence if she has any information which will shed light on this situation."

Speicher said he would recommend that his client accept the offer. He huddled with the 42-year-old defendant, then relayed her answer to the court:

"Claudia says the data she has is not conclusive. She is an intelligent girl and knows what that means."

To an informed observer of Reading's tradition concerning protection money, Claudia was saying, I paid the middleman, and I know you want The Man but I won't drop names because I want to stay healthy and continue to work in Reading.

Judge Ralph Body offered a similar interpretation:

"I assume she has been paying money to somebody, but she knows not where it goes. It means it goes from one hand to another. From what she says, she has been paying."

And that's as close as it got to an admission that boodle was an operating cost nobody wanted to fully expose. Speicher dwelled on the laxity of the police in failing to bring the case to court in the initial arrest of the robbers, stating they were "fined and sent off to go back to the house again. Their offenses were virtually excused." He claimed Claudia would be a scapegoat if her sentence was any longer than the usual three months in prison. Even that was far more severe than the measly penalties the robbers had paid.

Brubaker would not relent:

"She should be dealt with severely," he insisted. "This is not a light matter. It not only enraged the resident judge, me, Mr. Cianci and members of my staff, it should serve notice here and now, we don't want such a thing; serve notice by handing out a severe sentence to the defendant to show others we do not want it in our community."

When imposing sentence, Judge Body stated, "Shhas been a sore to this community, making a part of 7th Street a Barbary Coast. There are others in the same business. I believe it's the only business she knows, her profession, but it will not be her business after Friday."

She received an 11-month minimum term and fined $300. Court observers said they could not remember a longer prostitution sentence in Berks County Court.

Gov. David Lawrence and U.S. Sen. Joseph Clark were sick and tired of the national spotlight being aimed at their Pennsylvania Democratic Party because of the crime circus that Reading had become. In statements to the press they said it was an embarrassment they wanted to end.

Also that spring of 1962, Brubaker was busy battling what he perceived to be a vendetta being waged against him by the IRS. Things came to a head when he was involved in a collision with a government car driven by T-man James J. Baldwin. Brubaker believed the feds were tailing him about 8:45 p.m. on April 16, so he pulled over to the curb at Hampden Boulevard and Union Street. Baldwin, with another agent, drove past Fred's bronze colored sedan. Fred said he began a high-speed pursuit of them, both drivers ignoring stop signs and traffic lights. The chase lasted for several blocks through the northeast section of the city. When the government car stopped at Albright's Kelchner Field, Fred pulled his car in front of the agents' vehicle. Fred claimed the other driver then rammed his sedan from behind. Brubaker's two daughters were with him. Baldwin then drove away, and Brubaker went to City Hall to prefer charges against the other driver: assault and battery by auto, and leaving the scene of an accident without identifying himself.

The following week while he was in Philadelphia after testifying before the federal grand jury, Fred got into a squabble with the U.S. attorney. Fred complained by phone that the previous afternoon his father had received a telephone call from a federal agent who wanted to come to his house to talk with him. The ailing Oliver Brubaker was taken to Fred's house by a relative before the agent arrived. Fred told U.S. Attorney Drew T. J. O'Keefe that the agent who called his father was in violation of the IRS Code, which stated all questioning had to be performed during business hours. He was informed there was no such restriction in the code. In retaliation, the government filed petitions to gain jurisdiction in the case involving Fred's traffic charges against Baldwin. Reading Alderman Edward Heffner and the city police court received notices to turn over all material to the U.S. attorney's office in the case. O'Keefe piled on some more by charging Fred with harassment of federal agents while doing their duty.

A few days after the chase, Fred's suspicions increased when he thought his home and office phones might have been tapped. Bell Telephone sent a technician to inspect the lines but he found nothing amiss.

The charges and countercharges never reached the trial stage. After a postponement in July and a few more hearings with considerable bluster about who was chasing whom, the case quietly faded away on December 12 when both sides agreed it was just one big misunderstanding. All the charges were withdrawn.

Another story that made the rumor circuit was that one of the government agencies had hidden a bug under a certain table in Morey's Deli in the Berkshire Hotel, where several of Reading's criminal lawyers ate lunch every day. If so, the feds probably savored a few morsels out of those conversations. A lot of people in the city on both sides of the law were looking over their shoulders in 1962 and 1963.

# 31

## *With D.A. away, A.D.A. plays gangbuster*

The spring of 1962 was not a pleasant time for Abe Minker and his crumbling gambling empire. Federal agencies continued their relentless pursuit of him, and the state police were marshalling their forces to keep him from regaining his power. Although he had been convicted of tax charges the previous year, Minker would still be around for another year, but lying low. As Abe's fortunes went, so did John Kubacki's and Charlie Wade's. The federal grand jury had a lot of people squirming that season and Charlie was given his turn to answer some very hard questions on April 17. A few days earlier he had made a startling announcement that his department was launching a 7/24 check on all houses of prostitution. It might have been a sincere move to close down Mable Jones and friends, but it was too late to have any effect on the federal prosecutors who would interrogate him before the grand jury.

For two hours, Charlie, who said he would not lie to federal investigators because it would tarnish his reputation as a police chief, found himself lying profusely when questioned by U.S. Attorney Walter Alessandroni. His hopes of becoming Reading's greatest police chief were shattered that day. Alessandroni, who as Pennsylvania's attorney general in 1958 saw his strong case against the Minker mob go up in smoke when prosecution witnesses refused to testify, was now out for revenge.

Playing the innocent public servant at the whim of Mayor John Kubacki, Wade bobbed and weaved as Alessandroni peppered him with queries that if answered honestly he certainly would have incriminated himself. So he lied rather than taint his credibility by taking the 5th Amendment. It quickly became evident that the feds suspected Charlie of several irregularities regarding city contracts with two towing companies. Charlie explained that he had set a standard towing price for vehicles the city wanted moved, and one price only.

Alessandroni then got to the meat of the matter:

"In addition to that, I am asking you whether you also told them they should take one dollar per towing job for the city and pay it to you by mailing it to you in a plain envelope. Do you recall saying that?"

"I don't recall that," Charlie replied.

"You mean you might have said it?"

"You asked me if I recall. I just said I don't recall."

"Well, did you say it?"

"As I said, I don't recall saying it. I had a conversation about their towing."

"In other words, you understand my point. That would be a bribe, wouldn't it, if in fact it happened?"

"A bribe?"

"If they were to pay you a dollar per towing job for the city work?"

"They never paid me a cent. I never got a cent."

Then a member of the jury panel had a question:

"You say none of the money came to you … the dollar from the towing company … none of that money came to you? You were always working under the direction of the mayor? Do you feel that money may have gone to the mayor?"

"Well, ma'am, I cannot answer that for the simple reason I wouldn't know what he gets. He has never discussed it with me. It would be unfair to say … to give you my opinion on that, because I wouldn't want to hurt somebody I couldn't be sure of."

Other witnesses had informed the grand jury that Wade had suggested local automobile dealers should make kickbacks if they expected to win contracts for new cars the city was shopping for. When Alessandroni asked Charlie if there was any truth to those claims, the chief again stated he had no knowledge about any such malfeasance. And with each denial he knew he was only making matters worse. As the government continued its probe, it would be many months before Charlie began recanting his grand jury testimony, this time in private to investigators.

Wade was angry for having allowed himself to be drawn into corrupt deals that were of little financial gain to him. The kickbacks he received were a pittance compared to the money he was making from his home improvement businesses. He also felt cheated for not being allowed to run the police department as he wanted. Now that he had perjured himself, what next?

Out of the blue, and also out of the district attorney's office, strode another gangbuster that summer. Nobody had heard much about Asst. Dist. Atty. John Marx because not that many vice cases were reaching criminal court. His ascension came at an opportune time, coinciding with the arrival of Capt. Rocco Urella. A strong working relationship was developed by the pair. Wade's round-the-clock prostitution patrol had also closed down the girlie houses. This sudden burst of enthusiasm to step up the anti-vice activity by local law enforcement was too good to last. And who better than Mayor Kubacki to burst the bubble.

For six weeks, patrolmen and officers were detailed to make hourly checks on the bawdyhouses. Chief Wade proudly displayed the voluminous reports his watchdogs were turning in showing that the girlie business was kaput. Well, not quite. First Kubacki pulled the rug out from under Bill Lilley. Near the end of May at a City Council meeting, Kubacki introduced a list of police promotions and demotions. Lilley's name was on the list among the latter. Council, with no discussion, passed his recommendations.

The outraged reaction to Lilley being downgraded was that this was just John being John—sometimes getting mad but always getting even. Remember, it was Lilley who set up the numbers raid at Joe Fiorini's in January, much to the mayor's surprise.

Councilman Kobrin, who published a weekly newspaper, the *Reading Record*, used his little sheet to blast Kubacki for treating so shabbily the one man on the force who seemed to be fighting vice. The dailies, that rarely agreed with the *Record*, this time joined the chorus that was chastising the revengeful mayor. Times reporter Drex Bradley asked Kubacki to explain Lilley's demotion.

"Demotion?" the mayor sniffed. "He was transferred."

"All right," Drex persisted, "transferred down, why?"

"Do you want to know, off the record."

"No, on the record."

"I have no reason. I wanted those men moved around, and I will shift more around."

Later he offered another lame excuse:

"At this time we are very low on police patrol personnel, and I'm trying to utilize some of the younger men on patrol duty." What he did not reveal was that he was also disbanding Wade's brothel watch.

John Kubacki would be the first to agree you can't keep a good man down, but he'd rather Lilley had not proved it so soon after his reduction in rank. With the assistance of Trooper Don Holloway, Bill had been tracking Howard Himmelreich, a 48-year-old numbers writer. Two days after his demotion, he and Holloway arrested Himmelreich on Tulpehocken Street with a full book of bets in his pocket. The suspect was a tricky guy who had never before been arrested. During the weeks of tailing Howard, Lilley came in contact with a sumac shrub and suffered a severe rash. He had to take several days off after the numbers arrest, but soon was again chasing naughty girls and careless numbers peddlers. Over the next year, Lilley was treated like a yo-yo by the mayor: promoted to sergeant, then demoted again, only to be upgraded again. Bill's wife said that during that period he never knew from one day to the next what rank he would be when he reported for duty. Such was the capricious reign of John Kubacki.

It was another story by Don Barlett that revealed Kubacki had disbanded the prostitution squad, and Mable Jones and Freddie Williams were back in business. Wade staged a raid at Mable's but, probably forewarned, none of the beds were rocking by the time his cops looked in.

When Fred Brubaker took a summer vacation, his first assistant, John Marx, took exception to his boss's non-aggression policy regarding vice. According to Marx, he received a tip that a steady stream of male customers was seen paying short visits to 129 Lemon Street. He contacted the state police.

Capt. Rocco Urella marched into Mable Jones's place with a seven-man team on the evening of June 22, but the housemother wasn't home. So they arrested madam-for-the-night Gina "Fifi" Frey, Brenda Baker and Juil Smithers. Three frequenters were charged with disorderly conduct. Mable and Brenda were still awaiting court action rising out of the March scuffle with the pair of teenagers.

Without stopping for a drink at Mable's well-stocked, 20-foot-long bar, or plugging the jukebox to dance, Urella and part of his crew went to the 111 North 7th Street house. Again, no Mable. "We're not open for business," stated the lady who barred their way. Claudia Glenn, the former madam, had moved her operation to 8th and Green.

The importance of these actions at Mable's places was Marx's audacity in staging them while his boss was out of town. But the A.D.A. modestly claimed he was only doing what he was hired to do. He said he wanted to quit the job several times but Brubaker had urged him to stay until September, because Fred expected to be appointed to fill an empty seat on the county court.

"I told him I would stay, but only under my conditions and that was, as long as I was acting district attorney in his absence, the law would be enforced as it should be," Marx stated. "I received a complaint about the house, and since Mr. Brubaker was vacationing at the seashore and I didn't know where to reach him, I acted on it with the aid of the state police." Marx wasn't defying orders, but certainly wasn't following policy.

When he returned from vacation, Brubaker let Marx know he didn't appreciate his first assistant's freelancing while the boss was getting a little rest and relaxation. Marx renewed their ongoing argument about Brubaker's reluctance to take a stronger stance regarding vice investigations. Unlike Fred's passive approach, Marx believed it was the responsibility of the district attorney's office to investigate as well as prosecute criminal activities. Marx, having had a taste of popularity, was now working behind the scenes to prepare for his next opportunity.

In his private practice, Marx had a 29-year-old client, Joseph Senesac, a businessman with a taste for adventure. They had known each other for several years. Marx had handled legal problems for a couple of companies Joe owned. Senesac moved to Florida for a few years but on his recent return he and the A.D.A. renewed their friendship. Joe said he decided to get involved when he heard Reading was being referred to as Sin City. According to his later testimony in court, Joe said Marx suggested, "You can do something for me if you want to keep your eyes and ears open." With approval from Marx, Joe began his own investigation of prostitution. It wasn't long before he met a young woman at a party. He soon learned that Pat was a party girl plus. Through her, he met 40-year-old Ira "Ácie" Bates, the drummer in Frankie Scott's popular jazz band. Also, the little fellow told about drumming up business to a different beat, according to Senesac. Acie was bringing in high-priced call girls to his house at 26 North 2nd Street.

When Brubaker left for a seminar in Michigan to learn more about a new search and seizure law, Marx and Senesac were ready to do some seizing of their own. The day Fred left, Senesac was on the phone setting up an assignation for three girls that night, July 26. No girls available, Acie insisted, but he could fill the bill the next night. Joe had recruited a pair of married buddies to join his vigilante team, posing as johns. Marx contacted the state police the next day but Capt. Urella's men were not available, so he requested assistance from the city police. Just whom he contacted at City Hall was not revealed.

Acie's setup was not a smooth-running operation. When Senesac and friends arrived at Bates's house at the appointed hour, 11:30 p.m., the proprietor was in pajamas, ready for bed—but without the playmates he had promised. Acie, well schooled in improvisation, got on the phone to Coatesville where a lady was willing to travel if Bates sent a chauffeur. There was some bickering about price. Acie's "wife", Patricia Porter, got on the line and tried to hold the price down to $30, but the woman at the other end wouldn't budge below $50. More dickering, then Senesac handed Acie $50 of the $150 he had been given by Marx. Acie and Pat left in his 1956 Cadillac. Later he would explain that 24-year-old Patricia Porter wasn't quite his wife but they were committed to that end.

Having dispersed after the midnight false alarm, Lt. Paul Shipper, four other city cops, and Marx were notified by a lookout that the suspects were back in town. Senesac and friends, for the second time, soon arrived at the target house. Acie was still improvising. Did they have any objections to taking turns with Pat Porter—just her? Joe wanted his $50 back. Pat left to fetch Loretta Mitchell. A houseguest, Vivian Mobley, was asked to join the party after making a sudden appearance. The balance of the money was paid to Acie, and the three couples retired to the third floor.

On cue, Lt. Shipper knocked and Acie answered. The police entered with no trouble as Bates was shown a search warrant. But the little drummer bolted, running up the stairs shouting, "Up to the third floor!" Senesac, having paired off with Loretta, came out into the hall as Acie sprinted by. Things quickly settled down as Acie and his women were arrested and taken to City Hall.

Before doling out the $150, Marx had written down all the serial numbers on the $5 and $10 bills. Money confiscated from Acie matched the numbers of those Marx had noted. The raid itself was no more special than dozens of others in recent years, but the political fallout had a lasting effect on the Democratic Party.

Followers of the Marx-Brubaker soap opera, wondered how the D.A. was going to react to his assistant's temerity of again taking the law into his own hands while the boss was out of town. They remembered Fred's annoyance the last time Marx went off on his own. But Fred surprised everybody the following Monday by announcing he was appointing Marx to head up a county vice squad. Johnny was less than enthusiastic. He wanted a free hand to do as he saw fit, but was wary that Brubaker would hinder, rather than help, if he continued on his present course.

Brubaker gave every indication of helping by asking for, and getting assurances of assistance from Capt. Urella and city detective Capt. John Feltman in the formation of a county vice squad. Four men from each, the city and state police, would make up the county unit.

Capt. Feltman had headed the detective bureau for more than seven years, six of them with orders from successive mayors to avoid vice arrests. But now, Kubacki agreed to give him a freer hand. Questioned by the press, Marx did not try to conceal his doubts that Brubaker would not interfere with his new assignment. He felt their opposing viewpoints regarding law enforcement were not likely to be resolved. But he agreed to formulate a plan for the new vice squad. During negotiations, Marx made clear that he intended to have complete control of the eight men.

He met with Kubacki who promised full cooperation—if he were advised in advance of all operations, and if his members of the vice squad were available.

Too many ifs worried Marx, but he hoped for the best. Toward the end of a very busy week in August, Marx put the mayor's questionable promise to the test.

It was a Thursday morning, August 16, and Marx met with staties John Beemer and Don Holloway to discuss a case involving the possible bribing of a county official to allow gambling at the Kutztown Fair. Beemer mentioned he and Holloway had been surveilling what they believed was a warehouse at Moss and Amity streets suspected of housing gambling supplies. That morning they went to the building but could not find Earl Brumbach, a 63-year-old distributor of punchboards, whom they had seen entering and leaving the place.

At noon, Marx was driving to see a client when he spotted a parked car that matched the description of Brumbach's auto he had been given by the staties. It was parked at a gas station at Amity and North 9th streets. He stopped, looked into the car, and saw radios and clocks and other items known to be offered as bingo prizes. Using the station's phone he called the state police barracks but Beemer and Holloway had gone to Kutztown. A customer was in the filling station office during the phone conversation. When Marx went outside to ask an attendant who owned the car in question, he was told it belonged to Earl Brumbach, "That's him coming out."

Marx identified himself, then asked if Earl had punchboards in his car:

"Sure," Earl responded, maybe anticipating a sale.

"You're under arrest," was the A.D.A.'s surprise reply.

"Why, isn't everything all right?"

"Everything's all wrong."

"I thought it was cleared with everybody."

"It wasn't cleared with Johnny Marx."

"Who's he?"

"Me."

So Earl had to drive Marx to City Hall, wondering all the while why his "clearance" understanding was suddenly so unclear. When they parked, Marx confiscated the car keys before they went inside where the police department was headquartered. The head of the Berks County Vice Squad was aghast when officers in the detective bureau refused to take Earl Brumbach into custody. Police Chief Charlie Wade was in Pittsburgh, and Capt. Feltman was on vacation. So nobody wanted to take the responsibility of arresting the suspect.

According to Marx, he was told, "We have orders from the mayor not to handle any of your complaints or arrests." This was cooperation? Marx later praised the police for wanting to arrest Brumbach but not without direct orders from their superiors. After Marx located Don Holloway, the suspect was taken before an alderman and charged with gambling violations.

Later, Marx returned to the Amity Street building, opened the door with a key he had gotten from Brumbach, and was shocked at the huge cache of punchboards and merchandise prizes stored there. The next day he obtained a search warrant and went looking for additional loot at other locations. He was accompanied by Holloway and the 280-pound John Beemer. The 6-4 state police sergeant shouldered a rear door open in a small storage structure at 1122 Spring Street where 20 gambling machines were found. The property was owned by Kern Amusement, operated by H. Ronald Kern.

While they were taking inventory at the second building, a cellar containing cartons was spotted through a knothole in the floor. When Brumbach turned over a key to the cellar he mentioned "there's a few more boards down there." It turned out another 10,000 punchboards were found in the low-ceiling basement. Total worth of the stash was estimated at $10,000 to $15,000. A large trailer and a smaller truck were needed to carry away more than 15,000 punchboards, thousands of numbers slips, hundreds of merchandise prizes, pinball machines, and other gambling devices. The prizes included portable television sets, transistor radios, food mixers, tape recorders, clocks, toasters, fans, skillets, lamps, shotguns, shells, fishing tackle, luggage, baskets and all kinds of toys and novelties. It was the biggest haul in recent memory of this type of gambling material. The cache was taken to Troop C barracks.

Marx was very upset about the orders he believed Kubacki had handed down to his policemen. The A.D.A. informed the press:

"If that happens once more, that I don't get police protection when I have arrested a criminal on view and bring him in, I'm going right to court the next day with a writ of mandamus—a writ you serve on a public official which says 'why aren't you doing your job.'"

Marx also called the tax bureau in City Hall to find out who owned the building where the gambling stuff was stored. He was told there was no record of a warehouse at Moss and Amity. The assessor's office later said Marx called the wrong office to find out about the ownership. It was owned by Elmer K. Fidler and his wife, Mae, of Reifton. Marx admitted it was an honest error. Actually, the building had two apartments and the "warehouse" was formerly a store.

Enter John Kubacki. He was ready and willing to verbally duel with the assistant district attorney. The mayor said it was Marx who broke the agreement by not notifying him or department heads on the police force when an arrest was imminent so he could send his members on the Berks Vice Squad into action.

Marx retaliated by claiming he would never accept the rules Kubacki was insisting on. He did make one concession, however. He admitted the detectives on duty Thursday when he brought Brumbach to City Hall, had not made any comments about being ordered by the mayor not to cooperate with Marx. The A.D.A. said he had heard a report earlier that police had received such orders, and he was merely repeating second-hand information on Thursday. Kubacki said when he heard about the incident, he decided since Marx took Brumbach into custody, and the state police were working on the punchboard case, let them do the rest of the job by preferring the charges and hauling away the loot.

"I don't intend our city police, who have many multiple problems facing them, to be used on a spontaneous whim by Mr. Marx whenever he feels he wants to use them, especially in light of his having state police and county detectives in on the case and does not even extend to our police department the courtesy of informing them what he is planning to do in the city," Kubacki said. Then it got personal as he made the accusatory charge of politics:

"It isn't my intention to have Mr. Marx use our city police to foster his own personal ambitions to gain political office, which is well known to practically everyone except maybe himself, nor to foster any ideas that he may have with his disagreement with Dist. Atty. Frederick Brubaker. The question arises in my mind, as it does in many other people's way of thinking: Where was Mr. Marx during the past seven years as a crusader, and where was his white horse?"

Marx claimed the mayor was "talking through his hat. I'm willing to cooperate but not with the set of rules he's laying down, with all those ifs, ands, and buts—if he has enough men, if I clear it with a department head. My answer is that he's been doing it for the three years he's been in office, and now that it's catching up to him, he's trying to shove that dirty hat onto someone else."

The outcome of the case was a $350 fine and one year of probation for Brumbach. More important to Earl than the modest penalties was an order from the court to have 90 percent of the gambling prizes that had been seized by state police returned to him. Probably, Earl was a good example of those who had good friends in high places.

Marx did not let the hassle with Kubacki deter him from continuing his anti-vice campaign. Early on the Sunday evening following the punchboard raid, John Beemer and Don Holloway led another state police team that knocked off a poker game in the second-floor headquarters of the Penn Social Club, 827 Penn Street. Frank DeFazio, a 41-year-old city meter maintenance man, was named as the operator of the game. Ten players engaged in a game of seven-card stud were also arrested and $81.50 was seized from the table. Rather than advise Kubacki's police department that a raid was scheduled, Marx relied on the staties to do the job. The county vice squad was soon to be disbanded. Before Marx's short rebellion ended, he initiated 17 cases against the racketeers.

As the Bates case moved toward trial, the principal defendant spent six weeks in jail before bondsman Joseph "Gibraltar Joe" Biancone posted $8,000 bail. That same day Bates was indicted by the Berks grand jury and two new dope charges were placed against him. Gibraltar Joe came up with another $10,000 bond for his release. As payback for being scammed by Joe Senesac, Acie had his 15-year-old daughter file a "soliciting for prostitution" charge against the would-be private eye.

Then Brubaker found out that Senesac had been charged in Lancaster County by a woman who claimed she was defrauded when Joe installed an oil heater in her home. Fred initiated this latest row with Marx right before the new county vice chief had exchanged accusations with Mayor Kubacki about the punchboard bust.

Fred sent Marx a note ordering him not to let Joe testify at the Bates trial. But Marx came back at him with a vengeance. "He's clean as a whistle," Marx insisted, indicating he certainly would use Joe as his prime witness. He also accused Fred of "character assassination" and "sabotage." In a long written reply to Brubaker, Marx asked:

"Why are you so obviously trying to undermine the structure of my organization and trying to prevent us from accomplishing the job we set out to do at your orders?

"You know full well that your sudden attack, an unprovoked one, will only make it more difficult for me to secure other undercover men and women in the future.

"Both city and state police have performed flawlessly and with distinction in staging the last several raids in Reading against large scale gambling that has now suffered crippling blows."

Marx argued that even a grade school kid knows that exposing "inside" informants makes it almost impossible to win prosecutions in many cases.

"You yourself have always given the excuse that our county detectives are too well known to enable you to enforce the law, and thereby failed to make any arrests," reminded Marx. "The regret is that I feel for Joseph Senesac and his family as I read of your unbelievable assassination of the character of this young man, a man who served me willingly, without thought or hope of reward."

When preliminary hearings were held in the fraud case and the soliciting a minor case, neither the Lancaster county woman nor Bates's daughter showed up to testify. Charges were dismissed at both hearings.

Right after the 1961 *Eagle/Times* series showcasing the large number of gambling machines in Berks County, most of the slot machines disappeared from bars and clubs. By the following spring, however, just as many or more were plugged in again. The IRS started another campaign against places offering new and better multicoin machines for their customers. Several of the 14 devices agents seized in the initial raids were lacking $250 stamps. Some of the store and club operators said they were unaware of a $10 federal stamp requirement on pinball machines. For the next few months the feds canvassed numerous other service stations, clubs, and taverns as agents continued to hound even the county's smallest places that had always been ignored by law enforcement.

# 32

## *Fired, hired, tired of boss's theory*

If there were any hopes the Berks County Vice Squad could be revived, they were dashed at a meeting of the Berks County Democratic Committee. The final brick was loosened when John Marx appeared to be testing the political waters. Fred Brubaker and Marx presented written statements to the committee seeking support for their different views and commitments concerning vice. City Councilman Bruce Coleman, who also wore the hat of county chairman of the Democratic Party, recommended the committee not take sides. That happened, but by leaving that divisive issue unresolved, it further exposed how fragmented the party had become.

Since the party committee wouldn't back him, Brubaker took matters into his own hands the next day by firing Marx. Fred accused his first assistant of using his office "for personal political advantage," and contended that the type of work carried on by Marx in recent vice raids "is a function primarily for the police." Marx reiterated his anxiety to leave the D.A.'s office, and departed with a sigh of good riddance.

Adding salt to the wound, the annual salary of Marx's replacement, Peter Cianci, was boosted by $900 to $6,100. Then, in still another surprise 10 days later, Brubaker asked Marx to return as a special prosecutor of vice cases he had been involved with. In a most unusual deal, Marx was offered $200 per case for the 17 cases he was asked to try. Marx claimed the money was sufficient, but more importantly he felt obligated to tie up all the loose ends of cases he had initiated. But in the next 10 days before September term of criminal court began, numerous brush fires broke out leading up to what was expected to be a three-ring circus.

Two well publicized prostitution cases were scheduled for trial at the same time. Although Marx was rehired to try all the cases he had launched as head of the vice squad, Brubaker opted to handle the Mable Jones prosecution, leaving

Marx to try Acie Bates and company. Although the two cases were held without a hitch, Fred created still another confrontation in court.

Mable had escaped possible jail time that summer when a couple of teenagers refused to testify about a skirmish in her house the previous spring. In her case now about to begin, the principal witnesses were more reliable—state policemen. The main point of contention for Sam Liever as he defended Mable was to prove she was not the owner of the house at 129 Lemon Street. Although she was not at home the evening of the June 23 state police raid, it was generally believed she owned the property. Liever, however, claimed Mable Murray was the name on the title, therefore the prosecution had the wrong woman. It was no secret Mable had been married to a military man named Murray at the time she bought the place in 1956, and the D.A. had plenty of proof it was Mable who paid the electric bills, laundry bills, and soft drink bills. The state police had collected that evidence at the time of the raid.

During cross-examination, Chief County Detective Ed Strickland introduced a hint of how limited the pursuit of justice had been by the district attorney's office in recent years. Strickland testified that as a state police sergeant in 1958, he had led a raid at 129 Lemon. Mable Jones pleaded guilty to prostitution charges at that time. Liever then got Strickland to admit he had not raided the house again during the three years he was chief county detective. In his summation, Brubaker explained to the jury his opinion of how a district attorney should fulfill his duties:

"Liever will argue why the county detective didn't raid that house. I didn't tell him to, that's why. As district attorney I'm his boss. My principle is not to go out and make raids when we have 116 (sic) police in the city and 100 state police in the county. It's their job. It's what I expect them to do. I'm a lawyer. That's my job, to prosecute, to lay out the evidence for you. My county detectives help me. They are not supposed to go out and make raids. He's (Strickland) here all day. I don't expect him to make raids at 2 a.m. I know Mr. Liever will argue that. We have 285,000 people in the county and only two county detectives. We have 600 policemen in the county and that's their job,"

The jury convicted Mable Jones, Fifi Frey, Brenda Baker and Juil Smithers. At a sentencing hearing two weeks later, Brenda and Juil decided to get it over with and begin their prison terms of 4-to-12 months. Mable and Fifi said they wanted new trials. A few weeks later the *Reading Times* received a tip that Mable was convicted on a charge different from the violation listed on the warrant when she was arrested. In May at a preliminary hearing before Alderman Charlie Lease, he had held her for grand jury on the charge "illegally maintaining a disorderly house."

Her indictment carried the charge as "keeping a bawdyhouse." In the criminal code each charge had a different number. John Marx and Charlie Lease both recalled with certainty what the original charge was. They said they did not know when, how, or by whom the charge had been altered.

Brubaker shrugged away the difference:

"In common law, bawdyhouse and disorderly house are interchangeable terms."

"There's a big difference between the two charges when it comes to trying the case," Marx insisted. "I found out the district attorney did not follow the section Lilley swore to and which Lease cited in his transcript. Instead, the case came to trial on "keeping a bawdyhouse."

It proved to be much ado about nothing. Mable was granted a new trial because of Strickland's testimony about her being arrested on prostitution charges in 1958. Liever claimed the defendant's past police record should not have been introduced. The retrial was set for Monday March 1l, 1963, with Mable still charged with "keeping a bawdyhouse." But during the previous weekend, a suspect rash of maladies struck the ranks of beleaguered madams.

Jessie Maione's attorney, John Ruth, asked the court to offer his client early parole. She had served half of her 4-month minimum sentence in BCP and was now suffering heart problems as her weight approached 300 pounds on BCP food. Because of her weakened condition she had been transferred to the nearby former Berks County Tuberculosis Sanitarium. Judge Hess observed: "If she is that sick, she should go to a hospital and not her own home." She served another month and was then released to begin her retirement from the business.

Mable Jones was incapacitated the same weekend. On Saturday, Mable went to Reading Hospital with shoulder pains. She was admitted and tests were administered but nothing showed up positive as to the cause of pain. One doctor felt she was just trying to avoid going to trial. A second opinion was that it was a case of "untreatable fakery".

Mable's retrial was much the same as the original. Two soft drink delivery men and a route man for Pennsylvania Linen Rental Service all remember Mable as the woman who signed checks "Mable Murray." Elizabeth Ehrlich, later elected to the Berks County Court, testified that she was master at Mable's divorce hearing in December 1961. And the verdict was the same: guilty. Mable filed for a third trial. Another seven months passed before Judge Readinger presided at another hearing at which time he refused to grant her another go-round. By any other name, Mable Jones was still the madam of 129 Lemon Street. Fifi

Frey, like Mable and Josephine before her, also received a 4-to-12-month term. At 39, Fifi did her minimum time, the longest stretch of the several she served in the past 21 years.

On the same day Brubaker was handling the original case against Mable in September 1962, in another courtroom John Marx was beginning the prosecution of Acie Bates and company. The defense attorney, Fred Giorgi, tried to have the trial moved to another county because of excessive publicity. He also wanted Marx removed as prosecutor because he feared Brubaker might call Johnny as a defense witness in Mable's case. Judge Hess rejected Giorgi's requests. Marx withdrew the narcotics charges against Bates because he wasn't satisfied his evidence would hold up in court, although "bennies" and "goofballs," both illegal drugs, were found in Acie's house.

Joe Senesac, sharp in his business suit and fluent with his testimony, told of being recruited for undercover work by Marx, and detailed his part in convincing Acie Bates that he and his friends were legitimate johns willing to pay top dollar to frolic with Barbara Porter, Loretta Mitchell, and Vivian Mobley. The next day, Senesac's two friends, just doing their bit to help clean up the city and receiving no remuneration for doing so, also testified along the same lines. Whether their stories had convinced the jury was never known because on the third day of the trial three of the four defendants pleaded guilty. Charges against Ms. Mobley were dropped.

Uninvited, Fred Brubaker popped up in court where Judge Hess was in the process of determining sentences for Acie Bates and his women. By now, Fred was prosecuting a murder case in another courtroom. However, he saw fit to leave that trial in the hands of Peter Cianci, his new No. 1 A.D.A. In his march to Judge Hess's courtroom Fred brought along two other assistants and a stenographer to check on how John Marx was winding up the Bates trial. What followed was a bizarre intrusion that led Judge Hess to observe:

"If I was in Mr. Marx's position, I would resign." This was after Marx had resigned some weeks earlier.

Marx, outlining the case to Judge Hess when Fred entered, was explaining that Bates had pled guilty to charges of pandering, and misbranding drugs. He said two other drug charges had been withdrawn against Acie and the Porter woman.

At that point, Fred came forward, pointing out that six separate charges, each carrying a fine of $500 and a year in prison, had been placed against Bates. A wrangle about those and other charges broke out between the two strong-willed prosecutors. Among other comments, Brubaker mentioned that in his six and a half years as D.A., he had never moved to dismiss a charge of operating a disorderly house. Marx had dropped that charge against the drummer man.

As the bickering continued about the special prosecutor's handling of the sentencing, Judge Hess became exasperated. When Brubaker stated, "Justice is not to play with," Marx threw up his hands and let out a loud, "Oh, brother!" At this point Hess stated: "Let's have a recess and let the district attorney's office get together."

On a full stomach following lunch, the combatants were less hungry to devour each other. With Cpl. Don Holloway, Berks County Prison Warden Walter Scheipe, city detective John Habecker, and defense counsel Fred Giorgi also offering fact and opinion, the confusing debate over the mishmash of charges was finally ironed out.

Judge Hess sentenced Bates to 5-to-23 months on pandering and drug charges, and Porter and Mitchell each got 3-to-12 months.

There were no more face-to-face confrontations between Marx and Brubaker, but at a later State Pardons Board hearing their opinions were heard about whether a man's murder conviction should be commuted. Marx, who won a second-degree murder conviction in 1960, said the charge could have been voluntary manslaughter because the suspect was protecting himself, his wife, and family during a knife fight. Brubaker sent a letter to the board opposing commutation. The board agreed with Marx and several witnesses who supported his opinion. Angel Ortega served only two years of his 4-year minimum sentence.

With that case out of the way, Marx resigned as special prosecutor, declaring, "I want nothing more to do with him."

When Brubaker asked him to prepare a bill of indictment against Frank DeFazio, who faced gambling charges, Marx replied in a letter, "For some motive known only to yourself, you see fit to pass this responsibility on to me. What that motive might be, I don't know. However, I am certain of one thing, and that is, I don't trust it."

# 33

# *The Philly mob plays rough*

During the fall of 1962, the spotlight momentarily shifted from Abe Minker, the numbers writers, and prostitution, and focused on a little known Reading racketeer, Frank Donato. Like the Lucchese brothers, Donato had enough pull in organized crime circles to run a numbers game out of his home despite Abe Minker's dominance in his hometown. Frank was working for the Philadelphia Mafia run by Angelo Bruno.

The Donato tale began in 1961 when Treasury agents arrested him in his house at 29 South 2nd Street. Six boxes of gambling paraphernalia were seized and he was charged with accepting wagers without having a gambler's occupation stamp. He was described as a pickup man. Nothing was mentioned in the agents' public report about the raid indicating a large amount of money had also been seized. However, as the case evolved, the mob bosses felt Donato had short-changed them by a considerable amount.

On September 15, 1962, Donato was taking his dog for its nightly walk about 10:15 at 2nd and Franklin streets. Suddenly a black station wagon with five men in it pulled to the curb, a couple of the passengers jumped out, seized Frank and handcuffed him before wrestling him into the back seat of the vehicle. Frank thought he was being arrested by federal agents, therefore he did not call out for help or struggle to get free. Like so many in his trade, the 53-year-old racketeer was taken for a ride. His abductors dropped the dog off in West Lawn, continued on Penn Avenue, then turned onto Fritztown Road in Sinking Spring.

After exiting at Chapel Hill Road near Fritztown they stopped, stripped Frank of his T-shirt, removed the cuffs and tied his hands, then bound him to a tree with twine, facing the trunk. The gist of the interrogation that followed was:

"Where's the money?"

"What money?"

"You owe the boss $31,000."

"I ain't got that kind of money. I got a few hundred in the bank."

"That's peanuts. Where is it? You have only three minutes to live."

Threats continued well past the stated deadline as Frank pleaded for his life. He was unable or unwilling to tell where the money was, so the mobsters decided to take another tack. A gag was placed in Frank's mouth. He was told they were going back to his house and make his sister turn the money over to them. If she didn't come up with it, they warned, he could expect to see them again. They took $54 from his pocket and drove off.

On that warm autumn night the burly Donato was sweating profusely. He wiggled free of his bindings within a short time, removed the gag, but his cries for help went unanswered as he tried to arouse neighbors. At the second house Frank approached he was admitted by Philip Klahold who allowed him to telephone city and state police. Troopers Warren Werner and Jack Bednar soon arrived.

In the meantime, three of the five abductors were dropped off near Frank's 2nd Street house. The youngest of the group went to wait in a parked car down the street, while the other two rang the bell at No. 29. The other pair, Frank Townsend Sr. and George Sykes, started back to where they left Donato tied to the tree. Nearing that site, they saw the blinking lights of the state police car and turned around and headed back to the city. The troopers with Donato followed on Fritztown Road shortly thereafter and caught up with the mobsters' station wagon on Penn Avenue in West Lawn. Donato identified the vehicle, and it was pulled over by the troopers. Donato recognized Townsend and Sykes as two of his abductors.

Back in Reading, Jenny Donato, the 55-year-old sister with whom Frank lived, answered the doorbell and was confronted by two strangers, John Miller and James Porter. They did not wait for her to invite them in. With guns drawn, they pushed her back into the living room, and began ragging her about a large sum of money they claimed her brother owed to their employers in Philadelphia. The $31,000 … where was it hidden? Showing her Frank's keys, the pair warned that something bad would happen to him if she didn't cooperate. The frightened Jenny couldn't so the thugs went looking. After an unsuccessful search of the house, Miller and Porter returned Frank's keys to Jenny, but warned that her brother had better turn over the money if he knew what was good for him. They went outside and were standing on the front steps when the city police arrived. Five detectives and four patrolmen were sent after City Hall received Donato's phone call. Porter tried to flee but was quickly caught. Frank Townsend Jr. was arrested farther down 2nd Street, seated in a car with the engine running.

These were not made Mafioso, merely wise guys serving as collectors for the Bruno gang. And their intended enforcement job was hardly professional. Even a

Boy Scout could have tied a better knot than the one Donato loosened not long after his abductors left him hugging a tree. The five suspects, all with long criminal records, were charged with kidnapping.

Details about the mysterious $31,000 were never released by the government, but it is likely Bruno and company only learned Frank was holding out a short time before ordering his abduction. Another possibility was that Bruno's bunch found out soon after the December raid and gave Donato just so many months to replace the cash if it was seized by the government agents. Jenny always claimed she had no knowledge of the missing cash.

Although Donato knew the rules of the game, maybe he felt his debt to the mob was too heavy to ever repay. So when he was called as a witness before a newly formed federal grand jury in Philadelphia shortly after being abducted, whatever he talked about apparently sealed his fate. He and his sister each spent about 20 minutes in the jury room, long enough to relate the tale of Frank's seizure and Jenny's ordeal.

In far more detail on November 13, the Donatos repeated their story about the escapade at a preliminary hearing before Alderman John DeMott. Frank identified Frank Townsend Sr. and Sykes as the two who dragged him into the station wagon. Jenny remembered the faces of the men threatening her, but got the names mixed up when identifying them: she fingered Porter as the younger Townsend. These IDs were straightened out. She was sure John Miller was the other suspect who intimidated her.

While waiting for trial, Donato went about his daily business, taking no special precautions although he should have known he was a marked man. Having been a plumber's helper for 35 years, Frank was a good handyman, always willing to do home repairs for relatives and friends. He had spent the better part of two days fixing leaking pipes in the home of a relative on North 3rd Street. When he was about to leave for home shortly before 5:30 p.m., on January 25, 1963, he brought along a container of ashes to spread on the icy street under the tires of his 7-year-old white and maroon hardtop. Shortly after that, neighbors noticed a car with three men in it parked up the street on the west side of 3rd. Witnesses told police they had seen the late model Cadillac in the neighborhood a day or two earlier. This evening the front seat passenger was seen leaving the car and strolling down the street a short distance. By 5:45 he was back in the car when it eased away from the curb. At the same time Donato reappeared and was walking around the rear of his auto when the hit men's vehicle passed slowly by. Two shots were fired into Frank's chest, a third pierced his arm. The shooter was believed to have been in the left rear seat. Frank was flung back into the icy gutter in front of the house at 919. The Cadillac zoomed away, fishtailing down the slippery thoroughfare.

Taken to St. Joseph Hospital by ambulance, Donato died a short time later. The following day, the .38 caliber revolver used to kill Frank was found in a gutter at 5th and Greenwich streets, about six blocks from the murder scene. The weapon was traced to a doctor living near Marcus Hook, Delaware County, Pennsylvania. The doctor had reported the gun stolen more than two years earlier. Donato's death was the first mob-related murder in Reading since Tony Moran was shot and killed by Johnny Wittig in 1945.

Alderman DeMott received a phone call from a constable about the shooting shortly after it happened. On hanging up, his phone immediately rang again.

"You're next," was the clipped, chilling message he received.

DeMott had signed the arrest warrants of the alleged kidnappers, and later ordered them held for trial following their preliminary hearing. Police protection was provided for him and Jenny Donato, but no further threats were received.

The Philly Five who took Frank for a ride all had good alibis about their whereabouts at the time of the shooting. Chief Wade and Capt. Feldman had no doubts that hired guns from out of state were contracted to perform the hit.

Dan McDevitt, now serving in the State Legislature, requested help from the state police in solving the gangland slaying. For the time being, federal agencies made no comment about entering the investigation, although the IRS had now lost an important witness in its probe into the Philadelphia rackets. On the home front, there were ripples of anger and fear as church leaders again took up the cry about the disgrace brought on their city by local officials who allowed vice to go unchecked.

When the kidnapping case reached criminal court on March 14, 1963, Fred Brubaker asked Judge Wilson Austin to sequester the jury to assure their safety and prevent possible fixers from contacting them. During the 3-day trial, the jurors, when not in court, were housed in the Abraham Lincoln Hotel. Defense attorney Sam Liever's motion to have Frank Donato's testimony at the preliminary hearing ruled inadmissible was denied. The five suspects had all made $10,000 bail each, but it was revoked before the trial and they were confined to Berks County Prison and escorted to court each day.

Jenny again identified Porter and Miller as the pair who entered her house bent on recovering the money. Sykes and Townsend Sr. were identified by state troopers who had seized them in their station wagon. Donato's testimony at the preliminary hearing was read and that was enough for the jury to find all five guilty after short deliberation. Each suspect made his $20,000 bail and was freed while their appeals were reviewed.

Two days after the trial, Brubaker and Judge Hess were at odds again as Sam Liever was asking for a retrial claiming Fred had suppressed certain evidence. The defense attorney said two pieces of twine introduced as evidence did not match. One piece was used to tie Donato to the tree, and a second piece of smaller diameter was found in the station wagon and was said to have been used in the kidnapping.

Judge Hess stated, "That might be withholding evidence ... it comes very close to being fraud on the court." His tone particularly irked Brubaker who insisted the judge had, "questioned my integrity, and until I am cleared, I do not intend to try another case before his court."

Brubaker argued that he did tell Liever about the pieces of twine being different sizes, but Liever retorted, "After the trial was over."

Judge Hess later told the D.A. he would withdraw his remark about fraud on the court if Brubaker wished. But Brubaker said he might wait until the outcome of the new trial pleas were decided before determining whether his reputation was cleared. A lot of cases could have piled up if he had held to his threat, because that phase of the kidnapping case was not settled for seven months.

In his petitions for new trials, Liever claimed the district attorney had "intentionally" suppressed evidence. Brubaker denied that, saying he didn't know about the discrepancy until Liever mentioned it to the jury. At the same hearing, Judge Austin stated he thought the twine was the strongest piece of physical evidence needed to prove Donato was kidnapped. Petitions for new trials were argued before Judge Austin in November 1963, but were rejected. A month later Austin sentenced four of the five defendants to 5-to-15 years in a state prison. He dismissed charges against the 27-year-old Frank Townsend Jr. because no witness had specifically identified him as taking part in the kidnapping. While the case was under appeal to a higher court, Frank Townsend Sr., 49, died in January 1964.

Following more appeals before the State Superior Court, the three remaining defendants were awarded new trials. In March 1965 a retrial was held before Berks County Judge Albert Readinger, which ended with a hung jury. Dist. Atty. Dick Eshelman was determined not to let the case fade away.

Charges were refiled. In June 1966, almost five years after Frank Donato was kidnapped, threatened, beaten, robbed, and then murdered, the three remaining defendants went to court for the last time. A.D.A. Ralph J. Althouse handled the prosecution, again before Judge Readinger. It took three days to seat a jury, an ominous beginning. Memories had dimmed, identifications were shaky, the testimony notes of the preliminary hearing were beginning to fray as they were read once again. Also, the two different pieces of rope were dangled before the jury a second time.

On the sixth day of the trial, Judge Readinger turned down a defense request for a mistrial. Lawyers for the Philly thugs claimed the torn T-shirt Donato was wearing when abducted should not have been shown to his sister while she was testifying. On the seventh day it took the jury of three men and nine women five hours to decide the three defendants were innocent. Sykes, by now 48, and Porter, 44, walked free, but the 50-year-old Miller was sent back to Philadelphia to finish a 9-to-18 month sentence for burglary.

For the Donato family and the people of Reading, it was a shamefully disappointing ending to what appeared to be an open-and-shut case against five convicted associates of organized crime. To the long list of unsolved murders perpetrated by the Mafia, the name of Frank Donato was added.

Ironically, Donato's father, Frank Sr., also was an indirect victim of racketeering during Prohibition. When a large illegal still exploded in a building at 2nd and Washington Streets, on February 7, 1930, he rushed to the scene from his house two blocks away. After the excitement died down, he suffered a heart attack while returning to his home at 118 Franklin Street. He died a short time later at 61.

Many who followed this story to its conclusion wondered what happened to Donato's dog after the gangsters pushed it from the station wagon during the early stages of the eventful episode. The wandering pet was found by Wyomissing Patrolman Douglass Filbert and eventually returned to the Donatos.

# 34

# *Gritty little madam defies extortion attempt*

Angie Wilkerson and Charlie Wade were friends—special friends, according to Angie. Charlie described their relationship as just professional. He let her operate her whorehouse, she provided him with information. Oh, it was more intimate than that, Angie would testify in court.

Angeline Martin Wilkerson was 46 when she gained a large measure of notoriety starting in 1964. Unlike most women with two last names, Angie switched the usual alignment. Martin was inserted, rather than added, when she married John. By the time she became a headliner she was redheaded, not unattractive, but an obvious candidate for liposuction. The bright attire she usually wore to court only emphasized her girth, which was hard to camouflage on a 4-foot-8-inch frame. Despite a series of setbacks, the diminutive firebrand never lost her courage and continued defiance of the law.

Although Angie claimed a minor career in show business, most of her income over the years came from men who paid to join her act. Her prostitution arrests dated back to 1940 in Atlantic City.

Angie said she met Charlie Wade in the early 1950s "when I was a working girl at Mary Gruber's." That would be Dutch Mary's legendary whorehouses on Plum and Cherry streets. Charlie Wade was one of the detectives who raided Dutch Mary's in 1952 when Angie and others were hauled in. Angie claimed Dutch Mary did a thriving business all during the pearly gray administration of the Republicans. Wade agreed, saying there was no concerted effort to close down the notorious madam during those years 1952 to 1956. The Minker crowd was somewhat held at bay until the rackets revolution began when the Democrats regained City Hall.

Not too long after that '52 arrest, Charlie and Angie became better acquainted. According to her, it was a mutual acquaintance who brought Charlie to her home on Oley Street. Since Angie was in the business of pleasing men, it stands to reason she was telling the truth when testifying she and Charlie bedded down for the first time during that visit. Charlie, good-looking, dapper, and congenial, denied having sexual relations with her, but of course his devoted wife of 30 years was in the courtroom at the time his virtue was questioned.

About that same time in the early '50s, Angie decided to move up into management. From Oley Street she relocated to State Hill, a crossroad village a few miles northwest of Reading. She opened a small restaurant which was a front for her more profitable business upstairs. Then in 1959 it was back into town in a house on South 3rd Street just below Cherry. Years later, a 3rd Street man recalled that as a lad of 12 he was paid to do odd jobs for Angie, like cutting her lawn, running errands, or cleaning up around the house. He also remembers the girls she had living there but, "they never stayed more than a week or two. I was too young to understand, but my mother would always get mad when I told her Angie paid me good money."

Mayor Kubacki had a different opinion of Angie in 1961 when he felt she should divide some of her good money with him. When she refused to pay Kubacki a kickback, Patrolman John Halstead was ordered to close her down. Charged with running a bawdyhouse, she paid her $101.25 fine and found a new location a month later at 904 Penn Street. Her second-floor, two-bedroom apartment had a back entrance opening on Geigers Court.

Angie rented the apartment under her husband's name, John Martin. They lived in a rented house in Midvale Manor, Spring Township, where neighbors were unaware of her trade—for a while.

Angie and Charlie had remained friends over the years and she said he once gave her a radio for her birthday. Charlie denied he was ever so thoughtful. He admitted he paid occasional trips to her workplace and frequently talked with her on the phone, but only to obtain information. That's why he allowed her to remain open when he became chief of police. But Angie claimed she never had any tips that were helpful to Charlie, but she felt safe from arrest because of him. During their lengthy marriage, old Jack Martin was content to let his wife be the breadwinner in his declining years.

Unlike his police chief, the mayor had no personal interest in Angie and when he found out she was getting a free ride, he wanted to know why. What would the other madams think if they found out Angie had favored whore status? Kubacki didn't buy the information alibi, even though Charlie insisted she was feeding him some very confidential stuff. If the other houses paid, so should Angie, the mayor ruled. This conversation took place in his office in the fall of

1960. Like the good executive he was, John was constantly looking for additional sources of revenue. He ordered Wade to set up an appointment for him with Angie. Charlie argued that his friend had only one girl and couldn't really afford to pay. Also, she had an old, sickly husband to support. He stalled Kubacki for a few months, but John stuck to his all-inclusive philosophy of making the racketeers pay. So in March of 1961 he told the chief he was going to settle the matter personally with the recalcitrant procuress if Charlie didn't bring her in line.

On one of his Saturday morning visits to Minker's White House Market, Wade told Abe that Kubacki was determined to expand his protection racket. Abe was annoyed.

"I paid that man more than I've ever paid anyone in my life and he still is never satisfied," Minker is purported to have said, thoroughly disgusted with Kubacki's greed. But he knew when to respond to pressure and when to bluff. He knew he was up against someone who could be as ruthless as himself. Kubacki was threatening to close down the mob's Cherry Street gambling house and its numbers racket if he didn't get what he was asking for. Wade told Abe he was being pressured to set up a meeting between the mayor and Angie Wilkerson.

"Don't do nothing like that," Minker said. "I warned you before that you're going to get into trouble listening to him."

Kubacki was demanding $100 a week from Angie, Wade told "Pop," the term of affection he used for Abe. But she can't afford that much, Charlie insisted. Okay, Abe sighed, and offered to send Benny Bonanno to see her. Maybe she would agree to $75.

But the mayor, a man of action, was disgusted with his procrastinating police chief and decided to take matters into his own hands. Using a city detective, Mike DeMarco, as his private chauffeur he was driven to Geigers Court less than two blocks from City Hall. When Angie opened the door and saw who it was, she ordered, "Get going." Ignoring Angie's bad attitude, the mayor pushed his way into her apartment. Her lone employee, Susie, was seated on a couch reading a book. As DeMarco looked in the bedroom to see if any clientele were on the premises, Kubacki told Angie he was there because neighbors were grousing about late night pleasure seekers causing disturbances outside on Geigers Court. The mayor would later explain to a jury:

"I said we had received complaints about loud and boisterous noises in the area and told her I would place an officer in the area if it didn't cease." He didn't ask her for protection money, although a payoff was certainly implied. In defense of his nocturnal visit, he said, "Anyone who knows me knows I visited very many places in the city: playgrounds, fire companies." Mable Jones revealed as much when she told a reporter he often came to her house on Lemon Street to personally pick up the $300 dollars a week she was paying him. And here he was taking time out from his busy schedule to warn a whorehouse operator. He did not tell her to close up shop, or threaten her with arrest. Just, "Don't let your customers make so much noise. You'll hear from me later." As he and his driver left, they helped themselves to apples in a bowl, but did not sample the other forbidden fruit.

A few days later a fellow known as "Skidley" introduced Benny Bonanno to Angie. Benny was a high-ranking employee at the Cherry Street craps game and Skidley was a lugger. Benny and Angie negotiated a $75 weekly protection payoff, but the agreement wasn't sealed until Angie called Wade. Charlie advised her to pay, rather than have Kubacki do something rash. The first payment was made the following week. Angie met Bonanno at 10th and Penn, sat in his car and left money on the front seat when she got out. Kubacki was to get $50, and Benny $25 as the contact. Minker received nothing but "at least I'll have peace and he won't grab some detective and knock off the crap game or arrest numbers writers," Wade quoted Abe. "I'm glad everything is quiet now."

The truce lasted six weeks. After the first payoff in his car, Benny started going right to Angie's apartment to collect. He was so confident she was going to keep her end of the bargain he started paying Kubacki in advance. Then the bagman suddenly was left holding the bag. Angie said enough was enough. She called Charlie Wade to complain that the kickback was seriously hurting her profit margin. The chief told her to stop paying because he doubted Kubacki would be foolish enough to carry out his threat to close the dice game if she did not pay him. When Benny Bonanno arrived on week No. 7, Angie said the deal was off. Benny, understandably, was upset because he had already served the mayor his slice of the pie.

Kubacki learned from Minker that Angie was reneging. The mayor passed word to Wade, who also got an earful from Bonanno when they met in a cigar store a few days later. Kubacki told his police chief to "send Lilley up to scare her." Wade told Lilley to forget about Angie. Whenever the mayor brought up the kickback issue, Wade acted dumb and disturbed that Angie would display such independence, but it soon faded away.

Testing his memory again, the once-upon-a-time 12-year-old said he continued as Angie's handy boy at the 904 apartment. He recalled seeing the mayor pay Angie a visit and disappearing into the bedroom with the young lady of the week. Maybe another sort of deal had been set up. Madams were famous for offering girls gratis as payment for household bills. Dutch Mary often bartered with the plumber, electrician, or handyman by opening the bedroom door. If Angie did give the mayor a free ride, she never mentioned it in her court testimony.

Angie called Kubacki's bluff and got away with it. Neither he nor the Minker crowd harassed her any more. Reportedly the mayor was getting big money from Minker's numbers racket, the bawdyhouses, and the Cherry Street dice game. It was a very good year for anybody in the kickback business in 1961. Kubacki was not about to jeopardize all those perks just to get even with a little tart. She continued to operate at the same stand for another couple of years, bringing in new girls every Saturday for a weeklong solo engagement. Maybe in Greece it was never on Sundays, but Angie's girls worked every day in Reading before moving on to the next stop on the circuit. This constant rotation of fresh flesh kept her customers coming back. Like Jessie Maione, Angie always used white girls, whereas black girls were featured in the Lemon and Plum streets bordellos.

Soon, the little lady of the night would be involved in a series of misadventures worthy of a dime novel plot.

# 35

# *The voters speak: don't throw the rascals out*

The Reading clergy had been mounting attacks against the racketeers who infested their city for many years. From the pulpit, Wasp ministers had implored their congregations to support Prohibition and fight prostitution and gambling by using the power of the ballot to elect honest officials. But no matter which party was in office, Democratic, Republican, Socialist, or Fusion, the purveyors of vice survived every attempted purge.

By the beginning of 1962 when it was obvious that John Kubacki was no better than his predecessor, still another attempt was made by the clergy to run the rascals out of town. Civic-minded voters had unseated Mayor Dan McDevitt in 1959, hoping John Kubacki would be the golden boy who would finally adhere to the rule of law. But he was just more of the same.

Following the notoriety resulting from the Cherry Street and North 8$^{th}$ Street raids within one week, clergymen of the Greater Reading Council of Churches again spoke out. The Rev. Dr. Paul E. Schmoyer, the council president, urged local ministers to use the following Sunday for "repentance and prayers of guidance" in regard to vice conditions. Many did as they preached against the evil "that could eventually destroy us." In Dr. Schmoyer's own words about his community:

"It is controlled by men with no conscience and no soul, who care nothing about their fellow men and who love neither men nor God."

Although many churches celebrated "Youth Day" that Sabbath, Lutheran pastor Rev. Marvin Dewalt reminded other congregations, "While the fire is hot, let us each put our coals on the fire and keep it raging until we get action from our city officials."

Henry Sharp, branch president of the local Church of the Latter Day Saints, carried his coals right into the next Reading City Council meeting for a confrontation with Mayor Kubacki. He stated:

"Recently, '180 Club' tickets were sold by youngsters in which the prizes were bottles of whisky."

He accused Kubacki of breaking state law by lifting his ban on bingo for charitable organizations. Then he really raised some hackles by suggesting the mayor, Charlie Wade, and Fred Brubaker should all resign their posts. There was quite a back and forth until Kubacki said, "You'd better bring names and addresses in here and we'll prosecute those people. I've never heard of such a wild and fantastic charge as that. I dare you to bring them in here. Don't come here under the guise of being a teacher of God." He added that he would send detectives to investigate if he received the names. Sharp responded that it wasn't his duty to provide such evidence.

Two days later the church leader came up with a loaded question for Kubacki: "Will the mayor offer a signed statement that he will resign if the facts in my statement to council are substantiated?"

Kubacki's answer was to send two city detectives to question Sharp. The mayor also pointed out that Sharp had been a Democrat, but registered Republican in 1959, and was now GOP committeeman in Ontelaunee Township. Like many political brushfires, this one died out but not from a lack of oxygen.

Also in January 1962, the Junior Chamber of Commerce had joined the opposition by forming the Political Action Under Leadership committee. With Andrew Linette as chairman, PAUL's first major move to show it meant business was to invite the young mayor of Canton, Ohio, to speak in Reading. An audience of more than 600 in the Abraham Lincoln Hotel ballroom heard James H. Lawhun reveal how the vice situation in his city had been reversed in the past year. Canton, quite similar in size and population to Reading, had a mayor and safety director who refused to act against dozens of bordellos and gambling joints. A group of about 35 policemen united to take matters into their own hands. They obtained warrants to make gambling and prostitution arrests. When the director of safety refused to sign the warrants, that didn't stop them from raiding and closing down several brothels and gambling parlors. Honest candidates, including Lawhun, replaced the incumbents the previous November. The racketeers took the hint and left town. In the audience that night were Fred Brubaker and two city councilmen, Harold Guldin and Jerry Kobrin. The Reading police force never emulated their Canton brethren. Instead, Reading's boys in blue went along to get along and did as they were told.

A committee from the Ministerial Association of Reading met with Fred Brubaker at his request. The press was excluded, but Dr. Schmoyer later reported that Fred said he would support "very strongly" any organization willing to monitor vice activities. He told the clergymen that his office was not a law enforcement agency equipped to engage in large investigations. Again he emphasized, he and his associates were prosecutors, not policemen.

The churchmen were skeptical as Fred gave his job description, but they were heartened by his acceptance of a watchdog organization because they had already formed the Berks County Citizens Association, with Dr. Schmoyer as its leader. Instead of just criticizing the politicians for the criminal state of affairs, the BCCA initiated a plan to change the whole playing field. They blamed the commission form of government that Reading had adopted in 1912 for many of the current problems that nobody in City Hall seemed willing to, or capable of solving. With the mayor and each of the councilmen controlling a different department, there was no central power base. Since the police department was Kubacki's responsibility, the four councilmen could shrug off the furor over rampant vice with "that's no fault of ours."

The BCCA took up the torch and began campaigning to bring in a council-manager form of government that would have a professional administering all phases of government, while the mayor and council set policy. City Council was asked to place the issue on the 1961 general election ballot as a referendum. The incumbents refused, which told the public where the five of them stood. So BCCA took the high, hard road by soliciting neighborhoods and collecting enough signatures required for a referendum. In the 1961 general election the voters were asked whether they wanted a city charter commission formed to study the various forms of government for third class cities. Candidates running for seats on the commission were to be elected.

The fact that Jerry Kobrin and Joe Kuzminski were reelected as city councilmen in the '61 general election was secondary to the overwhelming "yes" vote for the formation of a city charter commission, 11,611 to 3,668. Elected to the commission after endorsement by the BCCA were Charles Seyfert, Mrs. Henrietta Leinbach, G. David Schlegel, Robert VanHoove, Dr. Mahlon Hellerich, Rev. Mark Gibson, Jane Bishop, and Harold Imber. Three seats on the commission were reserved for city councilmen. Bruce Coleman said he was not interested, so Kuzminski, Kobrin, and Guldin rounded out the 11-person study group. At its first meeting, Seyfert was elected president and Dr. Hellerich, vice chairman.

Running parallel with the citizens' war against organized gambling and prostitution in 1962 were the even more intense political battles being waged within the Democratic Party. Seeds for the 1963 general election were sown long before voters went to the polls. More and more active Democrats became disenchanted with Kubacki's brazen and confrontational approach to almost every issue he opposed. The ex-boxer rarely backed off in the political ring, so it was almost certain he was not going to give up the mayor's office without a fight in '63. Most of the old guard Democrats were leaning toward Councilman Guldin as their choice.

A group of influential regulars, including some old Socialists, worried that the party was so corrupted by recent administrations that they wanted to clean house. By the end of 1961, cracks in the Democratic organization were evident. The formal break came on June 29, 1962, when Berks Independent Democrats (BID) was formed. While the Republicans searched for a viable candidate for mayor in the heavily Democratic city, the incumbent Demos were in disarray, engaging in fratricide. Although the GOP had made some recent gains in voter registrations in the county, the Demos still held close to a 3-to-1 edge in Reading.

The charter study commission members debated the various types of government. Councilman Guldin was the leader of those who wanted to keep the present system. At one open discussion meeting in the YMCA, Guldin noted:

"You're not going to find a Utopia in any particular form. In one of our tours we found a form in which a shambles was made of civil service, where police and paid firemen were left 'acting' … so they could be removed at the whims of a politician if they were a bad boy."

The strong mayor type of government received support from Mark Brown and Dr. Earl S. Loder and others. But most vocal were those crowded into the YMCA auditorium who backed the council-manager form. The BID faction was well represented on the commission, but probably made a fatal mistake when it voted to let the debate be settled in a special election, rather than placing another referendum on the ballot in the November 1962 general election.

City Council's reaction was loud and convincing. Why spend $10,000 to settle the issue when a referendum tied to the general election would have the same result? The estimated cost of a special election was 10 cents per citizen. Kubacki suggested it might be closer to $17,000. The councilmen raged at this show of extravagance by the commission. The City Charter crowd wanted the special election, fearing a crowded ballot would cause some confusion that possibly would hurt its cause. "A waste of money" became the rallying cry of the "No" forces and it definitely swung many votes in its favor.

There were torrid debates that summer and fall, with churches offering seminars explaining how the different forms of government worked. The Reading School Board authorized evening seminars in public schools as long as they remained nonpartisan. The county Republican Committee sponsored three such forums, while criticizing the county Democratic Committee for taking a strong stand against change. The Charter Commission finally narrowed the choice down to two types of third-class city types of government. The daily newspapers ran a side-by-side explanation of the difference between the two types that would be on the ballot. A "yes" vote meant the voter favored the council-manager form of government; a "No" vote meant the voter did not want to change the current commission form of government. Reading Eagle Company's editorial policy agreed with BAAC that the commission form had not served the city well.

Some of the numerous civic organizations and fraternal clubs in Reading wrote proclamations supporting the "Yes" side. The clergy preached sermons, not so much supporting certain candidates, but opposing incumbents. Social clubs were less enthused with the idea of change. They were too financially dependent on gambling machines and punchboards to support the reformers.

Ironically, at the same time this political revolution was taking place, another movement was quietly gaining ground that would lead to major changes in the face of Reading. "Renewal" and "redevelopment" were buzzwords among the city planners. During the hubbub right after the 8th Street numbers raid, the Community Renewal Center opened at 843-45 Penn Street. With a city administration saturated with scandal, there were still many in City Hall who earnestly believed the city could replace notoriety with propriety. Leonidas G. Vastardis, director of the Department of Planning, spoke optimistically about emerging redevelopment concepts. Four days after opening his new office, Vastardis announced the city had received a $169,242 federal planning grant as a prelude to other funds available under the federal Downtown East Urban Renewal Project. Numerous other eastern cities were also vying for their share of the money, but to date, Reading's planning grant was the largest.

"We'll be blazing a lot of new trails," Vastardis predicted, when reporting to council on May 8, 1962, that the planning grant had been approved. Even more important, he announced, another $4.5 million would be held in reserve for Reading if the city's redevelopment plan was acceptable.

Former Mayor Jack Davis was chairman of the Reading Redevelopment Authority, charged with carrying out plans to remove numerous old buildings on

Penn Street from $6^{th}$ to $9^{th}$ streets, and improving others. It became a very slow process. The tearing down phase proceeded sporadically and the rebuilding stage straggled along for years. It is difficult to say the sluggish redevelopment of the city's main thoroughfare could be blamed on the long legacy of rackets-tainted administrations. Changing social and merchandising cultures certainly were a factor. Ironically, however, many old-timers equate the passing of Penn Street's glory days with the decline of the racketeers.

Even in the best of times, City Hall politics was no haven of tranquility. But with Kubacki at the helm, forecasts on the political scene were seldom sunny and clear. On one occasion when Guldin suggested there should be an investigation of organized crime in Reading, Kubacki offered to lend him six Reading cops to conduct such a probe. Guldin quickly backed off. He questioned whether the mayor could legally delegate police responsibilities to him. On a more personal note he stated, "If ever I've seen a grandstand play, this is it." A lack of on-the-spot creativity was never one of Kubacki's failings.

Another example of the mayor's utter disregard for his constituents: A mother went to his office for a permit to hold a dance for teenagers. After a considerable wait, the mayor came out and told her the permit was not available—but then decided it was, on one condition:

"You will stand and repeat after me, 'Mayor Kubacki is a good mayor. Mayor Kubacki is a good man.'"

It was this and many other displays of shameless behavior and inappropriate humor that caused Kubacki's former deep pool of political support to run dry.

BID had recruited veteran activists and others who were destined to make names for themselves in Reading politics. Several were educators: Victor Yarnell, serving his first term in the State Legislature, was to become the city's mayor in 1968; Anthony Carabello, eventually served many years as county commissioner; Mark Brown, an old Socialist and future Reading School Board member; Charles Raith, an Albright professor, was an important behind-the-scenes operator for BID. R. David Chelius, BID's first president, would soon be on City Council; Charlie Seyfert would be BID's candidate for mayor the following year. Marty Bookbinder, whose determined efforts to advance the party, was soon running for a seat on the Reading School Board. These and many others were willing to risk their positions of power in the Democratic establishment to fight corruption. The goals of BID and BCCA were somewhat different, but the two were of one mind to bring about changes in Reading's political system.

The "No" forces formed the Reading Defense Committee as the organized opposition to BCCA. The Defense Committee was dominated by City Hall leaders.

From the pulpit on "Good Government Sunday," numerous pastors beseeched their congregations to perform their civic duty by voting "Yes." The Greater Reading Council of Churches staffed several Q. and A. seminars on the issue that Sunday evening.

Leave it to John Kubacki to spice up the stew that was coming to a boil a week before the September special election. He had stayed above the fray and neither side had extended an invitation for him to trumpet its cause. The YMCA again was the site of the ongoing debate before another large audience. Kubacki stood quietly in the wings as spokesmen for each side exchanged assumptions, presumptions, and suppositions. The mayor eventually stepped to the microphone to propose a marriage of sorts to settle the issue: why not continue the present form of government, but hire a manager to run the show? He stated that he and each of the councilmen should take $2,000 yearly pay cuts to provide the $10,000 or $12,000 needed to hire a city manager. Now what's he up to? everybody wondered. Right away rumors started flying about Kubacki making a deal with BCCA, hoping to swing some votes his way. Dr. Schmoyer was quick to quash the notion that he would, in any way, be associated with the mayor.

Two days later, John topped his YMCA performance with another bit of mischief that caused a much bigger stir than his phony marriage proposal. This time he publicly announced he had uncovered an attempt by the four members of City Council to mace contributions from the police force to support the Defense Committee.

The source for this serious charge was his police chief, Charlie Wade. The previous day, the four councilmen had met to map strategy for the special election stretch drive. The question was asked: should the officers of the police department be asked to contribute to the Defense Committee? Wade carried that information to his boss. Kubacki saw an opportunity to make a little hay by casting aspersions on his Council cohorts. His revelation suggested the entire police department was being intimidated into forking over donations to help the "No" cause.

With indignation, Kubacki announced: "This unprecedented action disturbed and shocked me, particularly since the police department comes under Civil Service regulations. The police have not been known to participate in partisan politics.

"Because of the special election I have refrained from initiating any attacks on the four councilmen. I have worked independently with many of my friends for the present form of government, of which I am mayor. However, this has not been true of the other members who have tried to insert personalities so that the real issue of the election would be lost in the twisting of the facts."

Standing at the mayor's side, Wade nodded agreement.

The councilmen, now placed in the position of denying the charge, vociferously counterattacked with their own charges of twisting the facts.

Guldin: "Kubacki is now a "Yes" man."

Kobrin: "This was a vicious lie."

Kuzminski: "This statement made by Chief Wade and Mayor Kubacki is an outright, malicious lie."

Coleman: "Under no circumstances was there any discussion that led to any facet of macing any employee. And talks with Wade on the voluntary contributions that were talked about, he was to clear with the mayor. If the mayor said he shouldn't ask anybody to contribute, he shouldn't." He added that the discussion concerned police officers, including Wade as a prosperous businessman, not patrolmen.

City Treasurer John Hoch, also present when the alleged macing remarks were made, and included in the mayor's sweeping charge, smiled and said he had nothing to say. Later he indicated the whole affair was little more than City Hall politics as usual—probably more truthful than all the denials, claims, and accusations that whirled about for the next few days before the dust settled with no final resolution.

When the polling places closed on September 26, 1962, there was no conclusive result of the special election either. According to the first unofficial count of the paper ballots, the "No" vote was 14,154, and the "Yes" vote, 14,029. With only a 125-vote edge, the "No" camp knew a victory toast was premature.

The voters had spoken. The lopsided vote in the 1961 referendum had seemed to indicate change was assured. But twice as many people took the time to cast ballots in the special election, and that showed status quo forces running even with BAAC advocates. Change did not come easy in Reading.

Like Floyd Patterson fans, who watched Sonny Liston take away their champ's heavyweight title that same night, the "Yes" camp was shocked and frustrated. How could the voting majority still want the same type of government that had given the city such a bad name?

A recount was ordered in 41 of the city's 71 precincts. The process of re-examining the thousands of paper ballots took more than a month. Each day the "No" lead shrank: 91, 62, 58, 22, 8, 5. Then on October 31, Judges Warren Hess and Albert Readinger, in charge of the recount, announced the "Yes" camp had won by 31votes. Most of the votes questioned involved voters who wrote "No" or "Yes," instead of checking either the "Yes" or "No" boxes. The "No" group lost 156 votes because that many voters failed to follow ballot instructions. As expected, the final round of this struggle was still to be fought.

The first verbal punches were thrown the next day when City Council voted to hire a new city solicitor. With Kubacki abstaining, all four councilmen voted to promote Elliott Goldstan from assistant city solicitor to fill the post that had been empty since August when Wils Austin was appointed to the Berks County Court.

Much to the mayor's annoyance, Councilman Guldin had introduced the resolution for Goldstan's hiring. Kubacki said he should have been given the courtesy of introducing the measure. A second resolution approved would allow Goldstan to represent the "No" forces in any legal action growing out of the recount decision. Kubacki threatened to take legal action himself if the new solicitor tried to do that because, he said, it would be illegal for Goldstan to represent either side since City Council had no standing in the special election.

Prothonotary Paul A. Adams was directed to certify the election results to the county election board. Only an appeal to a higher court now stood in the way of Reading's switch to a different form of government. The RDC did appeal and the state Supreme Court quickly reacted by scheduling a special hearing on January 29, long before its next scheduled sitting on March 18. Both sides were well represented when the full court heard arguments in Philadelphia. Irving R. Segal of Philadelphia represented the Reading Defense Committee with Reading City Solicitor Elliott Goldstan allowed to speak one minute during the hour-long hearing. The "Yes" forces had Darlington Hoopes and former Berks Judge Paul N. Schaeffer presenting its case. Chief Justice John C. Bell Jr. gave the RDC ten days to file an additional brief of argument.

Even the 7-man Supreme Court was split in its interpretation of election laws after reviewing reams of election results. The final 4-3 decision in this drawn-out election was handed down on February 21, 1963. Another recount had been executed by the court and, as the saying goes, "You can't beat City Hall." The justices ruled the "Nos" won by six votes. Unlike the turmoil of the past five months, the two sides accepted the verdict without much fuss. Only Mayor Kubacki, whose support the RDC had spurned, made a sarcastic comment: "Now that the issue has been settled, perhaps Mr. Guldin can actively go back to his gutters, bus stops, and streets which today cause many inconveniences."

Harold's victory statement ignored his primary rival: "I am glad the State Supreme Court has seen fit to follow the will of the electorate of the city of Reading in carrying out their wish to continue our present form of government." Guldin and just about every other candidate were not so civil in their campaign debates as corruption was the core issue at every stop.

A week after the Supreme Court announced its decision, the losing faction still put up a bold front. The BCCA's publicity chairman, Douglas P. Fisher, was named winner of the Reading Chamber of Commerce Distinguished Service Award at its 11th Annual DSA banquet. The 29-year-old Fisher was chairman of the Junior Chamber of Commerce board of directors. After being lauded for his work in publicizing BCCA's campaign for change, Fisher said the battle must continue and said the organization would start a new membership drive the following week with a goal of 5,000 new members. But it was a hard sell after the long, contentious hostilities ended.

For another three decades Reading's commission form of government remained in place. In 1995 there was another special election and this time the council-manager forces came out on top. Starting in 1996, the city had a manager for the first time with a part-time council and full-time mayor. As for reducing the bickering, pettiness, and discontent at Council meetings, there was little change. It was as if ghosts of councils past possessed all who followed.

# 36

## *Enough is enough, D.A. sues*

The trial date for Fred Brubaker's libel case against Reading Eagle Company was finally set almost a year and a half after he filed suit. He had hired a Philadelphia lawyer, Alfred P. Filippone, to represent him. But two weeks before the May 27 opening of the trial, Filippone notified Fred he would be handling another case in Philadelphia that day. Fred requested a postponement, but Judge Herman M. Rodgers, who would try the civil case, turned him down. Brubaker had been granted a six-month continuance the previous year. All the Berks County judges had disqualified themselves, so the state attorney general's office appointed Rodgers, the president judge in Mercer County. Rather than hire a local attorney on short notice, Brubaker decided to handle his own prosecution.

There is a popular legal tenet that the attorney who defends himself has a fool for a lawyer. Fred was no fool and some suspect he was not at all disappointed at becoming a last minute substitute. Years of defending his method of running the D.A.'s office had provided him with plenty of motivation to go after the monopoly press, as he so often referred to it.

Fred would employ a David and Goliath strategy to win the sympathy of the jury of eight women and four men. Berks County juries were noted for taking the side of the underdog. Of the jurors, two were laborers and two were retired. Seven of the women were housewives and another was a clerk. Seven were city residents, and the rest lived in small towns or rural areas. Fred seemed pleased with the final selections—just plain folks. During the trial, most of the prosecutor's pointed remarks were directed at the *Reading Times* in general, and city editor Dick Peters in particular.

Lead attorney for the defense was John R. McConnell from Philadelphia, seconded by Charles H. Weidner of the Eagle Company's regular law firm, Stevens and Lee. McConnell's plan was to soften the bully image of the Eagle Company dailies that Fred was trying to promote. The attorney did not seek to bludgeon Brubaker about his lack of action against vice, rather he wanted to show it was the newspapers' responsibility to emphasize an indifferent and failed law enforcement system. Stevens and Lee lawyers would have preferred a frontal assault by showing it was the publisher's responsibility to run articles that Fred claimed were published to humiliate him, degrade him, blacken his character, and accuse him of criminal acts. McConnell advised reporters and editors who would be in the courtroom not to gather around Hawley Quier, the Eagle Company president. The attorney was afraid if editorial room personnel huddled around the boss it would give the impression of a big company ganging up on a lone defendant. But the congenial publisher, who was a regular at the 11-day trial, would occasionally motion company employees to come sit with him, providing the group portrait his lawyers had wanted to discourage.

The 15 stories and columns that were the basis of Brubaker's case were flashed on a movie screen for the jury to read. The Operation Vice Den series was shown, along with three Old Pete columns and five news articles. All had appeared in the Times between October 13, 1961, and January 19, 1962.

Hawley Quier, Dick Peters, and Donald Barlett, who no longer worked for the Times, were feature prosecution witnesses. When asked whether he or his employees had ever offered information about vice activities to the district attorney, Quier said the publication of stories about the vice issue was available to Brubaker as well as to the public. This was a constant theme throughout the trial: Fred claiming he acted when receiving complaints, so why didn't reporters and editors come to him if they had pertinent facts about gambling and prostitution.

To Peters he pointed out, "the only good information to a district attorney is the kind that would stand up in court. Do you have that kind?"

The city editor, who admitted not having any legal training, said he did not. Although Peters had very good and accurate sources about the 10$^{th}$ and Walnut gambling den that eventually moved to Cherry Street, it was true that these secondhand tales he could have offered to the D.A. probably would not have been accepted as evidence. But, as Peters pointed out, such information should have suggested to Brubaker that a city or state police investigation probably would have resulted in evidence he could have used before a judge and jury.

Brubaker called his secretary, Rosemary Drexler, to testify about the large number of criminal cases the district attorney's office had prosecuted since Fred became D.A. Defense counsel McConnell hopped on that bit of promotion by asking her if Abe Minker or John (sic) Fudeman had ever been prosecuted by Brubaker's office during that same six-year stretch.

The answer was no.

Brubaker and County Commissioner Peter Yonavick testified about the running debate the district attorney had with county officials regarding the hiring of a fifth assistant D.A. Fred had been requesting this during his first term in office. Finally in 1960, Fred got his fifth assistant at the cost of giving up one of the county detectives. Since assistant D.A.s were paid less than $5,000 a year, they were really only working part-time for the county in addition to their private practices. This issue was the basis of Fred's argument that he did not have the personnel to initiate investigations and stage raids. And this is what four witnesses, all district attorneys from other counties, talked about when testifying. Some were asked for their interpretations of their job descriptions according to the Pennsylvania Manual for Prosecuting Attorneys. But Judge Rodgers advised the jury to disregard any opinions of the visiting D.A.s, as he would take up this point in his instructions to the panel at the end of the trial.

District Attorney Carroll Noll of Lebanon County was a fellow officer in Brubaker's Air Force Reserve outfit, the 9202nd Air Force Recovery Squadron. He testified that the way Dick Peters taunted Fred in his columns possibly resulted in disrespect from some squadron personnel.

Dist. Atty. Paul Richard Thomas of Crawford County had attended Dickinson Law School with Brubaker. He testified that from reading Old Pete columns he felt the Times city editor did not like Fred, and was holding him up to ridicule and portraying him as incompetent. He said after reading Old Pete columns he had the impression that Fred was being accused of taking kickbacks or benefiting economically from the rampant gambling and prostitution. Thomas also answered "yes" when McConnell asked him if he agreed with a section in the state manual that stated a lazy or corrupt district attorney could take advantage of indefinite statutes when he fails to enforce the law.

All four of the D.A.s said a small staff, some on part-time status, could affect the amount of investigations and arrests a district attorney would be able to attempt. None of the four came right out with an opinion that supported the newspapers' veiled hints that Fred was in league with racketeers.

If the friendly D.A.s were a big plus for Brubaker, the clergy who were called to testify were not. And five of them admitted practically all of the information they had about Fred was from reading the Reading daily newspapers. And Fred made sure the jury was clear on that point each time he cross-examined a minister who said he believed Fred was less than diligent in his job performance. But all were careful not to accuse him of taking payoffs. Just like the press, none of the churchmen had any direct knowledge of graft.

In the past six years while racketeers were going to jail and police chief Charlie Wade was under federal indictment, no other elected or appointed local official had even been charged. And during the many grand jury sessions there was nothing to indicate Brubaker was even under suspicion. If the press had not pursued its muckraking course during his two administrations, possibly Fred would have escaped all the notoriety that pursued him during his time in office. Plenty of state prosecutors, federal prosecutors, a couple of state attorney generals, a couple of governors and judges, and a U.S. senator had stated organized crime could not exist in Reading without cooperation from the city and county's top law enforcement officials. The local newspaper could not ignore these complaints, but by being the messenger of bad news about the district attorney, Old Pete had added his satirical opinions.

In one of his turns on the stand, Brubaker said he could not walk down the street without somebody calling him Fearless Fred. This was Peters' favorite sobriquet for the district attorney. Brubaker testified he "withdrew himself" and "became depressed" and tried to keep newspaper articles away from his wife and daughters. His private law practice suffered, he testified. His sympathy strategy was working, although the Times staff did not realize it.

Reporter Nick Yost, who was covering City Hall at this time, was delegated by Peters, with Hawley Quier's approval, to cover the trial. It was feared by Times management that by allowing the usual court reporter, Gene Friedman, to report the trial, Brubaker might oppose that on the grounds of conflict of interest. Brubaker and Friedman had faced off on many matters over the last six years. Could Gene be trusted to put aside his true feelings when being selective in reporting what he saw as the most important testimony to pass on to the reading public? Yost and Brubaker had no issues between them, although Nick was a member of Fred's Army Reserve unit. So, Yost received strict orders to report the trial with no unnecessary adverbial or adjectival refinements; make no attempts to pep up the rather dry testimony with any exciting modifiers.

Fred's wife, Flora, stated that their family had been very active in the community until the newspapers began running unfavorable stories about her husband. She said he did not want to go out in public because it became unpleasant and uncomfortable.

As for the numerous federal, state, and city police raids on numbers banks, the Penn Hardware still, the Cherry Street dice game, scores of prostitution arrests, and frequent confiscation of hundreds of illegal gambling machines in the city and county, Brubaker said he knew of some of those criminal activities before they were knocked off, but felt the federal government was much better equipped to handle those jobs than his office was. He said he had always offered a willing hand but was constantly rejected by the state and federal agencies.

A defense witness with top credentials was former New York Judge Morris Ploscowe, the editor of a two-volume work, "Manual for Prosecuting Attorneys." The Harvard Law School graduate had served as a New York magistrate from 1945 to 1953. After the Kefauver Committee hearings, he wrote that panel's national report that included an extensive section regarding organized crime in Reading. So he was certainly familiar with vice conditions in the Pretzel City during the early years of the previous decade.

John McConnell read a passage from the judge's manual about indefinite statutes that a lazy or corrupt prosecuting attorney could take advantage of if he did not want to enforce the law. On the witness stand, Ploscowe said he still believed that to be the case. McConnell did not specifically ask the witness whether he felt Fred Brubaker had made a sincere effort to enforce the law. The words "lazy" and "corrupt," however, were bandied about several times during Ploscowe's two-hour stretch on the stand as he explained how a prosecutor, by harassing houses of prostitution, could put them out of business.

Brubaker read another passage in the manual that stated "there is no easy answer" to the question of whether a prosecuting attorney is a lawyer who presents evidence obtained by others or whether he has the broader role of a detective.

Ploscowe said he had written that opinion and still thought it to be true. It could be argued that Fred salvaged the argument he had been preaching for a long time.

Anticipated fireworks when John Marx was called by the defense to testify never happened. Unlike their accusatory and sarcastic debates in court the previous year, Fred and John were much more under control, with no major confrontations. The former A.D.A. gave a full report about the two prostitution raids he initiated while his superior was out of town. Brubaker pointed out Marx was not an actual participant of the raiding parties because he stayed outside while state police made up the strike force. When Brubaker cross-examined, Marx admitted that he had never been instructed NOT to conduct raids. But he also testified that he had wanted to quit his former job for almost a year because he was "sick and tired" of the pressure of working in the courthouse and in his private practice.

Fred made quite an issue about a picture that appeared in the *Reading Eagle*. Originally he was in the picture with two other people when it was taken. When it appeared in the paper, he had been cropped off. John Kunkleman, the military editor, explained that there was room only for a two-column picture, so Fred, having appeared in an Eagle photo a few days earlier, was eliminated. Fred was not the first, nor the last notable to suffer that indignity in the history of photo-journalism. But at the time, he saw it as just one more example of editors denying him good press.

Donald Barlett testified that he was critical in his Operation Vice Den series of the token prostitution raids because arrests in many instances were made without any apparent effort to secure evidence for a court case or an attempt to find "the persons really in control."

He had a lengthy stint on the witness stand detailing how he conducted his investigation of prostitution. He said he arrived at a figure of $500,000 as the total annual income at five houses of prostitution where he believed each accommodated at least 40 customers per day during a five-day week.

Times court reporter Gene Friedman, who visited the district attorney's office almost daily, was grilled by Brubaker about various raids and court appearances. Friedman was asked if he remembered U.S. Attorney Harold Wood, after a conference with Fred, saying he was "grateful to have the support of a public official of the caliber of District Attorney Fred Brubaker."

Friedman responded that such a statement "was never made in my presence."

Later, McConnell asked Friedman if he recalled any statements Wood did make about the still case.

Friedman said that during grand jury hearings in the illegal still case, Wood observed that such a major operation in the Penn Hardware building could not have existed "without the knowledge of public officials."

Back and forth it went, the prosecution claiming Fred's department was ill-equipped to carry out major investigations, but was subjected to continuous humiliation and scorn in the daily newspapers; the press denying its intent was to ridicule the D.A., and was only doing its job by informing the public that Brubaker was lax in performing his duties.

The jury deliberated for six hours before declaring Fred Brubaker the winner. It awarded him $100,000 in punitive damages, and $35,000 for general and special damages. Reading Eagle Company moved for a mistrial, claiming a witness's question had gone unanswered.

Six months later while the case was still under appeal, the U.S. Supreme Court heard arguments in *New York Times* vs. Sullivan, a noted civil rights case in which a Montgomery, Ala., city commissioner sued the newspaper for libel concerning an advertisement it had run. In its decision rendered on March 19, 1964, the high court ruled the 1st Amendment protected the publication of statements, even false ones, about the conduct of public officials except when statements were made with actual malice (with knowledge that they are false or in reckless disregard of their truth or falsity). Under this new standard, Sullivan's case collapsed.

And so did Fred Brubaker's case against Reading Eagle Company. The Pennsylvania Supreme Court overturned the Berks County Court ruling. The high court granted Reading Eagle Company a new trial on June 15, 1966. In a meeting of the two parties, a settlement was agreed to rather than go through another lengthy court proceeding. Instead of the $135,000 that the jury had awarded him, the newspaper management offered Fred a settlement to end the case, the amount sealed by the court. Brubaker agreed to accept a much smaller amount. Rumors, naturally, began to circulate, with $20,000 as the most persistent figure. Forty-four years later the records remained sealed.

The day before Thanksgiving 2007, I had the last of dozens and dozens of interviews for this book. It was a phone interview with 88-year-old Fred Brubaker. He had fallen last year and was now on a walker. Fred sounded fine and was ready for the holiday. I asked a very general question about the Minker era: Did he have anything to tell me about the overall experience of being district attorney at that time. On the spur of the moment he didn't, so we just talked about how times have changed. Then I posed a specific query:

"Do you still feel your policy of being strictly a prosecutor, not an investigator, was the right choice?"

"Absolutely," he stated without hesitation. "I never had any training in investigative work, I was not qualified to conduct investigations, I left the police work to the police." He believed in "You bring me the evidence and I'll prosecute the offenders."

Fred talked about how the district attorney's office has expanded 10-fold from the size it was when he started as D.A. in 1956. "I never had control of any of the money, not one cent. I had a budget but I needed permission from the commissioners to spend even a dime. Now the district attorney has a million dollars that he's responsible for." He was referring to the $1 million the recent D.A., Mark Baldwin, had been holding in confiscated drug money. Baldwin's decision to turn the money over to the Berks County Community Foundation for distribution instead of giving most of it to the Reading Police Department, cost him his job in the 2007 elections after having served 16 years in office.

And we discussed Fred's life before entering politics. After graduating from Reading High School, he attended Susquehanna University and earned his bachelor's degree in 1942. He received a commission on entering the Army. The next year he was sent to Sardinia, off Italy, as commanding officer of an anti-aircraft battery. He then transferred to the Army Air Corps. He commanded Headquarters Squadron of the 42nd Bomber Wing, serving in Corsica, France and Germany and attaining the rank of major.

After the war he continued his military career by becoming commanding officer of the 9202 Air Force Reserve Recovery Squadron at Reading's Spaatz field for 10 years before his unit was moved to the Middletown airport near Harrisburg. He retired as a lieutenant colonel.

Through the GI Bill he earned his law degree at Dickinson College. Fred entered politics in 1954, running for state legislator, but trailed John Kubacki and Albert Readinger in the primary election. The next year he ran for district attorney, defeating Henry Koch, the incumbent. Once out of politics in 1964, he returned to private practice which continues to this day. Selective about the cases he handles, he admits, "only the ones I know I can handle."

A story Fred recalled demonstrated to what extremes politics was carried in his day. At the Gregg American Legion Post at 10th and Penn streets one night, Eagle court reporter Irv Rollman was chatting with Fred. Irv mentioned that something should be done about the raunchy burlesque shows at the Park Theatre. Fred suggested Irv should complain to the mayor, not him. Irv said he had told Kubacki about the strippers, but was just brushed off. The reporter coaxed the district attorney to come with him to get a first-hand look at the Park just across Penn Street up in the next block.

"We ran into Jimmy Maurer, the theatre manager, in the lobby. I told him not to tell anybody we were there," Fred related. "We sat in the audience and the girl performing … her costume wasn't really too revealing, but her language was awful as she engaged the crowd in dirty talk. After the show I told Jimmy I wanted to talk with the girl. When she came out she was wearing street clothes with her hair in a knot. She looked like the girl next door. I told her I had no objection to what she wore on the stage, but I thought the remarks she was making were very offensive. She told me she had two children back in Baltimore where she lived when she wasn't out on the circuit. She told me she didn't want to offend anybody and tried to adhere to each community's moral standards. She promised to clean up her language.

"I told my wife about it when I went home that night. Then about midnight the phone rang. It was John Kubacki. He was outraged that I had gone to the theatre and talked with one of the performers. 'What do you mean by coming into my town snooping around. I am head of the police department and don't you ever do that again.' He bellowed at me for several minutes. My wife was shocked that he would talk like that. Kubacki and I never spoke to each other after that."

That story symbolized Reading's querulous Democratic politics during those never forgotten notorious times.

# 37

# *GOP finally wins at the ballot box*

John Kubacki knew his chance of becoming the first mayor in the history of Reading to win consecutive terms was rapidly declining as the 1963 campaign took shape. Few if any of the city's elected officials had ever faced greater odds within their own majority party. However, he knew several Democrats were after his job, so he hoped his diminished following would still outnumber those of each of his opponents.

Unlike their fractious foes, the Republicans settled early on their man for mayor. It would have been difficult to find a better Mr. Clean than Eugene L. Shirk, the athletic director, coach and math professor at Albright College. He was 62 years old, a novice in politics, but with a spotless reputation and a Pennsylvania German heritage, complete with strong Dutch accent. Although he was unopposed in the primary, he was still a long shot because of the big Democratic majority in the city. Many in that majority voted in the 1962 special election to keep the present form of commission government. But in the past six months, more and more rackets-related revelations had soured many of them on all the Democratic hopefuls.

In March the various Democratic factions began parading out their candidates for mayor, six before two dropped out preceding the May primary. The old guard Demos had settled on Councilman Harold Guldin as the party's choice for the top post. For many months, the former labor leader had been battling Kubacki in City Council meetings, obviously intent on replacing the incumbent.

Charlie "Buzz" Seyfert had improved his name recognition by serving as chairman of the City Charter Commission. So it was no surprise when BID elected him to run for mayor and lead its slate of six candidates. As president of the United Labor Council, Seyfert was positioned to split the labor vote with Guldin. Kubacki was counting on that to help his candidacy.

Watching closely as Kubacki almost systematically destroyed himself was Rep. Dan McDevitt, now in his second term as a state legislator. Although he had a better paying job, ($9,000 annually) and an easier work schedule in Harrisburg, McDevitt decided to take another crack at the mayor's office. After he talked with several civic leaders, he said they agreed "the city did progress, that I had a wonderful record in civic affairs" while serving as mayor from 1956 through 1959. If he won and eventually beat the GOP candidate in November, he would have to take a $1,000 pay cut. Like Kubacki, he certainly understood the perks available to a mayor of Reading.

McDevitt's surprise announcement stunned Guldin. Harold had stayed out of the 1959 race for mayor to give Danny a better chance of winning the primary four years ago. Now he was disappointed the ex-mayor had not afforded him the same consideration as he tried to unseat their mutual enemy.

Dr. Earl Yoder, who had fought City Hall by refusing to collect the city occupation tax from his employees, and Claude Focht, a recent heart attack victim, were the two dark horse mayoral candidates who could do little but serve as spoilers for the other four. Focht eventually dropped out, as did McDevitt, probably helping Guldin more than any of the others.

John Kubacki waited and waited to make his grand entrance. On the final day for filing, he threw his hat into the ring once again. It was no surprise, but all kinds of rumors were flying about last-minute deals, one of which had him running for City Council.

In March, Reading-Berks Chamber of Commerce joined the fray by sending letters to the four city councilmen requesting that planned downtown traffic changes be delayed for the time being. Thomas Cadmus, the C. of C. president, also sent letters to Gov. Scranton and U.S. Atty. Gen. Bobby Kennedy asking for state and federal aid to rid the city and county of racket influences. Feeling snubbed, the mayor naturally had to respond.

His letter to the Chamber claimed the traffic changes were proposed for "the protection of pedestrians and to insure that the motorist who desired to shop downtown would have an easier flow of traffic into and out of the business district. While other cities facing similar problems are progressing and moving forward, the C. of C. is doing everything possible to stifle these things which will help Reading."

Fred Brubaker had claimed that John Marx's motive for becoming a hyperactive assistant district attorney in 1962 was to boost his name before running against the district attorney in the coming primary. That did not happen, but

Marx did gain headlines again when he turned over to the federal government vice investigation reports of the previous year. He and Sheriff Harold Yetzer had appeared before the federal grand jury to be questioned about a state police probe of possible payoffs involving operators of games of chance at the Kutztown Fair in 1962. Tom McBride welcomed the notes as he continued his job as the Justice Department's special prosecutor of organized crime. He was informed that four concessionaires at the fair had paid Berks officials bribes to allow their gambling booths to remain open. The possibility of tax evasion interested the IRS. John Beemer and Don Holloway had conducted that investigation.

There was no lull in rackets-related news, which pleased the Republicans, BID, and any of the candidates running against those in office. The murder of Frank Donato proved that Reading was not immune to Mafia violence. With big money involved, it was inevitable blood eventually would be spilled.

Possibly more violence was averted on March 27 when the state police received a tip that three gunmen from Massachusetts were on their way to Reading to hold up a high-stakes poker game at the Berkshire Hotel. Not only the cops were informed, but before the would-be robbers arrived, operators of the game also were alerted. So the game was called off for that Tuesday night. Rocco Urella's men had hoped to seize the robbers during the game. The staties had information that several well-known businessmen and a city official often took part in the action. Urella posted troopers along the Allentown Pike and the suspects were nabbed before reaching Reading.

One of them was Thomas Guerro, a 34-year-old convicted criminal awaiting trial on bank-robbing charges in Massachusetts. Guerro and two buddies claimed they were coming to Reading looking for jobs. Apparently Guerro was in town several weeks earlier when it was learned he bought a hat in a local store and was known to be an acquaintance of a Reading gambler. Found in the trunk of the car from New England was a loaded sawed-off shotgun, three .38-caliber handguns, considerable .38-caliber ammunition and a leaded rubber hose.

John Kubacki, trying to make a little hay out of this additional bad news about the rackets, said he was not the city official who had recently lost more than $600 in the poker game. In all fairness, John stated, he thought the gambling official's name should be released to remove any taint from all others—but not by him. Guerro was charged with carrying a firearm without a license. Three months later he was tried, found guilty, and fined $100.

As the primary campaign continued to heat up, the federal government made a move that put the final seal of disapproval on Democratic office seekers. On April 9, the federal grand jury in Philadelphia indicted Charlie Wade for perjury in denying he arranged kickbacks to be paid to John Kubacki. If this didn't wipe out any slim possibilities of a Demo victory, the Republicans gloated, nothing could.

Along with the indictment, the government released for publication, the police chief's complete testimony before the grand jury just 12 months earlier. That report showed that Wade denied any role in suspected kickbacks involved in the purchase of parking meters. Employees from two parking meter companies had admitted to the grand jury paying bribe money to be awarded contracts from the city. Another charge indicated that before a garage operator received a towing contract, he agreed to pay $1 per towed car to an unnamed city official. In a third count, Wade was accused of arranging kickbacks from a Reading car dealer. Were more indictments pending, since Wade had stated that if the bribes ended up in the mayor's office, he (Charlie) knew nothing about it?

Wade announced he had no intention of resigning, denying all the accusations made against him. The mayor was equally ready to stonewall it. As his foes lined up to demand Kubacki at least suspend Wade, the mayor stated he had "complete confidence in him … and in his integrity … and he will continue as head of the bureau of police."

In the Democratic Party's civil war, a skirmish took place in City Hall at the April 16 Council meeting. The opening shot was fired by Kubacki when he read a letter regarding a threatened investigation by Fred Brubaker into a city contract to purchase a new fire alarm system. On February 6, Council had voted to buy the system from Sentinel Alarm Corp. for $390,000. Kubacki's had been the single dissenting vote. Now he was reading a letter from Asst. Dist. Atty. Gerald Ullman requesting a copy of the contract because his boss had received information that something was amiss. At the Council meeting, Kubacki got into a heated debate about why, after two months, he had not received the completed contract for his signature.

When Assistant City Solicitor Adam Krafczek reported that certain conditions in the contract had been changed since the resolution was passed, Kubacki attacked: "You mean to say you can go to the solicitor's office and get changes. Bids have been thrown out for less reasons than that." He aimed his remarks about the delay at his primary opponent, Harold Guldin, and Councilman Jerry Kobrin, who had claimed it was urgent that the contract be approved.

A full-scale battle broke out the next day as the mayor and councilmen met in a special session with Brubaker. As Fred patiently waited to explain his interest in the matter, Kobrin and Kubacki engaged in a preliminary vocal slugfest. Should

Council even accept Brubaker's letter with its hint of an unprecedented investigation into city business? Kubacki said it should, but Kobrin, the city's director of safety, said he was suspicious of Brubaker's motives.

"Really touching," Kobrin smirked. He questioned why the district attorney, who repeatedly stated it was not his job to investigate charges of corruption on rumors alone, was now initiating a probe into a city contract. Kobrin said he would welcome an investigation because Council had nothing to hide. Guldin was in complete agreement. When the dust settled, Brubaker had his say:

"I hate to interrupt in your private sandbox," but he was attending the session in his capacity as district attorney and acting on a complaint he had received. He stated it had been brought to his attention that Sentinel had little experience in fire alarm systems, and questioned whether the study committee assigned to investigate the alarm project was wined and dined by the Philadelphia company. And what about a trip to the racetrack they had taken with Sentinel people, he wanted to know.

The noisy, at times profane, debate raged for nearly 45 minutes when Brubaker suggested that Council members might have been guilty of malfeasance in negotiating the contract. All the combatants in this free-for-all were supposedly on the same political team, but for the moment most of them were thinking of the election and how to make points with the voters.

More than once Kubacki jumped into the fray by shouting at Kobrin: "Your remarks are out of order."

Guldin tossed a pointed query at his primary opponent: "Who challenges you when you're out of order."

Racketeering in Reading had reach such a state that politicians from both parties were not pulling any punches in the press. U.S. Sen. Joe Clark, the former Philadelphia mayor, complained that corruption in Reading was damaging Pennsylvania's state Democratic Party organization. This was at the time when the mob murder of Frank Donato was being reported in the national media. "The condition of the Democratic Party in Berks County is such as to require a pretty thorough housecleaning," Clark stated.

When Kubacki and Brubaker were asked to comment on the prominent senator's observations, the mayor offered the usual about Reading being no worse than other cities. Brubaker said it was his opinion that Clark was directing his remarks only at Reading, not Berks County.

This gave BID some fodder to chew on:

"As they have for many years, our city officials denied such influences, indeed, they denied that rackets existed. Nor will the people be fooled by the district attorney's weak attempt to evade responsibility." That was from a resolution BID passed at its next meeting.

On May 1, Gov. William Scranton came to Reading to give the Berks County Republican Committee a boost by labeling organized crime and vice conditions in Reading as "nothing short of deplorable." Kubacki and Brubaker were quick to respond. The governor was hardly on his way out of town before Fred sent a midnight telegram to him asking for the state to initiate a grand jury probe if he felt things were so bad in Reading. The district attorney also sent a message to Judge Hess calling for a local grand jury investigation. The judge had no trouble finding a motive in Fred's request and answered, "We will not be an instrument for furthering the political advantage of any candidate or party."

Kubacki called Scranton's remarks "oft-repeated hogwash." He offered to pay $100 into the state general fund if authorities could uncover any organized rackets or vice in Reading. Gene Shirk, not a betting man, was ready with an opinion:

"I am convinced that the mayor better have ready the $100 to which he referred. I'm sure he's going to lose it." Neither the state nor Berks County succumbed to the politicians' braggadocio by taking the grand jury bait. Scranton's rebuttal to Brubaker's request:

"Well, in the first place, I'm glad he wants to be cooperative in this. This is something new. As you know, he's been in office for some time and the problems of the Reading area have been pointed out to him point-blank by the newspapers, and he certainly has been anything but cooperative in stamping out the vice and gambling in that period of time."

At a political rally, Brubaker mentioned that it was no coincidence the governor had made uncomplimentary remarks about the district attorney shortly before Fred's libel trial against Reading Eagle Company was due to start. Questioned on this point, Scranton told the press he did not have any knowledge of the libel suit before he spoke before the Chamber of Commerce.

Rocco Urella's state troopers chipped in with a pair of gambling raids in Reading. Days before the election as a reminder that the city administration was still lax on gambling, state police arrested two numbers writers in a North 11th Street luncheonette. Then Thomas F. McBride, the Justice Department's special organized crime prosecutor, issued a timely flash: Police Chief Wade's trial might be held within a few weeks. Before the federal grand jury that day, McBride was questioning witnesses about irregularities in the $390,000 Sentinel fire alarm system the city had contracted to buy. And back in City Council chambers that morning, the contract was once again being hotly contested. It had been a prominent campaign issue for the past three weeks as Kubacki and Guldin made charges and countercharges at every political rally they attended.

Just five days before the May 21 primary election, a conflagration, even more heated than usual, broke out at a City Council meeting when Kubacki introduced a resolution to rescind the Sentinel contract. That started the ruckus that exploded into a fiery debate about the legality of even considering such an action. The resolution became so mired in parliamentary procedure that assistant solicitor Robert Shapiro was unable to free it for a vote. If Kubacki's proposal raised some hackles, an even more bizarre performance was yet to come.

Six policemen stationed at the rear of Council chamber were called to the Council table. Everybody, including the six, wondered why they were present. Then the mayor announced:

"Throughout the campaign, on many occasions I have said Reading was never cleaner ... even offering $100 to charity if proved wrong. As mayor of the city, I'm accepting responsibility. Since Mr. Guldin is aware of these things," the mayor stated, turning to the policemen, "you consult with Mr. Guldin ... work with him ... let him accept responsibility as a citizen and city official now."

Harold Guldin was furious. "If ever I have seen a grandstand play ... a political play. You want to throw all your responsibility in my lap." Guldin said he would talk with the city solicitor to determine the legality of such a move. Then, "I will accept the responsibility, but I'm not going to take all your rotten apples in my barrel."

When Kubacki tried to dismiss the bewildered policemen, Councilman Jerry Kobrin, enraged, jumped in: "Gentleman, you are not dismissed. You're still under old and new business."

And so it was just another average day at the office for a City Council that was good for a show practically every time the mayor and councilmen got together. Council's weekly performances should have been serialized as a TV comedy, but would anybody have believed their unrehearsed antics. Too bad that that gang was 45 years ahead of virtual reality television.

The final reminder to voters about the city's dismal record of flagrant racketeering was the publication of a 5-part biography of Abe Minker by Reading Eagle reporter Gerry Renner. His well-researched series gave a graphic account of Abe's long life of crime. The series started the day after Abe was taken into custody and shipped off to begin his 4-year sentence in the Lewisburg Federal Penitentiary.

In a four-man race for the Democratic nomination for mayor, Kubacki finished third. Guldin easily won by almost 1,700 votes over the BID candidate, Charlie Seyfert. Kubacki trailed Buzz by another 2,250 votes. The voters had spoken, awarding Kubacki only 3,481 votes, not even half of the 7,535 he received in the 1959 primary.

Although never charged with any wrongdoing, Fred Brubaker's lackluster record against the rackets cost him the Democratic nomination for a county judgeship. His opponent, Wils Austin, often a behind-the-scenes player in Democratic politics, 10 months earlier had been appointed to fill a vacancy on the bench Brubaker now hoped to win. In this primary, Brubaker failed to get half as many votes as Austin, a former city solicitor and county solicitor.

At City Council meeting the day after the election, Kubacki had the grace to congratulate the other successful Democratic candidates, including Harold Guldin. Then he took a shot at his conferees for the snub he received four years earlier when he was elected mayor:

"None of the councilmen had the courtesy or good sportsmanship to congratulate me."

Not so nice was Kubacki's reaction to subordinates who had not supported him. That same day several police officers were demoted, and two others who had attended political rallies—not his—while on duty, were suspended. As promised, another half a dozen officers were demoted the following Monday. The mayor was just playing the game of politics according to his rules.

The Sentinel Alarm system, a political hot potato before the election, eventually cooled off and probably had little effect on the primary outcome. After the election, City Council finally voted 4-1 to have the city solicitor complete the purchase of the Sentinel system. Kubacki's was the dissenting vote.

Although Dan McDevitt had dropped out of the race for mayor, he gained some unwanted attention two days after the primary with an appearance before the federal grand jury. He was questioned about the city's purchase of three fire trucks just before he left office four years earlier. It would be more than a year before that transaction was argued in criminal court.

Burlesque at the Park Theatre provided a flavor of show biz to the grand jury hearings. Employees of Jimmy Maurer, the theatre operator, were questioned about Mayor Kubacki's alleged visits backstage in regard to possible payoffs for allowing the strippers to perform. Witnesses told of seeing him behind the curtain, fueling the government's effort to prove John was not too humble to serve as his own personal bagman.

When Charlie Wade's trial was postponed in June, some took that as a sign more indictments were imminent. Fourth of July fireworks had barely ceased when the government lit up the political landscape on July 8. The grand jury indicted Kubacki and Abe Minker and Johnny Wittig for extorting $10,500 in city parking meter deals. Kubacki was not available for comment that night but issued a written statement declaring his innocence, insisting he would not resign.

That same day, Capt. Urella brought six of his vice team into Reading, returning to the scene of past crimes. Joe Fiorini and a 32-year-old partner, Shirley Otto, were arrested in the same row home at 872 North 8th Street, where Joe's numbers bank was raided 18 months earlier. The staties broke down a couple of doors and Trooper Richard Rafter climbed a ladder to a second-floor window. Rafter had to ward off a large attack dog as he entered. Shirley fled to the third floor, locked herself in a room and began burning betting slips and adding machine tapes. Fiorini, as he did in January 1962, came into the house while the raid was in progress. Several thousand dollars Joe had in his pockets were also seized. He had completed a four-month jail sentence in BCP only a few months ago.

Brothers John, 53, and Morris, 33, Pietrobone, were arrested in their grocery store on Franklin Street where they were charged with trafficking in lottery tickets supplied by Fiorini. With Cal Lieberman representing Joe and Shirley, a hearing before Alderman Larry Palmer ended abruptly when the Pietrobone brothers refused to testify against the other defendants. The state police said they needed the pair to make their case, Palmer dismissed the charges. No explanation was given why. As it turned out, the feds did not want evidence collected by the staties to be exposed before federal prosecutors completed their major investigation into Minker's empire.

At a second hearing, the alderman held the Pietrobones for grand jury action. The brothers eventually pleaded guilty to lottery charges, paid $500 fines and received 1-year probations.

When City Council met the day after Minker and Kubacki were indicted, the Council chamber was crowded with viewers anticipating some excitement, similar to the session right after Charlie Wade was indicted. Rumors were rife that as many as 13 more indictments were expected, but McBride denied that was about to happen. The anxious audience was disappointed as nobody mentioned the government charges against the mayor. The wear and tear of a council in turmoil had taken its toll. Only a few dull matters were discussed, with nary an accusation or insult.

Following his indictment in April 1963, Charlie Wade began considering his options, one of which was switching teams. In his City Hall office and at home he had been recording telephone conversations with other city and county officials. If he was going down, he planned to have company. When Wade met Johnny Wittig on back roads to accept bags of cash to be distributed to top police officials, the chief's hidden tape recorder in his car was turned on. He also carried a Miniphone tape recorder in his pocket that picked up conversations he had with other city officials in his office.

As summer wore on, Charlie had almost made up his mind to turn over a new leaf and cooperate with law enforcement. But he was worried sick that he would soon be a dead man if he did. He knew the Minker team had a spy on the grand jury who was providing Abe with information obtained by the government behind closed grand jury doors. That made the chief wary of what he could tell the feds confidentially, fearing it would get back to Minker. He decided to leak a false rumor to the agents who came to see him from time to time, sensing that Charlie wanted to tell them more, but couldn't quite bring himself to do it. He told them about the grandfather clock Karpack gave Kubacki claiming it was worth $2,000. If that report got back to Minker, the chief believed, then he'd know he could not trust the people who were trying to gain his trust. Finally he felt it was safe to inform the T-men about the suspect juror, who was immediately removed from the panel. It was then, in the fall of 1963, that Wade opened up.

Corp. Don Holloway, now in his role as head of the state police vice squad, occasionally spoke with Wade, letting him know the evidence against him and quite a few others was accumulating. Holloway told Charlie it was his choice: come in from the cold and talk, or continue to hold back and suffer the consequences. He believed Holloway and agreed to have a confab. Fearful of going to Troop C headquarters because too many people there knew him, he suggested the Holiday Inn near the Lancaster exit of the Pennsylvania Turnpike as a meeting place. It was there one afternoon that Charlie opened the floodgates to Holloway and Sgt. Leroy Lilly. Some of what he told the two state policemen they already knew. And there was other information about Minker's numerous payoffs to politicians and police officials that they had suspicions about. It was a fruitful beginning of Charlie's mea culpa that would be repeated several times in public over the next few years. Now that a stray had been split from the herd,

Lilly contacted federal interrogators. At subsequent meetings with the feds, Wade continued his narrative at the same Holiday Inn where he first began his rollover.

"I really liked Charlie," Holloway said 45 years later at his Chapel Hill Golf Course. "He wanted to do the right thing but he was one scared guy. He was a smart guy, but he wanted that chief's job so bad he made some bad choices."

On the motel parking lot, Charlie showed the state policemen an exterior security device he had installed on his Lincoln. It was a starter button attached under the rear bumper that could be activated by his foot. He had read about too many mob assassinations in which the victim turned the ignition key, setting off a bomb.

Life for Charlie and his family was not getting any easier. Threatening phone calls, drive-by harassment from racketeers at his Cumru Township home, and notes warning dire retaliation if he chose to sing were increasing. He began carrying a handgun. He installed security technology at his house. He also added several large, noisy watchdogs to his fortress. His was not the happiest of holidays as he was now expected to testify for the government at the parking meter trial due to begin in January.

Wade's fears were not just imagined. According to Johnny Wittig, who was interviewed by TV commentator Rod MacLeish, there was a contract of $20,000 for anyone willing to take the chief out.

"Nobody took it?" MacLeish asked.

"They say the man was too hot," Wittig said about Wade, who was still alive at the time of the interview in 1965. "I think one day there is a bullet for him. If they want to get a man it may take 20 years to get him." They never did get Charlie. He died at 59 of natural causes in 1973 after a prolonged illness.

The 1963 general election attracted the biggest voter turnout in years. Of the 32,700 votes cast in the race for mayor, Gene Shirk's margin of victory was more than 4,000. Obviously, many loyal Democrats could no longer justify voting for Guldin or other Democrats. Too many hints that other city officials, in addition to Kubacki, were on the take, doomed the Democratic party. The politicians' indifference to gambling and prostitution alone were not enough to sour the public in 1959, but revelations about extortion, perjury, and tax violations caused a wave of revulsion the Demos could not stem.

With Shirk's election, and Albert Schucker and William Laws winning seats on City Council, the Republicans held a 3-2 majority. Democratic Councilmen Jerry Kobrin and Joe Kuzminski were not up for reelection. The Republican landslide just about cleaned house in City Hall and the Courthouse. Only City

Treasurer John L. Hoch survived the purge, winning his seventh term in office. Democrat Wils Austin, weighed down by his reputation of power broker in the Democratic Party, was upset by James W. Bertolet, giving the Republicans a majority on the Berks County court.

W. Richard Eshelman scored a lopsided victory as Brubaker's replacement by beating Forrest Schaeffer by 7,000 votes. Eshelman would soon show his mettle as a district attorney more than willing to work with federal agencies to uproot the racketeers. He appointed a former Republican city councilman Sam Russell as a special prosecuting attorney who would concentrate on the mob's corrupting influence. The Justice Department was only too pleased to supply Eshelman with evidence and information it had gathered in Reading and Berks County over the past several years.

Possibly the happiest Democrat in Reading the day after the slaughter was John Kubacki. His capacity for getting even had not been sated by demoting and suspending "traitors" after the primary election. Having received no condolences following his defeat in May, the mayor was drooling to repay his detractors. He showed up at Wednesday's somber City Council meeting with a broad grin and brisk step. Before taking his seat he waved two face towels, one pink, one yellow, before the dour councilmen:

"I tried to get a few of these with "crying towel" printed on them," John joyfully stated, "but I couldn't find any. I brought these along in case anybody needs them. They're very absorbent." A showman to the end.

Among the several pre-election smears designed to heap more on the dung pile the Republicans had collected was the sale of the National Youth Center Administration tract. This former campsite along the Pricetown Road in Muhlenberg Township was a relic of the Prohibition era, one of FDR's social welfare programs to give young people employment to revive the economy. Part of the 59-acre parcel with 16 buildings had been leased by Howard and Thomas Huber in the early 1950s after it was turned over to the city of Reading by the federal government. In August 1960, the first year of the Kubacki administration, the Hubers bought the land for $22,000.

Four days before the 1963 general election on November 5, Walter Alessandroni came to Reading to speak at the American Legion's Gregg Post. Although Gov. Scranton ordered a state investigation into the land purchase on October 23, the state attorney general waited till his November 1 speech to reveal such a probe was underway. Claiming value of the tract was much higher than the purchase price, he charged there was no advertising of a sale of public land, no bids received, nor any evidence a competent appraisal having been made. The buyer was College Heights Enterprizes headed by the Hubers.

Daniel Huyett, county chairman of the GOP, claiming the land was worth in excess of $100,000, filed a taxpayers civil suit against the city, charging fraud and payoffs had been made. Since all three county judges had been involved in this sale of public land, they disqualified themselves from further litigation. Clinton County Judge Abraham Lipez was appointed to handle the case. Named as defendants in the suit were Mayor Kubacki, Councilmen Kobrin and Kuzminski, and former councilmen Guldin and Ruoff. During 1964 all the suspects except Kubacki gave statements denying they were involved in anything illegal, The councilmen and ex-councilmen also denied having any knowledge about Abe Minker being involved in the purchase. In August of 1965 Kubacki was still asking for more time to prepare an explanation in his role in the sale.

By November of '65, all parties had agreed to a settlement. Having obtained a 1960 fair market price from a Realtor, the Hubers agreed to pay the city an additional $23,000. After legal fees and other deductions, Reading was $18,725 richer.

This case turned out to be a sequel to the crane fiasco that ended with the buyer, who thought he had a bargain, eventually paying more than twice as much. No under-the-table business was verified in the NYA sale, but it was rather obvious everything was not above board.

A few days after the 1963 election, members of the Police Athletic League board of directors voted Charlie Wade PAL president. This seemed to be a strange selection. Charlie was not fully out of the closet at this time, although he was winning more and more points with the feds by feeding them the information about City Hall corruption and Minker's gambling ring. So Charlie was hardly a role model for PAL kids, unless the PAL board hoped to present him in a new light as the prodigal son turning over a new leaf.

Mayor Gene Shirk wasted no time realigning the city's major departments. The first new appointee after the winning candidates were sworn in was a replacement for Charlie Wade, who had refused to step down, although under indictment for eight months. After his election, Shirk had appointed a three-man panel to search for a new chief. Sidney M. Hilliard, a 26-year police veteran and recent chief in St. Petersburg, Florida, was chosen to reorganize Reading's much-maligned department that had a leadership crisis for eight years. Hilliard was given the title police commissioner at an annual salary of $10,000, substantially above Wade's $6,760. Charlie was demoted to detective and shortly thereafter retired to concentrate on becoming a government witness in a big way. John Feltman, captain of the detective bureau for seven years, retired in February, replaced by his longtime No. 2 man, Paul Hageman.

The long-smoldering fire alarm system issue flared again at the February 1964 meeting of the Firemen's Union. Copies of the secret contract with Sentinel Alarm were finally being circulated. Union members were dismayed to learn there was no audio system to notify volunteers to report to a fire scene. Nate McDevitt, honorary delegate from the Washington Fire Company, led the attack on Jerry Kobrin, still director of safety. Angrily, Kobrin denied there was any collusion when the contract with Sentinel Alarm was signed. But the union members asked what good was a system that does not notify volunteer firemen there was a fire to fight. Calling statements made by the ex-mayor's brother "inflammatory" and "derogatory," Kobrin promised a study would be made and reported on at the next meeting. The debate quieted down in March as Sentinel agreed to pick up the cost for two telephone lines to each firehouse.

# 38

# *Independents fill the void; staties react*

The IRS's interest in Reading gambling didn't completely relax when Jules Hanssens was transferred to head up the agency's Lancaster office covering Lebanon, York, Lancaster, and Adams counties. He still had a good line on what was happening up north in Berks. After Treasury agents made their presence felt on a St. Patrick's Day Saturday night, Hanssens and his deputy noticed how gambling tastes had changed following his war against the multicoin machines. Now Jules's men were going after punchboards, fishbowls, and other lottery and drawing games.

Led by the IRS local collection manager, Thomas Morgan, seven teams of Treasury agents dropped by several dozen places in Reading and its suburbs that rainy evening. They collected 40 samples of different types of boards, wheels and fishbowls as evidence to prove gambling was available at many of the 76 places visited. No slot machines were found, leading Hanssens to remark, "Drawings and lotteries have become big business since state authorities have instituted rigid enforcement of the coin-operated machines which cost $250 (for a federal stamp). Morgan added, "It's gambling, that's what it is." "This is a bonanza," Hanssens said. "By the time we visited the last place, the guy had been warned by phone eight times." But he didn't remove his punchboards.

Although Abe Minker had made his big killing in the numbers and slot machines, when he was expanding his illegal business he also had a hand in punchboards—a dirty hand. Most of the grocery stores and bars on North 9th Street had Abe's boards on display for customers. Tom Krause, president of T.G. Faust Inc., a body armor company, remembers his father, Ted, working part-time for Abe in the 1950s. Ted's job was pulling punchboards. He would make the rounds to check on Abe's boards. If most of the top prizes on a board had not yet been won, Ted would pull that board and return it to Abe. The store dealer would tell customers that the punchboard had been completely punched with all the winners paid off. This was just one more way the racketeers took advantage of gamblers. By depriving punchboard players of winning the best prizes, their profits were greatly increased. If most of the top prizes were gone, the board would not be pulled.

The places charged with ignoring their gambling tax obligations would receive notices of how much they owed. Hanssens mentioned a club operator cited in a recent raid in his area had anted up $27,000 in excise tax—and that amount represented only 10 per cent of the gross income from gambling activities.

It would take another 15 years before the Pennsylvania Legislature legalized the state lottery. Legislators were well aware of the gambling situation in Reading and Berks County. No other city or county in the state could match their disregard for state laws prohibiting gambling, although Schuylkill was not far behind with Matt Whitaker in charge of such matters.

Holloway's unit made a few gambling arrests during the summer of '63, including the Fiorini-Otto raid, but after that lull, things picked up dramatically during the months ahead. A $400 a day numbers/bookie operating in Bern and Cumru townships was uncovered in October after three months of surveillance. More unusual than the raid itself was a charge of attempted bribery against the operator, Henry Kotzen. Sgt. Lilly and Holloway headed the investigation that kept Kotzen in its sights while his 27 writers had numbers drops in several locations. Kotzen barricaded himself in his Greenfields house when the staties came knocking. He cut the phone wire in his den and disconnected the phone. When Lilly and Holloway eventually gained entrance, they spliced the wires, reconnected the phone and took incoming calls for the next half hour. In that time, almost $200 in numbers and horse bets were taken. Lilly said the numbers operation was bringing in between $4,000 and $5,000 weekly, plus $5,000 in racing bets.

The case took on added significance two months later when Kotzen was again arrested by Holloway and McAnally at a store operated by the suspect's son in the Antietam Shopping Center in St. Lawrence. They described Rich's Tile store as a sub-bank in Kotzen's numbers operation. A tip from another numbers writer led the state cops to the suspect. The state policemen waited until Kotzen arrived at his son's store to bust him. During a search of his person, numbers slips were found in his shoes, plus $794 in his pockets. He said the money was not from bets his writers had taken, but if they would forget about this entire incident, they could have the money. The two corporals accepted the money, kept on driving to the Troop C barracks where they charged Kotzen with attempted bribery in addition to gambling counts.

When Kotzen came to trial in 1965, he appealed to the court for a change of venue because he felt Don Holloway had become so well known as a gangbuster in Berks County that the jury would give too much credence to his testimony. Kotzen's bid was denied and he eventually pleaded guilty and got off with a stiff fine.

Another prominent figure in this transition period when veteran numbers writers and bookies scrambled to establish steady clientele was Richard "Slim" Rowe. This dapper racketeer apparently had enough clout with the Philadelphia mob to remain independent during the Minker reign. Slim served a few weeks in BCP on a numbers conviction in 1958, but avoided arrest for the next five years although never protected by the local mob.

Rowe's long winning streak ended on November 13, 1963, when he and Reading School Board Director William Sands were caught running a numbers/horse book. According to his confession, the 49-year-old Sands had been taught all there is to know about numbers and horse betting from the 50-year-old professor, Slim. Sands claimed he had just started his new night job at $75 a week before the staties nabbed him in his home. He was faced with the threat of losing his day job as business manager and secretary-treasurer of Local 155, Bartender, Hotel and Restaurant Employees Union, AFL-CIO. He resigned from the school board. Having admitted his folly he pleaded guilty to gambling charges. Sands appeared before a sympathetic Judge Austin for sentencing. As a first-time offender, Sands was placed on probation for two years. Rowe, too, pleaded guilty to reduced charges and received a 3-to-23 month sentence. He was allowed to spend Christmas at home, then served his minimum term before being paroled. Sidelined only a short time, this lifer in the gambling racket was soon turning a crooked buck again.

Not until May 1965 did the law catch up to him. This time Holloway and friends had been watching him for about five months. By springtime, Holloway said, Slim had built up a major operation he shared with John "Brick" Mainwaring, 56, one of the many players arrested in the 1962 Cherry Street dice raid. Abraham Smigelsky, 68, was named as a pickup man in Slim's latest venture. Also arrested was Daniel Wool, the owner of the luncheonette and cigar store at 501 Penn Street, where state policemen had placed bets. Several thousand dollars in betting slips were found in Mainwaring's apartment at 839 Chestnut Street. To gain entrance, Holloway dialed Mainwaring's number, then held the line open for 15 minutes. After a short time he repeated this maneuver. A bookie without a working telephone is about as handicapped as a three-legged horse. So, when a trooper, dressed as a telephone company repairman rang Mainwaring's doorbell, he put his alarm system on idle and opened up. The trooper led the way in for Holloway and others.

Smigelsky, anxious to avoid jail time at his advanced age, spoke freely to his captors about Rowe's enterprise in return for a suitable plea bargain. At Rowe's trial that began on June 25, 1965, mild, bald, bespectacled Abe Smigelsky testified, "I received what I thought was a good commission, 25 percent." He said Rowe would contact him each week about how much he had earned taking bets and as a pickup man. Then Abe would go to Rowe's apartment at 820 Penn and retrieve an envelope containing money from Slim's mailbox.

But when Slim took the stand he insisted his old buddy was mistaken about when they were associates. Slim admitted Abe wrote numbers for him back in '63, but since that time, the defendant claimed, he had no connection with gamblers. He said he had worked as a bartender at The Clique nightclub until November 1964, and for the past four or five months was learning dental technology with Dr. Ray Namy whose office was only a block from Slim's Penn Street apartment. Slim's wife and 16-year-old daughter testified they remembered Smigelsky coming to their apartment every Sunday in 1963 to settle accounts with Rowe, but he had not been there since then.

The dapper Slim, an acknowledged ladies man, might have had enough charisma to sway a pair on the jury when the 11-women panel arrived at a 9-2 vote for conviction. The 12$^{th}$ man, who had been ailing, was excused by Judge Readinger. But Dick Eshelman wasn't ready to throw in the towel. The D.A. filed new gaming charges. But long before the case was retried, Slim was behind bars again.

On August 8, Don Holloway was on a ladder peering in an open window and who did he see but Slim Rowe playing seven-card poker with some of the old gang. Don invited his buddy, Art McAnally and city detective Warren Hable to join him for a top-rung view. The setting for this lofty scene was on the Cumru Township property of Edith Lucchese, the widow of Charlie Lucchese whose weak heart had finally given out. Climbing down, the peekers, joined by five other city, county, and state policemen, broke into the small out-building less than 100 yards from Edith's house—the same house that was headquarters for her late husband's numbers bank three years earlier.

While on the ladder, Holloway had observed Tony Lucchese and Richard Miller taking cuts from the poker pots. This upped the status of the game to illegal gambling. So they were charged with running the game. The players, in addition to Slim Rowe, were Anthony Perry, Frank Gammino, and Patsy Pillo. Slim and the other three got off with paying $12 forfeits before being released. A few days later, however, Slim was back in BCP for breaking his parole. By removing a dollar from each pot, Lucchese and Miller, plus Pillo, a convicted felon, were the kind of people Slim was not supposed to mingle with while on probation. Rowe had to complete his original sentence in the 1963 numbers case before being released the following November. At that same time Brick Mainwaring was just getting used to his cell in BCP after pleading guilty as charged. He received a 30-day term.

Four months later Slim was back in court for his retrial after the hung jury had allowed him to walk. This time the jury vote was unanimous: guilty.

It wasn't till June 1966 that Lucchese and Miller pleaded guilty to running the poker game on Edith Lucchese's property. They got off with a year's probation and $500 fines. The charges against Edith were dropped on the recommendation of A.D.A. Norman Dettra, just as they were when her late husband was convicted of bookmaking and running a numbers game from their home.

The final chapter of Slim Rowe's life was more intriguing and grizzly than any of his other exploits as a gambler. But it was probably a gambling debt that was the motive behind his murder in April 1985.

At the age of 72, Rowe was still practicing his trade. This was 20 years after his previous arrest. The state lottery was prospering, but so were Slim and several other Reading racketeers who catered to bettors who liked to do things the old fashioned way. The numbers game was pretty much ignored by the police as illegal drugs were the rage, and kept law enforcement people busy in their dangerous pursuit of dealers and pushers.

The word on the street was that Slim owed up to $30,000. On February 12, 1985, three thugs broke into his first-floor apartment at 1040 Lancaster Avenue. He was pistol-whipped and the intruders robbed him of $2,635 and a $600 watch, he told police. Two years later, Lawrence Gaul Jr., 23 at the time, was convicted of the assault and sentenced to 3 ½ years in state prison. Three accomplices, Dennis Staten, David Seller and Karen Schwenk received shorter sentences.

Slim's luck finally ran out. His body was found in his apartment Sunday afternoon, April 6, 1986. Police said he was strangled and stabbed the previous night after admitting somebody he knew around midnight.

The suspected motive was that he was victimized by creditors. Then again, some wondered whether it was a revenge slaying. Nobody was ever arrested after years of investigation.

A side drama to this killing was the search for money that Slim might have left behind. His daughter, Cindy, was employed at the Spring Township Municipal Building. A search of the township safe revealed an envelope containing $45,000. An attached note signed by Cindy said that in the event of her death the money was to be turned over to her father. In her desk, another $6,400 was found. Since Spring officials found no township funds were missing the $51,400 was turned over to her. If it was gambling money, nobody came forward complaining it was money Slim owed. There was no sign the killer or killers searched Slim's apartment, and police recovered another $3,000 during their investigation. It was well known that the free-spending Slim usually kept large sums of money on his person or in his apartment. Therefore the robbery motive seemed unlikely when the killers left such a wad of cash behind.

The most recent local rackets murder before Slim was eliminated, was the fatal shooting of his brother, Harold "Red" Rowe, in 1948. The 37-year-old Red's body was found behind a billboard at Conner's Crossing, near Schuylkill Haven, with a bullet in his left temple. That case, just like Slim's, has never been solved, although city police have opened Slim's cold case file by having DNA evidence checked.

During 1964 and 1965, Holloway's crew made more than 30 raids in which gambling charges were entered against dozens of men and women. The city police department also kept the pressure on and cooperated with the state police in numerous raids during that period. The Pennsylvania Liquor Control Agency, on orders from Gov. Scranton, stepped up the prosecutions of liquor and gambling violators prevalent in the city's and county's many clubs.

Everybody who chanced to ignore the laws was red meat for the vociferous Holloway unit. The boss didn't pick and choose whom to chase down. Lester Miller had two wooden legs when he decided to distribute punchboards. Holloway stopped Miller's car on a back road and found 2,000 punchboards in the car. A further search of Miller's house revealed 12,000 fishbowl tickets. Although he wasn't charged because the punchboards and tickets were unused, Lester got the message that he was in an illegal business.

From the infirm to officialdom, nobody was untouchable. The secretary-treasurer of the Carpenter Steel Fellowship Association and public relations editor for the firm was knocked off and charged with operating a football pool. Carl S. Seigfried was fined $500 after pleading no defense. Judge Hess billed Carl an extra $6, the amount it cost the county to destroy the sizable amount of tickets seized.

Roy Danner operated a dairy bar in Kutztown, and Martin Ludwig ran a nearby service station on Route 222. They took horse bets—hundreds of dollars in horse bets weekly—and Danner phoned them in to Marty and Fat in Reading. After his arrest, Danner told Holloway either Fat or Marty would come to the dairy bar once a week to settle accounts, but other than their nicknames, he knew nothing else about them. Holloway took about 30 betting slips from Danner when he arrested him. The suspects were respected businessmen. If Danner, 70, and Ludwig, 51, gained a share of the racketeers' wealth for weeks, months, or years, they weren't saying. Both were convicted and fined. This was typical of the network the big boys in Reading had established throughout the county.

As for law enforcement, the next decade could be dubbed The Holloway Era. Don served under Sgt. Leroy Lilly, chief of Troop C's criminal division. In five years he would be promoted to Lilly's job, then be moved up to lieutenant while serving on an 11-county drug strike force in southeastern Pennsylvania. This unit gathered information about illegal narcotics activities and funneled it to individual troops for prosecution. Over his 38-year state police career, Holloway worked all types of cases, but his stretch on the high-profile vice squad made his a familiar name in Berks County.

With Minker already convicted when Holloway became the state police vice buster, Don didn't chase down any local legends, but he did go after the bad guys with the zeal of a Mike Reilly during Prohibition and later. Although he always worked in consort with other policemen, he was usually called on to be the prosecutor who had to appear at hearings and in court as the feature prosecution witness. In the next several years Don's name became synonymous with the ongoing state police crackdown on racketeers.

# 39

## *The meter runs out, pair convicted*

Charlie Wade arrived at the federal courthouse in Philadelphia on January 21, 1964, wearing a holstered pistol under his suit coat. "I have a license to carry a .38-caliber pistol, so I thought I might as well use it," Charlie announced.

Although he was smiling as he glanced around, constant threats from the mob had become no laughing matter. Making his second appearance before the grand jury, he delivered a long and detailed litany of corruption and vice in his town for the past four years. At a pair of four-hour sessions, the stories he told were a mother lode of evidence for prosecutors. This time Charlie told the truth.

And he was not the only one talking. Businessmen, City Hall employees, and salesmen were providing incriminating testimony about kickbacks being paid to elected officials in the city's purchase of cars, police emergency vans, fire trucks, and parking meters. Earlier, when representatives of local and national companies were called before the panel they identified those who extorted money and amounts that had exchanged hands. Wade was the inside man, confirming deals others had testified to. The government had not yet dismissed perjury charges against Charlie—that would depend on how he performed as the government's prize witness before a trial judge and jury.

Although the parking meter case for John Kubacki, Abe Minker, and Johnny Wittig was slated for trial in late January, a petition for postponement was granted to Kubacki. Minker, now languishing in prison, wanted to get the case over with, but his pleas for a speedy trial were rejected and it was rescheduled for March.

Still unable to accept the fact that elected officials, or former elected officials had to play by the same rules as Joe Public, Ex-Mayor Kubacki tried to get a parking ticket fixed in City Hall. The new police commissioner, Sidney Hilliard, turned him down, and Reading became $3.25 richer. John claimed Patrolman Gary Wenrich tagged his illegally parked car to satisfy a grudge against him.

Ever the optimist, Kubacki filed a petition to run for the Pennsylvania Legislature in the spring primary, seeking the same seat he surrendered in 1960 after being elected mayor. In the event he was found innocent in his forthcoming trial, he figured his chances were good of winning the Democratic nomination in the 5th Legislative District against Victor Yarnell, the incumbent. The 5th District covered the South of Penn area where John had grown up and had strong support.

As usual, Kubacki created a bit of theater before having his day in court, this time unintentionally. On Monday, March 30, Kubacki's attorney, Edwin P. Rome, asked the court for a last-minute postponement. The reason: blanched haunches. The previous Saturday, John had reclined too long under a sunlamp, searing the skin that the sun rarely illuminates. One day's delay was all the court would allow. As the jury was being selected on Tuesday, John gingerly entered the courtroom but spent much of the long day ambling along the courthouse corridors in obvious discomfort. He didn't complain, chatting with his wife and son and the press. He had an air cushion at the ready whenever he chose to sit. By Wednesday the jury was in place and John was tired of being the butt of gluteus maximus jokes.

Three government witnesses, Charlie Wade, Joe Liever, and George Gradel, were listed as unindicted co-conspirators. Wade, as expected, was the prosecution's star witness, but Gradel and Liever were never called to testify.

Minker and Kubacki, former partners in intrigue, ignored each other throughout the trial. Judge Alfred L. Luongo, who would preside, had been appointed to the federal bench at the age of 38, only three years earlier by President Kennedy. Luongo was also a former partner of Edwin Rome, Kubacki's attorney.

Instead of burning pain, Kubacki's discomfort was reduced to a persistent itch as opening statements were presented Wednesday morning. If physically annoyed, John was pleased with Rome, a veteran criminal lawyer who seemed to play to the predominant female jury with his gentle manner while picturing his client as a good civil servant, falsely accused. This contrasted with B. Nathaniel Richter's opener, which stressed the absurdity of the charges against Minker, who sat stone-faced as he had at so many court appearances over the past 40 years. Going up against the two noted Philadelphia lawyers for the next two and a half weeks were special organized crime prosecutors Thomas F. McBride and John S. Ruth Jr. Jake Kossman was Minker's first choice to represent him, but that respected criminal attorney was off in Florida still tied up with the Jimmy Hoffa matter.

Rodger Weidlich, sales representative for Koontz Equipment Corp., was the feature witness on day one. He repeated details of the story he had told investigators several times, and again before a federal grand jury. In brief, his tale was about first approaching Charlie Wade regarding the purchase of parking meters from his company. Weidlich told about meetings with John Kubacki and Abe Minker and Wade, and the subsequent dickering over how much kickback the company would have to pay to complete the deal. It was Minker who finally agreed to accept $6 for each meter head the city bought, Weidlich testified. When Weidlich brought a check for $3,000 to Reading, he said, he went with Charlie Wade to the bank to cash it. Instead of handing the cash to Wade, Weidlich said, the chief used a middleman to make the transfer to one of Charlie's employees. Charlie would testify later that he handed the cash to Kubacki, who counted the 30 one hundred dollar bills. Wade then admitted taking $300 the mayor offered him for his role in arranging the illegal transaction. The contract of almost $30,000 for 500 meters was signed in June, not quite six months after Kubacki took his oath as mayor.

Walter Hughes, general manager of Karpark Corp. of Starksville, Mississippi, was the main witness who testified about a second parking meter deal for an even bigger kickback than the first one. Hughes testified he received a call in March 1960 from Joe Liever that the mayor was in the market for more parking meters. In 1948, Liever had served as agent for Karpark when Jack Davis's administration made a large meter purchase. But Joe's contract with Karpark expired in 1959. Hughes said he came to Reading several weeks after Liever's call and discussed a deal with Joe and Abe Minker on the White House Market parking lot. He also met with Kubacki on that initial trip. Both parties agreed that there would be a kickback of $15 on each $51 meter head to be purchased. However, there was a hang-up: Kubacki also wanted a sizable gift, an $880 grandfather's clock, included in the deal. Later, Hughes, also plant superintendent of Herschede Hall Clock Co., a Karpark subsidiary, said the clock request could be arranged. Although the contract for 500 meters was signed in June 1960, the deal languished till the following summer when Hughes was looking for an agent because Liever had failed to renew his agreement. Hughes testified he then contacted a friend, George Gradel, a bookmaker in Covington, Kentucky, to be the middleman.

Hughes testified he received a $7,500 check from his company made out to Gradel. It was agreed, Hughes testified, that Gradel would pay income tax on the commission. In a Cincinnati bank, Hughes said he identified Gradel, who cashed the check. Hughes said he thought Gradel gave some of the money to his son, but he did not know how much. Of the remainder, Hughes said he took $385 to buy a Christmas gift for the widow of a Reading meter maintenance man, and Gradel took his 20 percent cut. That left about $6,000 for a payoff in Reading. Hughes later admitted he never bought the Christmas gift, but after being questioned by federal investigators the following year, he returned the money to Gradel because he felt it was part of his commission.

Hughes testified that the commission developed into an issue when he and Gradel arrived in Reading just before Christmas 1961. At a meeting in Joe Liever's office with Abe Minker, an argument developed concerning who should get the 20 percent fee. Abe backed Lievers's contention that he had brought the principals together to get the deal started, but Hughes claimed he had to use Gradel as the middleman because Joe turned down the job. Gradel won the argument. In a dark hallway outside Liever's office, Gradel had admitted to investigators, he handed an envelope with $6,000 to Johnny Wittig, who allegedly took it to the mayor's office in City Hall. Wittig, as a defendant, did not testify.

B. Nathaniel Richter, attorney for Minker, agreed with Hughes that the commission/kickback was perfectly legal in the parking meter trade. Hughes had testified, "We will not pay any kickbacks. We need a legal sales representative to pay the commission to. We'll even take a mayor's wife." This apparently cleared his conscience of any wrongdoing, although he knew full well that his gambler friend was handling the money just to take him off the hook. But it would be up to the jury to judge whether this was an underhanded system at work rather than an accepted business ploy as the man from Mississippi claimed.

The witness everybody was waiting to hear finally took the stand a week after the trial began. Ex-Police Chief Charlie Wade, dapper in a dark pinstripe suit with a gold tie, his silver, wavy locks stylishly groomed, made no bones about having lied to investigators and the grand jury. Under direct questioning, Wade made it known early that he was testifying under immunity. The jury had been assured by McBride that Charlie's tale about kickbacks would be the true story. Although Charlie appeared to hold back nothing, he tried to paint himself as a victim who wanted to do the right thing, but let ambition and vanity rule his actions. In the end, he confessed, he was now telling the truth because he wanted to protect his community.

Up to this point in the trial, witnesses had told about meetings they had with either Minker or Kubacki. Now, Wade placed Abe and Kubacki and himself together as they discussed ways to cover up their extra official deals with the parking meter companies. It was in August of 1962, several months after the contract was signed when they met in the back office of Joe Liever's place, Charlie testified. By then, Wade had informed Minker and Kubacki the feds were asking him very pointed questions about kickbacks.

Now on the witness stand, Wade admitted Kubacki gave him $300 after he handed the mayor the $3,000 payoff in the 1960 deal. Wade said he reluctantly took the money after Kubacki said, "I have to give the other councilmen $200 apiece. You did all the work, you're entitled to $100 more than the others are getting."

Quoting Minker, Charlie testified: "I have to fight with the mayor to give the councilmen their share. He wants to keep it all for himself, I don't get a nickel out of this, but I have to fight with him so there's peace." Council voted unanimously to buy the meters. It was never proven, however, that Harold Guldin, Bruce Coleman, Joe Kuzminski, and Bill Ruoff, the other four councilmen in 1960, ever received any money from Kubacki, and none was accused by the government.

Under relentless cross-examination by Rome, Kubacki's attorney, Wade was less at ease than when the prosecutors questioned him. During the trial he would not make eye contact with the defendants who also ignored each other. Wade continued to portray the role of the good guy who was forced into perjury and extortion to keep his job.

"I told Mr. McBride and Mr. Morris (federal investigator) that I paid for my job and I got short-changed." Charlie testified. "After two months, it was taken away from me." He added that he then began taping telephone conversations although he knew it was against the law to do so without authorization.

In another exchange with Rome, Charlie stated, "Irregardless of what happens to me, I want to see the town cleaned up. I've told the truth," he insisted, "and I'm happy. I've accomplished what I set out to do. I've exposed everyone. I don't care what happens to me now. If it costs me my life, I don't care"

Despite Charlie's expressed lack of concern, Judge Luongo was worried about Wade's safety because "He is an extremely critical witness in many respects."

The judge said he didn't intend "to put him in custody, either formal or informal," but questioned attorneys about the safety issue. He then assigned a deputy U.S. marshal to remain at Charlie's side in and outside the courtroom during the sessions he testified.

Charlie liked the public attention he had attracted when he stood up to a gunman and convinced him to surrender. He wanted to reclaim that stardom. According to Charlie, he was misled by Kubacki during the election campaign when John claimed he would have nothing to do with Minker. But the detective was experienced enough to know how politics had always worked in Reading. If he resented the company he had bought into, he had only himself to blame. Now in court, he was calling his former position "a stinking job," adding, "when in Rome, you do as the Romans do." He characterized himself as a one-man crusader who decided to work with the federal investigators over a period of several months. During that stage of the probe he hired Thomas D. McBride, the former Pennsylvania attorney general who had prosecuted Abe Minker, Johnny Wittig, Louie and Alex Fudeman for perjury. McBride, who was ordered by Luongo not to converse with Wade, sat in the courtroom as Charlie testified. Tom L. was not related to Tom D., the lead federal prosecutor in this case.

In an exchange with Richter, Wade admitted to his affection for Minker, as opposed to his opinion of Kubacki. He claimed to have fought with Kubacki more than any other chief had battled with his mayor. He admitted having used four-letter names to describe Kubacki many times. Questioned by Richter about his relationship with Abe:

"You had an affection for him, you called him Pop?"

"I still have," Wade admitted.

"Well, do you come here now and tell all these things because you love him so much?"

No reply.

"Do you love him?" the lawyer persisted.

"I tell my wife I love her."

"No, no. Do you love him?"

"I like him. I think a lot of him."

"Do you like yourself better?"

"I'm not in love with myself."

"Do you hate yourself?"

"Many times," Charlie said, "like when I took that $300."

Early in 1963, when the purchase of another 1,500 to 2,000 meter heads was being negotiated for the new Franklin Plaza parking garage, Wade recalled in court that Kubacki boasted to him that he, the mayor, would make the final decision, not Abe Minker, about how the deal would be handled.

Wade quoted Kubacki:

"I don't care what bids they're getting, I run the Parking Authority. As far as I'm concerned, when Abe tells me what kind of meters he wants, I don't care what any of the Parking Authority says. I put those fellows on the Parking Authority and they will get the meters I want to get."

At the end of his long ordeal on the witness stand, Wade said it had been more than a year since he had seen or talked with Abe. Not since a month before he was indicted in April 1963 had he and Abe discussed the mounting problems that were developing as the government marched more than a hundred witnesses before the grand jury. And after Minker was imprisoned in May 1963, Charlie began plotting how he could avoid the same fate.

During a four-day weekend recess of the trial, there was considerable speculation about whether John Kubacki would testify. Intimates, aware of the former mayor's powers of persuasion, felt he would. It was doubtful he would pass up the chance to disprove that he was the wily and greedy elected official several witnesses had made him out to be. He didn't disappoint those who hoped he would take the stand.

With Rome leading him through a reminiscence of his childhood and teen years, John performed, more than testified. With gestures and facial expressions he tried to present himself in a quiet, articulate manner that would sway the jury into believing this was the real John Kubacki, not the conniving, grasping politician the parking meter representatives and Charlie Wade had described. He told about his life as a youngster and teenager growing up in a middle class family "in the south end of town." The defendant calmly admitted to being aggressive and strong-willed as a high school and college athlete. And when he entered politics he used that same competitiveness to defeat political opponents and run the city as he saw fit. His answers to Rome's questions were expansive and detailed.

But when Tom McBride came at him with many more accusations, Kubacki's demeanor was quite erratic, his moods and temperament making sharp swings from cool detachment to obvious anger. But he never lost control, often trying to turn McBride's questions into debates. Frequently, Judge Luongo had to remind the witness he was entitled only to answer questions, not ask them.

Opening with an all-out attack, McBride fired a volley of intimations of malfeasance that had not previously been presented by the prosecution. Did Kubacki …

"… ever solicit boat tickets to Switzerland from Howard S. Lewis, a director of the Berks County Manufacturers Association?"

"… ever solicit $10,000 from William Goldman and Lester Krieger?"

"… ever receive $1,300 from two Reading automobile/truck salesmen, Bruce Ohlinger and Carl Ensslen?"

"… ever receive money from two Reading companies, South End Towing and Central Towing Service?"

"... ever solicit a stereo-television set from Mr. Noulett in connection with a police radio purchase by the city?"

"... ever possess a city-owned Colt gun?"

"... ever solicit anything from anyone?"

The 53-year-old former mayor answered "no" to most of the questions, and was unable to recall the names involved in others.

Rome objected midway through that line of questioning, wanting to know whether McBride "was prepared to prove the solicitations were ever made." The slender special prosecutor said he certainly was. However, Judge Luongo decided to halt further testimony on solicitations. This deprived the jury of hearing witnesses who had told the grand jury about their personal experiences regarding kickbacks to Kubacki.

The former mayor testified that he had received gifts during his four years in office from friends in City Hall. He also admitted accepting the grandfather clock from Walter Hughes, the Karpark general manager, but denied having solicited it. He estimated its price at $200.

Kubacki's association with Abe Minker was thoroughly examined by McBride. He questioned John about a trip to New York City two days after he was nominated to run for mayor. When McBride presented registration cards showing Minker and Mr. and Mrs. Kubacki were all registered at the Hotel Edison on May 22, 1959, the witness said he did not meet with the racketeer on that occasion or even run into him by chance. He said he didn't recall having dinner at Lindy's Restaurant with Minker on that same date. But he didn't deny he sometimes "bumped into" Abe while in Philadelphia, Harrisburg, Manhattan, or the Jewish Community Center steam bath, but never for the purpose of having a meeting. He said he never went to the White House Market where Abe supposedly tried to settle a dispute John had with Charlie; never met with Johnny Wittig in the basement of the YMCA, never met with his police chief in Wade's Moss Street factory to discuss police appointments, nor ever consulted with Abe about parking meter contracts in 1960, 1961, and 1963. No, he stated time and again, to questions about having any association with the wrong people.

Verna Minker, who had been sitting at the defense table between her husband and Richter, proved her devotion to Abe by testifying as a rebuttal witness. She told about her aging mate being a financial and business adviser to many people seeking his assistance. As for the chief of police, Verna said, Abe regarded Charlie Wade as a surrogate son. She sobbed when describing the bond between Charlie and the man he called "Pop."

Verna testified that Abe could not have been at certain places mentioned by other witnesses when negotiations were underway for the purchase of parking meters in early 1961. She said Abe underwent back surgery in late January and was confined to their apartment until March 20 of that winter. Three IRS agents were called to rebut that testimony, all claiming to have seen Abe away from home during the stated period.

The 12-day trial ended with Richter making a final plea that Abe Minker never made a penny out of any of the parking meter deals, and Rome calling Wade "a sanctimonious liar" during their summations. Rome also decried the prosecution's failure to put Joe Liever and Johnny Wittig on the stand because their testimony would have been damaging to the government's case, he stated.

The jury of 10 men and two women returned after more than nine hours of deliberation. The verdict: all three defendants guilty on all five counts of extortion. In his 68-page appeal, Kubacki argued that Wade, who had been charged with perjury, was not a reliable witness. In January 1965, Judge Luongo upheld three of the five conviction counts. He then handed down sentences that were far below the maximum for extortion (15 years in prison and a $30,000 fine). None of the defendants smiled when they heard "30 days in prison and a $5,000 fine, although many court observers thought those penalties were laughable. Lawyers familiar with the case couldn't believe the sentences were so light. An elevator operator commented: "I could get 30 days just for getting drunk."

Prosecutor Tom McBride who spent 18 months developing and trying the case snapped; "I have an angry no comment."

Kubacki was placed on three years probation but had to report to his parole office only once a year. The judge said he was convinced Kubacki "knew the difference between right and wrong." The five-years probation Minker received was to run concurrent with the four-year probation he received in his tax case.

Although nobody ever accused Kubacki of being a quitter, he now had no chance of winning another election so soon after the trial. Ten days after being convicted, he pulled out of the 5th Legislative District race since "circumstances beyond my control have prevented me from campaigning in the manner which could assure my nomination." He said he would support Rep. Victor Yarnell for reelection in the primary. He had already denounced the other two Democratic candidates, Danny McDevitt and Russell LaMarca, solicitor of the Reading Parking Authority.

After his victory in the tax case, McBride met with Dist. Atty. Dick Eshelman to discuss other reports of extortion coming out of City Hall. One case dated back to 1959 for the purchase of three pieces of fire equipment. That had been on the back burner for years because of the heavy load of rackets cases the various federal agencies were pursuing. Eshelman soon had Don Holloway and his state police vice squad retracing the feds' steps to learn more about the fire truck purchases.

Having recovered hardly any of Abe Minker's suspected wealth since his first conviction in 1961, the federal government resumed its crusade to bring Abe to justice again three months after winning the parking meter trial. On June 24, 1964, a federal grand jury indicted Abe Minker, Johnny Wittig and Joe Fiorini with failure to pay gambling occupation taxes. With an abundance of evidence provided by Charlie Wade, the grand jury was informed that Fiorini's numbers bank had collected about $250,000 in three months before being raided in January 1962. Although Fiorini had gone through the formality of purchasing a $50 federal gambling stamp, more importantly he had not bothered to file any income or excise tax forms on all the big money he was raking in. Neither had Minker nor Wittig.

Over the four decades of his criminal career dating back to the early 1920s, whenever Abe Minker was charged with a crime he almost always challenged prosecutors to prove their cases against him. Time after time he refused to take guilty pleas that might have meant reduced sentences. No, Abe was a gambler, willing to bet against the odds if there was a slim chance of beating the system. But now, at 67, he was losing his will to endure the aggravation of another trial.

Minker was brought down from Lewisburg to face the music one more time in April 1965. As usual, Abe was complaining of ill health. His attorney, B. Nathaniel Richter, had worked out a very good deal for his aging client. When Judge John Morgan Davis asked how he pleaded, in a strained voice Abe answered, "Guilty." His co-defendant, Johnny Wittig, similarly stated, "Guilty," but in a husky tone that intimated he was still contrite about possibly serving more time for his minor role in a cover-up that also involved Wade, Minker, and Fiorini. Joe was granted a separate trial.

Richter lined up an all-star character witness team for the May 4 sentencing. Adrian Bonnelly, the chief justice of the Philadelphia County Courts, equaled his performance of two years earlier when his laudatory speech failed to save Abe from a four-year sentence for failing to pay his taxes. Now the judge was back, reaching new heights as he made Abe sound like a prince of a fellow who just happened to get in with the wrong crowd. There were plenty of other businessmen, religious leaders, and lifelong friends willing to come forward to heap praise on Abe Minker. And Verna, as always stylishly dressed and loyal to her husband, described the turmoil in her life: "It really has been a nightmare," adding that she suffered from a heart ailment.

Judge Davis, taking into consideration that the aging Minker still had two years to serve on his current confinement, handed down a two-year sentence and a $5,000 fine. The jail time was to run concurrently with his present term, meaning that whenever Abe completed his four-year sentence, or if he were paroled short of four years, he would be released from the federal penitentiary.

Wittig, characterized by attorney Sam Liever as merely Fiorini's errand boy, was sentenced to a year and a day in federal prison, with a $1,000 fine and four years probation. Still on crutches after being hurt in a fight two months earlier, Wittig, 58, was allowed another 60 days to recuperate before being committed. Despite the charges he faced in a few other rackets-related cases over the past 15 years, this was the first time he drew jail time since his murder conviction in 1945.

The plea agreements were sweetened even further a month later by Judge Davis to overcome "technical violations." Without getting technical or explaining just what violations were at issue, the judge cut Wittig's jail sentence in half but added the time to his original 4-year probation period. Davis also revoked the three years probation he first levied on Minker. He then told Abe, "On September 11 you shall be eligible for parole. The court feels the probation (five years) imposed by Judge Kraft and Judge Luongo will be sufficient to keep you under control." However, the federal parole board once again rejected parole for Abe at its next session.

Fiorini changed his mind about standing trial again in the latest tax case. In April 1964 he pleaded guilty, received a $2,500 fine and one year of probation. That same year he was involved in the assault on Roy Frankhouser, a Ku Klux Klan activist, in the Court Tavern across from the Courthouse. Although Frankhouser lost an eye as he fought four assailants, he refused to testify in court and charges were dropped against Fiorini and three others. In 1966 Jules Hanssens was back in Reading to announce that Fiorini's house at 872 North 8$^{th}$ Street was seized by the IRS because he owed the government lots of back tax money. According to Jules, Joe had pulled in more than $250,000 lottery bets during the three-month period just before the first raid on his numbers bank in 1962.

At 49 in 1976, Joe Fiorini was killed in a car accident. Traveling at a high rate of speed and passing cars on two-lane Route 183 near the Bern Church, Joe lost control, struck a Metropolitan-Edison utility pole and was thrown from his car, as were his two passengers. Also killed was 62-year-old Angelo "Cowboy" DiFazio, a retired Reading Railroad car repairman. More fortunate was Samuel Lovello, 29, who survived the crash although seated in the front passenger seat. Lovello, a teacher at Tyson-Schoener Elementary School, went on to have an outstanding career as the wrestling coach at Brandywine High School. DiFazio had married Ruth Eppihimer only three days before his death.

# 40

# *Angie causes turmoil, decides to talk*

For a few years after her run-in with Mayor Kubacki, Angie Martin Wilkerson ran her small business without interference from the cops. By the summer of 1963, Troop C commander Urella knocked to include the little madam in his crackdown on Reading vice. Angie's employee of the week was Kim Hammer, a 25-year-old slim, attractive blonde just in from Philadelphia. It was a Tuesday, June 18, and Kim had already turned 20 tricks in her first three days, charging between $10 and $20 per customer, according to the madam.

Angelo Carcaca was the bait. He obtained Angie's phone number in a neighborhood bar and made an appointment. The next day he climbed the outside fire escape to Angie's second-floor rear apartment at 904 Penn Street. She answered the door. With little ado, a price was agreed to, he handed Kim a marked $50 bill, and received $30 change. Just after Kim and her customer retired to the bedroom, Capt. Urella knocked. Angie answered and was greeted by the captain and Don Holloway, and a few troopers. Kim came out of the bedroom in her bikini briefs followed by state police detective Angelo Carcaca, still dressed.

The 44-year-old Angie accepted the intrusion with no fuss. To her captors she was not shy about admitting Kim was the prostitute and she was the madam. She gave Holloway and his raiders a frank statement about her business, past and present, before being released on $2,000 bail.

During the next year, Angie's name and face became more familiar to newspaper readers in Berks County as her case moved slowly through the legal system. Refusing to retire, Angie kept the apartment at 904, and continued to rotate her girls. Teddy Bear Jones had the place and a john to herself in January 1964 when the state police intruded again. There was no doubt who the absentee madam was. Along with Teddy Bear, Angie was charged again with maintaining a whorehouse.

Angie and her elderly husband, Jack, rented a split-level in Midvale Manor west of Reading. After this latest arrest was publicized, Angie's landlord felt she was giving the neighborhood a bad name. Angie argued that all her girlie business was conducted in town, but eventually agreed to relocate. Without notifying her probation officer or anybody else about her change of address, she and Jack moved to a rented place in Earl Township off the beaten track near Pheasantland Park. The neighbors soon noticed increased traffic on the dirt lane leading to the unfinished two-story single home that was now a bawdyhouse.

While Angie was quietly trying to feather her nest in the country, back in town the political picture was undergoing a drastic change. As 1964 began, with the Republicans now running the show, Angie was still awaiting trial because Kim Hammer had not been located by the state police.

Among the many tales Charlie Wade had related to investigators, was his account of playing referee in Kubacki's kickback game. He told Sam Russell that for a short time Angie had paid the mayor $75 a week to stay in business. Sam immediately could see the makings of another extortion case.

Although Kim Hammer would eventually get caught, by June 1964 she was still a fugitive when Angie accepted a plea bargain: three of the five charges against her were dropped. For pleading guilty to assignation and establishing a bawdyhouse, she received a prison term of 30 days to one year, and a $250 fine.

When Sam Russell told her she was a principal in an extortion investigation, he hinted that an even sweeter deal could be arranged if she told the true story in court about Kubacki shaking her down. Aware that Abe Minker and Benny Bonanno would also be arrested, she was not anxious to testify against the mob. Angie said she would think about it. If she wanted legal advice, her lawyer, Sam Liever, was not the one to ask. He was also retained by Bonanno and Minker. So Angie dropped Sam and hired Forrest Schaeffer. Even though she hadn't yet agreed to the new bargain, Schaeffer managed to keep her out of jail for the time being. He appealed to the court that Angie's aging and long-suffering husband had nobody to take care of him if she was away serving her 30-day sentence. What nobody seemed to know was that Angie had moved Jack and all their belongings to Earl Township where she was once again a working wife. Then, on September 14, she appeared in court where her jail time was dismissed, but she was given one year's probation and her fine was upped to $500.

Russell now moved fast after he thought he had Angie in his pocket. Kubacki, Minker, and Bonanno were arrested and charged with extortion and conspiracy on September 19. Minker was charged for having told Benny Bonanno to work out a payment schedule for Angie. Benny had gotten himself further involved by keeping $25 for himself as middleman, the other $50 going to the mayor. A preliminary hearing was scheduled for the next day in the office of Alderman Larry Palmer. That Friday night before the hearing, Johnny Wittig and Joe Fiorini paid a visit to Angie in Earl Township. They were there as not-so-gentle persuaders. Joe suggested she shouldn't show up for the hearing the next morning, but if she insisted on going she should hide behind the 5th Amendment. Wittig was a little more forceful. Sounding like a Hollywood mogul, he told Angie, "If you testify, you'll never run a house in this town again." Then, looking to the future when friendlier politicians might make things easier for the racketeers, Johnny reminded her, "Remember this administration will be in only three more years." These were pretty convincing arguments to someone whose only visible means of support was prostitution.

Angie decided to take their advice and stay out of sight. For the next couple of days she didn't leave her rented house. The door that weekend was opened only for customers Angie could personally identify.

Some of the best theater in Reading that year was performed in the living room/office of Larry Palmer the day after the thugs did their James Cagney impersonations in the sticks. Palmer, a former New York policeman, hardly expected to become involved in a case of this dimension when he was elected alderman in Reading's 19th Ward. Parking fines, neighborhood spats, and complaints about unchained dogs were typical fare for local aldermen. On this Saturday morning, crammed into his parlor, were the three suspects, members of their families, three defense lawyers, the prosecution team including state policemen, and a U.S. marshal who had escorted Abe Minker from federal prison. And not least of all, Charlie Wade. A wag later mentioned: "Maybe it's just as well that Angie didn't show up—where would she sit?"

When Don Holloway and Trooper Arthur McAnally were dispatched to pick up Angie at her former home in Midvale Manor nobody answered the door. They reported to Russell, who was dismayed that what he feared would happen, did happen. Angie had skipped. Minker's henchmen had gotten to her.

Larry Palmer's small office was in turmoil: Sam Liever arguing that Benny Bonanno was illegally being held in Berks County Prison; Fred Noch, Kubacki's new lawyer, urging Palmer not to postpone the hearing; H. Nathaniel Richter, annoyed at being summoned from Philadelphia to represent Minker; Charlie Wade as vocal and upbeat as ever with Kubacki glaring at him; and Verna Minker voicing concern about her husband's health. At one point the federal marshal told Liever to stop talking with Minker. Sam was advised that only Abe's attorney could converse with him.

"I'm his local lawyer," Sam snapped, and insisted on seeing the marshal's ID.

Richter kept up a persistent harangue about the warrant for his client's arrest being illegal because it did not say what state statute had been violated. Russell shrugged and called Richter's complaint "legal public relations." Richter took Palmer's phone out to the kitchen to call Al Readinger. He wanted the judge to allow Minker to remain at Berks County Prison rather than being sent back to Lewisburg. That didn't work. Richter told Dick Eshelman to arrest Charlie Wade "for conspiracy." That didn't happen either. About the calmest guy in the room was Benny Bonanno who reportedly had been in the hospital for ulcer treatment until it was resolved that he was only treated for a cut.

After twice trying to reschedule the hearing for the following week, over the objections of just about everybody except Noch, Palmer decided not to set a date until Angie was available. Russell had won that round over the noisy objections of the majority of lawyers and defendants. Finally the shoving and shouting ended and Larry Palmer's living room was cleared out.

By Sunday, the distraught Angie had another change of heart. She called the state police barracks to tell them where she was. The staties didn't seem in any great hurry to bring her in. The next day they received a phone report about "a man lying dead on the floor" in an Earl Township house. This complaint they answered. Instead of a corpse, they found old Jack Martin in bed, not feeling too fit. Angie and Jack were taken to the courthouse for questioning. By 4 o'clock that afternoon, Fiorini and Wittig were in custody charged with hindering a witness. Angie was committed to Berks County Prison as a parole violator for not letting authorities know she had moved. Now, unless she testified, she faced a year in jail for parole violation. She agreed to accuse Minker, Kubacki, and Joe Bonnano of extortion.

Worried that things were getting out of hand, the district attorney sent out an SOS to the state. He asked the state attorney general, Walter Alessandroni, to assist in both the investigative and legal aspects of his corruption probe. Alessandroni agreed to lend a hand.

Although Fiorini had violated his parole by being arrested again, he was allowed to post bail and was released from BCP the day before he and Wittig were to become the second act in Larry Palmer's little theatre of the absurd.

For the second time in eight days, the Palmer living room was stuffed with a cast of dozens the following Saturday morning. H. Nathaniel Richter, Sam Liever, and other interested parties were again in full voice as Palmer tried to achieve some semblance of order out of the chaos swirling about him. In the end, he dodged all the legal maneuvers the pros threw at him. After listening to

Angie's tale about handing Benny Bonanno $75 for six weeks, and Wade's involvement with Kubacki and Minker, the alderman ordered the three defendants held for grand jury action. About the only concession Palmer made to Richter was to have Wade remove his holstered handgun while testifying.

Later that afternoon, Palmer held a second and less contentious hearing as Angie related how Fiorini and Wittig had threatened her if she testified against the extortion suspects. Despite the strong prosecution evidence Angie presented in her testimony, she was sent back to Berks County Prison for the time being. At a hearing three weeks later while pleading for Angie's release, Forrest Schaeffer said, "She's getting a little tired of the view." Judge Hess was not too sympathetic. When asked why she moved from Midvale Manor without notifying her probation officer, Angie explained, "The papers wrote me up so terrible, my landlady was undebatable about renting me a place."

Judge Hess ordered her remanded to jail, at least for the remaining time of her original 30-day term. Before leaving the courtroom the chunky redhead opened up on Don Holloway, who had reviewed her recent escapades: "You can take all your statements and stick them up your ass."

Judge Hess warned, "And if your attitude doesn't improve, you'll do a lot more than 30 days." The district attorney's office was worried that its volatile witness would waver again and blow its extortion case.

Angie was boiling. While she languished in BCP, Joe Fiorini, who also had been confined for parole violation, was again out on the street. When the case against Wittig and Fiorini was heard by the grand jury, that panel must have believed that Johnny and Joe hadn't really threatened Angie when they went to visit her in Oley Township, because the two racketeers were not indicted. Fiorini had been granted bail until he could have a hearing to determine whether he was a parole violator.

Judge Hess, who didn't hide his contempt for Angie, showed much more concern that every judicial consideration be afforded Fiorini to make sure the dapper gambler was not mistreated. After Angie was behind bars for five weeks, Hess relented. She was released with the warning that state police would be watching to see she didn't set up business again in her rural residence.

Teddy Bear Scott might have been the last prostitute to use the 904 Penn Street apartment. She failed to show up for her trial in September 1964, jumped bail and returned to Philadelphia. That's where she was caught five months later and ended up serving time in Berks County Prison.

But the little apartment where Angie catered to the sporting crowd soon found new tenants after she changed her base of operations. The boys began using it for card games. Chief county detective John Beemer got wind of this and decided to climb the metal stairway to heavenly delights to find out just what was going on in Angie's old digs.

On Sunday January 3, 1965, Beemer's team raided the place and found a bunch of well-known Reading gamblers sitting around. A few were playing gin rummy. The ten men were charged with gambling although there was no sign of chips or money on the table, no dice, nothing to indicate anybody was wagering. However, a total of $1,800 was seized from the suspects.

Among those arrested was the Philly transplant, Pasquale "Husky" Pillo, who had been a prominent defendant in the Cherry Street dice case. Others were Dominick "Mickey Shush" Quatieri, a pickup man in the Lancaster Avenue numbers case; Charlie Lucchese, who ran his own numbers racket from his rural home; and Leon Williams, another Cherry Street dice game alumnus.

Two days after the raid, Beemer reported there was no legal basis to charge them, so the $1,800 was returned. However, those who posted $30 bonds, and one who was bonded for $100, did not have the bail money returned to them because they failed to show up for hearings on Monday morning. Evidently they could not break the habit of automatically foregoing forfeitures after gambling raids.

The popular second floor racy rear apartment was typical of numerous locations in Reading. Once tainted as the haunt of racketeers, a garage, storefront, house or apartment often stayed in the family to be used as a base for a new operation.

# 41

# *A soliloquy reveals the underside of politics*

The reputations of former Reading office holders began falling like autumn leaves in 1964. Their appearances before the federal grand jury earlier that year hinted that questionable business deals they had made would come back to haunt them. Witnesses had told the jury panel about other kickbacks in addition to the parking meter payoffs that earned John Kubacki and Abe Minker extortion convictions in April of that year.

The September antics of Angie Wilkerson and the men trying to muzzle the aging harlot seemed like the topper of all the wild and crazy antics being staged. By October, after months of other legal and illegal spectacles that kept the good citizens laughing and crying and wondering when it would end, the best was yet to come. And the star attractions were leaders of the pack. The fruits of state police investigations of cases handed to them by federal officials were now about to be polished and exposed to public view.

Sam Russell's first target when he became special rackets prosecutor was an old adversary, Dan McDevitt. Dan and Sam had served together on City Council 10 years before. Now, McDevitt was finishing his second term as a state legislator. So it was with some trepidation Dick Eshelman and Russell revived a case that was threatened by the statute of limitations.

McDevitt's political career started to unravel when he was defeated in the 1964 spring primary. Running for a third term in the state Legislature, Dan was defeated by a newcomer to Democratic politics, Paul Hoh. This 29-year-old Church of Christ minister went on to win McDevitt's legislative seat in November.

Actually, the former mayor's troubles started in the summer of 1962, when representatives from a couple of Reading automobile dealers had appeared before the federal grand jury. Questioned by the feds about the purchase of city vehicles, the car people claimed kickbacks had been paid to city officials.

On May 23, 1963, McDevitt and Jimmy Maurer shared the hidden spotlight on the grand jury chair they occupied that day. Jimmy was there to answer questions about possible kickbacks to John Kubacki to allow his burlesque girls to continue to disrobe. Dan later took the hot seat, spending 55 minutes denying he had accepted tainted money in the car deals. When McDevitt was again subpoenaed for further questioning by Tom McBride the following November, rumors were rife about payoffs by a company to win a contract for three pieces of city fire apparatus shortly before his term as mayor ran out in 1959. Former Councilman Bruce Coleman also had been grilled earlier by McBride on the same subject.

In April 1958, McDevitt introduced a resolution to City Council to award Mack Truck Inc., Pottsville, the contract to purchase two pumpers and an aerial ladder truck at a total cost of $80,885. Later, Coleman seconded the resolution, which was passed by a 4-1 vote. John Kubacki, then on Council, opposed the purchase. Although another bid was $2,000 lower than the city's, it was not accepted, according to city records, because it did not meet the city's detailed specifications.

During the summer of 1964 when McDevitt found out Russell was having him investigated, he sent a letter to Eshelman inviting the district attorney to prove his (Dan's) administration had been involved in any type of corruption. A week later on July 1, McDevitt publicly waived "any inferred protection under the statute of limitations." The statute's five-year limit by this time had been exceeded. Accepting Dan's challenge, Eshelman issued arrest warrants for him and Coleman on October 15, charging them with extortion. Property bail was posted by their families.

Instead of going to Larry Palmer's office the day his preliminary hearing was scheduled on October 29, Dan showed up at the Courthouse that morning. First he went to the sheriff's office to surrender because he said his sister Elizabeth was withdrawing his $1,000 property bail. Next, accompanied by a sheriff's aide, he went to see the three county judges who were about to begin handling their daily caseload. Although not represented by counsel, Dan had drawn up a petition for a writ of habeas corpus claiming he had not received a speedy hearing. He insisted charges against him should be dismissed because they were motivated solely by politics.

What followed was a baffling proceeding before Judges Warren Hess, Albert Readinger, and James Bertolet. Sam Russell stated McDevitt's hearing was set for that morning in Larry Palmer's office, but McDevitt claimed he had not been notified. Accusations, loud and cynical, were exchanged by the prosecutor and the accused. The judges tried to maintain order, but barbs of "politics" were flying about like shrapnel in an arsenal explosion. Judge Hess postponed the preliminary hearing until the following afternoon. But, unless Dan renewed his bail, the judge said he would have to go to jail to ensure his appearance at the hearing. The jurist advised him several times to get an attorney.

Dan, playing the martyr, stated. "Were I to take what little savings I have to obtain a lawyer to go into this political jungle, these people will have gained their point by ruining me financially, as well as personally."

So Dan McDevitt became the first and only Berks County Prison inmate who had been Reading's mayor. It was just for a night, but it is a unique entry in the criminal record books.

The next day he was transported to Larry Palmer's office for the hearing, and the battle was resumed. Palmer advised, "Please get yourself a lawyer." Dan ranted, "I happen to be a man of principle. Where innocence is involved, I see no reason to get a lawyer." Bruce Coleman arrived in a more passive manner accompanied by his counsel, Joseph DeSantis.

The feature witness was Theodore Anderson, the salesman for Reading Mack Distributors, Inc., who submitted the bid for the fire equipment. After the contract was signed in 1959, Anderson said, he was summoned to City Hall by Coleman. The salesman testified the councilman took him to the mayor's office where McDevitt asked, "Could we (Mack) make a contribution to his political party? On the basis of the contract, McDevitt said, $2,000 would be the right amount."

Anderson testified he obtained checks for $1,200 and $400 from Clarence Bosler, a partner in Reading Mack Distributors, cashed the checks and turned the money over to Coleman in the councilman's home on North 4th Street. Four months later on October 1, Anderson said, he received another check from Bosler, cashed it and gave the $400 to Coleman in the Abe Lincoln Hotel.

Cross-examined by DeSantis, Anderson said the checks were made out to him with notations, "special commission and commission on fire trucks." Although Anderson was unable to answer questions put to him by attorney Dan about physical aspects of the mayor's office, the witness was steadfast in his description of the money exchange.

It was Dan who introduced politics into the hearing by calling several Republican and Democratic figures to the stand. Donald Bagenstose and Mrs. Minnie Pike Hurley, past and current secretary of the Democratic Party, said their records did not show any contributions from Reading Mack Distributing. None of the 10 witnesses except Anderson claimed knowing anything about the $2,000.

On the testimony of Ted Anderson, Alderman Palmer held Coleman and McDevitt for grand jury action.

Although enjoying celebrity status for one night in BCP, Rep. Dan McDevitt was in no mood for a return engagement. With his sister again securing his bail with her house, Dan was released. Now he would have to see whether the grand jury would decide the evidence was enough to make him stand trial.

The commotion stirred by McDevitt's appearances in court, was a mere temblor compared to what happened when Kubacki was charged with extortion a second time. Cpl. Don Holloway and his state police team's follow-up on the investigation involving kickbacks in the purchase of two city police emergency vehicles came to a head when a warrant was issued for Kubacki's arrest on November 7. Early that Saturday while Larry Palmer was preparing the warrants, Kubacki was getting ready for a family wedding. The daughter of Kubacki's brother, Stanley, was getting married.

Shortly after 9 a.m., Holloway arrived at Kubacki's Mineral Spring Road house. He was told the ex-mayor was not home, then left without serving the warrant. Preferring cuff links to handcuffs, Kubacki quickly contacted Palmer by phone. There was nothing he could do, Larry stated, but maybe the district attorney would hold the warrant over the weekend. It galled the future bride's uncle to ask Dick Eshelman for a favor, but he swallowed and dialed. Eshelman said he knew nothing about the wedding, but refused to relent by putting a hold on the warrant.

Holloway and other staties kept an eye on Kubacki's house and lingered near the wedding site, but Uncle John was a no-show. Kubacki's disappearing act went on for three days before he called the state police barracks to report he would surrender the next day at the office of Alderman Paul Brogley.

Mose Brogley was not your typical member of the minor judiciary. Some of the hearings held in the front room of his row house on South 6th Street became legend. On one occasion he scheduled four hearings at the same time leading to considerable confusion as might be expected. The managing editor of the *Reading Times*, Gordon Williams, was a longtime acquaintance of Mose. He was heard to say more than once:

"Mose played too many quarters without his helmet."

Brogley was indeed a football player when he attended the University of Pennsylvania. Maybe that's where he developed his love of classical music. Wife beaters, pickpockets, prostitutes, you name it … they all were treated to Bach and

Beethoven as they sat in his office waiting for prosecutors to present cases against them. On one occasion Mose halted proceedings so all present could soak up the wonders of a classical passage. Disorganized mayhem was the norm when he presided.

There were glares but no fireworks when Kubacki was first greeted by Brogley, with Holloway ready and waiting. Bail had been arranged by phone the previous night, with Stanley Kubacki taking the responsibility for $500 property bail. Holloway read the arrest warrant that stated Kubacki was charged with extorting $500 from a salesman and truck sales manager at A.W. Golden, Inc., an established Lancaster Avenue car dealer.

Having accomplished his mission, the veteran state policeman prepared to leave when the ex-mayor signaled him to remain. Holloway turned back into the room into a volley of verbal abuse that for the moment stunned him. Kubacki began raging about persecution and harassment, shaking a fist in Holloway's face. Holding his ground, Don vocally gave it right back to the husky former boxer. The press was well represented and recorded the threats and counter-threats that grew in volume but never quite reached the physical stage.

"You didn't have to harass my wife." Kubacki yelled. "Don't you ever use my children again to get to me."

Claiming he was just doing his job, Holloway insisted, "Nobody threatened anybody."

As the back-and-forth raged, Mose jumped in on the side of his close friend, the former mayor. He barked at Holloway, "You're going to work for 20 years and then moonlight and take away somebody else's job. That's what you're doing here."

Mose was a little off in his concern about Don's retirement plans.

The corporal still had another ten years to go before reaching the required 25-year state police policy on retirement, and it wasn't until Don was 60 that he hung up his campaign hat.

Then Kubacki issued a few complaints about Dick Eshelman for not having the decency to let the Kubacki family enjoy his niece's wedding before making the arrest. John said he went into hiding so as to not cause his family embarrassment that day.

Brogley brought an end to the bloodless brouhaha by ordering Holloway, "You better go, officer. You did your job."

"Are you telling me to get out of here?"

"I said you did your job, you better go."

With some reluctance, Holloway left, feeling his partner in upholding the law had deserted him. That ended the first act.

Now Kubacki was center stage alone. For the next half hour or more, he indulged himself by letting loose with much of the pent up frustration that had been building over the past months. He had not been shy about intimating, from time to time, that whatever he was being accused of, many others were guilty of the same. When the voters spoke in November by ousting the Democrats, John not too lightly chided his losing teammates on Council. His warning at that time was about him having lots of company on the sinking ship that was his administration. In Brogley's office, with his captivated audience, he enlarged on his previous complaints. He also dealt the persecution card over and over with such sincerity it appeared he truly saw himself as the fall guy who didn't deserve it. For years to come his attitude was that he didn't do anything worse than what those before him had done. Why hadn't they been singled out and put through the wringer like the GOP was now doing to him?

He toyed with the word corruption:

"Unfortunately it had to come to this impasse. Many people think it is politics. But it is worse than that. This is persecution at its worst. No one can prove I ever asked for one cent from anyone, nor did I threaten anyone," he insisted, despite very convincing testimony from several grand jury witnesses to the contrary. "Am I to be the scapegoat of all the ills of the Democratic Party?" As it eventually played out, he was. Some of his accusers received immunity by testifying against him to save their own necks. He frequently rationalized as he presented a remarkably lucid defense of his actions over the years, measuring them against the many others who played along to get along. He said he was never accused of conniving with any contractor to use inferior building materials to knock down costs on contracts, or of selling zoning permits or similar actions. "They come within the scope of corruption," he said.

Since John brought it up, could this be considerable standard procedure among builders who received city contracts? If he wasn't guilty of such acts, neither was he ever credited with exposing anybody engaged in such dirty work that, as mayor, he might have known about.

"Under none of these charges (against him), did they in any way cost the taxpayers one cent," he declared. Then he exposed his intimate knowledge of how business was conducted in the City of Reading.

"If I am guilty of shaking these people down," he stated, "then every politician, businessman, and banker is liable to be arrested for extortion and corruption."

That's what was eating at him, and justifiably so. Although he knew where the skeletons were hidden, he couldn't say where without including himself. He was trying to justify his own actions by spreading the blame among all parties in the extortion. Some took and some gave, but the givers also gave information to the prosecutors who in turn gave them immunity. Although it's not always the officeholder who initiates the extortion, it's usually the officeholder who loses if the businessman talks. But not always, as events would prove. In this case the investigators could always remind suspects to tell the truth because they had a witness who already offered first hand information about the extortion—Charlie Wade.

With a broad brush Kubacki was painting all businessmen and bankers and their trading counterparts in City Hall. It was a frightening accusation. Maybe corruption was much more prevalent than realized. But this was the master of manipulation talking, turning on his accusers to make it seem corruption was so pervasive there were snakes under every rock.

Kubacki told his small audience he had turned down a $10,000 offer made by "someone you fellows know" to make a zoning change. If he did reject such an offer, the question must be asked, why didn't he have his police force build a case against this unnamed extortionist? Other mayors and police chiefs revealed they too were targets of racketeers and businessmen with deep pockets, but the prosecution of such leeches never seemed to happen.

Then Kubacki turned to more personal issues. He complained that close friends had been questioned, embarrassed, and frightened while the feds and state police investigated him. That the men he had led on police raids would one day turn on him was particularly hurtful. As John told it, he could hardly pass a cop on the street without being baited or become the target of verbal abuse. This was probably true, a response to his cavalier attitude toward law enforcement that had embarrassed many on the force. John referred to his former police chief as despicable. And he bemoaned the fact that Mayor Shirk had not taken his complaints seriously about police harassment of his family.

His listeners in the alderman's office had heard bits and pieces of this dialogue before, but never so heartfelt, with unusual touches of submission. "I'm reeling. My head is bowed. But there's some things you have to let off steam about. Let's just call this a steam-letting session."

As the harried orator prepared to leave, Mose wished his buddy, "Good luck." Ambling out with his sailor's gait, he turned down 6$^{th}$ Street and around the corner where his wife was waiting in her car, wondering why the delay. He probably felt a brief sense of victory as he joined her. Maybe, he hoped, the reporters' readers would join him in his outrage at the Republican politicians who were determined to humble him.

Holloway's later reaction to Kubacki's bombastic outburst:

"You don't often serve warrants to people who go into a long oration about how honest they've been."

The Berks County Magistrates Association offered Holloway an invitation to air any complaints he had about Brogley's behavior, but the corporal saw the humor in Kubacki's surprise outburst and let it drop.

A week later John Kubacki found himself without a lawyer. With no explanation, Fred Noch announced he no longer would represent his client. There was speculation that John's long harangue at Brogley's was a confession of sorts to anyone reading between the lines. This was just the type of public lecturing by a client that criminal attorneys try to avoid. Not good at taking advice, would Kubacki emulate Dan McDevitt by testing the dangerous legal waters without legal counsel, too?

Court observers who anticipated still another riotous preliminary hearing on November 20 before Alderman Brogley were denied that pleasure when Kubacki announced he would waive his hearing and let the grand jury decide whether he should stand trial.

The December Berks grand jury had a full plate to chew on before returning indictments on the 3rd of the month. Having listened to a steady stream of serious accusations by a large assortment of witnesses over a period of several days, the 17-member panel returned indictments for two ex-mayors of Reading, an ex-councilman, and two racketeers in a pair of extortion cases. It was a dark day for Reading politics. In addition to Dan McDevitt and Bruce Coleman receiving bad news regarding the fire truck deal, John Kubacki, Abe Minker, and Joe Bonanno would now have to defend themselves in court against Angie Wilkerson's charges of a shakedown. The next day, the same grand jury indicted Kubacki again on charges he extorted $500 from a car dealer when the city bought two police emergency trucks in 1961.

McDevitt was still without counsel, but Kubacki had hired John Ruth and Alvin Woerle to represent him. Although they had seen their political careers reduced to shambles during the year, Dan and John were determined to fight to the end. Both were tentatively scheduled for trial on December 15. A not-too-merry Christmas loomed.

Kubacki petitioned the court to move his trial out of Reading because he felt the public had been inflamed by recent stories about the extortion cases. Judge

Hess rejected change of venue but he did postpone both Kubacki trials to allow the new attorneys time to catch up.

McDevitt made another bid to have charges against him dismissed by introducing a 10-page memorandum requesting the court to review his preliminary hearing notes. He argued that nowhere in the testimony was Theodore Anderson, the Mack Truck salesman, asked by Bruce Coleman or anybody else to pay them anything before the fire truck contract was signed. Dan also pointed out there was no testimony proving he had received any of the money Anderson said he gave to Coleman. Judge Hess agreed these were strong points in McDevitt's favor. During a 90-minute hearing, Judges Hess and Readinger and various lawyers in the audience advised Dan about certain rights he had, and warned him not to insert politics into the debate. It was finally agreed that the court would review notes from Palmer's hearing. Soon it would be the Republicans howling politics.

Three days before Christmas, the court announced its 2-1 opinion that the district attorney had no case against McDevitt. Republican Judge Bertolet cast the dissenting vote. The two Democratic judges, Hess and Readinger, agreed with McDevitt's analysis that the salesman's testimony did not prove Dan was guilty of extortion. Eshelman and Russell made no comment about the court's decision but stood by an earlier statement made by the special prosecutor that he would not harass the former mayor by filing further appeals.

Bruce Coleman's case was not included in the judicial opinion. Although McDevitt was off the hook, Russell indicated he would still try to show that McDevitt conspired with Coleman to extort money from the truck distributors.

Coleman's trial, after a 6-month postponement, began on June 17, 1965, with Dick Eshelman as the lead prosecutor, and Russell now in the second chair. Judge Readinger let the trial run until the afternoon session of the second day was about to start. Then he announced that the district attorney lacked evidence to prove Coleman had, indeed, extorted $2,000 from Reading Mack Distributors. Theodore Anderson, the Mack salesman, had repeated his testimony that McDevitt and Coleman had asked for a $2,000 political contribution to the Democratic Party, and said he eventually gave the money to Coleman in two payments. Eshelman did not have a Charlie Wade to back up the prosecution charges. City and Democratic Party records introduced at the trial did not indicate Mack Distributors had made such a donation.

Judge Readinger dismissed the charges. The official ending to this extortion case occurred five days later when Dick Eshelman announced he was letting the appeal deadline for McDevitt pass without taking any further action. Eshelman said his office "did not have sufficient time and resources to warrant a retrial".

The amateur attorney had saved himself considerable legal fees and won the case to boot. He could now claim he was not guilty of corruption, but the voters had already spoken when they voted him out of office. His police force, following his orders, had not aggressively pursued obvious organized crime figures who profited from gambling and prostitution. Three months after the case went into the closed file, Dan McDevitt died of a heart attack. He was 49.

# 42

# *Local trials end colorful era*

The opening chapter of John Kubacki's legal battles did not have a happy ending for him. The federal government had won its extortion case at the parking meter trial but sentencing would not come for more than a year after conviction. But as 1965 began, the former mayor faced two more trials involving kickbacks that would be tried in Berks County Court. He hoped to fare better defending himself before a local jury.

Kubacki's next trial date was January 25, only three days before he was scheduled to be tried with Abe Minker and Benny Bonanno in the Angie Wilkerson extortion case. And that's where things stood when Judge Hess gaveled the court to order that Monday morning.

Unlike some of the previous complicated and drawn out rackets trials, this one was a matter of which of three witnesses the jury would believe. Charlie Wade and Carl Ensslen Sr. testified there was a $500 kickback to Kubacki when the city purchased two police emergency trucks in 1961. Kubacki claimed he never received a cent.

As usual, Wade's testimony was some of the most damaging to the defendant. Charlie said he quoted prices to the mayor after having discussed the purchase of the "paddy wagons" with Ensslen, an A.W. Golden salesman.

Quoting Kubacki, Wade testified, "The price we're getting on the wagons, did you put anything in it?"

Wade's answer: "No, I didn't know you wanted anything in."

Again recalling the mayor's words, Wade said, "If I got $200 for cars, I should get at least $350 per wagon."

After discussions about buying different models of the vehicles, Wade said he approached Ensslen about a kickback of $350 on each truck, but Ensslen would settle only for $250. That was the figure arrived at between the two parties when the truck agreement was signed, Wade stated. He added, Ensslen came to the chief's office some time after the vehicles were delivered and offered him an envelope. Charlie told the salesman to take it upstairs to the mayor. After a phone call to Kubacki's office, Wade stated, Ensslen left and that was all Charlie knew about the alleged exchange of money. The chief's secretary, Thelma Reinhart, testified that she saw Charlie refuse to take the envelope before directing Ensslen to deliver it to the second-floor office of the mayor.

(On the evening of the first day of the trial, Col. E. Wilson Purdy, the state police commissioner, was guest speaker at a Rotary Club function in the Berkshire Hotel. "Organized crime cannot exist without corruption" was the commissioner's message. "No police department can exist with political interference either." Purdy admitted that when he took over as leader of the state police in 1963 he found his organization "deeply infiltrated with political influence."

A year before that, Rocco Urella became Troop C's commander. He formed a vice squad that launched an assault on Reading vice that was continuing as the big boss spoke to the Rotarians. Abe Minker was in prison and his organization no longer had any influence with the Shirk administration. The independent bookies and numbers operators were filling the rackets vacuum, despite strong resistance from the staties and city police. So Purdy's speech was rather inopportune for local attorney John Ruth who was in the midst of a trial trying to clear former mayor John Kubacki of an extortion charge.)

On the second day of the trial, Carl Ensslen supported the prosecution by insisting he handed the alleged kickback to Kubacki who accepted the envelope with $500. Nobody else was in the mayor's office to witness the exchange, Ensslen said. He also mentioned it was the only time he had ever paid booty to any city, township, or county official in the sale of cars or trucks. Ensslen admitted to Ruth that he was promised immunity by prosecutor Sam Russell if he testified.

In his closing address, Ruth offered a scenario in which Wade and Ensslen were the sole negotiators in the truck sale. Despite claims by Wade that Kubacki wanted a kickback, as an indicted perjuror Charlie's testimony was worthless, according to Ruth. Since nobody witnessed Ensslen giving the envelope containing $500 to Kubacki, it was only the salesman's word that it happened.

The jury deliberated for five hours before returning a verdict of not guilty. Among the eight women and four men on the panel, several said they were displeased that Wade and Ensslen were given immunity instead of being charged. The defense strategy to keep Kubacki off the witness stand proved successful. Acquitted, Kubacki now evened his court record of one win and one loss.

Of the numerous trials that made headlines during the wide open Minker era, the extortion trial involving Angie Wilkerson promised to be the juiciest scandal of them all. And it lived up to expectations. Testimony by and against Charlie Wade weighed heavily on his credibility when an all-star local cast appeared in Berks County Court on March 17, 1965.

Sam Russell was anxious for a second chance to prosecute John Kubacki in this highly anticipated trial, with Angie ready and willing to repeat her story about being forced to pay Kubacki to stay in business. Judge Hess, who was at the judicial center of numerous rackets cases over the past decade, would once again officiate as Abe Minker occupied a seat at the defense table. Only John Kubacki of the three defendants would testify. Minker and John Bonanno were kept off the witness stand by their attorneys. Kubacki, however, wanted a platform to deny he ever asked for, or received payoffs from Angie.

Kubacki admitted going with detective Mike DeMarco to see Angie Wilkerson in April 1961, but it was just a goodwill call, to his way of thinking. He disagreed with the prosecution's suggestion that this was unseemly behavior for the city's top official. He claimed he did not threaten to close her down. His mission was merely to advise her that he had received a complaint about Angie's customers being too noisy. This was grassroots management at its best, the mayor rationalized.

Kubacki, when first testifying, claimed he didn't know Wade from Adam when he decided to run against Danny McDevitt in the 1959 primary. However, Wade, Mrs. Wade, and Patrolman Charles Beamsderfer recalled Kubacki coming to Wade's home during a political meeting before the primary. John made big promises at that time about cleaning up the city, Wade testified. Later in the trial, Kubacki admitted he knew Wade but didn't ask for his assistance in getting elected. He also denied telling Wade he would have to pay $10,000 to Abe Minker for the police chief job.

Kubacki admitted he had known Abe Minker for eight years, even had attended a cocktail party in Abe's residence. But Judge Hess refused to permit a question asked by Russell about a trip to New York Kubacki took with Minker in the spring of 1959 during the primary campaign. Russell had learned that Abe and John were seen together in a Manhattan restaurant with Fat Tony Salerno, the Mafia's top numbers operator in Harlem.

The defense's ace in the hole at the trial was a surprise witness—a well-traveled call girl with roots in Berks County. When she completed her testimony, Charlie Wade felt more like the accused than the accuser. Trying to discredit Wade, Minker's new Philadelphia attorney, Bernard Edelson, called Gail "Connie" Lutz Amorosa to the stand. The petite, shapely blonde with an upsweep hairdo, who began charging while attending Wilson High School, related her odyssey as a prostitute in Reading, Schuylkill County, Hazleton and points west and south. Miami was her latest place of business.

Connie testified that she met Wade at a party in 1957 in a North 10th Street bar. As for those trips she made to the detective bureau in the wee hours of Charlie's graveyard shift, she said she was "an accommodating girl," offering her favors gratis. But she also testified making "$50 payoffs for protection" off and on during a period from 1959 to 1961.

These revelations came after Angie had given an extended rundown on her long-running relationship with Charlie. Betty Wade apparently didn't believe any of it as her testimony pictured Charlie as a model husband during the "thirty wonderful years" of marriage. Charlie agreed with her, denying he knew Connie Lutz, and accused the young, aggressive Edelson and his witness of stooping to new depths.

Prosecutor Sam Russell asked Connie whether she knew Joe Fiorini. The woman admitted meeting him at the Kutztown Fair but denied taking any money from him. The introduction of Fiorini's name raised the possibility that the Minker mob might have paid Connie to testify.

Angie offered no new surprises when she testified, repeating her tale about the roles of Abe, Joe, and John in the $75 weekly payoffs she made for six weeks. Then on the advice of Charlie Wade, she stopped paying her protection money, but still managed to run the best little whorehouse on Penn Street for another three years before being closed down.

It was an emotional trial, sometimes getting out of hand as attorneys, defendants, and Judge Hess were all shouting at the same time. But the jury had no trouble coming to a decision. After four days of testimony, the panel returned with a verdict in just one hour: all three defendants were guilty as charged.

On the third try, the district attorney's office had finally won an extortion case against one of Reading's ex-mayors. It was the second time in a year Kubacki and Minker had gone down together. Their wives, good and respectable women, wept as their husbands again brought embarrassment and shame to their families.

Kubacki was found guilty of conspiracy to do an unlawful act and extortion by color (power) of office. Minker and Bonanno were convicted of conspiracy and aiding and abetting extortion. Their convictions were immediately appealed, but Judge Hess refused to overturn them. In December he sentenced each of them to six months to a year in Berks County Prison with fines of $500.

Before sentencing, the judge noted he had never received so many sympathy calls for a defendant's family as he had for Kubacki's. The calls, he noted, were not from politicians but from industrialists and others.

In his verbal plea for clemency to the judge, Kubacki wondered if anyone realized the "humiliations and ridicule I've been placed under" for two years. About Wade he stated, "Little did I know of the despicable trickery he would resort to." He was referring to Wade's rollover to the feds after being indicted for perjury, then promised immunity. Petitions were filed with state appellate courts, but before they were acted on, Angie Wilkerson was up to her old tricks. The careers of Abe Minker and John Kubacki were finished, but Angie Wilkerson, in an age-old profession not too concerned with reputation, was not quite ready to call it quits.

By February 1966 the state police again started receiving complaints about the number of gentlemen visitors to her Earl Township home. Surveillance continued for two months before the staties moved in. This time Trooper Joseph Zaun played the john role. Driving his own pickup truck, Zaun was greeted outside by the madam. She certainly did not resemble your typical Hollywood and Vine hooker, but Zaun really didn't care. Off in the woods, two county detectives, Raymond Miller and John Beemer, had binoculars trained on the pair. Zaun said to the dumpy, grandmotherly woman who approached his pickup that he was looking for Angie.

"I'm Angie, baby," she smiled.

If Joe had really been looking for action he might have backed up and driven away, but this was business before pleasure. Angie told him to park behind the house, out of sight of her nosy neighbors. Once inside, she showed Joe around, including a tour of the cellar and garage where an old, blue Cadillac was parked. She said it was "a gift from a friend," but times were tough and she pointed to an area from which a portable bar had been removed. She had to sell it, she explained, because she needed money. Joe asked whether she was alone.

"I had two other girls working for me, but they fought all the time so I got rid of them," Angie said. The menu was pretty light and she was special of the day. She escorted Joe down a hallway past a room where her husband was bedfast with a heart condition. Old, white-haired Jack was still being nursed by his wife of 10 years.

Having entered Angie's bedroom, they discussed money. "Baby, I get paid before I do anything," she said, quoting fees of $10 and $15. "I'm back in the rent, so I hope you take the higher price." Joe didn't quibble, handing her two marked bills, a five and a ten. She placed the money in a dresser drawer and started to take off her blouse. As Joe leaned over to remove his shoes, he identified himself as a state cop.

This was not the mild Angie of three years ago when she was raided in her Penn Street apartment. This time she went wild. Zaun was cursed with every obscenity in Angie's extensive vocabulary. She resisted as he grabbed her arm to take her away. Joe pulled her outside to signal Beemer and Miller for assistance. Angie broke free, ran inside and locked the door. She immediately called the state police barracks in Reading to report she had been assaulted by an unknown man. Old Jack wasn't as infirm as Angie had led Zaun to believe. He opened the door to let the raiders in despite his wife's profane objections.

Attorney Calvin Lieberman defended her in court, making a big deal about entrapment. He called Angie's arrest "a travesty of justice. A sweet person like Angie, two years reformed." He asked the jury of nine men and three women whether they thought Angie was a sex symbol who men would pay for her favors. To make his point, Lieberman said:

"I must apologize to my client, but if her livelihood had to come from sexual attraction, she would starve to death. Sexually, she would have unmotivated any man." Then, to further emphasize her lack of appeal, he held up the patched and frayed tan shorts she was wearing when enticing Joe Zaun to her bedroom.

"This is more like what a person would wear working in the garden," the attorney declared.

Cruel to someone who always was conscious of her appearance in public, but effective. And it worked.

The jury acquitted Angie Wilkerson. She was elated. Sobbing, she hugged her husky lawyer whose devastating assessment of her professional resources might have driven a lesser woman into retirement, but Angie was resilient.

Trying to perk up her appearance she dyed her hair blonde. This didn't necessarily mean that life would suddenly be more fun while waiting for news from the State Superior Court in the extortion case. In November 1966 the appellate court announced its decision: Kubacki, Minker, and Bonanno were awarded new trials. Their convictions were overturned because the Berks court had failed to permit the defense attorneys to examine a transcript (tape recording) of a statement given by former Police Chief Charlie Wade. The press tried to obtain a copy of the tape when it was discussed during an appeals hearing the previous year. Judge Hess refused to release the tape but said he would pass it on to the higher court. The Superior Court decided portions of the statement would have been helpful in the defense of the convicted trio. On that basis, the three defendants were granted new trials.

Now it was Dick Eshelman's turn to take the appellate route. In December he asked the State Supreme Court to overturn the lower court's ruling. That didn't happen, so Eshelman started preparing for a retrial. All of the principals appeared before Judge Hess as the retrial was about to begin, but this time Angie would not cooperate. She refused to retell the story she had related so often before—no, not again. On this occasion, however, she availed herself of her 5th Amendment rights not to testify if it might incriminate her. Eshelman said by now nothing surprised him where Angie was concerned. Without her testimony, the D.A. dropped the charges and the case was officially closed on June 21, 1967.

Abe Minker showed no emotion as his long string of court appearances finally ended. Some suspected Abe squeezed out of this latest jam by greasing Angie's palm. Heaven knows her legal problems of late had just about drained her dry. But nobody worked overtime to uncover yet another hush money event in the eventful life of little Angie Martin Wilkerson. Judge Hess delivered a brief opinion about Angie's change of heart.

"A result like this is not fair to anybody. It's not fair to the defendants who are entitled to a clearcut answer to 'Are you guilty?' or 'Are you innocent?' No answer will ever be given."

With that final reversal, Dick Eshelman and his hard working team of assistants and state policemen were now batting 0 for 3. Despite his all-out attempts to convict Kubacki, McDevitt, and Minker on extortion charges, all three had slipped the noose. Once again his efforts proved how difficult it was to win an extortion conviction that sticks.

According to the Third Class City Code, it was the city controller's job to prepare an annual report on the various duties of his department during the previous year. Not for several years had such a report been issued in Reading. In January 1965, the current controller, Earl Patterson, put a five-page report together that started tongues wagging. One of the points he made was that he had cooperated with the district attorney's office by providing files it requested in a probe regarding corruption in city contracts. This was the first inkling that such an investigation was underway. Eshelman was far more specific in July when he made public the results of the probe.

Eshelman's annoyance was not masked in his report. No matter how hard the state police and his county detectives tried—plus a much improved performance by the city police—prosecuting corruption in Berks County was still a frustrating business. He announced in a six-page report the discouraging results of a yearlong investigation of local transactions between elected officials of earlier administrations and businesses. Public apathy and the lack of cooperation by people who dealt with the city was the principal reason corruption continued to flourish, the report claimed. Sam Russell, who headed the probe, described the roadblocks caused by current laws, and the need for new legislation. He cited 100 municipal transactions that were reviewed and 41 that were "investigated intensively."

Eshelman said, "It is almost unbelievable that Reading and Berks County within a period of 10 years after having experienced the alleged corruption of the late 1940s, resulting in the U.S. Senate crime investigation, then went right back to the same thing or even worse in the latter 1950s."

As an example of uncooperative action, Russell told of a routine city permit, which remained unauthorized until the property owner and his agent turned over $750 in cash to an intermediary, "who refused to discuss to whom he paid the money." The permit was then signed and issued.

Another case, which was referred to federal authorities, involved a transaction "by a local municipal corporation and a seller." A day after the transaction, $20,000 was paid as a "commission" by the seller to one of its officers, who helped to arrange the sale. The next day, the seller's officer drew a personal check for $10,000 and drove to Manhattan to cash it, then returned to Reading with that amount of cash, Russell continued, "He has refused, without the advice of counsel, to answer whether all or any part of the $10,000 in cash was paid to any public official who participated in the transaction."

The report described numerous other suspect deals that the D.A.'s office pursued, but were stymied by stonewalling businessmen and politicians who refused to embarrass or incriminate themselves with the truth. The recent cases lost by Eshelman and Russell against McDevitt and Kubacki obviously rankled these two honest and determined law enforcement officers. Russell stated that the most significant result was that the investigation "into the conduct of local public officials ever took place at all." Russell said if the need arose for such an investigation in the future, it could be launched more readily because of the existence of a precedent. The memory of such an investigation "may be of some guidance for our future local public officials." He worried that no convictions of any kind would be possible, despite the arduous work of county detectives and assistant district attorneys.

Expressing some optimism at the end of the dire report, Russell concluded: "On the other hand, the many businessmen and others who have taken refuge in the privilege against self-incrimination have asserted their presently existing right, but have earned the respect of no one, including themselves." Sadly, those reluctant enablers of the rackets were never fully exposed. Only rumors about them circulated and soon were forgotten.

Angie was beginning to think her troubles would never end. The day after her refusal to testify one more time in her extortion case, a bench warrant was served at her latest residence on Reading Crest Avenue in Muhlenberg Park. Judge Hess, at the urging of the county probation officer, Mrs. Dorothy Beidler, had issued the warrant reminding Angie she had failed to pay a $500 fine levied three years earlier. She took care of that the next day with a $589 check, which included interest. A year later she was in trouble again.

State Trooper Robert "Tex" Kaunert had been observing the heavy male traffic to the room of 35-year-old Joan Farris at West Reading's Penn View Motel. Joan had worked a week for Angie a few years earlier. On August 31, 1968, Tex arrested the Pittsburgh woman and took her to the D.A.'s office where she gave a seven-page statement. She detailed Angie's color code used by clients to gain entrance to Joan's motel boudoir. The code wasn't too sophisticated and it eliminated haggling. If Don Juan arrived at Joan's room with a black slip of paper, he was a big spender ready with $20 for elite action. A green slip gave him the green light for the $15 special, and a red paper might match the shade of his face if he needed change to scratch together 10 bucks for basic.

Whatever occurred on Joan's mattress could hardly have matched the excitement at Angie's domicile that evening when Holloway, Kaunert, and Zaun arrived at her place with an arrest warrant. These guys were trained to subdue dangerous drug dealers and Hells Angels, but they should have taken a refresher course in bobcat defense before tangling with Angie. She tore up the warrant, kicked Tex, scratched Zaun, and sicced her dog on Holloway, whose pants were chewed. Cursing and biting, Angie was cuffed and bodily hauled off to an alderman.

At her trial the following March, Angie insisted she acted like a lady when Holloway and company arrested her, and denied color-coding her connection with Joan Farris. Mrs. Farris, however, repeated her story about being contacted by Angie to come to Reading where she offered the prostitute a 50-50 split on customer fees and room rent. Farris said her 7-year-old daughter stayed with Angie during their four-day partnership. The jury found Angie guilty on three counts.

The IRS added to her woes by filing a $98,400 lien against her for unpaid income taxes dating from 1954 to 1962. But she was more concerned with staying out of jail on the prostitution conviction.

Her attorney, James Potter, filed a petition for a new trial with Judge Readinger, but as the year progressed Angie could no longer pay her legal fees. She showed up at a December 1968 hearing without a lawyer, telling the court she was now waitressing six days a week in Birdsboro. The judge granted her one last postponement, but in March 1969 she was sentenced by Judge James Bertolet to 4 to 14 months in Berks County Prison. She cajoled the judge to let her remain free one more day to find a home for her dog and close down her Birdsboro home.

On leaving the courtroom, Angie had the last word for Holloway, who she accused of harassing her and costing her job opportunities. He denied that. Angie also made serious threats against him that cost her an additional four months in jail as Bertolet increased her sentence to 9 to 23 months. The little lady with the big mouth served her minimum time in BCP and was home for Christmas.

When last heard from, Angie used a false name to get hired as a bartender at the Dolphin Lounge on Shillington Road. Don Holloway chanced to stop in the lounge one day. Did Angie greet him as a long last friend? No, she shrugged and sighed, resignedly:

"Well, there goes this job."

The Pennsylvania Liquor Control Board bans people with criminal records from tending bar. Time to move on again for the aging vagabond.

# 43

# *Long ordeal ends, retirement at last*

A federal parole board, after twice having rejected Abe's release from the federal penitentiary at Lewisburg, finally gave him his freedom on May 24, 1966. He had served 3 years and 8 days of his 4-year sentence. Of the IRS $1.95 million tax lien the government held against him, Abe had not paid a cent towards reducing it. He claimed he was broke and ailing with lingering infirmities that would restrict his wage earning options. Still under appeal was his conviction for conspiring to extort payoff money from Angie Wilkerson. His 6-month prison sentence in that case was still in abeyance.

At 68, Abe was finally a free man but still faced a lengthy period of probation. Along with his jail sentence in May 1961, his total fines had reached $45,000 and his probation time climbed to 10 years. A month after sentencing, Judge John Morgan Davis had second thoughts, declaring that Abe would be eligible for parole the following September. The judge also knocked off three years of probation. The parole board again turned down Abe's plea for release and it would be another nine months before he got out.

The same year Abe was released from prison, the U.S. Supreme Court ruled the $50 gambling occupation stamp tax was unconstitutional. It took the top court in the land 15 years to repeal the 1951 legislation that had put quite a few Reading numbers operators behind bars and others who had paid substantial fines. The law's revocation was of some help to Abe as the courts began chipping away at his probation time.

During her husband's imprisonment, Verna, for the most part, remained in their Hampden Boulevard apartment. She paid Abe regular visits for the first year, then in October 1964 was hurt in a fall outside the Mount Penn Post Office. Stepping from her car, she slipped on loose stones, fell and injured her back and broke her left arm. In 1965 she filed a $20,000 personal injury suit against the U.S. government. The case dragged on for a few years before she was awarded $6,349 in 1969. The government appealed but eventually withdrew its petition and paid the settlement.

After Abe was released from prison in 1966, the Minkers enjoyed their first summer of his retirement in the Phoenix house he had built in 1961. Finally he was retired. He had no visible income or the IRS would have tried harder to pry loose some of it. But he certainly was no pauper. Wherever he kept his stash, the government never found it.

When Johnny Wittig was interviewed for "The Corrupt City" television documentary in 1971, he told commentator Rod MacLeish:

"He contributed large sums to his church, he never drove anything near a big car, maybe 3 or 4 years old. He wanted people to think he was a poor man. Today he is worth three or four million in cash." Just how knowledgeable Wittig was about his old boss' financial standing is questionable, but Abe never had to worry about where the next buck was coming from for the rest of his life.

By the spring of 1967 he moved from the rancher to a $250-a-month luxury apartment about two miles away. Like his former residence, the apartment complex had a swimming pool. Whenever he visited Reading or Philadelphia on legal matters, he sported a mellow tan. That's how he appeared when he was in the Quaker City on March 28, 1968, to make one final bid to expunge the sizable period of probation he still faced. His petition was reviewed by the three federal judges instrumental in his sentencing: Alfred Luongo, John Morgan Davis, and C. William Kraft. With Kraft as spokesman at the March hearing, Minker was informed that the panel had rejected his plea. Abe again brought up his health issue, stating he had undergone still another back operation, his fifth, six months earlier.

"I'm an old man," he pleaded. He would turn 70 the following October. "If God gives me time, I want to go to Israel. If God spares me I want to live in peace. I've paid for everything I've done. I'm old and sick."

Judge Kraft reminded Abe he had not paid anything to reduce the government's $2-million tax lien. "How could I pay anything?" Abe questioned, claiming the IRS had attached all he had, plus that of his wife and daughter. He also complained that since the law regarding an occupation tax on gamblers was recently ruled unconstitutional, the $2-million lien against him was twice what it should be because most of his earnings came from gambling during the period he was being prosecuted.

Judge Kraft said the judicial panel had considered all the factors and decided it was best for everybody if Abe continued his monthly visits to his parole officer in Phoenix, and if his health failed the P.O. would visit him. With the threat of going back to jail hanging over him if he violated his parole, Judge Kraft said, he felt Abe would not be tempted to return to his old trade.

It was on that court visit to Philly that he chanced to run into Skinny Barrett in the federal courthouse. Barrett, a honcho who operated the renowned interstate dice games in Reading from 1956 to 1962, was also cleaning up some legal business that day. Their brief reunion was interrupted by a press photographer who recognized them. Abe and Verna hustled away. Skinny, hiding his face from the cameraman, drifted off in another direction.

In 1969, Abe and Verna moved into a house in Scranton that they rented from Verna's sister, Ethel McKinney. The house had been left to Ethel by their parents. Nothing fancy this time, just a two-and-a-half story frame home with aluminum siding valued at $15,000 in a middle class neighborhood. The Minkers stayed for less than two years. Abe was 72 but still leaving a long shadow in his hometown.

Some of the folks in Reading felt he was still a threat to their community. Or was it the GOP who fostered this notion on the electorate? Republican Party plotters, using Minker's notoriety, planted a seed of doubt to win the mayoral election in 1971, the same year Abe and Verna were getting settled in a Fort Lauderdale apartment. They would live out the rest of their lives there.

During the 1971 primary election campaign, Gene Shirk was seeking to regain the mayor's office he had lost four years earlier to Victor Yarnell. He suggested one or more of the six Democratic candidates might have links to the rackets. Councilman Joe Kuzminski beat the BID candidate Tony Carabello, setting up a race for mayor with Shirk. Shirk, assistant to the president of Albright College, now drew some support from Dr. Charlie Raith, a BID pioneer and professor at Albright and a close friend of the old Dutchman.

A week before the general election, state Rep. James Gallen spoke at a political function, inferring that if Kuzminski were elected, Minker was waiting in the wings to return Reading to the good old rackets days of the past. Gallen, GOP county chairman, theorized that since the mayor of Scranton had attended a Kuzminski rally a few days earlier, and since Minker had lived in Scranton earlier that year, there must be collusion afoot. He exhumed a quote by Police Chief Bernie Dobinsky from the television documentary. Dobinsky had responded to a question about the possibility of the rackets returning to Reading:

"'I'm sure there are some elements just poised on a springboard waiting to get back in,'" Gallen recalled. "Abe Minker is one small step away. Now, we know what he (Dobinsky) meant. I think it is more than a coincidence," meaning the link between Kuzminski, the mayor of Scranton, and Abe.

The Reading Times sent a reporter to Scranton to find out if Gallen's assumption had any validity. Mayor Eugene Peters, when asked if he knew Abe Minker, responded, "Abe who?" When the scenario presented by Gallen was explained to him, he laughed.

"If that's not wild. I don't know Abe Minker. That's about as ridiculous as it can get. I won't even reply to something like that it's so far out." Peters said he attended the political rally in Reading believing it was a banquet for Kuzminski, because the two had become good friends while both served on the board of the Pennsylvania League of Cities.

As it turned out, Minker had left Scranton ten months earlier. A federal official commenting on Minker's current status placed him in the "sweet, lovable old man category rather than one of the baddies." He thought the 72-year-old Abe was 82.

It seems likely this was one dirty trick that actually worked. With a big advantage in Democratic voter registration, Kuzminski was regarded as a lopsided favorite. Mayor Victor Yarnell had left a clean government legacy for Kuzminski to build on, and even though Shirk had been a popular mayor, the Democrats voted him out of office in 1967. Reading voters, however, lived up to their reputation of unpredictability. Shirk won by almost 900 votes.

Years later, Kuzminski blamed Raith for swinging the BID vote over to the Republicans. Who can say how many Demos feared the Minker rumors were true and decided to back Shirk, who they felt was incorruptible. Abe, basking in the Florida sun, must have chuckled at the outcome, possibly proud that his notoriety still carried plenty of weight in the Pretzel City he once owned.

Despite his infirmities and lack of funds, somehow, Abe managed to live almost another 17 years after moving to Fort Lauderdale to a well-appointed apartment. It remained a secret wherever Abe got the money to live well above the poverty level.

Abe Minker died in Fort Lauderdale in 1985 at 87. After more than 45 years of marriage to Abe, Verna died nine years later at 93. Isadore Minker outlived his brother by 10 years, dying in 1995.

# 44

## *All in the family for years and years*

Reading never had a crime organization that could be regarded as a Mafia family per se where blood oaths and hit men were part of the legend. A local branch of the Black Hand, an extortionist gang, played pretty rough more than 80 years ago, but tales from those days are long forgotten. Max Hassel, Tony Moran, Abe Minker, and other local racketeers certainly had influential friends in the Mafia that were financially rewarding at times. And there was one connected family of recent vintage that extended its racketeering activities over three generations into the present decade.

The Damianos became active in the local underworld back in the late Depression years. Santo and Samuel Damiano took the high road at first, gaining recognition throughout the East Coast states as members of the "Four Aces" acrobatic act in vaudeville. As the closing act in many of their appearances from 1931 to 1936, the Damiano brothers teamed with Roy Lukens and Chester "Chet" Farrara in the aerial derring-do. Santo and Sam, who also went by "Salvo," supplied the brawn and were the catchers. Chet and Roy were the daring young men on the trapeze as the flyers.

They appeared with such headliners as the Mills Brothers, comedians Andy Devine and Eddie Foy Jr., and Mary Martin. After five years in show business at the height of the Depression, they hung up their tights and settled in Reading. Lukens went to work in Lukens Gym operated by his father and uncle on Thorn Street. It was there the Aces and other acrobats learned their trade. Farrara became a bartender at the Franklin AC and later drifted into numbers writing before opening his men's store at 5$^{th}$ and Cherry streets. The Damianos tried raising chickens on a small farm they bought at Blue Marsh, but compared to the challenge and exhilaration of their high-flying act, this was chicken feed. So they opened a beer distributorship at 7$^{th}$ and Bingaman. Sam also was handy with a hammer and saw, working at times as a carpenter. As young men willing to take risks, maybe it was inevitable that they drifted into the fast-money racket of writing numbers.

By April 1940 Santo had advanced to pickup man in Tony Moran's organization when he was arrested by Sgt. Mike Reilly, still the state police nemesis of racketeers. Over the next four decades Santo gained a sizeable police record, sometimes serving jail time, other times winning his cases, but always returning to the line of work he knew best, the lottery. In the early '50s he teamed with a neighborhood buddy, Patsy Lepera, running a numbers game. That was before Patsy moved up in the underworld as a conman. Patsy, a self-professed fashion plate, recorded his dirty work around the country in a published book: "Memoirs of a Scam Man."

Santo built enough of a reputation in gambling circles to be included on a list of major Pennsylvania racketeers named in a 1961 report released by a U.S. Senate subcommittee investigating racketeering. The report said Santo subscribed to a horse race betting service and was a known numbers operator. When Charlie Wade saw the report he announced Santo would be one of his targets in the city police clampdown on numbers writers and bookmakers.

Charlie apparently wasn't keeping tabs on Santo, because the IRS beat him to his target by pinching the big fellow in his pool hall at 7th and Cherry streets on December 16. Six other places were also hit that day. The agents collected quite a bit of evidence showing races were being booked and lottery tickets were being sold in Santo's pool hall. Also, Santo was not displaying a federal gambling stamp on the wall. What really upset him, however, was the feds impounded his black 1960 Cadillac parked nearby. Eleven large bottles of liquor lacking state stamps were found in the car's trunk. The Caddy was eventually towed to Philadelphia.

When Minker took over as the vice lord in 1956, one of the very few fellows in the numbers racket NOT threatened if he didn't pay for protection was Santo. With imposing brawn, dark complexion, a prominent nose and a full crop of wavy, silver hair, Santo looked the part of a godfather. He supposedly held that distinction locally because of his ties with the Philly mob. When the feds were chasing down Minker, they didn't seem too interested in him because he wasn't operating on the scale that Abe was.

By 1961 Santo was living in the suburbs, but maintained a home at the northwest corner of Franklin and Apple streets. Across Franklin Street and up toward 2nd was the home of Patsy Spadafora. The IRS agents nabbed Patsy for not having a gambling stamp in his restaurant around the corner on South 2nd where numbers were being sold. Patsy's arrest meant nothing to his neighbors who would shortly elect him their alderman.

Others charged with failure to buy federal stamps in the December 16 raids were John Ocksrider, David Pizzo, John Palladino, Robert Schearer, and Frank Donato. The latter would soon be in far greater trouble with Bruno's mob in Philadelphia. Seventeen months later, Damiano was still battling the government to return his car. The feds wanted to turn it over to a finance company where Damiano owed money on a loan.

The state police ran into Santo eight years later when they raided a floating dice game in an Alsace Manor Township picnic grove in the summer of 1969. Santo got into a shoving match when a trooper tried to sweep the dice table clean of $350 in the pot. At 61, Santo was still a very large force to deal with as others joined the fray. Thirteen were arrested and four more escaped through a window in the grove's pavilion. Gibraltar Joe Biancone added his girth as a combatant in this heavyweight tussle. Anthony Sottasanti, who had to be pried off a trooper's back, was charged with running the game.

Although Chief Wade missed his chance to nab Santo Damiano, two months later city cops nabbed brother Sam in his own pool room/poker parlor across the tracks from Santo's place. Five years younger than his brother, Sam had succumbed to the lure and profitability of illegal gambling. He didn't miss the hard labor of running a beer distributorship. In 1962, he was being watched by Bill Lilley who did the spadework before the chief led the pack into Sam's house at 48 South 7th. Nine card players were also arrested. But the city cops didn't look upstairs where the numbers and horse betting slips were plentiful in Sam's apartment. That would come later.

At Sam's trial the following December, the prosecution had no witnesses to testify he was taking a cut out of the poker game. None of the nine players, who forfeited the $50 bonds they posted after their arrests, would come forward to testify Sam was cutting the game. He claimed he was in the kitchen eating a sandwich when Charlie's raiders broke in. That is when Judge Hess stepped in:

"The commonwealth lacks evidence showing that the defendant got anything out of it, that it was a professional activity. I can't let the jury guess." So he dismissed the charges and sent the jury home.

Ten months later on October 29, 1963, the state police looked in on another game in progress in Sam's card room. The row house was now being called the S&S Smoke Shop although pool could still be played in the front room. This time the raiders checked out the second floor, well aware that's where a numbers bank was located. A door blocking the way upstairs was knocked down as the staties raced up to grab Sam in his apartment just as he was coming out of the bathroom where he had flushed slips down the toilet. Evidence on the second and third floors was found showing Sam had 18 numbers writers working for him in a bank that was averaging $1,100 a week. His weekly take was estimated at $700. Three others in the card room were arrested along with two more upstairs.

The city police took a different tack trying to nab Sam again. On May 10, 1964, two patrolmen closed down the S&S Smoke Shop because pool was being played, a violation of the state blue laws prohibiting pool operations on Sunday. Patrolmen Joseph Kolasa and Michael Perate swore out warrants for the arrests of Samuel Damiano and Luis Ruiz, who managed the pool room. But when they served the warrants it was Santo, not Sam, who was there in 48 South 7th that Sunday evening. The argument grew pretty heated and Santo was arrested for disorderly conduct. The close resemblance of the brothers made the mistaken identity understandable. So everybody including Sam Liever showed up the next day at police court—except Paul Brogley. Mose was the magistrate who had issued the warrants. Finally on June 5 the matter was straightened out when charges were dismissed against Santo. Ruiz also was cleared after he explained the pool game in question was merely a friendly match between him and a close friend.

When Sam's trial in the earlier numbers case was about to start on September 22, 1964, he pleaded guilty to the lottery charge, and the poker charge was dismissed. When his lawyer, Sam Liever, told Judge Hess his client planned to get out of the gambling racket and return to his former jobs, carpenter or beer distributor, he was let off with a year of probation.

If that was the end of Sam's racketeering career, the family tradition was being carried on by the younger generation. Sam's 26-year-old son, Sammy, got into big trouble passing counterfeit $100 bills in a 1959 poker game in Lancaster. This activity was soon linked to a major bogus money ring that was cracked in Chicago. Sammy proved to be one of the many passers the syndicate employed in the exchange of false money for honest cash. Sammy had passed $1,000 in phony bills in the Philadelphia area before being caught. Secret Service officials reported the ring had printed more than $1 million in spurious money, with $750,000 recovered. Sammy was convicted by a federal jury. His 5-year sentence was later reduced to 3.

Although Sammy always claimed he was not Mafia-connected, many law enforcement officials believed he was. A 1990 Pennsylvania Crime Commission annual report stated his uncle, Santo, was a close associate of the late Angelo

Bruno, and that Sammy was friendly with several members of the Scarfo family in Philly.

Out of the building at 529 Cherry Street, years before the headquarters of one of Tony Moran's numbers games, Sammy operated both legal and illegal businesses in Reading. He ran The Clique, a South 8th Street nightclub that was demolished by a mysterious explosion and fire in January 1978. In 1992, with his 21-year-old son, Troy, Sammy was convicted on cocaine trafficking charges. At the time of his death from heart failure in 1997 in a federal prison in Kentucky, he had served seven years of a 15-year sentence. He did not leave Vicki, his wife of 33 years, penniless. In 2005, she sold two houses in Cumru township for a total of $700,000.

In 1997 Troy was released from federal prison with 5 years of parole remaining. During an argument with his girlfriend in July 1999, an Exeter Township policeman tried to intervene and was punched by Troy. Although the charge was simple assault, a jury convicted him and Judge Stephen Lieberman sentenced him to 9-to-23-months in BCP. After a few days in jail he was released on bail by the judge while the conviction was under appeal. Troy raised the necessary $250,000 bail. A year later while the case was still being appealed, a federal judge ordered Troy remanded to prison for another 10 months for having violated his parole.

The third generation racketeer is currently in a federal prison having pleaded guilty to a series of charges in May 2006 and October 2007. The most serious charges involved heroin and methamphetamines. He was sentenced to 7 to 14 years, and fined $50,000.

# 45

# *Wincanton and its citizens fare badly in report*

A few years after the dust had settled and Reading was no longer the target of federal investigations, the city still remained a curiosity to the national media and academics researching organized crime.

In 1967, "The Wincanton Report," a federally funded study, was published about corruption and organized crime in a small city. Four years after that, Reading was again exposed to a national audience when an independent television company, Group W Corp., produced an hour-long documentary, "The Corrupt City." The film was revived in 2006 at the Goggleworks art museum in Reading during a film festival organized by Reading Arts Council.

Fifteen years after the 1951 Kefauver hearings exposed Reading for what it was, the federal government was again in an anti-Mafia mode. The President's Commission on Law Enforcement and Administration of Justice formed a task force to prepare a report on the state of organized crime. Reading became a good source of information for commission investigators. In the previous 10 years, various agencies of the Justice Department had, at considerable cost, developed high-profile gambling, tax, and bootlegging cases in Reading that were successfully prosecuted in federal courts. Ironically, by the time Wincanton became a familiar name nationally, Berks County and Reading law enforcement officials had launched their own attack on local racketeering.

A pair of young University of Wisconsin political science professors arrived in Reading unannounced in May 1966. Dr. John A. Gardiner and David J. Olson said they had received a grant from New York City's Russell Sage Foundation to write a book on small city politics. They said Reading was one of three or four cities whose political setup they would be analyzing. Actually, the President's Commission was financing their study, fully aware of Reading's history as a city where the rackets had flourished since Prohibition.

Using a list of 120 questions, commission survey crews interviewed hundreds of citizens, businessmen, politicians, professionals, and policemen. Gardiner and Olson pored through newspaper files and compiled a short history of illegal gambling, bootlegging, prostitution, and extortion in Reading. Their final report was entitled, "Wincanton: The Politics of Corruption." Their findings were included in "Task Force Report: Organized Crime," a document published in 1967 by the President's Commission. It was the only section of the task force study dealing specifically with one city's corruption problems.

Gardiner and Olson stated, "Although the facts and events of this report are true, every attempt has been made to hide the identity of actual people by the use of fictitious names, descriptions and dates." They were about as successful in this subterfuge as was "Anonymous" in his 1997 novel "Primary Colors." Only a Reading reader who didn't recognize President Clinton's character in that book might not have been able to identify Irv Stern as Abe Minker in the task force report.

More important than the rehash of the long reign of the racketeers, Gardiner and Olson probed deeply into the psyche of a community that put up with corruption for so long. The professors drew heavily on the findings of the Kefauver Committee, and from data compiled during the series of federal raids and trials during the McDevitt and Kubacki administrations.

Not at any time in the 20th Century, the investigators learned, had the Reading police force been allowed to completely run its own show. At one time, elected constables and policemen shared equal arresting powers. In 1907, the local Chamber of Commerce hired the New York Bureau of Municipal Research to look into the sad state of Reading's police force. The bureau's report of more than 100 pages was a broad indictment of mismanagement in law enforcement. It was also an early warning that was rarely heeded by the politicians for the next 10 years.

Instead of hiring the best applicants in those early years, it was solely a case of whom you knew. The politicians controlled all appointments. The New York experts found that in the previous 17 years, Reading police personnel had completely changed seven times. Rookies received on the job training, learning from "veterans" who knew their number was up after the next election. Men were being hired as cops at an age other cities would have forced them to retire. Since no physicals were required, many came aboard with chronic illnesses, but were paid full salary when out sick. Some could barely write their names, which didn't really matter because few written records were kept. In police court cops told their version of the arrest, the magistrate passed judgment, and that was it. That future scourge, paperwork, had not yet infested Reading's police department. The seven holding cells in the basement of City Hall were described as unsanitary "ancient torture dungeons." City Hall at that time was on the northeast corner of South 5$^{th}$ and Franklin streets.

That old and forgotten study pointed out that the 94-man department was too small for a growing city approaching 100,000 population. It recommended hiring through civil service tests, including physical and mental examinations. Over the next 60 years, gradual improvements were made toward the goal of establishing a professional department, but one important change never happened—the police department remained at the mercy of each succeeding mayor.

"The Wincanton Report" illustrated this merry-go-round pattern in the case of Police Chief Robert Elliott. He had curbed outside racketeering as best he could during the pearly gray administration of James Bamford. When Dan McDevitt took office, he demoted Elliott because the chief said he would continue to go after organized crime wherever he found it.

One of the idiosyncrasies of Reading voters until 1984 was that they never reelected an incumbent mayor. A few mayors won second terms but never twice in a row. Because each new mayor invariably reshuffled the police brass, the department usually lacked stability and experienced officers who had administrative training. This weakened morale and played into the hands of the racketeers who were always ready with gifts for the disenchanted, underpaid patrolmen who had little respect for their superiors.

The activities of Abe Minker were thoroughly examined by the Wincanton authors. With sound federal government sources, they were able to assess records about Abe's rise to power in 1945. By the time U.S. Sen. Estes Kefauver and his committee investigated the interstate activities of organized crime, Minker still shared power with other local racketeers. Abe and his brother, Isadore, were far less candid when they appeared before the committee than was Ralph Kreitz. But the questions they refused to answer by taking the 5th Amendment exposed not only their gambling operations, but also their reliance on the Philadelphia and New York mobs.

"Two basic principles were involved in Minker's protection system," the Wincanton Report stated. "Pay top personnel as much as necessary to keep them happy (and quiet), and pay something to as many others as possible to implicate them in the system to keep them from talking. The range of the system thus went from a weekly salary for some public officials to a Christmas turkey for patrolmen on the beat. Records from the numbers banks listed payments totaling $2,400 each week to locally elected officials, state legislators, the police chief, a captain in charge of detectives, and persons mysteriously labeled "county" and "state." While lists of persons to be paid remained fairly constant, the amounts distributed varied according to fluctuating profitability of gambling operations at the time. Payoff figures dropped sharply when the FBI put the Cherry Street dice game out of business. When the game was running, one official was receiving $750 a week, the chief, $100, and a few captains, lieutenants, and detectives lesser amounts."

The report pointed out that patrolmen learned the hard way to keep their mouths shut about reporting or making unassigned arrests for gambling or prostitution. Those who dared to buck the system ended up on the midnight shift. Despite these assumptions that numerous Reading elected officials were taking payoffs, one of a very few were ever charged with bribery.

When high school teachers complained about burlesque shows in the Park Theater, Jimmy Maurer was paying the mayor $25 a week to allow his nudies to perform, the report stated. Unnamed township officials were said to have paid a county official $5,000 to operate gambling tents for five nights each summer. State police were never called to close down that annual rural gambling event, the report claimed.

"Many other city and county officials must be termed guilty of nonfeasance," the report continued, "although there is no evidence that they received payoffs, and although they could present reasonable excuses for their inaction." Local judges did request an investigation by the state attorney general, but refused to approve his suggestion that a grand jury be convened to continue the investigation. For each of these instances of inaction, a tenable excuse might be offered: the best patrolman should not be expected to endure harassment from his superior officers; state police gambling raids in a hostile city might jeopardize state-local cooperation on more serious crimes; and a grand jury probe might easily be turned into a whitewash by a corrupt district attorney."

Charlie Wade was guilty of malfeasance when he paid $5,000 to Abe Minker to be appointed chief of police, the report stated. And Dan McDevitt was guilty of macing, a violation of his oath of office, by informing City Hall employees they were expected to contribute 2 percent of their salaries to the Democratic Party. By asking salesmen who sold equipment to the city to make voluntary contributions to the party, McDevitt and Kubacki were guilty of malfeasance, not just honest graft as Reading politicians came to regard such donations. And McDevitt's revenge campaign of ticketing Reading Eagle Company delivery trucks was identified in the report as an act of misfeasance.

About the only positive finding in the study about Abe Minker: "He never, it might be added, permitted narcotics traffic in the city while he controlled it." This could also be said about McDevitt and Kubacki. Detective John Feltman was given a direct order not to investigate gambling or prostitution, but also was given a free hand to undertake any investigation of illegal drugs he wanted to. During those two administrations very few drug arrests were made, but it wasn't too many years later that the long war started, and continues to this day.

When Kubacki became mayor in 1960 he maneuvered to gain control of the bureaus of building and plumbing inspection. The Wincanton Report explained why: "With this power to approve or deny building permits, Kubacki 'sat on' applications, waiting until the petitioner contributed $50 or $75, or threatened to sue to get his permit. Some building designs were not approved until a favored architect was retained as a consultant. At least three instances are known in which developers were forced to pay for zoning variances before apartment buildings or supermarkets could be erected. Businessmen who wanted to encourage rapid turnover of curb space in front of their stores were told to pay a police sergeant to erect "10-minute parking" signs. The report questioned whether this was honest graft.

Attempting to offer a fair and realistic big picture of Reading's city government, Gardiner and Olson came to this conclusion:

"This cataloging of acts of nonfeasance, malfeasance, and misfeasance by Wincanton officials raises a danger of confusing variety with universality, of assuming that every employee of the city was either engaged in corrupt activities or was being paid to ignore the corruption of others. On the contrary, both official investigations and private research led to the conclusion that there is no reason whatsoever to question the honesty of the vast number of employees of the city of Wincanton. Certainly, no more than 10 of the 155 members of the Wincanton police force were on Irv Stern's (Minker's) payroll (although as many as half of them might have accepted petty Christmas presents (turkeys or liquor.) The only charge that can be justly leveled against the mass of employees is that they were unwilling to jeopardize their employment by publicly exposing what was going on."

Some employees agreed to cooperate with federal investigators when they were convinced an honest attempt was being made to convict Minker and Kubacki. These few brave souls risked the mayor's wrath by testifying before the grand jury in Philadelphia. Charlie Wade, at the risk of facing trial for perjury, really opened up, giving the government first-hand information on how the mob had thoroughly corrupted city officials during his time as chief.

Gambling became so imbedded in the social structure of Reading, the report pointed out, that reform movements seldom had a lasting effect on politics. In one year alone, it was estimated 272,000 persons paid to play bingo in the city. Fringe mobsters had an interest in the more profitable bingo establishments.

Most candidates for office grew up in neighborhoods where numbers were sold in most corner grocery stores. They or their parents belonged to social, political, athletic, or fire company clubs where slot machines and punchboards were as much a part of the milieu as jars of pickled eggs and sausage on the bar. However, it could be said that while a majority of the voters who felt no qualms about placing a bet with a bookie or playing the daily number, these same citizens would prefer honest politicians to those who weren't. It was because of this hypocritical attitude, so prevalent all over the city, that victorious reform candidates never stayed in office long enough to change the system.

"While gambling and corruption are easy to judge in the abstract," the report said, "they are never encountered in the abstract—they are encountered in the form of a slot machine which is helping to pay off your club's mortgage, or a chance to fix your son's speeding ticket, or an opportunity to hasten the completion of your new building by overlooking a few violations of the building code. In these forms the choices seem less clear.

"Furthermore, to obtain a final appraisal of what took place in Wincanton one must weigh the manifest functions served—providing income for the participants, recreation for the consumers of vice and gambling, etc.—against the latent functions, the unintended or unrecognized consequences of these events."

Not only clubs relied on gambling for financial support. Business groups used lotteries to advertise "Downtown Reading Days." Playground associations and churches sponsored lotteries, bingo and Las Vegas nights to pay for equipment in youth leagues. Union halls were hotbeds of all types of gambling. Far more than most cities of its size, Reading allowed itself to drift into a situation that left many, many of its organizations dependent upon gambling to survive. The direct consequence of this dependency was the election of officials who also relied heavily on gambling for financial support.

And the betting cancer spread even to our hallowed institutions, the report stated. It noted that "leading gamblers and racketeers were generous supporters of Reading charities." Going back to Max Hassel and Dutch Mary, the city's underworld folk heroes had promotional agendas, including spreading the wealth among the poor on holidays. Today it would be called marketing, akin to Nike's giveaway programs in the sports community. Tony Moran won civic support by underwriting athletic teams. Abe Minker donated a $10,000 stained glass window to his synagogue and aided welfare groups and hospitals in Reading and other cities. Ralph Kreitz, with annual incomes of more than $100,000, gave much of his money to churches, hospitals and the underprivileged. Before his downfall, Ralph bought 7,000 Christmas trees for the poor, and chartered buses to take slum kids to Philadelphia baseball games.

This paradox of the Reading racketeer personality had deep roots. The public built an image of Max Hassel, Dutch Mary, and Tony Moran as honest-to-goodness benefactors to the downtrodden. Minker never gained that status. The publicity about Minker's dominance of the rackets brought to light by federal prosecutors and disgruntled gambling machine operators, finally soured voters on the sad condition of the city's politics.

Business in general suffered because of the rackets. Cigar and candy storeowners who succumbed to the numbers rackets, were pinched financially during the occasional crackdowns on gambling by state or federal investigations. Because of the easy money, the storeowners had not established solid profit bases. The same could be said for contractors who relied on illicit deals with the city. Taking the crooked road usually left these outmoded businessmen behind in the technology race. They were often the uneducated and untrained who gained a certain social status by being in league with racketeers and politicians of their own ilk. Reputable businessmen who didn't fall into the kickback trap profited in the long run.

A review of Reading's political history offered researchers further understanding of why corruption was allowed to exist decade after decade. Things creaked along under many administrations that resisted innovation. During the '20s and early '30s when the population was growing, construction was booming with the advent of several new schools, the Lindbergh Viaduct, the Courthouse, the Abraham Lincoln Hotel, a new county prison, and several other major buildings. In 1925 the city and county discussed building a city hall/courthouse. But the city took the cheaper route by renovating the former boys high school building at 8th and Washington. Almost 80 years later, after alterations and an addition used by the police department, City Hall still serves the city.

The report was critical of the city's commission form of government. It was not until 1996 that the voters finally caught up with the rest of the country by changing to the strong mayor-manager form.

In 1966, eight female pollsters from the Wisconsin Survey Research Laboratory randomly interviewed several hundred Reading residents. Using a lengthy questionnaire that took 45 to 75 minutes to complete, the pollsters tried to get people to answer all the queries. In a nutshell this is what the pollsters found out:

"The people of Wincanton apparently want both easily accessible gambling and freedom from racket domination."

The professors heading the study had other opinions:

"On balance, it seems far more likely to conclude that gambling and corruption will soon return to Wincanton (although possibly in less blatant forms) for two reasons—first, a significant number of people want to be able to gamble or make improper deals with the city government. (This assumes, of course, that racketeers will be available to provide gambling if a complacent city administration permits it.) Second, and numerically far more important, most voters think that the problem has been permanently solved, and thus they will not be choosing candidates based on these issues in future elections."

Five years after The Wincanton Report was published, Reading was reminded once again of its recent past when "The Corrupt City" was being shown on national television. As viewers were told, racketeering was not as visible in 1971, but the threat of its revival seemed possible.

This documentary was a spinoff of Wincanton, but it was graphic evidence of why the city had gained its terrible reputation one decade earlier. The film introduced a shadowy figure, identified only as a convicted murderer who had killed a former racketeer leader. It was Johnny Wittig telling how he transferred Abe Minker's payoff money to Police Chief Charlie Wade on a lonely country road. Then there was Wade in his automobile telling the interviewer how his tape recorder picked up conversations with passengers at that same money exchange site in the country. Also Charlie and his German shepherds were seen at his fenced in Cumru Township home where he feared the mob would come after him because of his incriminating testimony in court.

Conversations with political club members were taped, documenting that many citizens still wanted illegal gambling although they didn't like political shakedowns.

Tom McBride, the Pennsylvania attorney general, had this to say about the political picture and the role Abe Minker played:

"Reading seemed to me to always be in a vacuum, a vacuum of leadership, a vacuum of people who cared deeply enough about the city, and a single man driven by single-minded objectives moved in to fill that vacuum. The usual business leadership and political focus seemed to evaporate and he took over. And once the pattern was set, he held control, almost in a feudal sense."

Victor Yarnell, mayor at the time of filming, and his police chief, Bernie Dobinsky, were quite open about the threat of racketeers making a comeback in the near future. Dobinsky frankly stated it was a strong possibility that could happen. He told about a mobster offering him weekly sums to allow a gambling joint to operate. He rejected the offer, but said the realization was that "this guy was ready to pay to stay in business. I don't think it would take too long because I really think there are people poised just waiting for this department to relax. From information given to me and my personal contacts, I don't doubt that there would be a racket element ready to move in."

The film's narrator, Rod MacLeish, asked Yarnell about this rackets group Dobinsky was talking about and recent offers made to people in his administration.

"Well, it occurred very soon after I took over this job," Yarnell stated. "He visited me and said he would be an ideal man to have as a go-between with the police and the racketeers he knew very well. He did this with a straight face and I thought he really felt this was a good idea. But I didn't think too much about it and I tended to laugh it off, and that was all we heard about it."

Paul Galan, director of the Group W Urban American film, recalled that City Hall personnel were not overly cooperative when his TV interviewers arrived in town. But the production crew overcame this reluctance and succeeded in talking to enough people to gain an overview of how things operated during the corrupt years. He said at the 2006 film festival that he was amazed by the Runyonesque characters his crew met in Reading.

"Charlie Wade was one of a kind," Galan said. "He was fascinating in that he really seemed driven to have a good police force but wanted the prestige even more. He was a complex individual."

Although racketeering in Reading declined during the late 1960s, it did not disappear. Numbers writing continued even after 1978 when the Pennsylvania State Lottery was introduced. With the loss of many industrial jobs in recent years, the later purveyors of sports betting and numbers have sharply decreased. Former factories gave each numbers bank a strong base in which to operate. But it remained a profitable business for a greatly reduced number of independents.

When the state legalized off track betting, Berks County was awarded the first OTB parlor.

The arrest of a numbers writer or bookie has been a rare event in recent years as police spend much of their time and resources waging war on drug gangs. Put in prospective, the present battle seems to belittle the long fight against vice back in the mid-20th Century. The violence and overall social problems resulting from today's sale of illegal drugs and its resultant violence is certainly of far greater concern than was the gambling and prostitution of that distant era. But the political base of today's society is certainly an improvement over city government then. As predicted by many, gambling became legal.

In another 50 years will prostitution and all drugs be taxable, rather than illegal?

# *Sources*

Reading Times
Reading Eagle
Philadelphia Inquirer
New York Times
Reading Record
Berks County Recorder of Deeds archives
Berks County Register of Wills archives
Berks County Clerk of Criminal Courts archives
Berks County Prothonotary Archives Center
The Historical Society of Berks County
Historical Review of Berks County
Reading City Council archives
Reading Public Library and its Pennsylvania Room
Albright College archives
Federal Court Archives of Philadelphia
U.S. Senate subcommittee hearing on illegal gambling, 1961
U.S. Supreme Court, United States v, Minker, 350 U.S. 179, 1956
U.S. District Court for the Eastern District of Pennsylvania, 15 arrest and search warrants
U.S. Attorneys Office, Eastern District of Pennsylvania, 13 pretrial depositions
Pennsylvania Crime Commission, 1980 report
Pennsylvania Crime Commission, The Changing Face of Organized Crime, 1986 report
Dr. John A. Gardiner and David J. Olson, Wincanton: The Politics of Corruption, President's Commission on Organized Crime, 1966.
Dr. John A. Gardiner, The Politics of Corruption, Organized Crime in an American City, 1970
Carl Sifakis, Encyclopedia of American Crime, 1982

# Index

978-0-595-49689-1
0-595-49689-X

Printed in the United States
203691BV00005B/34-36/P